Discovering Children's Literature

Third Edition

JUDITH HILLMAN

Saint Michael's College

Merrill
Prentice Hall

Upper Saddle River, New Jersey
Columbus, Ohio

Library of Congress Cataloging-in-Publication Data.

Hillman, Judith.
    Discovering children's literature/Judith Hillman.—3rd ed.
      p. cm.
    Includes bibliographical references and index.
    ISBN 0-13-042332-7
      1. Children's literature—History and criticism. I. Title.

PN1009.A1 H554 2003
809'.89282—dc21   2002016619

Vice President and Publisher: Jeffery W. Johnston
Editor: Linda Ashe Montgomery
Production Editor: Mary M. Irvin
Design Coordinator: Diane C. Lorenzo
Text Design and Production Coordination: Carlisle Publishers Services
Cover Designer: Ali Mohrman
Cover Photo: Corbis Stock Market
Production Manager: Pamela D. Bennett
Director of Marketing: Ann Castel Davis
Marketing Manager: Krista Groshong
Marketing Coordinator: Tyra Cooper

This book was set in Garamond by Carlisle Communications, Ltd., and was printed and bound by R. R. Donnelley & Sons Company. The cover was printed by Phoenix Color Corp.

Photo Credits: Jeff Clark, p. 329; Judith Hillman, p. 136; Anne Vega/Merrill, pp. 8, 97, 131.

Poetry Credits: From THE COLLECTED POEMS OF LANGSTON HUGHES by Langston Hughes, copyright © 1994 by The Estate of Langston Hughes. Used by permission of Alfred A. Knopf, a division of Random House, Inc., p. 145; Excerpted from the poem "What in the World?" by Eve Merriam which is now the full text of the picture book WHAT IN THE WORLD? by Eve Merriam, HarperFestival, copyright ©1962, 1990 Eve Merriam. Used by permission of Marian Reiner.

Pearson Education Ltd.
Pearson Education Australia Pty. Limited
Pearson Education Singapore Pte. Ltd.
Pearson Education North Asia Ltd.
Pearson Education Canada, Ltd.
Pearson Educación de Mexico, S.A. de C.V.
Pearson Education—Japan
Pearson Education Malaysia Pte. Ltd.
Pearson Education,*Upper Saddle River, New Jersey*

10 9 8 7 6 5 4 3 2 1
ISBN 0-13-042332-7

To Donald, with love and gratitude

Preface

This third edition of *Discovering Children's Literature* includes and extends the previous edition. However, the basic premise remains the same: to guide interested adults into a serious study of children's literature through an exploration of books written for infants, children, and adolescents.

Those who work with children as teachers, prospective teachers, librarians, and parents will find this text useful because it succinctly explains the field of children's literature—how it is organized by genre, how it is defined, and the criteria used to evaluate children's literature selections. The text presents readers with many examples of fine children's literature and teaching suggestions. As in the previous edition, the text is deliberately brief, highlighting significant aspects of children's literature and encouraging students to read children's books as they learn about children's literature.

As an introduction to the field, this edition can serve as a primary text in children's literature courses for preservice and inservice teachers, or as a supplementary text in reading and literature-based instruction. English departments and library information schools as well may have courses that call for a text with just this emphasis on children's and adolescent literature.

Discovering Children's Literature, Third Edition, includes many special features, some of which have been added or expanded since the previous edition. It is organized systematically to reveal the history, structure, and content of children's literature, establishing a foundation as new books and authors are considered. This edition contains two picture-book chapters, in response to the accelerated growth of picture books for a wide age range. The accompanying CD contains bibliographic information on many books mentioned in the text and more than a thousand new books. Four new literature units, three text sets, and many teaching suggestions, activities, and projects encourage the reader to delve into children's books and create exciting learning experiences for children. Interactive throughout, the text invites questions, opinions, and reflections from students.

Evaluating children's books is a major theme in all chapters. Evaluation criteria are clearly articulated and related to the genre that is presented. A new feature of this edition is a four-point scale for every genre, which sharpens the process of evaluation and encourages discussion among evaluators.

Every chapter has been revised and updated. Books of national and international diversity permeate each chapter, and specific bibliographies that address diversity are found in Chapters 7, 9, 10, and 11. Similarly, books that include characters with special needs and individual differences infuse many chapters, with special mention in Chapters 6 and 12. Another new feature is the inclusion in Chapter 12 of recent Orbis Pictus award and honor books. Chapter 12, Books of Information, has been reorganized to match disciplines in school curricula, and teaching suggestions are explicit. Award winners, including the Newbery, Caldecott, and Coretta Scott King recipients, are found in Appendix A, and updated website addresses, storytelling, and additional resources are in Appendix B. A glossary provides further information for the interested student.

Children's literature is a vibrant, interdisciplinary field. I hope this edition helps you celebrate the joy of discovery as you recall old favorites and delight in new books, authors, and ideas.

ACKNOWLEDGMENTS

I am especially grateful to the educational community within which I work. Many teachers, student teachers, librarians, children, and booksellers have helped me formulate ideas for this edition. There are too many to name, but all are so important to this work. My colleagues at Saint Michael's College are particularly supportive and valued. The children's literature community in Vermont and New England forms a network that sustains and motivates me. My professional associates in state, regional, and national organizations continually amaze me with their learned contributions.

I appreciate very much the support and clear advice of Linda Montgomery, editor of curriculum and instruction, and production editor Mary Irvin at Merrill/Prentice Hall. Also, I thank Marilee Aschenbrenner and her colleagues at Carlisle Publishers Services. The technical quality and accuracy of the text is due to the fine efforts of all these people, and what you are reading now is much the result of their knowledge and creativity.

The reviewers were extremely helpful, and I thank them: Dorothy Bowen, Eastern Kentucky University; Nancy Williams, DePaul University; Diane E. Bushner, Salem State College; Angela M. Ferree, Western Illinois University; and Hollis Lowery-Moore, Sam Houston State University.

Last, and still best, I thank my family, who read, discuss, argue, and enjoy literature of all kinds: Donald, my husband, and Cara, Jonathan, Stephanie, and Emily Rose.

Discover the Companion Website Accompanying This Book

THE PRENTICE HALL COMPANION WEBSITE: A VIRTUAL LEARNING ENVIRONMENT

Technology is a constantly growing and changing aspect of our field that is creating a need for content and resources. To address this emerging need, Prentice Hall has developed an online learning environment for students and professors alike—Companion Websites–to support our textbooks.

In creating a Companion Website, our goal is to build on and enhance what the textbook already offers. For this reason, the content for each user-friendly website is organized by topic and provides the professor and student with a variety of meaningful resources. Common features of a Companion Website include:

FOR THE PROFESSOR

Every Companion Website integrates **Syllabus Manager**™, an online syllabus creation and management utility.

- **Syllabus Manager**™ provides you, the instructor, with an easy, step-by-step process to create and revise syllabi, with direct links into Companion Website and other online content without having to learn HTML.

- Students may logon to your syllabus during any study session. All they need to know is the web address for the Companion Website and the password you've assigned to your syllabus.
- After you have created a syllabus using **Syllabus Manager**™, students may enter the syllabus for their course section from any point in the Companion Website.
- Clicking on a date, the student is shown the list of activities for the assignment. The activities for each assignment are linked directly to actual content, saving time for students.
- Adding assignments consists of clicking on the desired due date, then filling in the details of the assignment—name of the assignment, instructions, and whether or not it is a one-time or repeating assignment.
- In addition, links to other activities can be created easily. If the activity is on-line, a URL can be entered in the space provided, and it will be linked automatically in the final syllabus.
- Your completed syllabus is hosted on our servers, allowing convenient updates from any computer on the Internet. Changes you make to your syllabus are immediately available to your students at their next logon.

FOR THE STUDENT

- **Topic Overviews**—outline key concepts in literacy topic areas.
- **Strategies**—these websites provide suggestions and information on how to implement instructional strategies and activities for each topic.
- **Web Links**—a wide range of websites that allow the students to access current information on everything from rationales for specific types of instruction, to research on related topics, to compilations of useful articles and more.
- **Electronic Bluebook**—send homework or essays directly to your instructor's email with this paperless form.
- **Message Board**—serves as a virtual bulletin board to post–or to respond to–quesitons or comments to/from a national audience.
- **Chat**—real-time chat with anyone who is using the text anywhere in the country–ideal for discussion and study groups, class projects, etc.

To take advantage of these and other resources, please visit the *Discovering Children's Literature* Companion Website at

www.prenhall.com/hillman

Brief Contents

1 THE CHILD, THE BOOK, AND LITERACY   1

2 CHILDHOOD, CHILDREN, AND HISTORY   21

3 EVALUATING CHILDREN'S BOOKS   41

4 ONCE UPON A TIME . . . AND TRADITION CONTINUES   67

5 PICTURE BOOKS FOR THE VERY YOUNG   91

6 PICTURE BOOKS FOR ALL   111

7 THE PLEASURE AND POWER OF POETRY   135

8 IMAGINARY WORLDS OF FANTASY   159

9 REALISM IN THE HERE AND NOW   183

10 REALISM IN THE PAST   207

11 BIOGRAPHY: THE STORY OF A LIFE   227

12 BOOKS OF INFORMATION   243

Contents

1 THE CHILD, THE BOOK, AND LITERACY   1

Introduction and Response   1

Defining Children's Literature   2

Differences Between Children's Literature and Adult Literature   4

How to Evaluate Children's Books   5

Aspects of Child Development   6

Infancy Through Preschool   6

Primary Childhood   7

Middle Childhood   9

Adolescence   9

Principles of a Literature-Based Program in School Classrooms   10

Three Guiding Principles   11

Describing Literature Units   12

A Preview of Units in Chapters 3, 6, and 10   12

Text Sets for a Literature-Based Program   13

How This Book Is Organized   15

Summary   16

Implications for Instruction   16

Projects   16

Activities for the Primary Level   17

Activities for the Intermediate and Middle Levels   17

References   18

   Children's Works   18

   Professional Works   18

   Additional Resources   18

2   CHILDHOOD, CHILDREN, AND HISTORY   21

Introduction and Response   21

In the Distant Past   22

   From the Oral Tradition to Print   24

1500 A.D. to 1600 A.D.   24

1600 A.D. to 1700 A.D.   26

   Fairy Tales and Mother Goose   28

1700 A.D. to 1800 A.D.   28

   Novels of Adventure and Satire   30

   John Newbery & Co.   31

   Scientific Didacticism   31

1800 A.D. to 1900 A.D.   33

   The Golden Age of Children's Literature   34

1900 A.D. to 2000 A.D.   36

2001 A.D. to the Future   37

Summary   37

Implications for Instruction   38

   Projects   38

References   39

   Children's Works   39

   Professional Works   39

   Additional Resources   40

3   EVALUATING CHILDREN'S BOOKS   41

Introduction and Response   41

Other Approaches to Classification   43

A Rationale for Genres   44

Literary Elements   46

   Theme   46

   Plot   46

   Character   48

   Setting   49

Style   *49*

Point of View   *51*

Evaluation of Literary Elements   51

Literary Elements Related to Genres   53

Summary   54

Implications for Instruction   55

Projects   *55*

Activities for the Primary Level: A Unit on Wings   *56*

Activities for the Intermediate and Middle Levels: A Unit on Flight   *61*

References   64

Children's Works   *64*

Professional Works   *64*

Additional Resources   *65*

4 ONCE UPON A TIME ... AND TRADITION CONTINUES   67

Introduction and Response   67

History of Traditional Literature   68

The Universality of Folklore   *69*

Subgenres of Traditional Literature   70

Folk Rhymes, Songs, and Proverbs   *71*

Parables and Fables   *72*

Folktales and Fairy Tales   *72*

Myths and Legends   76

Evaluating Traditional Literature   78

The World's Traditional Literature   80

Traditional Literature from Africa and the Middle East   *80*

Traditional Literature from Asia   *81*

Traditional Literature from the Americas   *82*

Traditional Literature from Europe   *84*

Retellings Too Good To Miss (for Young and Old)   85

Summary   86

Implications for Instruction   86

Projects   *86*

Activities for the Primary Level   *87*

Activities for the Intermediate and Middle Levels   *87*

References   88

Children's Works   *88*

Professional Works   *88*

Additional Resources   *89*

5 PICTURE BOOKS FOR THE VERY YOUNG   91

Introduction and Response   91

History of the Children's Picture Book   92

Pre-Literacy and Child Development   95

Definition of Picture Books for the Very Young   98

Subgenres of Picture Books for Young Children   99

Artistic Elements in Picture Books   101

Recognizing Media and Style   103

Evaluating Picture Books for the Very Young   104

Summary   106

Implications for Instruction   107

Projects   107

Activities for Very Young Children (ages 0–2)   108

Activities for Young Preschoolers (ages 2, 3, and 4)   108

References   109

Children's Works   109

Professional Works   110

Additional Resources   110

6 PICTURE BOOKS FOR ALL   111

Introduction and Response   111

Definition and Rationale   113

Genres, Examples, and Curriculum Value of Picture Storybooks   113

Recognizing Media and Style   115

Characters and Themes in Picture Storybooks   116

Evaluating Picture Books   117

Controversies, Sensitive Issues, and Current Trends   118

Picture Books for Older Readers   121

Summary   123

Implications for Instruction   123

Projects   123

A Unit for the Primary Grades   124

Activities for the Intermediate and Middle Levels   131

References   132

Children's Works   *132*

Professional Works   *132*

Additional Resources   *133*

7 THE PLEASURE AND POWER OF POETRY   **135**

Introduction and Response   135

Defining Poetry   137

History of Poetry for Children   138

Children's Poetry Preferences   139

Evaluating Poetry   140

Subgenres of Poetry   142

Ballads   *142*

Narrative Poetry   *144*

Lyrical Poetry   *144*

Free Verse   *145*

Haiku   *145*

Limericks   *146*

Concrete Poetry   *147*

Cinquain, Diamante, and Other Forms   *148*

Elements of Poetry   149

Contemporary Poets   150

Recent Anthologies and Collections: A Bibliography   151

Anthologies   *151*

Themed Collections and Anthologies   *151*

African and African-American Collections and Anthologies   153

Asian and Asian-American Collections and Anthologies   153

Hispanic and Caribbean Collections and Anthologies   153

Native American Collections and Anthologies   153

Summary   154

Implication for Instruction   154

Projects   *154*

Activities for the Primary Level   *155*

Activities for the Intermediate and Middle Levels   *156*

References   157

Poetry and Children's Works   *157*

Professional Works   *158*

Additional Resources   *158*

8 IMAGINARY WORLDS OF FANTASY   159

Introduction and Response   159

History of Modern Fantasy   161

Subgenres of Modern Fantasy   165

Animal Fantasies   165

High Fantasy   167

Time Fantasy   171

Science-Fiction Fantasy   172

Extraordinary Characters and Inventions   173

Evaluating Fantasy   175

Summary   176

Implications for Instruction   177

Projects   177

Activities for the Primary Level   177

Activities for the Intermediate and Middle Levels   178

References   179

Children's Works   179

Professional Works   181

Additional Resources   181

9 REALISM IN THE HERE AND NOW   183

Introduction and Response   183

Defining Contemporary Realism   185

Value of Contemporary Realism   186

History of Contemporary Realism   186

Evaluation of Contemporary Realism   189

Subgenres of Contemporary Realism   190

Focus on Character   190

Focus on Plot   194

Combating Censorship   198

National Diversity: A Bibliography   199

African-American   199

Asian-American   199

European-American   199

Hispanic   199

Native American   200

Gay and Lesbian   200

International Diversity: A Bibliography   200
Summary   201
Implications for Instruction   201
   Projects   201
   Activities for the Primary Level   202
   Activities for the Intermediate and Middle Levels   203
References   204
   Children's Works   204
   Professional Works   205
   Additional Resources   205
   Children's Book Clubs   206

10   REALISM IN THE PAST   207

Introduction and Response   207
Defining Historical Fiction   208
History of Historical Fiction   209
Value of Historical Realism   211
Evaluating Historical Fiction   212
Subgenres of Historical Fiction   213
   The Ancient World   214
   The Medieval and Renaissance Worlds   215
   Exploration and Colonization   215
   Western Expansion and Industrialization   216
   The Early and Mid-20th Century   217
Diversity in Historical Realism: A Bibliography   217
   African-American   218
   Asian-American   218
   Native American and Creole   218
   Gay and Lesbian   218
Summary   218
   *When Children Went to War: Text Set and Teaching
   Suggestions   219*
Implications for Instruction   222
   Projects   222
   Activities for the Primary Level   222
   Activities for the Intermediate and Middle Levels   222
References   224
   Children's Works   224

Professional Works   225
Additional Resources   226

11 BIOGRAPHY: THE STORY OF A LIFE   227

Introduction and Response   227

History of Biography and Autobiography for Children   229

Defining Biography   231

Value of Biography for Children   232

Evaluating Biography   233

Subgenres of Biography   234

   Biographies of Historical Figures   235

   Biographies of Contemporary Figures   236

Recent Biographies Too Good To Miss   236

Summary   236

Implications for Instruction   238

   Projects   238

   Activities for the Primary Level   239

   Activities for the Intermediate and Middle Levels   239

References   240

   Children's Works   240

   Professional Works   241

   Additional Resources   241

   Author Information   241

12 BOOKS OF INFORMATION   243

Introduction and Response   243

History of Information Books for Children   244

Defining Informational Books   245

   Types of Information Books   246

Structures of Expository Writing   247

   Definitions and Examples of Patterns in Expository Writing   248

Evaluating Informational Books   249

Subgenres of Nonfiction   252

   Humanities (The Arts)   252

   Mathematics and Technology   253

   Science   254

Social Studies   255
Award-Winning Nonfiction for Children   257
Sensitive Issues, Special Needs, and Individual Differences   258
Summary   258
Implications for Instruction   259
  Projects   259
  Activities for the Primary Level   260
  Activities for the Intermediate and Middle Levels   260
References   262
  Children's Works   262
  Professional Works   263
  Additional Resources   263

APPENDIX A: CHILDREN'S BOOK AWARDS   **265**

Newbery Medal Winners and Honor Books   265
Caldecott Medal Winners and Honor Books   274
Coretta Scott King Awards   282

APPENDIX B: INTERNET ADDRESSES AND ADDITIONAL RESOURCES   **289**

GLOSSARY   **291**

AUTHOR AND TITLE INDEX   **295**

SUBJECT INDEX   **323**

ABOUT THE AUTHOR   **329**

NOTE: Every effort has been made to provide accurate and current Internet information in this book. However, the Internet and information posted on it are constantly changing, so it is inevitable that some of the Internet addresses listed in this textbook will change.

CHAPTER 1

The Child, the Book, and Literacy

INTRODUCTION AND RESPONSE

What happens when a child reads a book? Surely, imagination, the drama of fiction and nonfiction, knowledge, and curiosity are all engaged in the powerful process we call reading. Children's books bring compelling stories, interesting characters, and intriguing facts to readers and listeners from early ages through adulthood. The link between children, books, and literacy spotlights the field of endeavor called children's literature. What does the phrase *children's literature* mean to you? Does it summon memories of looking at a favorite picture book on a parent's lap, or reading a great story outdoors on a lazy summer day? Mention children's literature to a group of adults and most will smile with a remembered fondness for special books or authors. Do you recall a particular book, such as *Charlotte's Web* (White, 1952) or *Goodnight Moon* (Brown, 1947)?

Children's literature today enjoys unprecedented visibility; children can choose from about 5,000 books published annually in the United States alone. Worldwide estimates of the total number of children's books in print are as high as 90,000 (Huck et al., 2001). School classrooms and libraries display an abundant selection of literature for all age levels because of the popularity and pedagogical importance of literature-based reading programs (Tompkins, 2001). Most bookstores house large children's sections with a variety of appealing books.

Children's literature has captured the interest of the marketplace as well as those in academia who believe that children need quality literature. It has become a legitimate field of study for scholars in literature, and it crosses interdisciplinary lines to education, child development, folklore, and fine arts as well. Truly multidisciplinary and international in scope, children's literature of today represents cultural richness and diversity.

In this chapter, a new discovery of literature for children begins. Because children's literature is multifaceted and there is much to discover, begin to think about what you would like to know. What are your interests in the field of children's literature? New books? Trends in popularity and publishing? Multicultural stories? Why are you embarking on this voyage of discovery now? Identify some personal goals as you begin to look closely at children's books from today and the past.

This chapter lays the foundation for your study, defining children's literature and suggesting a way to organize this diverse field. The evaluation system is first explained here, and continues through remaining chapters. Understanding children's growth and development helps teachers and parents choose appropriate books and, moreover, forms the basis for principles of literature-based reading and language-arts programs in schools. These principles find expression in text sets, units, projects, and activities within chapters.

Here begins a remarkable, thought-provoking journey into children's literature that will not end when you finish this book. Your discoveries will continue as each year brings new children's books that delight and challenge readers of all ages.

REFLECTION   What children's book had a significant effect on you as you were growing up? Do you remember a special book, one that had lasting influence? What is it?

DEFINING CHILDREN'S LITERATURE

Children's literature is a somewhat subjective term, because literature implies that some value has been added to separate "good" books from the mediocre ones. This value is associated with literary standards, the notion of fine writing, profound ideas, and memorable plots and characters. The term *literature* suggests that some judgment, or critical evaluation, has been applied to a book. There are many children's books, but how many do we consider to be literature? Children's story and informational books—also called **trade books** to distinguish them from textbooks—are concrete, tangible, real, and heavy. Children's literature is an abstract concept, loaded with ingrained notions of worth and value. To distinguish between books and literature is the challenge of the adult and child who read and want to recognize the best. Distinguishing between books and literature is an evaluative judgment based on specific characteristics that define literature.

A definition of *children's literature* has two parts: One deals with *content* and the other with *quality*. The first part, content, is relatively straightforward. Children's literature is material written for infants, children, and adolescents that contains the following:

- Typical childhood experiences written from a child's perspective
- Children or childlike characters
- Simple and direct plots that focus on action

- A feeling of optimism and innocence (e.g., happy endings are the norm)
- A tendency toward combining reality and fantasy

Two scholars of children's literature, Perry Nodelman (1996) and Rebecca Lukens (1999) insist that literature should first of all be pleasurable. The stories in fiction and the factual writing in nonfiction should be interesting and entertaining while allowing readers to gain new insights and to use their imaginations.

In describing children's literature, Nodelman (1996) adds that it is often **didactic,** with strong cultural messages designed to teach children how to behave and what to think. Throughout its history, children's literature has been viewed as a socializing agent, a way to instill values and norms into following generations. This should be subtle, however, and the literary qualities that render a good story should not be sacrificed to the message. Heavy-handed, overt didacticism should not be evident in children's literature.

Although content is quite easy to describe, the second part, quality, is not. Quality is the subjective dimension of literature, a judgment made as to whether a children's book is "good" or "poor." If it is deemed good, it becomes literature, and if it is really good, it joins the **canon** of what has been recognized as the best. If the book is "flawed," it is not literature. Some common flaws include stodgy writing, plots that are either too predictable or too illogical, too many voices telling the story, and socially conscious themes that outweigh the slender story that supports them (i.e., the story is too didactic).

REFLECTION   What children's books would figure prominently in your personal canon of children's literature?

Literature can be defined by characteristics that refer to its power to satisfy, explain, invite, and compel. Which books do you know that do the following:

- Evoke strong emotions while engaging the intellect
- Empower readers with a will to act
- Express a feeling or an act in beautiful language
- Reveal deep and subtle human motives
- Allow readers to experience vicariously a different time, place, and character

If a book does such things, it may be called literature. In his essay "Why I Value Literature," Richard Hoggart says that literature "seeks for the meanings in human experience" (Chambers, 1983, p. 8). These meanings allow each of us to explore our humanity. Literature gives us words to describe and explore our thoughts, dreams, hopes, fears, and longings.

Charlotte's Web has long been recognized as exemplifying the best in children's literature. It is a delightful story, riveting and emotionally satisfying, combined with superb craftsmanship to create a deeply moving aesthetic experience. For many,

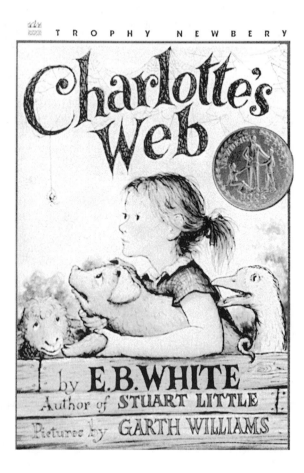

Charlotte's Web represents a touchstone against which other books are measured. (Matthew Arnold, the noted English poet and critic, first used the term *touchstone* to signify the best and truly excellent.)

REFLECTION   Which children's book best represents children's literature to you? Do you have a touchstone that helps you compare and judge the best?

Differences Between Children's Literature and Adult Literature

Is children's literature different from adult literature? (Note that many adult books do not necessarily qualify as literature.) Superficial aspects of children's literature—such as fewer characters, simpler plots, shorter sentences, and larger print—mark obvious differences when comparing material written for children with that written for adults. However, issues of quality should be the same: the depth and range of emotion, the profundity of ideas. Many authors, Jill Paton Walsh among them, do not shrink from expressing a theme or an idea in children's literature in the best comprehensive prose (Hunt, 1991). She does not "write down" to a child audience. Lukens (1999) supports this similarity in quality when she says literature for young readers differs from adult literature in *degree* but not in *kind*. Literary quality should be a hallmark of books for every audience: infants, toddlers, children, adolescents, and adults.

Because our definition of literature hinges on synonymous qualities of adult and children's literature, we bring the same standards of evaluation to both. In other words, we do not lower our standards because a book is written especially for children. Lower expectations would be patronizing and condescending to child readers.

REFLECTION   Do you think some books, considered children's books, are mislabeled because they seem to be adultlike, nostalgic, or inappropriate? What are they, and why do you think so?

HOW TO EVALUATE CHILDREN'S BOOKS

Evaluation is an ongoing process with many aspects. First, we like or dislike a book based on personal responses to characters, plot, setting, and other literary elements. Next, an evaluation may be colored by knowledge of the author, the purpose of the book (how it will be used), and how it matches our expectations of what literature is.

In this text, many suggestions, questions, and methods are given so that books can be evaluated in a variety of ways. Sometimes wholistically, sometimes in parts, the discerning reader of children's books is asked to focus on a personal response, then to compare a book to others, and finally to think about specific points that signify literary quality. The following three steps mirror this process:

1. Evaluate the book by applying your definition of literature: Does it evoke strong emotion? Is the plot coherent? Is it well written, pleasurable, and empowering? Does it explore the human condition in a unique way?

2. Evaluate the book by comparing it with others you hold in high esteem: Is it as good as *Charlotte's Web, Island of the Blue Dolphins* (O'Dell, 1960), *Goodnight Moon,* or your own choice? Does it have the same depth, range of emotion, beautiful language? Using these books as touchstones helps anchor the concept of *literature* in your mind, invites comparison, and sets a standard by which to judge other works.

3. Evaluate the book by identifying your purpose and the audience you wish the book to reach, then determine if the book fits. If the book does not suit, then search for the best book—the "best" fit.

This is actually the beginning of evaluation. Evaluation continues with knowledge of genre—that is, what is important in the evaluation of fantasy, of poetry, and of contemporary realistic fiction? Chapter 3 continues an in-depth look at evaluation, and then each chapter adds genre information, an evaluation pattern, and a four-point scale to aid in book selection. Clearly, evaluation of children's books is crucial, time-consuming, interesting, and sometimes frustrating and perilous.

ASPECTS OF CHILD DEVELOPMENT

Defining the *child* in children's literature is just about as difficult as determining quality in a literary work. Have children changed in the last generation? Has *childhood* been redefined? Clearly cultural and social influences exist that impinge on children now that were not present a generation ago. However, psychologists identify predictable stages of development stemming from human biological and psychological imperatives that transcend culture and society.

REFLECTION   What do you consider to be major influences on children now? Has your definition of "childhood" changed?

Although several theories exist about how and why human beings develop as they do, these basic characteristics in behavior and language generally typify age groups. Figure 1.1 summarizes major points of development, called "psychosocial markers" because they mark unique characteristics in development.

Infancy Through Preschool

As infants begin their journey into childhood, their primary tasks are to acquire language, to develop locomotor skills, and to form attachments or bond with a primary caregiver while at the same time learning the autonomy necessary to function independently. Each of these tasks continues to develop in complexity through the preschool period, forming a foundation for future cognitive, social, and personality development.

As children learn to talk, their language is a window into their minds. A fascinating study of a young child named Anna (Crago & Crago, 1983) responding to literature from the age of 12 months to 5 years demonstrated how she learned vocabulary and story structures, used pictures to predict text, and learned to love books. Like Anna, children who are surrounded by a rich language environment, full of experiences with books, can gain linguistic facility through their exposure to stories, poems, songs, and chants.

Developmental theories of Erik Erikson (1963), Jean Piaget (1952), and Lev Vygotsky (1962)—notable psychologists of the early 20th century—have been cast into educational practices particularly relevant to reading and language-arts pro-

Figure 1.1
Descriptions of
Developmental
Characteristics

Source: From
*Developmental
Psychology Today* (5th
ed.) by L. Hoffman, S.
Paris, E. Hall, and R.
Schell, 1988, New York:
McGraw-Hill. Copyright
1988 by McGraw-Hill.
Adapted by permission.

Ages	Psychosocial Markers
Infancy through preschool (ages birth to 4)	Acquiring language Forming attachments Mastering locomotor skills Beginning to learn autonomy Enjoying parallel and pretend play
Primary childhood (ages 5 to 8)	Developing language Enjoying achievements (learning to read) Imitating adult roles Using "concrete" thought Projecting an optimistic view
Middle childhood (ages 9 to 12)	Becoming more logical and rule-oriented Growing dependency on peer group Perfecting skills Employing metacognitive thought Moving toward independence from parents
Adolescence	Maturing biologically Establishing sexual identity Becoming autonomous while retaining strong attachment to peer group Employing abstract thought

grams. The relationship between language and thought flourishes when pleasurable literature stimulates the senses and the imagination. From pat-a-cake to picture books, young children need to hear language, particularly the connected discourse in story and description, song and poem. Most children are surrounded by snippets of conversation, a quick question or direction from adults, and from that they learn words, phrases, and meanings. They also need to hear how language extends, to understand how stories begin and end, and to see how written language symbolizes spoken language.

In addition to language development, emotional and social aspects are enhanced through literature. Developing trust, learning empathy, using imagination, and identifying with role models are all important human traits that can be developed by reading aloud to young children, beginning at birth.

Our basic personality characteristics, cognitive styles, and ideas about the world are formed very early in life. Exposure to children's literature can widen, extend, and enrich that formation.

Primary Childhood

Most children ages 5 through 8 participate in a structured educational system. Much of their time and energy is spent learning to read, enjoying achievements, gaining competence, and imitating adult roles. At these ages, children still believe that adults can offer something useful to their lives. There is a general optimism about the world among children whose world is still somewhat carefree and innocent. Family life, school, and community represent the child's wider world. Parents, stepparents, and siblings play a large part in determining the developing values and attitudes of the individual.

In this vital period of beginning formalized instruction, "language not only speeds the acquisition of new concepts, but allows children to reason more effectively as well" (Hoffman, Paris, Hall, & Schell, 1988, p. 278). Language is also fundamental to the development of self-control, aiding necessary socialization in school and family. Thus language development provides the foundation for learning and the control of behavior in primary children.

When the renowned Swiss psychologist Jean Piaget studied the origins of intelligence, his insight led to revolutionary educational practices. He determined that children in this stage learn best by manipulating concrete objects that represent abstract concepts (Flavell, 1985). Particularly in math and science, children profit from describing, sorting, and classifying objects. From this they can learn numerical concepts such as adding and dividing. When language is an integral part of the activity, concepts become entrenched in both long-term and short-term memory.

Because children this age are curious, ready to try new things, and increasingly confident, they should find children's books an ever widening source of information and pleasure. Learning about other cultures or about scientific topics becomes an exciting project in a primary classroom. Truly soaking up information like sponges, children benefit from exposure to all kinds of books and magazines.

This child, reading independently, enjoys the classic *Where the Wild Things Are* (Sendak, 1963).

Middle Childhood

Children at this stage—roughly from ages 9 through 12—are asserting their individuality so much that generalizations are difficult and rife with error. Perhaps that is the hallmark of this stage: the lack of a stable, consistent way to describe childhood. Louv (1990), a writer and reporter, suggests that the nature of childhood has changed dramatically in one generation due to societal and electronic forces. From new constellations of family definitions to the new television environment, aspects of modern society change preconceived notions of childhood. Clearly, in most middle or junior high schools, a casual observer would notice many changes in learning and social contexts.

Nevertheless, children in this stage are becoming more like adults in logical thought patterns. Piaget referred to the "formal-operations" stage, which most children enter at about age 11. Manipulation of concrete objects is no longer so necessary; more abstract notions can be internalized without the preliminary movement of physical properties. Also, children gain an ability to reflect on their thought processes, an ability called *metacognition*. Metacognition is a sophisticated way to monitor one's own language and thought. It is the mental process of becoming aware of how one derives meaning from written and oral language.

Peer-group influence grows while parental influence diminishes. As children continue to work on establishing an identity (and this task continues through adolescence), their industriousness is evident. For example, many children work unhesitatingly on perfecting skills in swimming, basketball, or tennis, or playing a musical instrument. Team play is important, as the team represents identification with a peer group, a marker of growing competence, and the chance to practice governance by rules.

At this time, boys and girls express different interests in book selection. Boys select more nonfiction than girls, and the types of fiction vary between genders (Childress, 1985). Boys tend to choose action and adventure, while girls prefer stories based on strong interpersonal relationships.

REFLECTION   Are you aware of noticeable gender differences in book selection? Do other marked differences emerge in selection patterns—between fantasy and realism, for example, or others?

Adolescence

Dramatic changes in adolescence affecting young men and women are most noticeable in physical appearance, but of equal importance is the development in thinking abilities and social–emotional discoveries. Many psychologists believe that the strongest characteristic of adolescence is the quest for autonomy, as the growing urge to define oneself forces shifts in perceptions and attitudes (Hoffman et al., 1988). The emerging sense of self is a hallmark of this period as biological, intellectual, and personality changes work together to establish an adult identity apart from family and friends.

Intellectual development is seen in the capacity to think abstractly and to understand complexities in concepts such as justice, community, and freedom. Teenagers can discuss controversial issues, entertain others' points of view, and forge new opinions. In the social–emotional realm, family roles change as adolescents experiment with new identities.

The inevitable conflicts of adolescence are portrayed realistically in children's literature. The particular interests and needs of this age group are found in a relatively new category called "young adult" literature. Cultural demands, choices (or lack of them), and the risks and joys of emerging independence are all presented in literature as well as other media. Literature such as *Monster* (Myers, 1999) helps young teenagers to reflect, to identify with a time, place, and character, and to reach into their imaginations. Young-adult literature fills an important niche between children's and adult literature for many readers, especially when skillful authors create incidents about making decisions and taking responsibility (Nilsen & Donelson, 1997).

A strong call for enhanced language development through literature permeates these periods of child and adolescent development. As language is every person's birthright, so literature is the supreme expression of how human beings use this birthright artistically.

PRINCIPLES OF A LITERATURE-BASED PROGRAM IN SCHOOL CLASSROOMS

With appropriate knowledge and selection criteria, teachers can use children's literature to provide the base for the reading and language-arts curriculum of any primary or middle school. *Reading* is defined as "a purposeful, active, strategic search for meaning in which readers use everything they know to make sense of written language" (Wepner & Feeley, 1993, p. 5). Learning to read effectively is probably the main purpose of attending school, especially in the early years. The overriding goal is to ensure that every child becomes literate and values reading as a lifelong activity.

Literacy is the result of a complex process, with most facets of cognition engaged while reading and writing. It may be one of the most difficult, demanding tasks we perform as human beings. Even seeing a letter "A," recognizing it as upper or lower case, and understanding what it means in context is a very sophisticated skill. Because reading and writing are complex and dynamic, there are many methods, strategies, techniques, and philosophies of reading instruction, and most include some use of literature. It is often the case today that scholars support a "balanced" approach to reading instruction because of the complexity (Au et al., 2001). Literature is the base, while strategy and skill instruction comes from activities generated from the literature and thematically related material. State and national standards are also aligned with activities derived from the literature.

While no single correct way exists for using literature productively, some suggestions promote the wise use of literature. The following principles come from many successful literature-based classroom programs and a deeply held belief that literature, if used effectively, has the power to reach and teach all learners. When literature-based approaches form the foundation of school reading programs, children and teachers "grow into a community of learners and view themselves as readers and writers" (Wepner & Feeley, 1993, p. 28).

Three Guiding Principles

1. Teachers must know a wide range of children's literature. They should read extensively, understand how literature works, be familiar with reviewing sources, and enjoy the richness literature offers.

2. In a classroom program, there must be *time* for children to read silently every day, *trust* that each child can choose books appropriately (with adult help) and respond honestly, and a *connection* to a home reading program.

3. Activities based on literature should closely reflect the integrity of the story, the purpose of the teacher, and the children's needs. Music, the visual arts, science, math, and other fields are allied with literature to create meaningful activities, often in a topic-centered or thematic unit approach to learning.

Elaborating briefly on these points will perhaps clarify and extend their practical use. In the first principle, the responsibility lies with the teacher (or librarian, or parent) to become knowledgeable. Only a secure, comprehensive, and up-to-date knowledge base will equip an adult to make a positive contribution to a child's literacy and love for books.

The second point focuses on classroom organization and an attitude about children's responses. There are many demands on time in a school day, and at home, too. However, since a major purpose of school is improving reading, writing, and computing, time for literature should not be at risk. Usually class time can be reorganized, allowing more time for discussions and projects and less time for busy work with workbooks. Exciting projects, planned *with* children instead of *for* them, ensure their enthusiasm and trigger the needed support from home. Parents need to be kept well informed about the literature program and how it works, as well as encouraged to become a part of it. Teacher-produced letters or student-produced newsletters can help accomplish this goal. Inviting parents to the classroom to read aloud is also a proven technique.

The third point has to do with planning activities within the context of a thematic unit that help children respond to literature with depth and understanding. A reconsideration of the kind of appropriate activities, prompted by Rosenblatt's work (1978), pervades many successful classroom programs. She introduced a *transactional* view of reading, also called *reader response,* in which the reader's background, experiences, and view of the world interact with the text to create meaning. Activities, therefore, are more open-ended, not fill-in-the-blank busy work, and they ask for honest reactions and critical thinking and often entail projects, writing, and longer, more involved assignments.

DESCRIBING LITERATURE UNITS

A literature unit is "a set of instructional activities linked by a unifying element" (Cox & Zarillo, 1993, p. 121). The unifying element may be a theme, a genre, an author or illustrator, or a school-related subject. For example, literature units may focus on journeys, poetry, Katherine Paterson, or protecting the environment.

There is no single model for a literature unit; there is instead a varied pattern of activities coming from the purposes and objectives of the curriculum and the teacher, the needs and interests of the students, the resources available, and the time limits imposed by a school schedule. However, guiding principles to the formulation of units arise from beliefs about the value of literature and a conviction that children learn by interacting with text in myriad ways. Common features of literature-based programs typically include the following:

- Children are read to daily.
- Children have time to read books of their own choosing.
- Children discuss and reflect on the books they read.
- Children respond to books through writing, art, drama, music, and talk.
- Children write on topics of their own choosing.
- Children share their reading, writing, and art products with the class.
- Children use a variety of good books as an essential part of any theme or unit of study.
- The daily schedule is flexible (DeLapp, 1989).

A literature-based classroom would find children being read to, children reading silently and aloud in pairs or small groups, all responding to literature holistically and analytically. Responses are seen in a variety of written work, as well as in artwork, drama, three-dimensional constructions, musical productions, and lots of discussion. Reflecting a reader's authentic interpretation of story, essay, chapter, or poem, responses are valued because they show what and how children are thinking, not because they are "right" or "wrong." The transaction between the reader and the text creates a context for learning to occur (Rosenblatt, 1978). When many disciplines (science, art, music, math) are included, the unit encompasses different kinds of thinking, or the "multiple intelligences" theory that psychologist Howard Gardner hypothesizes (1983). Figure 1.2 demonstrates how different disciplines are utilized through activities in the *Penguin Power!* unit, found in chapter 6.

A Preview of Units in Chapters 3, 6, and 10

To demonstrate how literature units may operate in classrooms, four units are interspersed throughout the text.

- In chapter 3, children learn genre classification and other reading skills through *Wings* for primary classrooms (grades K–3), and
- *Flight* for grades 4–7, which complement each other.

Figure 1.2
Integration of
Disciplines in
Penguin Power!

Discipline	Activities
Literature	Listening to and reading fiction and nonfiction
Art	Drawing penguins; making dioramas, puppets, and masks
Mathematics	Graphing penguin height
Science	Learning characteristics of penguin behavior and habitats
Social Studies	Plotting penguin habitats on a map of the Southern Hemisphere

- In chapter 6 is a multidisciplinary unit entitled *Penguin Power!* for grades 2–4 (approximately).
- In chapter 10, the unit focuses on one genre, historical realism, through the theme *When Children Went to War: Text Set and Teaching Suggestions.*

This unit outline and teaching suggestions were created for children in a heterogeneous classroom of grades 4 to 7. It dovetails with the text set *Holocaust,* which follows in this chapter.

TEXT SETS FOR A LITERATURE-BASED PROGRAM

Occasionally, a theme might develop as a result of several books that seem to explore an issue or topic that fits into plans and purposes. Cairney (1990) suggests that the most delicate aspect of creating literature units is careful, thoughtful attention to selecting books, then allowing the power of literature to generate applications that call for authentic responses. Clearly, a careful selection of literature is the heart of successful literature-based instruction. Inherent in the selection process is a regard for the best possible match between book and reader. A text set is a group of books, usually five or six, covering a similar theme and disparate reading levels, from which ad hoc reading groups may be organized in a classroom (Leu & Kinzer, 1999). Discussion groups may form around each of the books, or each person in a group of five or six could be reading a different book.

Figure 1.3 illustrates some text sets that could be the genesis of units, or could simply be highly recommended books for book clubs, literature circles, or other literacy groups in a class. The first, focused on the Holocaust, provides a bibliography for this important topic frequently found in schools (see also books mentioned in chapter 10, activity 5, for intermediate- and middle-grade students). An author study is next, with Walter Dean Myers the focus of this text set. Third, a genre study for young readers, Mysteries, is presented. (Please note that the bibliographies are complete in the text sets and are not referenced at the end of this chapter.)

Text Set: Holocaust books, websites, and resources

These nonfiction books suitable for children in grades 4 through 7, are personal stories of Holocaust survivors and those who had the courage to help them.

Friedman, I. (1990). *The other victims: First person stories of non-jews persecuted by the Nazis.* Boston: Houghton Mifflin.

Nieuwsma, M. J. (ed.) (1998). *Kinderlager: An oral history of young Holocaust survivors.* New York: Holiday.

Radin, R. Y. (2000). *Escape to the forest: Based on a true story of the Holocaust.* New York: HarperCollins.

Talbott, H. (2000). *Forging freedom: A true story of heroism.* New York: Putnam.

Vos, I. (2000). *The key Is lost.* New York: HarperCollins.

Warren, A. (2001). *Surviving Hitler: A boy in the Nazi death camps.* New York: HarperCollins.

United States Holocaust Memorial Museum, Washington, D. C.
   http://www.ushmm.org/education
Holocaust Teacher Resource Center, Newport News, VA
   http://www.Holocaust-trc.org/

Johnson, N. J. & C. Giorgis. (2001). Children's books: Interacting with the curriculum, in *The reading teacher, 55(2),* 204–213.

Rochman, H. (1998). Bearing witness to the Holocaust, *Book Links, 7(3),* 8–14.

Rochman, H. (1999). Holocaust survivors, rescuers and bystanders, *Book Links, 8(3),* 54–57.

Text Set: Walter Dean Myers, with websites and resources

Walter Dean Myers is a popular, award-winning author who writes in several genres: contemporary realism, historical realism, poetry, biography, and information. Recent books for intermediate through middle grades form this text set.

Myers, W. D. (1998). *Amistad: A long road to freedom.* New York: Dutton.

Myers, W. D. (1999a). *At Her Majesty's request: An African princess in Victorian England.* New York: Scholastic.

Myers, W. D. (1999b). *Monster.* New York: HarperCollins.

Myers, W. D. (2000). *145th street: Short stories.* New York: Delacorte.

Myers, W. D. (2001a). *Bad boy: A memoir.* New York: HarperCollins.

Myers, W. D. (2001b). *The journal of Biddy Owens: The Negro leagues.* New York: Scholastic.

For author information on Walter Dean Myers, see
   http://teacher.scholastic.com/authorsandbooks/authors/myers/bio.htm
   http://www.scils.rutgers.edu/special/kay

Text Set: Mysteries, with websites and resources

These mysteries were selected for children in grades 1 through 4. Each author has a series of mysteries so that if one proves to be popular with some readers, several more are available.

Adler, D. A. (2000). *Young Cam Jansen and the pizza shop mystery.* New York: Viking.

Brooks, W. (1958/2000). *Freddy and the dragon.* New York: Overlook.

Cushman, D. (2000). *Inspector Hopper.* New York: HarperCollins.

Hale, B. (2000). *The chameleon wore chartreuse: From the tattered casebook of Chet Gekko, private eye.* New York: Harcourt.

Joose, B. M. (2000). *Alien brain fryout: A Wild Willie mystery.* New York: Clarion.

Rylant, C. (2000). *The high rise private eyes: The case of the climbing cat.* New York: Greenwillow.

Van Draanen, W. (2000). *Sammy Keyes and the curse of Moustache Mary.* New York: Knopf.

Figure 1.3 Text Sets

For additional mysteries for young readers and the website for the Mystery Writers of America, see chapter 9.
For software, see "Spy Masters: UnMask the Prankster" at www.knowledgeadventure.com.

Figure 1.3   Continued

HOW THIS BOOK IS ORGANIZED

The chapters in this text are organized so that knowledge proceeds from a historical viewpoint and builds to current practices. In chapter 2, classic children's books demonstrate attitudes toward children and literature that still influence books and schooling today.

Chapter 3 provides an explanation of how literature works, so that evaluating books becomes easier. Similarities of form and content create categories of literature called *genres*. Genre distinctions and literary elements are described and exemplified through several outstanding books, most notably *Charlotte's Web* (White, 1952) and *Island of the Blue Dolphins* (O'Dell, 1960). Chapters 4 through 12 focus on each of the genres, with an in-depth look at how each is defined, its historical development, and many examples.

Figure 1.4 displays the relationships among genres, with prose, poetry, and picture books identified as fiction or nonfiction. (Numbers after the terms refer to chapters in which the genre is located.)

This text has threads running through all chapters that tie the book together and form a matrix for you to use to gather information. The first is an evaluation scheme for every genre that asks for a personal response related to purpose and audience.

Content/Form	Picture Books	Prose	Poetry (7)

Fiction	Realism (5, 6)
	Fantasy (5, 6)
	Traditional
	  Literature (4)
	Alphabet and
	  counting books
	  (5, 6)
		Realism
		Contemporary (9)
		Historical (10)
		Fantasy
		  Modern (8)
		  Traditional (4)
			(Poetry can be fiction
			  or nonfiction)

Nonfiction	Concept books
	  (5, 6)
	Alphabet and
	  counting (5, 6)
		Information (12)
		Biography (11)
			(Poetry can be
			  fiction or
			  nonfiction)

Forms	Nursery Rhymes Poetry Stories	Novels Short Stories Essays Drama	Lyric Ballad Haiku Others

Figure 1.4   Genres of Children's Literature

After a personal response is elicited, a four-point scale is introduced that models a rubric. Based on statements, the responder is asked to rate the book on a scale from 1 ("very good" or "yes") to 4 ("unsatisfactory" or "no").

Also, the pattern of each chapter is similar. Chapters begin with an Introduction and Response section designed to help recall knowledge. Chapters 4 through 12 each describe a single genre and include an evaluation scheme and a summary. Implications for Instruction sections include teaching ideas for young readers, and additional resources are listed after the references to direct you to other related ideas.

SUMMARY

Literature is powerful and pleasurable and has the capacity to entice readers into realistic stories, books of fact, or imaginary kingdoms. Because children's literature is gaining attention as an integral part of reading programs, teachers, librarians, and all adults who interact with children are turning to resources to find out how to best utilize the richness literature offers. This chapter (and, in fact, this book) provides a close look at the field of children's literature and its current strength and diversity.

This chapter began with an introduction that asked for involvement. Identifying needs, recalling background knowledge, and setting purposes were the first responses demanded from this text, and each following chapter opens with a similar invitation to explore different aspects of children's literature.

Children's literature was defined by qualitative statements: It is powerful and mesmerizing, causing readers to think and act. Many children's books exist; some of them have the requisite qualities to be considered literature, and some do not. Suggestions for evaluation were considered, and stages of child development helped focus on the primary audience and its characteristics that have a special bearing on language and literature.

Principles for a literature-based reading program, derived from developmental and educational axioms, were given. Essentially, principles suggested that adults know the field and read widely; that school organizations support the kind of responses children can make; and that integrated, authentic, and multidisciplinary activities arise from the literature and the needs of the children.

IMPLICATIONS FOR INSTRUCTION

In this section, projects are suggested so that you can actively become engaged with some children's literature, and classroom activities are listed for your interaction with primary (ages 5 through 8) and intermediate- and middle-school children (ages 9 through 13).

Projects

1. If you have not already started a reading list, start one now. Also, develop a system that will record your responses to books as you read them. You may want to jot your ideas on small cards, or type them into a computer-

ized database, or begin a notebook just for this purpose. If your school or colleagues have one, join a children's-literature book club. If not, start one and begin with some books you have always wanted to read.

2. Create a text set on a topic or theme that is unique or timely, such as the Arab World and Islam, or something else that has meaning for you.

3. Read five new children's books and determine if they are literature. Evaluate them by the methods suggested in this chapter. What did you discover?

4. Find an author who writes both children's and adult books. Read some of both and see if there are differences in style, substance, or quality. You could begin with Roald Dahl, Jane Langton, John Steinbeck, Madeleine L'Engle, or Judy Blume.

Activities for the Primary Level

1. Read aloud a popular picture book to a group of 6-year-olds. List their responses and reflect on "what they got" from the literature. Were you surprised? Did the children think of aspects that you did not?

2. Visit a primary classroom to note what children's books are being read by and to the children, and find out from the teacher the place of literature in the reading program. Is literature balanced with a "skills" approach?

3. Visit a child-care center or a primary classroom and look for the psychosocial markers for the stages of development. Do children manipulate concrete objects for math? Do they seem optimistic about their capabilities and feelings? What oral language patterns are noticeable in children's speech? What kinds of activities has the teacher planned that seem to be particularly developmentally appropriate?

4. Visit the children's room of a public library and notice how books are displayed and how posters and other visual aids "sell" books. Find out what kind of programming is done to connect children and books. You may want to ask the children's librarian about book selection, budgets, frequency, attendance at story hours, and other facets of this position.

Activities for the Intermediate and Middle Levels

1. Survey some middle-schoolers to see what their favorite books are. Do they have a touchstone or a significant book by which to judge others?

2. Visit a middle-school library and ask the librarian what books are popular and what programs are in place to encourage reading. Are any of the books entangled in censorship issues? Are the books displayed in a visually inviting manner?

3. Discuss with a group of children how they select literature to read. How do they know when a book is too easy or too difficult? What influence does the peer group have?

REFERENCES

Children's Works

Brown, M. W. (1947). *Goodnight moon*. New York: Harper & Row.

Myers, W. D. (1999). *Monster*. New York: HarperCollins.

O'Dell, S. (1960). *Island of the blue dolphins*. Boston: Houghton Mifflin.

Sendak, M. (1963). *Where the wild things are*. New York: Harper & Row.

White, E. B. (1952). *Charlotte's web*. New York: Harper & Row.

Professional Works

Au, K. H., Carroll, J. H., & Scheu, J. A. (2001). *Balanced literacy instruction: A teacher's resource book* (2nd ed.). Norwood, MA: Christopher Gordon.

Cairney, T. (1990). *Other worlds: The endless possibilities of literature*. Portsmouth, NH: Heinemann.

Chambers, A. (1983). *Introducing books to children* (2nd ed.) (p. 8). Boston: Horn Book.

Childress, G. (1985). Gender gap in the library: Different choices for boys and girls. *Top of the news, 42,* 69–73.

Cox, C., & Zarillo, J. (1993). *Teaching reading with children's literature* (p. 121). Upper Saddle River, NJ: Merrill/Prentice Hall.

Crago, M., & Crago, H. (1983). *Prelude to literacy: A preschool child's encounter with picture and story*. Carbondale: Southern Illinois University.

DeLapp, S. (1989). Administrative support for literature-based reading programs. In J. Hickman & B. Cullinan (Eds.), *Children's literature in the classroom: Weaving Charlotte's web* (pp. 221–229). Norwood, MA: Christopher Gordon.

Erikson, E. (1963). *Childhood and society*. New York: Norton.

Flavell, J. (1985). *Cognitive development* (2nd ed.). Upper Saddle River, NJ: Prentice Hall.

Gardner, H. (1983). *Frames of mind*. New York: Basic.

Hoffman, L., Paris, S., Hall, E., & Schell, R. (1988). *Developmental psychology today* (5th ed.) (p. 278). New York: McGraw-Hill.

Huck, C., Hepler, S., Hickman, J., & Kiefer, B. Z. (2001). *Children's literature in the elementary school* (7th ed., revised by Barbara Kiefer) (p. 5.). Boston: McGraw-Hill.

Hunt, P. (1991). *Criticism, theory, and children's literature*. Cambridge, MA: Basil Blackwell.

Leu, D. J., & Kinzer, C. K. (1999). *Effective reading instruction, K–8.* (4th ed.). Upper Saddle River, NJ: Merrill/Prentice Hall.

Louv, R. (1990). *Childhood's future*. New York: Anchor-Doubleday.

Lukens, R. (1999). *A critical handbook of children's literature* (6th ed.). New York: HarperCollins.

Nilsen, A., & Donelson, K. (1997). *Literature for today's young adults* (5th ed.). New York: Addison-Wesley.

Nodelman, P. (1996). *The pleasures of children's literature* (2nd ed.). New York: Longman.

Piaget, J. (1952). *The origins of intelligence in children*. New York: International University Press.

Rosenblatt, L. (1978). *The reader, the text, the poem: The transactional theory of the literary work*. Carbondale: Southern Illinois University.

Tompkins, G. E. (2001). *Literacy for the 21st century: A balanced approach* (2nd ed). Upper Saddle River, NJ: Prentice Hall.

Vygotsky, L. S. (1962). *Thought and language*. Cambridge, MA: MIT Press.

Wepner, S. B., & Feeley, J. T. (1993). *Moving forward with literature: Basals, books, and beyond* (p. 5). Upper Saddle River, NJ: Merrill/Prentice Hall.

Additional Resources

Fox, M. (2001). *Reading magic: Why reading aloud to our children will change their lives forever*. New York: Harvest/Harcourt.
    Well-known Australian children's book author and professor of literacy, Fox writes persuasively about the importance of reading aloud. She also offers practical tips.

Marcus, L. (Ed. and Comp.). (1998). *Dear genius: The letters of Ursula Nordstrom*. New York: HarperCollins.
    An influential person in children's literature from 1940 to 1973 (some would say the most influential), Nordstrom oversaw the growth and development of the industry and brought Charlotte's Web, Where the Wild Things Are, *and many other classics to the public.*

Silvey, A. (1995/2002). *Children's books and their creators.* (2nd ed.). Boston: Houghton Mifflin.
An outstanding collection of themes, authors' profiles, and trends and issues in children's literature, updated and enlarged.

Van Orden, P. (2000). *Selecting books for the elementary school library media center: A complete guide.* New York: Neal-Schuman.
An excellent, comprehensive guide to managing a library, and a crash course for beginners or detailed enough for experienced librarians.

CHAPTER 2

Childhood, Children, and History

INTRODUCTION AND RESPONSE

> It is summer. Sunk deep in the soft bed among feather pillows, with the inconstant rumble of carts on the cobblestones outside the window. . . in the grey village of Saint-Sauveur-en-Puisaye, an eight-year-old girl is silently reading Victor Hugo's *Les Miserables*. She doesn't read many books, she rereads the same ones over and over again. She loves *Les Miserables* with what she'll later call "a reasoning passion"; she feels she can nestle in its pages "like a dog in its kennel." Every night she longs to follow Jean Valjean on his agonizing peregrinations, meet Cosette again, meet Marius, even the dreaded Javert. (Manguel, 1996, p. 149)

This quote by the French author Colette describes herself as a young girl at the end of the 19th century. Several things are important to note as we consider the history of children's literature. First, the child is reading an "adult" book, and children have always appropriated literature from the adult world, from traditional literature to stories of adventure and romance. Second, she wants to read the same text again and again, a familiar pattern to all of us who have read to children and, even as adults, have a favorite story that means so much. Moreover, many children's books were not available at this time to Colette, so perhaps this paucity of choice added incentive to her rereading. Third, a young girl is reading, and in the history of books and reading, women and girls have been discouraged, even forbidden, from reading, though by the late 1800s this was not true for Colette. However, in other parts of the world, and among disenfranchised people, learning to read and write was and is an act of political defiance. Last, Colette expresses the mesmerizing, addictive power of literacy, the longing to enter the world of the novel and live among its characters. When and how did children come to acquire all these factors—enjoying the ability to read, the leisure time that allows literacy to flourish, and control over the choices of reading material?

•◆•

REFLECTION   How is Colette different from, or similar to, an 8-year-old whom you know? Or how and what were you reading at age 8?

To understand the history of children's literature is to understand how the human race invented and began to practice a period of time called "childhood." The invention of childhood did not happen quickly but came about as attitudes and knowledge of medicine, nutrition, human worth, communication, art, and culture allowed men and women slowly to gain control of their lives. Literacy and literature developed hand in hand, each depending on and fostering the other. Discoveries triggered startling innovations in technology, knowledge, and creativity. Beginning early in humankind's brief history of recorded time on Earth, our passion for language, story, and metaphor have brought us to today's wealth of children's books.

In this chapter, several chronological charts summarize certain accomplishments in writing and publishing throughout the last few centuries. You can begin a chronology of your own, and think about "old" books, people, or inventions that you think were instrumental in shaping society. What would be the first entry?

IN THE DISTANT PAST

In the distant past, most people were nonliterate because they had neither the opportunity nor the means to learn to read. Before the 15th century, literature for the common people (that is, neither clerics nor nobility) was expressed in the oral tradition. A vast repertoire of tales, songs, proverbs, and ditties passed from generation to generation in spoken form or sung. Called **traditional literature,** or the *oral tradition,* this repertoire forms the foundation of all literature today. In the fourth chapter, we will examine traditional literature and examples from long ago and more modern times.

Traditional literature began when our ancestors in caves told stories about and drew pictures of real and metaphorical beasts. Unexplainable forces of nature—lightning, thunder, fire, the sun, and the moon—were explained through stories about their creation and their purpose. Wise elders and shamen intuited creation myths about how the society, or tribe, began. The deities were sometimes female, sometimes male, and reflected each group's environment. For example, if people depended on the ocean for sustenance, then sea creatures, turtles, whales, dolphins, and such would figure prominently in the creation story. Creation stories described how animals and people came to be in a particular kind of community. *In the Beginning: Creation Stories Around the* World (Hamilton, 1988), a Newbery honor book, is a powerful collection of 25 of these stories. They show the diversity, the imagination, and the linguistic ability of primitive people to explain supernatural and scientific forces. In this collection, many societies—including Native American, Greek, African, South American, and Icelandic—seek to understand their place in the early fabric of their existence. As Virginia Hamilton says, "Lonely as they were, by themselves, early people looked inside themselves and expressed a longing to discover, to explain who they were, why they were, and from what and where they came" (p. xi). Creation, or genesis myths, came before the "Once Upon a Time" stories and before time itself was discovered.

As early people continued to rationalize their lives by "storying," many purposes were served. The myths, fables, and folklore bound the tribe together, providing a common body of knowledge. Children were taught what to believe, how to act, and what roles to play. Storytelling revealed common psychological impulses, as fears, needs, and universal human problems appeared in stories from geographically distant cultures (see the many versions of *Cinderella, Snow White,* and *Sleeping Beauty,* for example, in Bettelheim, 1976). It socialized children into the linguistic and moral practices of the tribe. Traditional literature was the mortar that held communities together; it was an expression for religious, social, and educational beliefs.

Panchatantra fables from India written in one of the earliest languages, Sanskrit, and fables from Aesop (probably dating from the 6th century B.C.E.) are among the earliest examples of traditional literature that identified human behavior and satirized it. If we say "sour grapes," "cry wolf," or "Slow but steady wins the race," we know immediately that these phrases allude to Aesop. It is amazing that these pithy, short allegorical narratives are so true to human nature that they speak to us across thousands of years. From earliest times, Aesop's fables were known to peasants, kings, and clergy, and often were instrumental in teaching young boys to read. The fables, frequently the only secular readings, "became the common coin of European childhood" (Bader, 1991, p. 11).

Aesop's fables were also passed down orally through storytelling from generation to generation. Storytelling was a mode of communication, and storytellers often were entrusted with the history of the community as well as the tales. This dual role of the storyteller emerged in primitive society: a historian, responsible for committing to memory the genealogy and important events of the tribe, and a fantasist, who created or retold stories to entertain and instruct listeners in the values and mores of society. Storytellers were often transient, traveling from castle to cottage to earn their keep. Stories were told and retold, expanded or diminished according to the magical bond between teller and listener. Special names were given to storytellers: *bards* in the British Isles, *troubadours* in Europe, *skalds* in Scandinavia, and *griots* in Africa.

Illuminated manuscripts were painstakingly drawn and copied by monks in medieval monasteries, and handmade books were available only to a few. Most of the populace had no access to reading material. The few books that were available were enjoyed by everyone who could read, and age was no indicator of reading ability. Chaucer's *Canterbury Tales* (c. 1400/McCaughrean, 1984) was surely enjoyed by the reading public. Also, manuscripts called *courtesy books* flourished in the 15th century. Very instructive and often written in rhyme, these books of lessons exhorted children, and everyone else, to behave properly.

In the medieval world and before, there was no place for childhood (Aries, 1962). As soon as infants gained physical independence, they were expected to be supporting members of the family. To be sure, the life span of the populace was much shorter, as most individuals had to work for the most basic needs—food and shelter—and socialization into the adult world occurred very quickly for economic reasons. If they managed to live through a treacherous childhood vulnerable to disease, the plague, poverty, and sometimes uncaring parents, at age 7, children were apprenticed to craftsmen or taverners, or into the houses of the aristocracy and landed gentry. A great many children of all social and economic classes died before their first birthday.

From the Oral Tradition to Print

Traditional literature collided with the invention of the printing press in the middle 1400s. The new technology, movable type, changed forever the course of language and literature. Social, political, and economic forces soon dictated the need for a literate populace, and the fledgling production of books provided opportunities for more people to learn to read. Schooling became possible for the rising European middle class, and boys (and to some extent, girls) had to have books.

Publication of the first books associated with children's literature is attributed to the Englishman William Caxton, who produced *Aesop's Fables* (1484), *Morte D'Arthur* (1485), and the *History of Reynard the Fox* (1481), among others. These tales came from the oral tradition and were popular with everyone. As printed books gained in abundance and popularity, folk literature began to be associated with a new audience, a first-time audience: children.

1500 A.D. TO 1600 A.D.

Wynken de Worde assumed William Caxton's printing business in London, and in 1504 he published the romantic French folktale *Valentine and Orson* (Burkert, 1989). (See Figure 2.1.) It promptly became popular, finding its audience among young, old, and middle-aged people. Similarly, Robert Whittington translated *A Lytell Book of Good Manners for Children* from the writings of Erasmus, the famous philosopher who influenced Henry VIII, among others. Printed by de Worde in 1532 in Latin and in English, the book exemplifies the courtesy books mentioned earlier. It was highly unusual for a scholar of Erasmus's reputation to pay any attention to children, even when the subject was courteous behavior (Bingham & Scholt, 1980).

The 1500s became embroiled in turmoil as King Henry VIII of England challenged the Roman Catholic Church in Rome. Religious controversies rocked all of Europe as Martin Luther pounded his *95 Theses* on the cathedral door in Germany in 1517 to spark the Protestant Reformation. Publication of the Gutenberg Bible contributed to the religious unease as the dichotomy between Catholic and Protestant beliefs grew, paving the way for the *religious didacticism* in children's literature that

Date	Milestones
1504	The folktale *Valentine and Orson* is translated and published by Wynken de Worde in London.
1532	*A Lytell Book of Good Manners for Children,* a courtesy book probably by the philosopher Erasmus, is published.
1540	King Henry VIII writes *King Henry's Primers* to teach the populace about his religious views.
1563	John Foxe's *Book of Martyrs* fuels the fires of the Protestant Reformation and is considered appropriate for children.
Late 1500s	Hornbooks and chapbooks become available in classrooms and countryside.

Figure 2.1 Milestones in the 1500s

followed. Henry VIII published *King Henry's Primers* in 1540, a set of simple English books that contained his own religious dogma. While not expressly for children, the primers were nevertheless suitable for young readers.

As literacy became more necessary for participating in commerce, so did it also become a focal point in the religious controversies of the 16th century. Protestantism, with its emphasis on personal salvation gained apart from the intercession of priests and saints, required each of the "elect," to use Calvinist terminology, to study the Bible and other religious tracts. John Foxe's *Book of Martyrs* (1563/Foxe, 1997), containing horrendous accounts of torture and suffering, was considered highly suitable for children. Written to provide life stories of the Christian martyrs who sacrificed their lives, the short and bloody accounts were exciting, and did much to stiffen the Protestant resolve when "Bloody Mary," Henry VIII's Roman Catholic daughter, came to the throne and persecuted all those who didn't follow Rome's teaching. When her five-year reign ended and Elizabeth I ascended to the throne, Protestant literature was again sweeping the country and the rest of Europe.

This period of didacticism was lightened somewhat by the availability of the **chapbook.** Analogous to inexpensive paperbacks today, chapbooks were small paper booklets sold by peddlers, or "chapmen," who roamed the countryside and hawked their wares, including humorous and romantic stories. Printed on cheap paper, sometimes with crude woodcuts the only illustrations, these chapbooks were available to common people and contained familiar and well-loved stories. For example, a rhymed story of a tiny hero—*Tom Thumb: His Life and Death*—was found in a chapbook printed in 1630 (Sutherland, 1997).

In the late 1500s, another kind of book appeared that is associated with the beginnings of children's literature. Prevalent in English classrooms, **hornbooks** were

A page from *Orbis Pictus*.

(1)

Orbis Sensualium Pictus,

A World of Things Obvious to the Senses drawn in Pictures.

Invitation.   I.   Invitatio.

The Master and the Boy. | *Magister & Puer.*

M. Come, Boy, learn to | M. Veni, Puer, disce sa-
. be wise. | pere.

P. What doth this mean, | P. Quid hoc est, *Sapere?*
to be wise?

M. To understand right- | M. Intelligere recte,
ly,

small wooden boards shaped like paddles and covered with a thin layer of transparent horn. In the next century, when the American colonies began, New England classrooms were replete with these small samplers from which, for example, children chanted the alphabet, then written as *ab, ac, ad,* and so on. The Lord's Prayer and biblical verses also were often displayed. Significant books and dates are summarized in Figure 2.1: Milestones in the 1500s.

1600 A.D. TO 1700 A.D.

In 1658, John Comenius wrote and published the first picture book expressly for children, *Orbis Pictus,* or *The World Illustrated*. Bishop Comenius was a Moravian minister who wrote and printed this little scientific book, as he explained in the preface, "to entice witty children to it" (Sutherland, 1997). Woodcuts by Michael Endter illustrated common plants and animals, accompanied by explanatory text in German and in Latin. Truly a milestone in publishing for children, this book not only repre- sented a deviation from religious stories, but also identified an audience heretofore largely ignored.

From the impetus of the break with Roman Catholicism, literature emerged that typified the personal search for a heavenly end. John Bunyan's *Pilgrim's Progress* (1678/1994) is a prime example. Writing in prison, Bunyan created this allegorical, didactic odyssey of a Christian seeking salvation, which struck a chord in younger readers as an adventurous journey. Didacticism prevailed, however, and most ma- terial written and published for children had as its primary purpose the instruction of young souls so that they would be worthy to die. An example of religious di- dacticism is one of the first books for children published in North America, John Cotton's *Milk for Babes Drawn Out of the Breasts of Both Testaments, Chiefly for the Spiritual Nourishment of Boston Babes in Either England, but May Be of Like Use to Any Children,* which was published in England in 1646 and in Boston in 1684 (Rosenbach, 1971).

The first *New England Primer,* known to have been published before 1690, be- gins as follows:

A In Adam's fall
We sinned all.

B Thy life to mend
This Book attend.

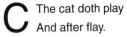

C The cat doth play
And after flay.

Small block woodcuts depict the Garden of Eden, with *A*dam standing by the tree, then the open *B*ible, and a *c*at playing with a mouse accompanied the couplets. Thus were all Pilgrim and Puritan children informed of the burden of their sinful be- ginnings in this life.

REFLECTION   What are some didactic books of today? Do we have mod- ern versions of the religious didacticism or the "good manners" books of past centuries? Is this didacticism still a feature of children's literature?

Another event of great importance happened at the turn of this century. When the English philosopher John Locke wrote *Some Thoughts Concerning Education* (c. 1693), a quiet revolution began. Departing from the conventional wisdom, which preached that children were born with the taint of "original sin," Locke argued that infants come into the world with no burden of the sins of the forefathers, but with a *tabula rasa,* or blank slate. Thus, all impressions and experiences were instru- mental in forming the personalities of human beings. Innocence replaced original sin, and the idea of a formative period, a period of childhood, began to gain acceptance. What an antidote to the stern puritanical views of childhood and education com- monly held! These views of the importance of the social environment were also the

Date	Milestones
1600	Hornbooks and chapbooks continue to educate and delight children.
1646–1684	John Cotton's *Milk for Babes Drawn Out of the Breasts of Both Testaments, Chiefly for the Spiritual Nourishment of Boston Babes in Either England, but May Be of Like Use to Any Children* is standard reading for everyone.
1658	*Orbis Pictus* is written "to entice witty children."
1678	John Bunyan's prison epic, *Pilgrim's Progress,* achieves great popularity.
1690	The first *New England Primer* makes its appearance.
1693	Childhood is forecast in John Locke's *Some Thoughts Concerning Education.*
1697	*Mother Goose Tales,* published by Charles Perrault in France, lightens the heavy tone of reading material for children and adults.

Figure 2.2   Milestones in the 1600s

beginning of nature versus nurture controversies still theorized and researched to-day in human psychological development.

Fairy Tales and Mother Goose

Although religious material was much more prevalent, another kind of literature made its presence known at the end of the 1600s. Through the efforts of Charles Per-rault in France, and later the Brothers Grimm in Germany, old tales common in the oral tradition were collected and frozen in print, to the delight of children, linguists, folklorists, and other scholars. In 1697 Charles Perrault (or possibly his son, Pierre d'Armancourt) published *Mother Goose Tales* in France. These eight tales included "Cinderella," "Puss in Boots," "Sleeping Beauty," and a version of "Little Red Riding Hood" (Ehrlich, 1985).

At the turn of the 17th century, the heavy-handedness of religious didacticism was offset somewhat by these ephemeral fairy tales, a welcome addition to literature for children. Figure 2.2: Milestones in the 1600s summarizes significant events and books of this century.

1700 A.D. TO 1800 A.D.

Mother Goose nursery rhymes had been part of the oral tradition in England in an-other form (not the stories collected by Perrault/d'Armancourt). Short verses, or ditties, such as *Humpty Dumpty, Jack and Jill, Little Miss Muffet,* and so on predate the 1700s, and were enjoyed by adults because many were thought to be political satires. This interpretation of *Humpty Dumpty* suggests that Henry VIII, King of England, is the main character of this ditty.

Humpty Dumpty sat on a wall (Henry VIII torn between Roman Catholicism and the desire to divorce his wife).

Humpty Dumpty had a great fall (the King fell away from the church).

All the King's horses and All the King's men (the ministers, the dukes, political and religious allies).

Couldn't put Humpty together again (the Kingdom would never be the same, and Henry VIII lost his reputation).

These rhymes provided a way to characterize the nobility as foolish or worse without impugning an aristocrat's name. After all, it was treasonous to speak out, as freedom of speech was only a dream in the minds of a few. To show how a simple rhyme can have wide-ranging interpretations, *Sing a Song of Sixpence* has been described as alluding to the choirs of Tudor monasteries, the printing of the English Bible, the malpractices of the Romish clergy, or the infinite workings of the solar system (Opie & Opie, 1951). That is, the 24 blackbirds baked into the pie stood for the choirs of the soon-to-be-dissolved monasteries under Henry VIII's reign, or the 24 letters of the alphabet in the movable type of the printing press, or the 24 hours of the solar clock. Certainly, political satire was not the only interpretation of nursery rhymes, as some were just nonsensical, and some related to the weather, to human traits, or to human folly.

Mother Goose, whose real identity will never be known, if indeed such a person existed, lends her name to two important contributions to children's literature: verse and fairy tale. Reasons for linking the name to collections of nursery rhymes or fairy tales have been lost in historical obscurity, but several theories explain why and how the name is so closely associated with children's literature. One of the earliest theories is that the ditties were from the repertoire of medieval storyteller Goose-footed Bertha, who could have been the mother of Charlemagne (742–814) or the wife of Robert II of France (970–1031). Apparently both of these women entertained children with stories and verses while spinning or sewing at court (Gillespie, 1970). It is possible to imagine that a clubfoot, or some other physical impairment, contributed to the reason that a "goose-footed" Bertha remained sedentary and delighted listeners as she worked.

One of the later theories suggests that an American in Boston, "Dame Goose," was the true embodiment of the legend. Her tombstone can be found in the Old Granary Burying Ground and notes her fame. This claim is supported by the fact that in 1715 her daughter married Thomas Fleet, a publisher who may have published the first American version of *Mother Goose's Melodies* (Gillespie, 1970). Whatever the circumstances and whoever began the tradition make no difference now. We can enjoy speculating about all the possibilities and imagining even more. The value of the rhymes, their variations, and modern evocations of Mother Goose will be considered further in Chapters 5 and 6.

A page from Swift's *Gulliver's Travels.*

Novels of Adventure and Satire

Two books whose importance cannot be overstated emerged from the puritanical world of the early 1700s. First, *The Life and Adventures of Robinson Crusoe* appeared in 1719 at the end of Daniel Defoe's career. The story became immensely popular in the English-speaking world and was soon translated into other languages. The love of adventure, independence, and ingenuity of the main character, a sailor in the best British tradition, struck a chord in youthful readers and the general public. Defoe's (1719/1965) work was instrumental in the development of a new form in literature: the *novel.*

The second book followed fast and was equally devoured by the reading public. It had an especially compelling storyline for children. In 1726, Jonathan Swift, an Irishman writing anonymously because of possible repercussions from his heavy-handed satire, published *Gulliver's Travels* (1726/1995). Upon reading of the allegorical journey of the character Lemuel Gulliver, children immediately saw humor and delight in the now famous Lilliput and Brobdingnag. Margaret Hodges, a well-known reteller and illustrator, introduces young children to Gulliver in her picture book, *Gulliver in Lilliput* (1995).

Dog licking the Porridge Pot.

COW and CALF

Cat cleaning the Frying Pan.

The Hoop does run   the Doll makes fun.

A battledore adapted by the Colonial Williamsburg Foundation. Copyright © 1985. Used by permission.

John Newbery & Co.

John Newbery put his mark on children's literature in 1744 when he published the first books expressly for children. Newbery can be viewed as the father—or at least the midwife—of modern children's literature. He published stories written either by himself or by others (Oliver Goldsmith, for one) such as *A Little Pretty Pocket-Book* (1744) and *Goody Two Shoes* (1745). Remembered as an energetic entrepreneur who also sold quack medicines, Newbery can be honored for his vision of providing children with entertaining, as well as instructive, books (Hearn, 1997). The Newbery Medal, awarded each year by the American Library Association to designate the best children's book published in the United States by a U.S. author, appropriately pays homage to Newbery's memory.

According to legend, one of Newbery's employees invented the **battledore,** a large piece of cardboard folded in three leaves. It contained alphabets, numerals, and easy reading lessons. Battledores were the only instructional material many children had.

Scientific Didacticism

As the 18th century produced more authors and books for children, religious didacticism was replaced with a fervor to instruct children about the natural world. Books were now seen as teaching devices and were an indispensable part of schools and

Date	Milestones
1700s	Battledores add to the reading fare of children, and *scientific didacticism* replaces religious didacticism for children.
(?)1715	Possibly the American title *Mother Goose's Melodies* was published in Boston.
1719	*Robinson Crusoe,* by Daniel Defoe, captures the imagination of the world and is immensely popular.
1726	Witty and satirical, *Gulliver's Travels* by Jonathan Swift is published.
1744	John Newbery, from his children's bookstore in London, publishes *A Little Pretty Pocket-Book.*
1762	Jean-Jacques Rousseau writes *Émile* to celebrate the "natural" upbringing of children.
1789	William Blake establishes a standard of poetry for children in *Songs of Innocence.*

Figure 2.3   Milestones in the 1700s

classrooms. Educational theorists, such as Locke, Rousseau, and Comenius, gave impetus to new ideas about the importance of childhood and the kinds of books that should be available to children.

"The influence of Jean-Jacques Rousseau (1712–78) on English language children's literature is comparable with that of Locke" (Townsend, 1987, p. 25). Rousseau, another philosopher/reformer, wrote *Émile* (1762/1969) and thus provided an example of the child brought up naturally, with the freedom to explore woods, fields, and streams unhampered by direct instruction. Physical activity was important, natural curiosity was encouraged, and "moral" education and even learning to read were postponed until adolescence. (When the intellectual stimulation of reading was approved, the first book Rousseau recommended was *Robinson Crusoe.*)

Although childhood was now recognized as a developmental period, and education, primarily reading, writing, and arithmetic, was seen as the birthright of many children, the urge to provide thinly disguised moral lessons in story form still characterized most of children's literature. The end of the 18th century saw a "stock literary character emerging in books for children—the all-wise and beneficent friend, teacher, or parent, who was constantly available to answer all questions propounded by the children in the books" (Gillespie, 1970, p. 22). This adult figure represented the voice of maturity and common sense, and would inevitably turn the dialogue into a sermon. Needless to say, such a character impeded the narrative flow and rendered a story dull and lifeless. Figure 2.3 summarizes the significant events and books of the 1700s.

1800 A.D. TO 1900 A.D.

The first notable spotlight of the 19th century focuses on the Brothers Grimm—Jacob and Wilhelm—who collected folktales. As scholars in linguistics, they were interested in how language forms changed, and they used the old tales of their nurse and others to find archaic forms of vocabulary, grammar, and usage. A by-product of their research is, of course, more than 200 tales and "the inspiration of an entirely new attitude towards the human imagination" (Alderson, 1985, unpaged). The tales were published first in Germany in 1812 as *Kinder und Hausmarchen Gesammelt Durch Die Bruder Grimm* (roughly, *Little Tales for Children and for the Family Collected by the Brothers Grimm*). The English version was known popularly as *Grimms' Fairy Tales* (1823/1973). It is important to remember that the folktales were of the oral tradition first, and even though the title mentions an audience of children and families, the tales were really for everyone.

At this same time, Hans Christian Andersen of Denmark was composing original fairy tales, which were translated into and published in English in 1846 to the wonder of the rest of the world. His tales, such as "The Emperor's New Clothes," "Thumbelina," "The Steadfast Tin Soldier," and "The Ugly Duckling" speak so clearly with wisdom and insight that it seems they sprang from folklore. Their charm and poignancy come from universal human truths and foibles, but they have a lyrical quality unmatched in any other body of work (Hazard, 1944).

With the burgeoning industrial revolution and the technology in book design and publishing that sprang from it, children's books became plentiful and handsome. Outstanding books were published, books that are readily acknowledged as classics, such as *A Christmas Carol* (Charles Dickens, 1843/1997), *Alice's Adventures in Wonderland* (Charles Dodgson writing as Lewis Carroll, 1865/1985), and *Little Women* (Louisa May Alcott, 1868/1987). Many other books were sentimental, provincial, and didactic: *Tales of Peter Parley* (Samuel Goodrich, 1827 through 1850), *Ragged Dick* (Horatio Alger, 1867), and *Elsie Dinsmore* (Martha Farquharson Finley, 1867).

REFLECTION   Many of our classics were written in this "Golden Age." In retrospect, some of the books are criticized for racial, ethnic, gender, and other stereotypes. Are these criticisms important enough to warrant ignoring the books?

In *Alice's Adventures in Wonderland,* the "wordplay, nonsense, adult-baiting, violence, nightmare, and comedy pushed the whole concept of writing for children light years ahead of the generally safe and sentimental didacticism of the earlier literature" (Frey & Griffith, 1987, p. 116). This book emphatically revolutionized ideas about what was appropriate or permissible for children and still amazes and sometimes unsettles us today. Rich in theme, imagery, and whimsy, *Alice* and its companion, *Through the Looking Glass* (1872/1994), propelled literature for children into a different and wholly new creative dimension.

The Golden Age of Children's Literature

The Victorian era in England is known for its middle-class ethos, an ethos that exalted books, reading, and the innocence and beauty of childhood. A rising middle class wanted its children to have books on manners, morals, and the mores of society. Children were even entertained by some of them. While Mark Twain was writing *The Adventures of Tom Sawyer* (1876/1989) in the United States, Anna Sewell was writing *Black Beauty* (1877/1990), a story from a horse's point of view. An early animal-rights activist, Sewell wrote the story to point out harsh and cruel treatment of horses.

Meanwhile, in 1873, Mary Mapes Dodge became editor of one of the most famous magazines for children, *St. Nicholas*. Her interest in and understanding of young people, combined with her literary ability, made it the "outstanding magazine for children of all time" (Gillespie, 1970, p. 73). Other children's magazines also enjoyed unprecedented popularity in this last half of the 19th century and provided new outlets for authors and illustrators.

The beginning of technical artistry and illustration in this period brought forth a unique art form, the **picture book.** As the industrial revolution changed so much of commerce and industry, so did it spur the invention of technology related to printing and reproducing illustrations. A pioneer in this field, Edmund Evans, can be credited with charting the course of modern book illustration because of his work in the late 1800s. He was an illustrator, engraver, printer, and businessman, but his true genius seemed to be the recognition of artistic ability in others. His expertise allowed the

From *Randolph Caldecott's Favorite Nursery Rhymes.* (p. 57), 1980, New York: Castle Book Sales. Copyright © 1980, F. S. Oppel, Castle Book Sales. Reprinted by permission.

artist's vision to remain true in the mass production of book after book. Evans developed a full-color printing process, providing illustrators with the technology to realize images more consistently. His artistry graces some early stories, but he was instrumental in encouraging and marketing the work of Walter Crane, Randolph Caldecott, and Kate Greenaway, the triumvirate of the best in early children's book artistry, and those who set standards for 20th-century work. Caldecott, especially, drew with such imagination and grace that he set standards for picture book artistry. It is fitting that the most prestigious award given in the United States for picture books is the Caldecott Award. (See Chapter 5 for a more comprehensive history of the picture book.)

By the turn of the century, children's literature and compulsory education had become firmly established in the fabric of society. Books were plentiful, and in this "Golden Age of Victorian children's books, literature was for pleasure rather than for admonition" (Egoff, 1980, p. 416). Because of the increasing number of notable books, each of the following chapters includes a brief account of literary development in that genre. See Figure 2.4 for a summary of significant books and events of the 1800s.

Date	Milestones
1812	Jacob and Wilhelm Grimm collect and publish *Little Tales for Children and for the Family,* which became famous the world over. (Translated to English, 1823.)
1843	Charles Dickens writes *A Christmas Carol,* beloved by everyone.
1846	The imaginative Hans Christian Andersen composes his unique fairy tales very much in the tradition of folk literature.
1865	*Alice's Adventures in Wonderland* establishes modern fantasy as a genre.
mid-1800s	The Victorian era encourages modern views of childhood and family, and the *Golden Age* of children's literature ensues.
1870s and on	Technology combines art and text so that *picture books* assume importance in industry and economics.
1873	*St. Nicholas,* a forerunner of modern magazines for children, is published.
By late 1800s	Touchstone books are published in genres such as historical fiction, contemporary realism, and animal fantasy, and children's literature classics are recognized.

Figure 2.4   Milestones in the 1800s

1900 A.D. TO 2000 A.D.

The early 20th century was marked by an explosion of picture books, made possible by new technology in color printing. In chapter books, a variety of genres became apparent as children began to enjoy the same breadth and depth that characterized all literature. Realistic adventure, animal stories, folklore, fantasy, poetry, family stories, school stories, and so on became readily accessible. The European literary industry was devastated by World War I, and leadership in publishing shifted to the United States.

Views of childhood in the 1920s and 1930s were marked by an interest in individual differences, prompted as the new discipline of psychology began to explain human growth and development in intelligence, language, and social behavior. Progressive ideas of schooling advanced by John Dewey and others allowed children much more freedom. Immigrant children filled city schools, and literature for children reflected some of the melting-pot philosophy that society then articulated. Generally the literature was optimistic, even during the Great Depression of the early 1930s, as evidenced by a number of happy family stories. Some excellent examples are the Laura Ingalls Wilder "Little House" books, which began to be published in 1932. The rise of children's libraries, an influx of talented writers and illustrators from Europe, and advances in medicine, transportation, and communication affected children's book publishing positively.

Although World War II caused havoc among institutions and individuals, the decades of the 1940s and 1950s still saw happy family stories or domestic stories, fantasies, historical fiction, and, indeed, memorable books in all genres. The launch of a Russian sputnik in 1957 precipitated a crisis in education, and the growing interest in the psychological theories of the Swiss psychologist Jean Piaget created a context for educational reform. A host of political changes in the late 1950s and 1960s forced an awareness of social inequity as it became apparent that too many children's books reflected a middle-class, Caucasian, Judeo–Christian, suburban lifestyle unlike that of many of the children for whom the books were written. A new realism—the breaking of taboos in content—permeated children's books of the 1970s, continuing through the 1980s and into the 1990s. Each of the following chapters includes a brief accounting of the history of important books and events in the genre of that chapter.

REFLECTION   The new realism in children's literature after the 1960s and 1970s blurred again the distinction between childhood and adulthood. Almost any subject is now considered suitable for children's stories. Do you have some examples of books that seem too "adult" or unsuitable for an audience of children?

As is evident by now, this historical accounting of the development of a body of literature known as children's literature focused primarily on English-language books and events. Even though England led the world into book publishing, it seems short-sighted, if not prejudicial, to presume that everything of significance happened in England or the United States. However, with rare exceptions, it is difficult to find information about the rise of childhood and children's literature in other parts of the world. This is a necessary endeavor as we acknowledge and celebrate diversity among all children today.

2001 A.D. TO THE FUTURE

The early years of this 3rd millennium give evidence to a thriving children's book industry. Internationalism, scholarly and popular attention, and political support for literacy ensure strong growth and development of children's books, and even encourage some creativity and risk taking in the marketplace. This new millennium is so new that trends in the late 20th century are viable today, and can be summarized thusly:

- More picture books and a wider audience for picture books
- Continued proliferation of nonfiction for all ages in high-quality texts
- Fiction and nonfiction for the 7–10 age group (developmental readers from "emerging" to "fluent")
- Multimedia combinations with books (including CD-ROMs, movie tie-ins, toys, games, and so on)
- Contemporary realism that focuses on abandonment, abuse, racial conflict, and other aspects of the reality many children face in all parts of the globe
- An interest in science fiction/fantasy as J. K. Rowling's *Harry Potter* books and Philip Pullman's *His Dark Materials* series typify (see Chapter 8 for a discussion and complete bibliographic information of these books and others)
- Historical realism for elementary and middle school children that reflects a darker, more realistic stance toward the atrocities committed in the name of nationalism or religious fervor.

Children's literature reflects society's views. Still occasionally didactic, it should also offer hope and solace. In the best writing, by fine writers, it does. Sheila Egoff and Wendy Sutton (1996) contend that there is a fairly consistent theme in children's literary fiction that places the child (main character) in difficult situations (as in *Harry Potter,* for example). They say, "The best of modern writers are not concerned, as their predecessors were, with a state called childhood, either distinct from or in tandem with adulthood, but rather with an investigation of those conundrums of life most evident in the psychological transitions from childhood to adulthood" (p. 393).

SUMMARY

Two themes prevail in this chapter on the historical development of children's literature. The first theme is that children's literature emerged when societal and cultural forces defined a period of childhood—that is, until childhood was recognized, there could be no literature for children. The second theme underscores the double nature of children's literature, because it has always had two purposes: to entertain and to instruct. Heavy-handed didacticism, prevalent in religious tracts, then in socially moralistic tomes, is still a concern in children's literature today. This characteristic—using literature to instruct—probably affects children's literature more than any other characteristic. Indeed, when one talks about the unique qualities of a literature for children, this **didacticism** must be considered. Because the audience for whom the books are intended has not fully developed its critical powers, adult intercession in the form of authorship and critical judgment ensures the imposition of adult values and societal messages, but how much adult intercession should be tolerated in the creation of literature for children and the opposite force, censorship, is open to debate.

What are the future directions, characteristics, and issues in children's literature as we approach the 21st century? We have seen how social, religious, and economic forces play on the tapestry of human history and influence entertainment and instruction for children. How do we define *childhood* in this modern era? Children are expected to be independent at an early age; some say they are hurried into adolescence and adulthood. The definition of *childhood* will no doubt continue to evolve, and continue to have a remarkable effect on books produced for children of the next century.

REFLECTION   What will childhood in the 21st century be? What salient characteristics do you predict?

IMPLICATIONS FOR INSTRUCTION

The following projects encourage you to research in more detail significant events and people who affected the development of children's literature. Activities for primary, intermediate, and middle school children are found in Chapter 4 and other chapters because they are based on traditional literature.

Projects

1. John Newbery was an exceptionally talented and quick-thinking person who became financially successful and left a fortune to his descendants. To find out more about this successful entrepreneur, see John Rowe Townsend's *John Newbery and His Books: Trade and Plumb-cake Forever, Huzza!* (1994).

2. Because many of the Mother Goose rhymes are politically charged, continue the precedent by creating some new rhymes that reflect the political situation today.

3. If you search the web for "New England Primer," thousands of sites pop up. Recent New England primers are associated with religious conservatism, home schooling, and supporting school prayer. What do you think of this use of historical artifacts in children's books? To see an early edition of the *New England Primer,* consult www.gettysburg.edu/~tshannon/his341/hep1805c.

4. The Elizabeth Nesbitt Room (www.pitt.edu/~enroom) has information on early editions of children's books, and in particular a very early *Aesop's Fables* is discussed and pictured.

REFERENCES

Children's Works

Alcott, L. M. (1868/1987). *Little women.* New York: Dell Yearling Classics.

Alger, H., Jr. (1867/1990). *Ragged Dick.* New York: Penguin.

Bader, B. (1991). *Aesop & company* (p. 11). Boston: Houghton Mifflin.

Blake, W. (1789/1992). *Songs of innocence and experience.* London: Folio Society.

Bunyan, J. (1678/1994). *Pilgrim's progress.* (G. D. Schmidt, ed.). New York: Eerdmans.

Burkert, N. E. (1989). *Valentine and Orson.* New York: Farrar, Strauss & Giroux.

Carroll, L. (1865/1985). *Alice's adventures in wonderland.* New York: Puffin.

Carroll, L. (1994). *The complete works of Lewis Carroll.* New York: Barnes and Noble.

Defoe, D. (1719/1965). *The life and adventures of Robinson Crusoe.* Baltimore: Penguin Books.

Dickens, C. (1843/1997). *A Christmas carol.* New York: Stewart, Tabori and Chang.

Ehrlich, A. (Adapter). (1985). *The Random House book of fairy tales.* (B. Bettelheim, Intro.; D. Goode, Illus.). New York: Random House.

Finley, M. F. (1867/c. 1920?). *Elsie Dinsmore.* London: Routledge.

Foxe, J. (1997). *Foxe's book of martyrs.* Greenville, SC: Ambassador.

Goodrich, S. (1864). *Peter Parley's own story.* New York: Sheldon and Company.

Goody two shoes. (1745/1993). Warwick, NY: Book Look.

Grimms' fairy tales: Twenty stories. (1823/1973). Illustrated by Arthur Rackham. New York: Viking Press.

Hamilton, V. (1988). *In the beginning: Creation stories around the world.* New York: Harcourt.

Hodges, M. (1995). *Gulliver in Lilliput.* New York: Holiday.

McCaughrean, G. (1984). *Canterbury tales.* Oxford: Oxford University Press.

Newbery, J. (1744/1967). *A little pretty pocket-book.* New York: Harcourt, Brace & World.

Rousseau, J. J. (1762/1969). *Émile.* New York: Dutton.

Sewell, A. (1877/1990). *Black Beauty.* New York: Dell Yearling Classics.

Swift, J. (1726/1995). *Gulliver's travels.* New York: Gramercy Books.

Twain, M. (1876/1989). *The adventures of Tom Sawyer.* New York: Penguin.

Wilder, L. I. (1932). *Little house in the big woods.* New York: Harper Collins.

Professional Works

Alderson, B. (1985). *Grimm tales in English.* London: British Library Exhibition Notes.

Aries, P. (1962). *Centuries of childhood.* New York: Vintage Books.

Bettelheim, B. (1976). *The uses of enchantment.* New York: Knopf.

Bingham, J., & Scholt, G. (1980). *Fifteen centuries of children's literature.* Westport, CT: Greenwood Press.

Egoff, S. (1980). Precepts, pleasures, and portents: Changing emphases in children's literature. In Egoff,

Stubbs, & Ashley (Eds.), *Only connect* (pp. 405–433). Toronto: Oxford University Press.

Egoff, S., & Sutton, W. (1996). Epilogue: Some thoughts on connecting (p. 393). In Egoff, Stubbs, Ashley, & Sutton (Eds.). *Only connect* (3rd ed.). Toronto: Oxford University Press.

Frey, C., & Griffith, J. (1987). *The literary heritage of childhood* (p. 116). New York: Greenwood Press.

Gillespie, M. (1970). *History and trends* (pp. 22, 73). Dubuque, IA: Wm. C. Brown.

Hazard, P. (1944). *Books, children, and men*. Boston: The Horn Book, Inc.

Hearn, M. P. (1997). John Newbery, "Friend of all mankind." *TALL, 6,* 38–46.

Manguel, A. (1996). *A history of reading* (p. 149). New York: Viking.

Opie, I., & Opie, P. (Eds.). (1951). *The Oxford dictionary of nursery rhymes*. Oxford: The Clarendon Press.

Rosenbach, A. S. W. (1971). *Early American children's books*. New York: Dover Publications.

Sutherland, Z. (1997). *Children and books* (9th ed.). New York: Addison-Wesley Longman.

Townsend, J. R. (1987). *Written for children* (3rd ed.) (p. 25). New York: Lippincott.

Townsend, J. R. (Ed.). (1994). *John Newbery and his books: Trade and plumb-cake forever, huzza!* New York: Scarecrow.

Additional Resources

Try bookfinder.com for hard-to-find books in the following and future additional resources.

Griffith, J. W., & Frey, C. H. (Eds.). (2000). *Classics of children's literature* (5th ed.). Upper Saddle River, NJ: Prentice Hall.

This anthology of traditional and modern literature includes some of Perrault, the Grimms, and Andersen, as well as the complete Pinocchio and Treasure Island.

Hunt, P. (Ed.). (2001). *Children's literature: An anthology 1801–1902*. Malden, MA: Blackwell.

Peter Hunt, a preeminent British scholar, edits this volume of over 120 works from the Golden Age in the United Kingdom, United States, Canada, Australia, and New Zealand.

Meigs, C., Eaton, A., Nesbit, E., & Viguers, R. H. (1953). *A critical history of children's literature*. Upper Saddle River, NJ: Merrill/Prentice Hall.

This is the classic history of U.S. children's literature by well-known and entertaining writers. This volume particularly sheds light on the 19th and early 20th centuries.

Three periodicals and a newsletter consistently bring thoughtful analysis, criticism, and historical information about children's literature to interested readers:

Children's Literature Association Quarterly, published by the Children's Literature Association. The Children's Literature Association is a nonprofit organization formed to encourage serious scholarship and research in children's literature.

Children's Literature in Education is an international quarterly published by Human Sciences Press, Inc.

The Five Owls, a newsletter, is published bimonthly by the Jara Society in Minneapolis, Minnesota.

The Lion and the Unicorn, a critical journal of children's literature, is published by the Johns Hopkins University Press in Baltimore, Maryland.

CHAPTER 3

Evaluating Children's Books

INTRODUCTION AND RESPONSE

Recalling what you know about two classics of children's literature, how are *Island of the Blue Dolphins* (O'Dell, 1960) and *Charlotte's Web* (White, 1952) alike? What do they have in common? How are they different? What is distinctive about each one? To respond to these books, and to literature in general, certain questions are asked to allow comparisons among different stories. When comparisons are made, evaluations inevitably follow. Comparisons help to shape a critical response to books, and then may lead to an evaluation of the worth of each book, or several books.

Comparisons also form the basis for classification according to similar types of literature. The classification, or grouping, of similar traits and structures in literature leads to identification of a distinct group, a **genre.** Genre simply means a category or a family of closely related characteristics based on a single premise. A genre in literature is a category of literature, such as poetry. Even though there are many kinds of poems, they are nevertheless distinguishable from other kinds of literature and thus form a genre.

"Correct classification is one of the first steps in a scientific investigation. The accuracy of all further study depends on the accuracy of classification" (Propp, 1968, p. 5). This statement reflects the opinion of a scholar who collected and analyzed Russian folktales in the early part of the 20th century. Then, as now, in literature and in other fields, scientific inquiry began with classification and led to further study and understanding. In this chapter a classification scheme of children's literature is explored so that this field, with all its rich variety, can be better understood and evaluated. Literature for children covers a wide range of topics, from the realistic to the improbable to the wildly fantastic. Its audience ranges from infancy to adulthood, and many styles, types, and kinds of writing mark its pages. This breadth and depth

necessitates schemes of classification so that diversity is recognized and appreciated, yet function and value remain clear.

What are your responses to the comparison of *Island of the Blue Dolphins* and *Charlotte's Web?* How are they similar? Different? If these novels are unfamiliar to you, a quick perusal might be helpful. These are very different books: One is set in the past, on an island; the other turns into a fantasy after a realistic beginning on a farm in the Midwest. There are similarities, too: Both have females as main characters (one of the females is a spider), and both follow a fairly straightforward plot. Both are fiction, and both address a theme that relates to the importance of survival and the extent to which a character works to achieve it.

REFLECTION If you are familiar with these two children's literature classics, what are your thoughts as you compare the books? Some points have been raised; what are others? If you are unfamiliar with these books, compare two others that you know are representative of some of the best in children's books.

After reflection and discussion, certain concepts of classification emerge: Stories that are set in the past, are realistic, or "could have happened," may be called **historical realism**; stories with talking animals must be **fantasy**, because fantasy is based on the impossible—it "could not have happened." When the content of narrative prose is classified into certain types, the patterns form genres. Genre distinctions do not always form unbreakable or clearly defined categories; in fact, they can be somewhat fluid because certain traits or elements may not be present when one expects them to be. Nevertheless, from reading and being read to, we have internalized the definitions of fantasy, poetry, biography, and so on, and we recognize the conventions of that particular group, or genre. As the critic Peter Hunt (1991, p. 136) affirms, "knowing what is or what is not permissible in a certain genre controls our reactions to a text." Our intuitive knowledge of genres gives us cues as we read a text and allows us to decide what is permissible and what is not. We can then decide what is good, or acceptable, and what is not.

Classification into genres comes from what we know about literature, and it is also influenced by social and cultural contexts (Mikkelsen, 2000). The formation of genres is sometimes the result of societal movements and values. When new or different kinds of books appear, the classification system extends to incorporate them. For example, in the last decade attention has been drawn to "multicultural" books in order to support diversity in society and in school curricula. Welcoming diversity is an articulated value in schools, and books that mirror the positive effects of cross-cultural friendships, or that tell a good story while set in a minority culture, may reside in a special category—that is, a genre—in libraries and classrooms.

REFLECTION   Can you think of other genres, or subsets of genres, formed from societal constructs or personal preferences?

After briefly presenting other classification approaches, this chapter focuses on genres as they are defined in this and in other studies of children's literature. Definitions and examples of each genre follow; then literary elements such as theme, plot, character, and so on are defined and related to *Island of the Blue Dolphins* and *Charlotte's Web*. Literary elements give us the vocabulary of literary analysis and criticism. With this theoretical framework, you will be better prepared to enjoy, evaluate, remember, and use books effectively in a classroom or a library or at home.

OTHER APPROACHES TO CLASSIFICATION

Most approaches to the study of children's literature include methods of classifying. Common methods use literary forms, age levels, and topics, in addition to genres based on content. Each method is useful in certain instances, and gives another perspective on the many children's books published today.

Literary forms such as novel, drama, poetry, novella, and short story are sometimes the basis for classifying literary works. All these prose forms have a distinct length, as well as other characteristics. The visual appearance of a literary work determines whether it is a poem, a play, or a novel.

The eminent Canadian critic Northrop Frye (1957) identified four forms of fiction for genre study. Glenna Davis Sloan (1991), professor at Teachers College, Columbia University, applied the ideas to children's literature and identified the four types as **comedy**, **romance**, **tragedy**, and **irony–satire**. (See the Glossary for a short description of each form and an example.)

Age distinctions refer to grouping by the age of the intended audience—that is, books for infants from birth to 2; books for toddlers; books for preschoolers; and so on through adolescence. This approach is helpful for school-related use (see Developmental Aspects of Picture Books in Chapters 5 and 6).

Topical categories allow a focus on current issues, a subject area, or a cultural group. For example, Sims (1982) reported on analysis and evaluation of realistic books depicting the African-American experience. Similarly, current issues such as gender roles, heritage, special needs, old age, and so on form the basis for many annotated bibliographies.

REFLECTION   What are other ways that books are organized? What classification schemes are used by libraries? By bookstores? How can you find what you want?

A RATIONALE FOR GENRES

When we consider that one definition of *literature* is "the whole body of valued writing in society" (Eagleton, 1983, p. 17), we again see the necessity to categorize. From the categories, or genres, we will eventually have a sense of what is good and what is poor. From the content of stories and expository writing, the "valued writing" and basic categorizing questions such as "Could it happen?" and "When?" we find that **contemporary** and **historical realism** and **fantasy** emerge as genres. If we ask "Did it happen?" and thus expect some truth (facts) in the writing, then **biography**, **autobiography**, and **information** form distinct genres. *Traditional literature* forms a genre because it is a definable body of literature that existed before printing presses. Similarly, the *picture book* is a genre because of its unique blend of artwork and text. Thus we have the following genres based on content, and, in the case of picture books and *poetry*, on the appearance or visual form of the literary work:

Traditional literature—anonymous stories, wise sayings, and rhymes coming from the oral tradition

Picture books—books usually intended for a young audience that use art as well as text to convey meaning (in most picture books, art is the primary vehicle for meaning)

Figure 3.1 Genres
and subgenres

Genre	Examples of Subgenres
Poetry	Narrative poetry, lyric poetry, sonnets, haikus, limericks, ballads, free verse, and more
Traditional literature	Rhymes, chants, proverbs, fables, folktales, myths, legends, tall tales
Picture books	Alphabet and counting books, concept books, picture storybooks, realism, fantasy, nursery rhymes, wordless books
Fantasy	High fantasy, talking-animal tales, science fiction, time fantasies, ghost stories, unbelievable characters
Contemporary realism	Set in the present, realistic stories of family and school, mysteries, sports, animals, survival, adventure
Historical realism	Set in the past and often including a historical person or event; subgenres indicated by time periods: medieval and Renaissance, exploration and colonization, and so on
Biography and autobiography	Historical and contemporary accounts of persons' lives
Information	Factual writing in content areas such as science, history, math, technology, and psychology

Poetry—words and sentences that conform to certain definitions of length, rhyme, and meter

Fantasy—a story with at least one impossible element

Contemporary realism—a story mirroring our contemporary world as we understand it

Historical realism—a realistic story that could have happened in the past

Biography and *Autobiography*—a factual account of a person's life

Information—factual writing about human and natural phenomena

Notice some of the similar traits and structures among genres: the element of a past, present, or future time; the factual writing in biography and information; and the narrative stories in traditional literature, fantasy, and realism.

Each of these genres, as it has evolved through time and the fertile imaginations of storytellers and scribes, can be expressed in a variety of *subgenres*. Subgenres are more detailed classifications of literary works based on the fundamental premise that unites the category; for example, there are several kinds of fantasy writing. Figure 3.1 details how each genre can be divided into a variety of subgenres.

Hereafter, in each chapter, a genre will be discussed first within a historical context with classic examples, then further divided into subgenres with definitions and current examples.

LITERARY ELEMENTS

Aspects of analysis, as mentioned previously, give all who study literature a vocabulary with which to discuss and evaluate it. Indispensable to any genre is an understanding of **theme**, **plot**, **character**, **setting**, **style**, and **point of view**. Authors decide how each of these will work within a story; their decisions create either memorable writings that live on in our literary tradition or dull, lifeless works.

Theme **Descriptors of theme: Explicit and implicit**

Authors thread through a tale a common idea that unifies a story. The common idea, or thread, is sometimes stated by the author, in which case it is an **explicit theme.** Usually it is not directly stated, but left to the reader to infer. In that case we have an **implicit theme.** Whether it is explicitly stated or implicit, the theme can be drawn out of a story or poem by asking "What does the author seem to say?" If, for example, the author seems to convey an idea that "Cooperation is better than conflict" or "Adversity builds character," then characters, plot, and other elements exist in harmony with that idea. Theme is more than an explanation of what the story is about; it is a value-laden statement. In children's books, themes usually are "unifying truths" (Lukens, 1999), because they embody the meaning of a story.

Themes are sometimes difficult to articulate, because they can be obscure, or inconsistently demonstrated by characters, or meaningless. Because literature is complex, stories also can have multiple themes and secondary themes. In *The Wanderer* (Creech, 2000), for example, the title explicitly names the sailboat that Sophie, her uncles, and cousins take on the trans-Atlantic voyage. "Wanderer" also implies that the characters, especially Sophie, are on a journey of self-discovery and wonder.

Plot **Descriptors of plot: Linear, cumulative, and episodic, with flashback, foreshadowing, a cliffhanger, and/or conflict**

If you answer the question "What happens in this story?" you are describing the *plot*. Plot is action, the narrative order of events as the story unfolds. Plot usually has a predictable structure. Three basic structural patterns are called linear, cumulative (or circular), and episodic. A **linear plot** has a beginning (introduction and statement of the problem), a middle (rising action, or action and consequence pattern), and an

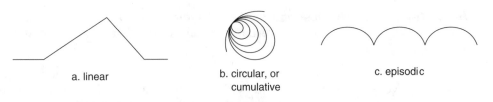

Figure 3.2   Patterns of Plot Structure

end (climax and resolution). This linear pattern is sometimes referred to as *story structure* or *story grammar.*

Cumulative plots are composed of phrases, sentences, or events repeated with one new aspect added each time. It is almost as if the plot is continuing in ever widening circles.

Episodic plots are exemplified by books in which chapters are almost complete stories in themselves. There is an introduction, problem, action and consequence, climax, and resolution with each episode.

Diagrams of each pattern can be seen in Figure 3.2. Because the first two patterns figure prominently in traditional literature, they are also addressed in Chapter 4.

Although one of these three basic patterns is found in almost every story, authors can alter a pattern to achieve other purposes. A **flashback** allows the linear progression to stop and an earlier event to be interjected. This creates suspense and excitement, and adds another dimension to the story. The opposite dimension, **foreshadowing**, is used by authors to allow readers to anticipate and to look forward to events. The forthcoming event, character, or action is hinted at in the text.

Authors use a technique to sustain tension when they leave a chapter or a part in the midst of some dangerous or suspenseful action. A **cliffhanger** is unresolved action at the end of a chapter. This inconclusive ending leads the reader to the next chapter in breathless anticipation of what might happen next.

Conflict, a term that refers to the interaction of plot and character, is necessary so that a literary work has some tension. Tension derived from conflict provides motivation for characters and it keeps readers interested in the story. Four types of conflict occur in most stories:

person against self

person against other

person against society

person against nature

REFLECTION   What are some examples of conflicts in children's books?

Character **Descriptors of character: Round, flat, foil, dynamic, static, stereotypical, protagonist, and antagonist**

Characters in literature, as creations of authors' imaginations, can be as real as people we know or the most impossibly fantastic creatures inhabiting another planet. From ordinary males and females to ghosts, talking animals, and creatures from outer space, *characters* form another indispensable element of story. Occasionally, they move the action forward in poetry and nonfiction, too. Characters voice or imply theme, they act or react to events, and they enhance setting with their motives and dialogue. Sometimes readers identify with the ideal traits of a character—characteristics of honesty, truth, courage, and intelligence. Identifying with characters is an important aspect of reading and enjoying literature.

Different types of characters balance a story. A fully developed, complex character—sometimes called a main or **round character**—has many traits. **Flat** characters, however, have only a few dimensions, sometimes only one or two. The rat Templeton in *Charlotte's Web,* a flat character, is greedy and sarcastic from beginning to end. He plays an important part, as he adds humor and provides a **foil** for Wilbur. A foil is a character whose traits are opposite those of the main character; without foils the main character's traits could not be so sharply etched in the story. Foils are usually flat characters. Comic book characters are flat, as are most minor characters in television sitcoms.

When characters change, grow, and develop, they are said to be **dynamic**. Dynamic characters make self-discoveries, influence others, and cause events to happen, and they create movement in the plot. In contrast, characters who do not change are **static.** They can be varied and complex, or exhibit very few traits, but they remain essentially the same. Because she has to survive, Karana, in *Island of the Blue Dolphins,* gains knowledge, competence, and personal insight. She is a dynamic character.

When a character mirrors traits that society dictates instead of idiosyncratic traits that an author attributes, a **stereotype** is created. Stereotypes can be destructive in literature because they are derogatory at worst; even at best, they often reveal an author's lack of imagination and sensitivity. When Native American characters are depicted only as "savage Indians" or Asian-Americans as bespectacled computer geniuses, readers lose the variety and richness that fully developed characters bring to a story.

REFLECTION   Can stereotyped characters be found in well-known books? Would qualities of stereotyping change over time?

The literary terms **protagonist** and **antagonist** refer to main characters who oppose each other. This opposition is frequently found in the person-against-other conflict. Usually the protagonist is the "good" character, while the antagonist is the opposite.

Setting   **Descriptors of setting: Time, place, mood, and symbol**

Setting includes both *time* and *place*. A story may be set in the late 1800s (time) on a remote island (place), such as *Island of the Blue Dolphins*. Setting can range from very realistic—a time and place we readily recognize—to the most abstract—a time and place existing in an imaginary world.

Setting anchors a story, as it provides the backdrop against which the action occurs and the characters speak. It can be much more important than backdrop, however, and establishes the mood of a literary work. **Mood,** a subjective emotional state, adds to the tension of a plot and colors everything in the story. In *Where the Wild Things Are* (1963), Maurice Sendak manipulated the setting by enlarging the forest in Max's room until it completely enveloped the fantasy. Night turned into day and reflected the change from anger to joy in Max's mood as he tamed the wild things.

Setting can also be a **symbol** of what the story is about. The symbol harmonizes with theme, character, and plot. The island, in *Island of the Blue Dolphins,* works as a symbol to denote separation; it is a symbol of Karana and her solitude, independence, and completeness. When the setting is the title of a book, as in this one, you can be sure it functions as a major element of the work. In fantasy, setting is especially important because it creates the fantasy world that is crucial to the narrative. In realistic stories that pit person against nature, the setting can be viewed as an antagonist. Thus it also assumes a major function in survival stories.

Style   **Descriptors of style: Figurative language, metaphor, simile, personification, alliteration, tone, archetype, symbol, allusion, irony, and humor**

Style refers to the many ways an author uses words to express ideas resulting in prose or poetry. As we read, we take words for granted, but they stand between us and our comprehension of a work. Because words are the building blocks of character, theme, plot, and so on, they must be selected with care and precision. Language patterns, dialects in characters' speech, words used to create alliteration and rhythm, and connotations and denotations are all aspects of style. Style can be described holistically or specifically. We could summarize the style of Scott O'Dell's work by saying the language seems matter-of-fact and even slightly flat as Karana describes her work, her thoughts, and her solitude. The style is unadorned and unemotional, as Karana is.

Figurative language encompasses terms that use words to stand for something else. We have the ability through language to create metaphors, to personify anything, to allude to something indirectly, and to name symbols that connote a host of meanings.

Metaphors and **similes** create images in our minds as they connect what the author is trying to say to a concrete referent we can recognize. Metaphors and similes compare unlike things, and the unlikely comparison helps us see things in a fresh way. For example, a passage at the beginning of Chapter 15 in *Charlotte's Web* demonstrates a feast of figurative language: "The crickets sang in the grasses. They sang a song of summer ending, a sad, monotonous song. 'Summer is over and gone,' they sang" (White, 1952, p. 113). The idea that crickets can sing is an example of **personification**, while "sang a song of summer" exemplifies **alliteration**, or using the same sound to begin words in a series. The sad, monotonous song compares to summer's ending, which is a metaphor, and last, the **tone** of sadness is created in that passage and what follows it, which speaks of summer as over, gone, and dying. In this beautiful, poetic paragraph E. B. White used the rhythm and sounds of language to create imagery and tone.

Even more deeply felt in the passage is the idea that summer is turning into fall—the year is beginning to die. Besides foreshadowing Wilbur or Charlotte's death, White draws on an **archetype** of seasonal change to convey meaning. Archetypes are universal ideas that probably spring from our unconscious. They are images, situations, themes, and characters that stand for universally held beliefs and meanings. They are found in mythology and religious ritual and are depicted in artistic forms all over the world. Archetypes in literature can relate to the seasons: Spring is linked with rebirth and beginnings, summer with triumph and celebration, autumn with tragedy, and winter with death and despair (Frye, 1957). Other archetypes are linked with plot and character as the recurring plot of the hero-quest (Odysseus) and also as a miraculous overturning of a helpless maiden's plight (Cinderella). Settings of ancient forests or waterways are archetypal, with forests regarded as places of terror, unknown and dangerous, while waterways are associated with journeys. Water, by itself, can be an archetype of baptism, conversion, or birth.

As archetypes are universal patterns of form and structure, deeply symbolic of what human beings have regarded as mysterious and wonderful for centuries, *symbols* are more recent and not quite so universal. The U.S. flag, a song, *Charlotte's Web*—all can symbolize something quite specific and personal. Although symbols are visible signs, they resist total explanation because they "suggest, reveal, and conceal all at the same time" (Cullinan, 1971, p. 69).

Allusions are indirect references to someone or something well known. To allude to something creates an association with a common concept or person; we can allude to the "Midas touch," for example. In using *Walk Two Moons* (1994, a Newbery award winner in 1995) as the title of her book, Sharon Creech alludes to the Native American connection with Salamanca, the main character. She also suggests through the allusion to a well-known Native American proverb that the reader should not "judge a man until you've walked two moons in his moccasins."

Irony and **humor** can be used very effectively in prose or poetry. *Irony* is the juxtaposition of two opposite ideas; it is sometimes the discrepancy between what is stated and what is known to be true. There is an irony in *Charlotte's Web* because Charlotte was saving Wilbur's life at the same time she was preparing for her own death. The juxtaposition of life and death creates the irony. Opposite forces balanced ironically make a story more interesting and more surprising at the conclusion. Irony has a larger reference than simply stylistic use, as it is identified in literary criticism as forming one of the four forms of story (Sloan, 1991).

Humor comes from the use of words with double meanings to create jokes, puns, riddles, and witty sayings. Writing comedic lines is truly an art—what may be funny to one person may not necessarily be funny to someone else. Because of language, comedy is also sometimes culturally based, as there are relatively few universal funny images. Figurative language and surprising word choices can provide humor, as Jon Scieszka does repeatedly in his Time Warp Trio series, such as *See You Later, Gladiator* (2000).

Point of View   **Descriptors of point of view: First person, omniscient, and limited omniscient**

Point of view suggests a vantage point from which everything in a story or a poem is seen. That is, we can see the action from one character's point of view or from many characters' points of view. When a character tells the story, and uses *I* in the telling, the point of view is **first person**, as in the grammatical first-person-singular construction. In contrast to first person is the **omniscient** point of view. With omniscience, or knowledge of everything, an author uses all the characters to tell a story. Thoughts, motives, and descriptions unfold from everyone to advance the plot and delineate character. It is as if the author can read everyone's mind and occupies a lofty position from which to regard everything and describe it.

An author may develop a combination by alternating first person or creating two or three *limited omniscient* characters. The possibilities are practically limitless. Point of view provides focus to a literary work and allows an easy identification with the first person narrator in many realistic novels.

EVALUATION OF LITERARY ELEMENTS

Three principal criteria seem to be most important in judging quality: vitality, freshness, and balance. *Vitality* is energy, a life-giving force that speaks to a driving current in prose or poetry that keeps us interested, curious, and engaged. *Freshness* refers to the creation of new characters, situations, plots; it is the inventiveness of taking basic themes, motifs, and archetypes that are universal, well loved, and familiar and generating new stories and new perspectives. It is creating and re-creating. It is not using cliches, the same old tired lines, hackneyed phrases, trite jokes, or stereotypical characters. Freshness means "new," but it also means building on the enduring truths of traditional literature in modern ways.

Balance is the cohesive integration of all literary elements. The literary work is an entity with all parts in balance. Plot depends on character development and conflict; theme draws from both plot and character—and everything meshes to create the whole. Setting supports the framework of a story, and style permeates practically every word an author chooses. To have strong characters and a weak plot, or to have a well-developed setting and nothing happening, is a flaw that balance would correct.

Criteria	Your personal response
Vitality	Is this theme worthwhile? Does it seem current, i.e., does it reflect values that are important culturally? Is the theme too didactic? Too subtle?
Freshness	Is this a version of other, similar themes? If this is a coming-of-age novel, e.g., how has the author made it new and intriguing? If this is a picture book, how does the artwork add a fresh dimension to the theme?
Balance	Does the author impose a personal view? Too much? Too little? Is the theme present in how the action moves the plot forward? Is the theme consistent with the development of the characters? Do other literary elements (point of view, setting, style) support the theme?

Figure 3.3 Evaluating literary elements: *Theme*

In each of the succeeding chapters related to genre, two types of evaluation strategies are suggested. In the first evaluation strategy, an open-ended personal response is required. In the second evaluation strategy, a four-point scale is used to quantify a response. The four-point scale allows for a numerical analysis, while the open-ended response in the first evaluation strategy may provide a more thoughtful, in-depth analysis of the book. The four-point scale is useful for individuals who take their evaluations to a group and use the statements to start a discussion, and the open-ended response may better serve the evaluator when a written report is necessary. Each strategy has advantages and disadvantages. Figure 3.3 demonstrates an open-ended evaluation based on the literary element of *theme*, followed by an example of a four-point scale using just the literary element of *point of view*.

A Four-Point Scale for Evaluating Point of View

Name of Book: _____

Author (and illustrator): _____

1 stands for "very good —yes," 2 is "good," 3 is "marginal," and 4 is "unsatisfactory—no," rate the book according to

Vitality

    I. If fiction, the point of view adds strength, drama, and depth to the story.

        1 _____ 2 _____ 3 _____ 4 _____

    II. If nonfiction, the point of view is objective, clear, and accurate.

        1 _____ 2 _____ 3 _____ 4 _____

Freshness

    III. The author successfully gives an unexpected perspective with point of view.

        1 _____ 2 _____ 3 _____ 4 _____

    IV. The point of view seems natural and unforced even though it can be unusual and unpredictable.

        1 _____ 2 _____ 3 _____ 4 _____

Balance

    V. The point of view gives insight into how the characters develop.

        1 _____ 2 _____ 3 _____ 4 _____

    VI. The point of view accommodates plot turns, changes of setting, stylistic language (dialect, conversation, figurative language).

        1 _____ 2 _____ 3 _____ 4 _____

LITERARY ELEMENTS RELATED TO GENRES

Characterization, point of view, theme, and plot may work differently in certain genres. Although authors impose their best creative efforts on their work, nevertheless generic expectations dictate certain literary conventions that allow readers to understand how a text is constructed and why characters act in predictable ways.

Key differences in realism and fantasy are most pronounced when we consider characterization, which is essentially narrow and static in fantasy and traditional literature. Stylized figures that expand into psychological archetypes are predominant. Thus Cinderella, the wicked stepmother, and the hero, as well as the sly fox and the trickster coyote, are examples of psychological archetypes. In modern fantasy, particularly in the subgenre of high fantasy, flat characters also predominate. With the exception of a dynamic hero and a small number of round characters, high fantasy is full of one-dimensional characters who are either good or bad. This is as it should be, because the purpose of fantasy is to create a mythlike otherworld, an abstraction based on what we know to be true but one that carries the truth into a different dimension. Flat characters allow this abstraction to occur more easily.

Compare this with our expectations when we read realistic prose fiction. We expect fully developed characters like ourselves and our friends. Multidimensional characters who show conflicting emotions and motives give realism its power. This is as it should be, so that identification with characters can occur more easily.

Fantasy, as an abstraction of reality, gives rise to differences in setting as well. In fantasy, setting is a more integral part of the story, because time and place in the fantasy world drives much of the action. For example, in science fiction, a subgenre of fantasy, a spaceship may harbor the community and help to define community boundaries in action and thought.

Theme in fantasy seems to be loftier, as it is often related to the idealized world of truth and goodness created in the setting. Thus we have good and bad characters, firmly on one side or the other, and a predominant theme of "good triumphing

Elements	Realism	Fantasy
Theme	Related to contemporary life	Lofty, as in good vs. evil
Plot	Variety of patterns, with flashbacks, conflicts, etc.	Usually linear
Characterization	Realistic, with multidimensional characters	Idealized, often one-dimensional (good or bad)
Setting	Generalized from reality	Integral part of the story (the fantasy world)
Point of view	First person and omniscient, sometimes with a variety of points of view	Usually omniscient

Figure 3.4 Generalizations about realism and fantasy

over evil in spite of great odds." Again, high fantasy and science fiction seem to articulate this theme more than other subgenres of fantasy.

Realistic plots are more apt to meander and to include flashbacks or other events that impede the resolution; in fantasy the plot is usually straightforward, or linear, with few digressions. Point of view is likely to be omniscient in fantasy and traditional literature, while a variety of points of view may be found in realism. First-person narration is common in young adult realistic novels, probably because the reader's identification with an adolescent narrator makes the story more immediate and timely.

Understanding these differences in literary elements helps us classify literature and shows us how the genres work to reveal structure and cohesion. Figure 3.4 summarizes the differences in literary elements between realism and fantasy. Please note that these are generalizations; not all books follow these rules predictably.

SUMMARY

A rationale for classifying and studying literature preceded an explanation of genre theory, definitions of genres, and examples. Providing a theoretical framework for this chapter and others that follow, the genres of poetry, traditional literature, picture books, fantasy, contemporary and historical realism, biography and autobiography, and information were presented.

Next, specific literary elements such as theme, plot, character, setting, style, and point of view were described and related to several well-known children's books.

The key attributes of vitality, freshness, and balance were proposed as criteria for evaluating how literary elements work in story, poem, and factual writing. Two kinds of evaluation demonstrated first an open-ended strategy, then a more objective, quantifiable strategy. Finally, this chapter presented differences in characterization, plot, theme, and point of view as they appear in fantasy and realism and relate to our generic expectations.

Knowledge of literature and how literature works is crucial to those who want to guide children toward lifelong reading enjoyment. This is not so that children will be subjected to analysis in a formal, lifeless way, but so this knowledge will allow adults to suggest, find patterns, guide, and promulgate a rich interpretation of meaning. Literature is every child's birthright, and it deserves our best efforts to search for meanings, to understand, and to delight in it. To this end, critical theory related to children's literature is becoming more obvious in scholarly journals and reviewing sources. An important trend, the focus of criticism and attention will result in better literature and a surer foundation of knowledge for readers.

IMPLICATIONS FOR INSTRUCTION

Because literary theory and criticism are the focus of this chapter, this section asks you to react to theoretical ideas. Projects will allow you to pursue aspects of genre theory and literary elements, while activities comprise two units: *Wings* for primary classrooms and *Flight* for intermediate or middle school classrooms.

Projects

1. Select five children's books that appeal to you and classify them according to genres identified in this chapter. Then look at plot structures and note conflicts and anything else that the authors have used to make the stories compelling. How would you articulate the books' themes?

2. Continue your analysis with the books selected (or choose others) and explore point of view, the importance of setting in each one, and specific stylistic language patterns, such as figurative language. Compare your notes with those of a friend.

3. Compare reviews of the same children's book from two sources, such as *The Horn Book Magazine* and *The Bulletin of the Center for Children's Books*. Note how descriptive, analytical, or evaluative each review is. Are the reviews similar, or do they focus on different aspects? Which literary elements are mentioned?

4. Can you think of other books that reveal the setting in the title, as does *Island of the Blue Dolphins?* In your examples, do settings have a symbolic function? A literary map may be made by using push pins or flags to locate the setting on a geographical map. The literary map helps to demonstrate the importance of setting in a political, geographical, or cultural context.

Activities for the Primary Level: A Unit on Wings

Instead of several discrete activities, an outline of a literature unit on Wings is presented using a reader-response mode of teaching. Children in kindergarten through third grade can participate in these activities designed to teach these *goals:* some genre recognition (fiction and nonfiction); word recognition; the comprehension strategies of recalling, comparing, locating, organizing, evaluating, and analyzing; and other critical thinking strategies. The *purpose* of the unit is to encourage imagination, to reinforce concepts in the natural world related to the science of aeronautical engineering, and to enjoy literature in nonfiction and fictional prose. Teaching suggestions are listed and defined below: Word Wall; Story Retelling; Word Web; Partner Reading; and Think, Pair and Tomorrow/Today Share (Cunningham, 2000; Donoghue, 2001; Morrow, 2001). Other activities include silent reading, drawing, whole group discussions, creating a mural, taking notes, and others which may occur to a teacher as the unit progresses. The unit does not specify national or state curriculum standards so that teachers may use the particular standard or language describing the standard that best fits their districts' requirements. After reading the unit, direct connections to state and national standards in reading and language arts, as well as some in science and social studies, should be clear.

The five-day unit of about 45 minutes per day has been created for a heterogeneous classroom of about 20 children. A bibliography is presented and may be incorporated in the unit for intermediate and middle grades (Flight) which follows. In the following unit, brackets indicate what the teacher will do and why; when there are no brackets, the statements are directed toward the children in a conversational tone. A different read-aloud is the heart of each day's lesson, along with other activities.

The following bibliography for *Wings* is complete here and is not referenced again at the end of this chapter. See also the CD-ROM accompanying this text.

Bibliography

Allen, D. (2000). *Dancing in the wings.* (Ill. by K. Nelson). New York: Dial.

Blake, R. J. (2000). *Fledgling.* New York: Philomel.

Burton J., & Taylor, K. (1998). *The nature and science of wings.* New York: Gareth.

Conover, C. (2000). *The lion's share.* New York: Farrar.

Graham, B. (2000). *Max.* Cambridge, MA: Candlewick.

Hunter, R. A. (2000). *Take off!* (Ill. by E. Miller). New York: Holiday.

Krensky, S. (2000). *Taking flight: The story of the Wright brothers.* (Ill. by L. Day). New York: Simon & Schuster.

Myers, C. (2000). *Wings.* New York: Scholastic.

O'Brien, P. (2000). *The Hindenburg.* New York: Holt.

*Ormerod, J. (2001). *Miss Mouse takes off.* New York: HarperCollins.

*This book is for preschool children, but would be suitable for a special child, perhaps a Down syndrome or developmentally delayed child, in a primary classroom.

Ryder, J. (2000). *Rainbow wings*. (Ill. by V. Lee). New York: HarperCollins.

Seymour, T. (1999). *Our neighbor is a strange, strange man*. (Ill. by W. L. Krudop). New York: Orchard.

Wallner, A. (1996). *The first air voyage in the United States: The story of Jean-Pierre Blanchard*. New York: Holiday.

Teaching Suggestions

Word Wall—A graphic display of words on a classroom wall, bulletin board, or other place where children will be confronted with words and will have easy access to them. Words should be movable, and they may be displayed alphabetically, thematically, in rhyming patterns, or in other ways the teacher and children may generate (Cunningham, 2000).

Story Retelling—Retellings involve active participation in a literacy experience that helps children develop language structures, comprehension, and sense of story structure (Morrow, 2001). Individually, children retell a story to an adult (assessor) who notes various kinds of language, thinking, organization, and confidence demonstrated by the children.

Word Web—Teacher and children create a semantic web with the main idea (word) in the middle, and they build associations out from the middle in spokes.

Partner Reading—Children pair with each other (or the teacher designates the pair) for oral reading in turn. (It is not necessary to pair a good reader with a struggling reader, although that may sometimes happen. Pairs should be fairly fluid so that children have a chance to read to and be read to by all their classmates.) In the next unit for older students, **Buddy Reading** is scheduled so that the younger children in this classroom may be paired with older children who are studying *Flight*.

Think, Pair, and Tomorrow/Today Share—Teachers ask questions, and they give children time to think about their responses and a partner with whom to talk over their ideas. Children come back together as a group to share their ideas (Morrow, 2001). Sometimes the group reconvenes the next day, and sometimes the sharing is done immediately.

Introduction (First Day)   [Have books displayed and blank poster paper with an outline of wings that is ready to write on. Note that square brackets [ ] denote what the teacher will do. Where there are no brackets, the teacher will speak directly to the class.] We're going to be reading, discussing, and thinking about wings with some good books in the next several days. Here are some questions to get us started: Why are wings important? Who has wings? How can wings help an organism? What are your questions? Are wings real? What beings have wings, and which ones don't? Let's put some of our ideas on this word web, and some of our questions, too. This word web will grow and in a few days we'll include it in our mural about wings.

[The children's ideas are included in the word web in Figure 3.5. As you can see, they were sure about some things, but had questions about others. This brainstorming activity was designed to help children focus on what they know, to articulate questions they have, and to build enthusiasm for the unit.] Listen to this story, *Wings*

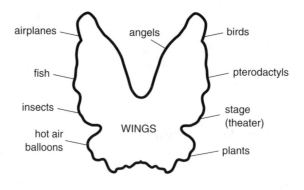

Figure 3.5   Word web

(Myers, 2000), to see if you think it could really happen. After the read-aloud, we'll have a Think, Pair, and Tomorrow/Today Share. Here are the questions to think about:

- If you were Ikarus, how would you feel when you were flying?
- How would you feel when the boys and girls made fun of you and your wings?
- How would you feel when the narrator (classmate) complimented you?

[After the read-aloud, pair up the children, and suggest that they jot down their responses to the questions or figure out a way to remember them. For second- and third-graders, their reader-response notebooks would be a great place to record their ideas. Depending on the sophistication of kindergarteners and first-graders, written notes or drawn pictures may be possible, too. The book display will initiate questions and encourage books to be chosen for silent reading. Children may choose today, or tomorrow, or the teacher may assign books to certain children or groups.]

Second Day   Let's recall our questions about Ikarus and *Wings* from yesterday. Who would like to volunteer his or her responses? [After a short discussion and review of the three questions, discuss the terms *fiction,* and *nonfiction* and elicit words for the word wall.] Could this really happen? Is this fiction? Has anyone ever heard a story something like this, a myth? How do we know it is fiction? Who has some interesting words for our word wall? I heard these words: *soar, long, strong, beautiful,* and *Thursday.* [Or use words that the children offer, and think of ways to emphasize the phonic regularity or visual pattern.] Yes, we know that *soar* is an r-controlled word, *long* and *strong* rhyme, and *beautiful* and *Thursday* are sight words. Where would they go on our word wall? [Word recognition could be extended; then the lesson will proceed with another read-aloud.]

Today we're going to hear another book about wings. Listen to this story about Max, and compare it to the book *Wings* from yesterday. Listen for two differences and two similarities, and I will give you a diagram to help you compare [see Figure 3.6].

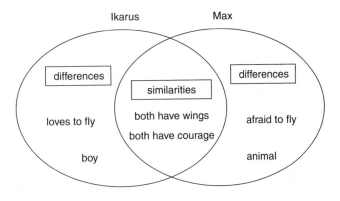

Figure 3.6   Comparing Ikarus and Max (venn diagram)

[Read *Max* (2000), a picture book written and illustrated by Bob Graham. Max is the son of two superheroes, Captain Lightning and Madam Thunderbolt, but he is afraid to fly. The desire to help a falling baby bird gives Max the necessary courage. Give the children a blank venn diagram (as in Figure 3.6) so that they can think of similarities and differences. Also, make sure that every child has a book about wings from the book display so that she or he can read silently at school, during *DEAR* (Drop Everything and Read), *SSR* (Sustained Silent Reading), and at home for a specified time each evening.]

Third Day   [Begin the reading period with a discussion of the children's comparison diagrams.] What were the similarities and differences between Ikarus and Max? Which story did you like better? Why? Are they fiction, or nonfiction? How do you know? If they are fiction, are they realistic, or fantasy? What clues are given that tell us a book is realistic or fantastic? [After the discussion, *paired reading* starts. Children have been reading their books silently and now are ready to read orally. Depending on the class, paired reading could take from 15 to 30 minutes. As a teacher, it is worthwhile to circulate and listen to children read, or to read with a child. If time allows, elicit more words for the word wall, or ask the children to add words in their journals.]

[After paired reading, introduce children to *retelling*. When a child is asked to tell the story, the retelling may be evaluated for many different comprehension tasks. A qualitative analysis of a retelling is an invaluable aid to a teacher when assessing a child's reading and language development. A protocol should be established by primary teachers, or by the district so that some uniform standard is applied and a child's learning is documented. For this unit, the Retelling Center is located in a corner of the classroom, in the adjacent activity room, or even out in the hall. The Retelling Center sometimes has a tape recorder, or children pair up and one plays the part of the "teacher" to record ideas and prompt occasionally with questions. Children who are new at retelling may take pictures, key words, or artifacts with them to aid in recall (see Morrow, 2001, pp. 220–225 for more ideas).]

You will have three more days to complete the retelling. Sign up at my desk for a good time to meet with me and share your book. I can't wait to hear about it! We'll finish today's class with another read-aloud. Today is another story about wings. Listen to this story to see what happened when two men wanted to fly, and you can draw a picture of one of the scenes.

[*Taking Flight: The Story of the Wright Brothers,* by Stephen Krensky, 2000, and illustrated by Larry Day, is a beginning biography in the "Ready to Read" series. It tells about Wilbur and Orville Wright as they arrive at Kitty Hawk and the inhospitable conditions there. The book conveys principles of flight and the human story of perseverance through struggle.]

Fourth Day   Yesterday we heard about an important event in history. Who can recall the first Americans to use their wings? What did their wings look like? [Share pictures.] Was this story fiction or nonfiction? Nonfiction is based on truth. Yes, this really happened. [Introduce the read-aloud for today.]

We're going to go further back in time to see what else people have invented to give them wings. Can anyone think of an invention that flew? Listen to this book about an early attempt to fly and remember if it is fiction or nonfiction. Then you can choose one of four activities. [*The First Air Voyage in the United States: The Story of Jean-Pierre Blanchard* (written and illustrated by Alexandra Wallner, 1996) is about the man who made 44 hot-air balloon flights over Europe. Then, in 1793, he ballooned from Philadelphia to southern New Jersey, becoming the first human to fly in the United States.]

Here are the activities from which to choose:

- Compare Jean-Pierre Blanchard to Orville and Wilbur Wright.
- Practice retellings, and sign up to have your retelling documented for this period.
- Add five to ten words from today's book or your silent reading to the word wall.
- Choose a partner and read to each other.

Fifth Day   Let's review what we've learned this week. [Elicit from the children these concepts: (1) Differences between fiction and nonfiction; (2) why wings are important and who has wings; (3) vocabulary development, as evidenced by the word wall; (4) Ikarus as a retelling of Icarus, a Greek myth; (5) facts from the Wright Brothers flight, as well as principles of flight; (6) information about Jean-Pierre Blanchard; (7) how a retelling strategy helps language development; and (8) many others. Children will recall specific concepts and details from the books they are reading.]

Culminating activity: Let's listen to this book about wings [*The Nature and Science of Wings* (Burton & Taylor, 1998).] to reaffirm what we know and to learn some more insects, animals, and plants with wings. Then, we'll do an activity or complete the mural for our classroom.

[This is a concise, well-paced picture book illustrated with color photos. The teacher may choose to read a part of it or all of it. Several ideas for activities are appended to it.]

This concludes the unit. Assessment strategies are embedded in each day's activities. Most importantly, retellings may be scored to reveal reading growth and enthusiasm.

Activities for the Intermediate and Middle Levels: A Unit on Flight

A five-day unit on flight for heterogeneous classes in grades 4 to 7 is outlined below. The imagined classroom is one that employs a literature-based reading and language arts program, so the children are fairly independent and ready to do individual and group work based on reader-response theory. Books were selected at various reading levels so that a wide range of reading abilities are well served. There are undoubtedly many more books available, so colleagues may be consulted, as well as school and public librarians. While the purpose and goals of the unit are stated, there are no precise national or state standards listed because of the variation from state to state and differing adherence to national standards among school districts nationwide. It is proposed that teachers and curriculum developers take the mandated language of their standards and match those to the activities of the unit.

The *purposes* of the Unit are (1) to acquaint children with different concepts of flight as represented by genres in literature; (2) to present the history of the Wright brothers and other courageous pilots during the early part of the 20th century; and (3) to explore this phenomenon in airborne insects, plants, and birds. *Goals* are that children will read with comprehension, identify genres, write analytically and expressively (poetry and prose), enjoy content and authors' styles, and learn new vocabulary related to flight.

The following annotated bibliography consists of books from which children may choose (or a teacher may assign) as they progress through and complete their unit. The book list contains all bibliographic information and these publications are not referenced again at the end of this chapter. (See also books in the preceding wings unit, particularly the ones appropriate for emergent readers by Wallner, O'Brien, Burton and Taylor, and Krensky. As with the previous bibliography, please read about these books on the CD-ROM accompanying this text.)

Bibliography

Borden, L., & Kroeger, M. K. (2001). *Fly high: The story of Bessie Coleman.* (Ill. by R. Flavin). New York: McElderry.

Cummins, J. (2001). *Tomboy of the air: Daredevil pilot Blanche Stuart Scott.* New York: HarperCollins.

Freedman, R. (1991). *The Wright brothers: How they invented the airplane.* New York: Holiday House.

Ingold, J. (1999). *Airfield.* New York: Harcourt.

Joose, B. M. (2001). *Ghost wings.* New York: Chronicle.

Lerner, C. (2001). *On the wing: American birds in migration.* New York: HarperCollins.

Lester, J. (2001). *Ackamarackus: Julius Lester's sumptuously silly fantastically funny fables*. New York: Scholastic.

Murphy, R. (2000). *Night flying*. New York: Delacorte. (Young Adult).

Old, W. C. (2000). *The Wright brothers: Inventors of the airplane*. New York: Enslow.

Prelutsky, J. (1984). *The new kid on the block*. New York: Greenwillow.

Spinner, S., & Bisson, T. (2001). *Expiration date: Never*. New York: Delacorte.

Sproule, A. (1999). *The Wright brothers: The birth of modern aviation*. New York: Blackbirch.

Zaunders, B. (2001). *Feathers, flaps & flops: Fabulous early fliers*. New York: Dutton.

Teaching Suggestions

Whole class meeting—This is the beginning 10 minutes or so of every day in which children report on assignments completed and clarify expectations for the coming days' activities. There is a teacher's agenda for this time, though sometimes children may create the agenda.

Buddy reading—Matched with a young classroom, each child in a pair will read to the other.

Writing poetry—(Second day's assignment) Using a structure such as cinquain, haiku, or limerick, a teacher models the form and then assigns the form.

Plot Profile or *Expository Text Profile*—In fiction, this is a graph with an "excitement" or "tension" variable to plot for each chapter (Tompkins, 2001). In expository text, it would be a representation of the kinds of expository text structures (see Chapter 12 for further explanations) in nonfiction: sequence, description, cause and effect, comparison, and enumeration.

Essay—Students are assigned a short essay in which characteristics of the genre they are reading are described and exemplified in their book.

Alphabet/Dictionary Sheet—New words found in their books are written on an alphabet sheet (for younger learners) or in the part of their journals for new words (for older learners).

Short story or *Create something that flies unaided for at least 5 seconds*—final assignment.

First Day   Today we're going to begin a unit on flight. Let's start with a concept web to predict what we might learn in this unit. What is flight, and who/what flies?

Flight	**Things that fly**
a journey	airplanes
a migration	hot-air balloons
an escape	kites
a quest	_____
a desire to fly	_____

[Children will generate more concepts in response to the question. Ask: What are some books we've read that describe a flight?]

Who can describe the feeling of flight? Jack Prelutsky (*The New Kid on the Block,* 1984, p. 90) describes it this way:

"I am flying! I am flying!/I am riding on the breeze/I am soaring over meadows/I am sailing over seas."

In this unit, you may choose a book to read from the books displayed. You'll notice that the books represent different genres, such as fantasy, biography, contemporary and historical realism, and information. We have talked about the characteristics of genres, and one of your writing assignments has to do with describing and then finding examples in your book to demonstrate the genre. As we begin, let's make sure we have the next week planned. [With the class, or ready to hand out, list the daily assignments and determine the criteria for evaluation for each. Discuss the final, culminating assignment and determine criteria to evaluate. Last, have the children select their books after a short talk about each book and then create a reading schedule for each day so that they know how much to read.] The assignment is to begin reading and begin your alphabet sheet or journal with new words (about ten) to our class meeting tomorrow.

Second Day   Let's check on some new words that we are learning. Who would like to start? [Continue with vocabulary development for 10 to 15 minutes, then discuss assignments for tomorrow: to write a cinquain, haiku, or limerick about a character or event in the chosen book.] Let's read silently, then be ready to go to Ms._____'s classroom to listen to the first-graders read. You should have a page or two of your book ready to read, too. And, the assignment for tomorrow is to write the short poem. Any questions?

Third Day   [At the class meeting, ask about their silent reading, SSR, and homework (reading at home for about 20 to 25 minutes per night). Encourage the children to talk about their books, and reinforce the different genres as the children volunteer things that happen and things they've learned.] Today we're going to talk about plot profiles and expository text patterns. [While children who are reading nonfiction are reading silently, present the concept of a graph to children who are reading fiction. Then, the children who are reading fiction read silently while you remind all the children about sequence, cause and effect, comparisons, and so on.] *Assignment:* Please hand in the plot profile sheet tomorrow or the expository text examples drawn from the books.

Fourth Day   How are you enjoying the books on flight? Who has a really good example of an exciting chapter from *Feathers, Flaps & Flops* (Zaunders, 2001)? What are some other things you've learned? [After a brief discussion, begin to outline the essay that is due tomorrow.] In your journals, think about the characteristics of the genre you are reading. For example, if you are reading fiction like *Ghost Wings* (Joose, 2001), who are the characters and how do they interact? What is the conflict in the story? What is the resolution? What makes this a contemporary story, as compared to a historical one? Divide your essay into five parts, and write a paragraph about each aspect: character development, plot conflict, and so on. Now, if you are reading an information book, what do you expect to find? Are there characters? Is it written from an objective point of view? Are the facts accurate? Reflect tonight on these questions and others in your journal as you continue to read your book. *Assignment:* Tomorrow please hand in the essay on genre characteristics and examples from reading.

Fifth Day   [At the class meeting, have children read from some of their essays. Reiterate genre distinctions, and ask for more examples that help to define genre. Ask why it is important to categorize literature into fiction, nonfiction, then genres of each. Does this help children to understand the writing a bit better?] Are we ready for the final assignment? I know that some of you are already working on it. How are the flying inventions? I know 5 seconds is a long time when you're hoping your invention will stay aloft, isn't it? Tomorrow you may present your final assignment. Some of you are writing stories, and I can't wait to hear them. We'll also go outside to see the flying inventions, and I can't wait to see those, too. You may write a short evaluation of your book. Please let me know what you thought of it.

[This concludes the unit outline on flight. For an extra assignment, or for special credit, the students could use the Web to find out more about the authors whose books they have read or some topic in their books.]

REFERENCES

Children's Works

Creech, S. (1994). *Walk two moons*. New York: Harper-Collins.

Creech, S. (2000). *The Wanderer*. New York: Harper-Collins.

O'Dell, S. (1960). *Island of the blue dolphins*. Boston: Houghton Mifflin.

Scieszka, J. (2000). *See you later, gladiator*. New York: Viking.

Sendak, M. (1963). *Where the wild things are*. New York: Harper & Row.

White, E. B. (1952). *Charlotte's web*. New York: Harper & Row.

Professional Works

Cullinan, B. (1971). *Children's literature: Its discipline and content*. Dubuque, IA: Wm. C. Brown.

Cunningham, P. (2000). *Phonics they use: Words for reading and writing* (3rd ed.). New York: Longman.

Donoghue, M. R. (2001). *Using literature activities to teach content areas to emergent readers*. Boston: Allyn & Bacon.

Eagleton, T. (1983). *Literary theory: An introduction*. Minneapolis: University of Minnesota Press.

Frye, N. (1957). *Anatomy of criticism*. Princeton, NJ: Princeton University Press.

Hunt, P. (1991). *Criticism, theory, and children's literature*. Cambridge, MA: Basil Blackwell.

Lukens, R. (1999). *A critical handbook of children's literature* (6th ed.). New York: HarperCollins.

May, J. P. (1995). *Children's literature and critical theory*. New York: Oxford.

Mikkelsen, N. (2000). *Words and pictures: Lessons in children's literature and literacies*. Boston: McGraw Hill Higher Education.

Morrow, L. M. (2001). *Literacy development in the early years: Helping children read and write* (4th ed.). Boston: Allyn & Bacon.

Propp, V. (1968). *Morphology of the folktale* (2nd ed.). Austin: University of Texas Press.

Rosenblatt, L. (1978). *The reader, the text, the poem: The transactional theory of the literary work*. Carbondale: Southern Illinois University Press.

Sims, R. (1982). *Shadow and substance*. Urbana, IL: National Council of Teachers of English.

Sloan, G. (1991). *The child as critic* (3rd ed.). New York: Teachers College Press.

Stevenson, D. (Ed.). *The Bulletin of the Center for Children's Books*. [Published monthly, except August.]

Sutton, R. (Ed.). *The Horn Book Magazine*. [Published bimonthly.]

Tompkins, G. (2001). *Literacy for the 21st century*. Upper Saddle River, NJ: Merrill/Prentice Hall.

Additional Resources

Buss, K., & Karnowski, L. (2000). *Reading and writing literary genres*. Newark, DE: International Reading Association.

For grades 3 to 6, this has a variety of teaching suggestions and activities related to genre theory.

Hill, B. C., Noe, K. L. S., & Johnson, N. J. (2001). *Literature circles resource guide: Teaching suggestions, forms, sample book lists and databases*. Norwood, MA: Christopher Gordon.

This resource guide, with an accompanying CD-ROM, lists over 2,000 titles and describes the uses of literature circles.

Hunt, P. (2001). *Children's literature*. Malden, MA: Blackwell.

In this thorough overview of children's literature, the author, a British professor, advances critical theory, important authors, and the development of a defensible scholarly field.

West, M. I. (1997). *Everyone's guide to children's literature*. Ft. Atkinson, WI: Highsmith.

West lists many resources: reference works, periodicals, organizations, and the Internet. His brief annotations of major works of criticism related to children's literature are helpful.

CHAPTER 4

Once Upon a Time . . . and Tradition Continues

INTRODUCTION AND RESPONSE

Old, old stories, the authors' names lost in antiquity, have been a part of the world's literature for centuries. Stories told around fires at the cave's mouth or the riverbank, proverbs to codify conventional wisdom, and myths about real and imaginary happenings—all these formed the language and culture that held together a group of intelligent, yet primitive, people. The oral tradition preceded written expression, as it brought a community together by expressing common values and accepted truths through a storyteller's magic and ritual. Our vast heritage of traditional literature, coming to us over time and space, finds new expression through modern multicultural stories based on old truths and modern adaptations.

Hallmarks of traditional literature include the following:

> "Once upon a time . . .
> a beautiful heroine,
> a brave hero,
> had a problem,
> resolved it, and lived
> happily ever after."

What is the first fairy tale that pops into your mind? Identify a story and match its parts to the previous short plot description. You may take, for example, *Cinderella, Snow White,* or *Rapunzel,* and determine who the heroine and hero are, what the problem is, and how it is resolved. Called **story grammar** or **story structure,** this basic narrative flow is a blueprint for traditional literature and, indeed, for most modern stories.

While many myths, legends, folktales, and so on fit into this story structure, some do not. Keep the framework in mind as other tales are discussed, but realize also that traditional literature comes in many forms and motifs, with different characters, elements, settings, and language conventions. This chapter points out rich variations in the oral tradition by highlighting folklore from all over the world. Many of the single-story books that are listed and recommended are picture books; however, collections are noted as well.

Traditional literature will sometimes be referred to as **folklore,** a term which has a somewhat broader meaning, but the two terms will be used interchangeably to denote linguistic expressions, from stories to songs to "wise sayings" coming from the oral tradition.

REFLECTION   Why is folklore found most often in a picture book format? Typically, these familiar stories are associated with ages 3 to 8, and most of the books listed in this chapter are *picture books*. Originally folklore was meant for everyone; why has the focus changed?

HISTORY OF TRADITIONAL LITERATURE

The compelling nature of story, the desire and the need to frame words around events, evolved as our ancestors began to form social communities. Folklore from prehistoric times, told again and again, never the same way twice, and in every cultural group, entertained and instructed listeners of all ages. Before the printing press and even the scant literacy of medieval times, the common people built a heritage of literary works. Royalty also contributed, and tales, songs, ditties, wise sayings, and myths were gradually added as cultures grew and changed.

From early scholars' work we see that folklorists first were captivated by a theory of *monogenesis* to explain these literary phenomena. Monogenesis means one (mono) beginning (genesis), and refers to the former belief that all stories came from one place, namely northern Europe. This thought has since been refuted with a more logical *polygenesis* theory, which insists that human beings in every culture express the same basic needs and desires—to love, to hate, to search for meaning, to laugh—and therefore generate similar patterns, characters, themes, and situations (Sutherland, 1997).

In the 1800s, while the Brothers Grimm were collecting and publishing household stories in Germany, Hans Christian Andersen wrote his original tales in the folkloric style in Denmark (Haugaard, 1983). Other collections of old stories signaled an ever expanding multicultural base that resulted in significant contributions and influenced the development of modern literature in theme and form. *The Arabian Nights,* translated a century earlier in 1704, was such a collection. Lady Charlotte Guest, translating and adapting *The Mabinogion* (see a recent children's version, Thomas & Crossley-Holland, 1985) from ancient Welsh to English in the mid-1800s, did so in spite of resistance from some scholars who questioned that a woman could accomplish such a feat (Wrenn, 1976). Russian folktales were collected by Afanas'ev in the mid-1800s, Norwegian tales by Asbjornsen and Moe (1953). Japan, with its rich tradition of story and art, and propelled to some extent by the opening of its borders by Commodore Perry, revealed its flourishing literary and publishing enterprise at that time. *Pinocchio,* an original story written by Carlo Collodi (1880/1996), popularized Italian folklore; Andrew Lang began his series of adapted fairy tales in the *Blue Fairy Book* (1889) and the *Red Fairy Book* (1890). In 1908, Herbert Giles translated the Chinese collection of folklore gathered by Pu Song Ling in the late 17th century (Chang & Chang, 1997).

In the 1920s, *The Morphology of the Folktale* (Propp, 1968), a landmark study, gave credibility to the formal exploration of literary structures and paved the way for cross-cultural studies. As evidence of this kind of exploration, *Cinderella* has perhaps been studied more than any other tale, as at least five "types" and more than 500 variants of the tale have been identified (Dundes, 1983). Hearne's (1989) study of *Beauty and the Beast* points out how global versions of this famous story reverberate with similar themes and adapt to changing social and political contexts.

The Universality of Folklore

As we become more sensitive to differences and similarities among works of folklore, it becomes obvious that certain patterns and themes cannot be present in all cultures; nevertheless, striking similarities remain. Modern analyses of folklore tend to take points of view from philosophy, political science, and psychology to explain the origins and functions of these stories and sayings. Thus there are psychoanalytic interpretations, as in Bruno Bettelheim's well-known *The Uses of Enchantment* (1976). When the noted psychologist Carl Jung related modern dreams to primitive myths and rites in an effort to explain how symbols organize and give meaning to life (Jung, 1964), renewed interest and attention focused on folklore and, in particular, on mythology. Studies of myths figured prominently in the work of Joseph Campbell, who revealed hero myths throughout world cultures (Campbell, 1968). By providing a thorough cross-cultural basis to traditional literature, Campbell advanced the study of folklore and implied that knowledge of the universality of mythmaking could be a step toward cross-cultural understanding.

These analyses show that folklore has been and remains the continuing study of several academic disciplines. It merits research and analysis because of the richness and complexity of seemingly simple patterns, verses, and elements. Perhaps this irony—that the most complex of our enduring truths can be expressed in language a child can understand—explains the appeal of traditional literature.

SUBGENRES OF TRADITIONAL LITERATURE

For purposes of easy classification, traditional forms seem to fall into groups that share many characteristics. Figure 4.1 identifies subgenres and defines them.

Figure 4.1
Traditional literature: Subgenres and definitions

Subgenre	Definition
Folk rhymes, songs, and proverbs	Succinct ideas expressed rhythmically, and sometimes in song. Folk songs are most apt to tell a story through a recurring melodic pattern (many verses). Proverbs express a truth in one sentence.
Parables and fables	Brief narratives that describe a behavior and then explicitly or implicitly contain a moral. Parables usually have human characters while fables have animal characters.
Folktales and fairy tales	Narratives that include human or talking animal characters, and a clean and direct plot with unambiguous right and wrong in the decisive resolution. Folktales are more likely to be about common people, while fairy tales are more likely to be associated with magic and royalty.
Myths and legends	Narratives that explain why natural or cosmic phenomena occur; who our heroes and heroines are; what the relationships of the gods are to human beings or to each other. Myths seem to be more otherworldly, or more abstract, while legends begin with a kernel of truth and become exaggerated. When legends about astonishing superhuman feats or people become too exaggerated, they are tall tales.

Folk Rhymes, Songs, and Proverbs

Examples of this subgenre are Mother Goose rhymes and songs, chants, finger plays, riddles, jump-rope rhymes, proverbs, superstitions, jokes, tongue twisters, and probably more. These verbal phrases demonstrate common wisdom or just simple nonsense, as in "Red sky at night, a sailor's delight" or "Simple Simon met a pieman."

Proverbs hold the conventional wisdom of the ages in one-sentence utterances, as in "Don't cry over spilt milk," "A stitch in time saves nine," or "A bird in the hand is worth two in the bush."

"It can be safely stated that the overwhelming majority of nursery rhymes were not in the first place composed for children" (Opie & Opie, 1951, p. 3). There are many different explanations as to the origin of what we now call nursery rhymes: fragments of ballads, folk songs, proverbs, or political statements satirizing the nobility. The singing game "Ring o' Roses" has a particularly gruesome origin, some suggest.

> Ring-a ring o' roses,
> A pocket full of posies,
> A-tishoo! A-tishoo!
> We all fall down.

The rhyme may date back to the great plague of Europe, spread by rats in the 1300s. A rosy rash was a symptom of the disease, and posies or herbs were carried for protection and to keep the smell away from one's nose. Sneezing was a fatal symptom (marked by the "A-tishoo!"), and the last line mimics death. But another version has a second verse in which "we all get up again" (Opie & Opie, 1951, p. 365).

It is further testament to the power of these seemingly frivolous and nonsensical rhymes that they survive and, indeed, spawn imitations and parodies. Some are truly charming and memorable, giving young children a sense of story, interesting characters, a taste of whimsy, and a shared literary experience. For more discussion of nursery rhymes, particularly Mother Goose, see Chapters 5 and 6 for picture-book examples and Chapter 2 for a more detailed historical account.

Folk songs use the rhythm and pattern of spoken verses but add elements of music—melody and harmony—to make common wisdom, a story, or simple nonsense more memorable. They include spirituals, ballads, lullabies, work songs, and sea chanteys. Some of these are about heroes and heroines, and some describe the cruelty of war, the pompous and foolish, or the uncertainties of love.

REFLECTION Can you think of some proverbs that were said in your family? Have some family expressions become proverbs? Are bumper stickers on cars becoming the modern proverbs of our age?

Recent and Recommended Books of Folk Songs and Rhymes

From Sea to Shining Sea: A Treasury of American Folklore and Folk Songs.
     A. Cohn (1993)
This Is My Song: A Collection of Gospel Music for the Family. V. Higginsen (1995)
Here Comes Mother Goose, I. Opie (1999)

Parables and Fables

These brief narratives use their short length and terse style to illuminate human foibles. Undesirable human traits, such as arrogance and pride, are ridiculed, and positive traits are rewarded. Relatively few traditional parables exist in children's literature, with the exception of biblical stories rewritten for a young audience. Fables are not numerous either, but three great collections have been accessible to children from earliest times: Aesop from ancient Greece; La Fontaine from France; and the Panchantantra, a collection of fables from India. A second well-known source of Indian fables is the Jatakas, which are fables depicting Buddha's reincarnations as various animals. Many modern stories are reminiscent of fables in their brevity and pointed moral lessons.

Recent and Recommended Books of Parables and Fables

Buddha Stories, Demi. (1997)
The Lion and the Mouse and Other Aesop's Fables. D. Orgel, (2000)
Aesop's Fables. J. Pinkney (2000)

Folktales and Fairy Tales

These are by far the most numerous works in all of folklore and create the body of literature that most people associate with the oral tradition. Although the terms are often used interchangeably, there is a difference between **folktales,** which are closer to the oral tradition, and **fairy tales,** which are literary creations drawn from folktale elements (Mikkelsen, 2000). However, in our modern retellings and inventions based on folklore, some subtle differences are notable. As a case in point, William Steig composed a literary fairy tale when he wrote *Shrek* (1990) and turned all the folklore elements inside out. Everything we've been led to expect in fairy tales is upended in this story of Shrek, the ugly, uncouth hero who is delightfully proud of his unfortunate effect on everyone. His quest to meet the princess of his dreams (uglier than he) is fulfilled. The movie, *Shrek,* released in the summer of 2001, goes back to some of the conventions of folklore: The princess is beautiful and the plot is much more substantial. As noted earlier in Figure 4.1, folktales are more likely to be about common people, talking animals, and conventional wisdom, while fairy tales offer royalty, castles, and magic. Frequently the traditional stories include both—commoners and royalty, cottages and castles, and magical animals and spirits. In the following discussion the distinction between the two forms is blurred. Narrative patterns and stylistic language, stock characters and themes, and common folkloric elements abound in thousands and thousands of stories referred to primarily as folktales or, in the more encompassing term, as traditional literature.

●◆●

REFLECTION Retellings of folktales and fairy tales, either in additional stories or in movie versions, can change substantially folktale elements of character, setting, and plot. What do you think of these changes? Can you think of some examples of retellings that you liked, and some that you didn't, and why?

Narrative Patterns and Stylistic Language

Story structure, introduced at the beginning of this chapter, is a common narrative pattern. Folktales begin with a brief introduction that uses "Once upon a time" or "Long ago and far away" or other stylistic language to alert the listener–reader to the folk quality of the work.

In the following example from "The Fisherman and His Wife," *setting*—denoting time and place—is quickly established with the phrase "There was once a fisherman who lived with his wife in a pigsty not far from the sea, and every day the fisherman went fishing" (Manheim, 1983, p. 70).

Following this introduction of setting and characters, an event occurs that galvanizes the action; this event is called the **problem.** It can also be a supernatural task undertaken by one of the characters, usually the hero. In this well-known story collected by the Brothers Grimm, "The Fisherman and His Wife," the problem takes shape when the husband catches a talking flounder who promises anything in return for its life. When the fisherman's wife hears that her husband let the fish go without wishing for anything, she urges him to go back to the sea and try again. He does, with the refrain "Little man whoever you be,/ Flounder, flounder in the sea,/ My wife, her name is Ilsebil,/ Has sent me here against my will" (Manheim, 1983, pp. 70–71). Very often these tales employ a repetitive language pattern that becomes predictable and adds to the escalating tension in the plot as grander and grander events occur. This is called "rising action" or, in the terms of story structure, a series of action/consequence, action/consequence. In this story, the wife wishes first for a cottage, then a stone castle, and next for a palace in which she is king. (Notice the pattern of three events.) Greed grows, and with the flounder's magical help triggered by the magical refrain, she becomes emperor, then pope, and finally she wants to be "like God" (again a series of three). With a storm raging to show that the climax is near, the problem is solved by sending the woman back to the original cottage/hovel with her husband, and her life returns to what it was before her greed caused the uproar. A retelling for young children set in Norway in which the fisherman and his wife are cats is *The Fisherman and His Wife: A Brand New Version* (Wells, 1998).

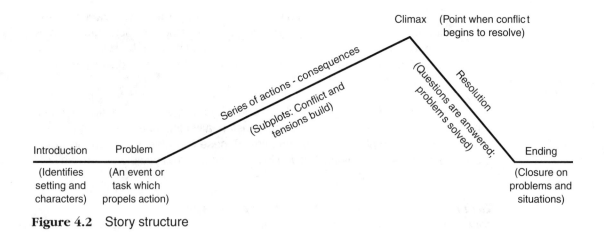

Figure 4.2   Story structure

    This common narrative pattern, or story structure, may be diagrammed, as in Figure 4.2.

    The structure of folktales has gained attention in recent years because it is believed that children implicitly internalize the structure when listening to many stories. Then when they read, they show better comprehension because they can predict what might happen. Thus, knowledge of story structure aids reading–listening comprehension and underscores the value of reading aloud to children.

    Quite often, the action–consequence sequence is based on a quest undertaken by the hero or heroine. Subplots occur in which a character meets other characters along the journey and has other adventures, leading to the climax, which is that period in the story when tension explodes from all the action and excitement leading up to it. The action–consequence sequence occurs in "The Fisherman and His Wife" when the fisherman entreats the flounder on behalf of his wife each time, and the consequence is a bigger home.

    Another narrative pattern in folktales is called the *cumulative tale*. It is a circular pattern in which events are repeated with one more added each time (see Figure 4.3). *The House that Jack Built* is just such a story (Winter, 2000). *The Little Red Hen (Makes A Pizza)* (Sturges, 1999) is a common cumulative pattern as well, with the new event coming at the beginning of the chain, but the unfolding of events continuing in the same order. Cumulative aspects are evident in songs and nursery rhymes, too. With the predictability in language and plot, cumulative tales are usually excellent for beginning readers.

    Language in folktales tends to reflect some stylized patterns, such as "Once upon a time," and repeated sayings, such as "Mirror, mirror, on the wall," but generally stories are told in unadorned prose, simple and direct. Modern storytellers use contemporary language so that new listeners can understand. In the spirit of the oral tradition, tales weren't memorized verbatim but rather grew out of the rapport between storyteller and audience. Thus, modern versions can be a welcome addition to this genre, if the essential nature of folklore is left unchanged.

Figure 4.3 Cumulative
Story Structure

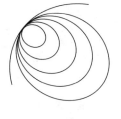

REFLECTION Do the Disney versions of folktales retain the essential nature of folklore?

Stock Characters

Characters in folktales are often one-dimensional or flat. They exist as undeveloped types to serve the plot. In "The Fisherman," for example, the fisherman is simply a messenger, we know nothing else about him. His wife is portrayed only as greedy. Narrow characterization paradoxically allows the story to have broader appeal because these single, specific traits are universal.

Characters fall into personality types and roles so that the action can be fast-paced and eventful. Following is a list of typical characters in folktales:

Beautiful maiden	Handsome prince/hero
Eldest son/daughter	Youngest son/daughter
Evil twin or jealous siblings	Stepmother
Elderly childless couple	Wise elderly person
Fool, or noodlehead	Trickster
Witch/wizard	Talking animals
Personified object (broom, trees, clouds, and more)	Fantasy character (leprechaun, elf, fairy, gnome, giant, ogre, mermaid/merman, and many more)

Folktales are often criticized because characterization is so narrow that characters become stereotypical or a caricature of a type. In other words, the stepmother is always and only evil, and the maiden is always and only passively innocent. These characters are archetypes, and the folktales do not represent reality, as even young children intuit (Bettelheim, 1976; Chukovsky, 1971).

REFLECTION Is it fair to criticize folktales for stereotyping characters when, in traditional literature, characters are supposed to have only one or two traits?

Folktale Themes and Elements

Common themes in folklore reflected values, and the values of a pretechnological society dictated that harmony, truth, and goodness be rewarded, while cruelty, deception, and greed be chastised. Fairness and justice ruled eventually. Hard work was honored, wit and intelligence were prized. Sometimes a struggle for power precipitated the outcome, but good always vanquished evil. From folktales our definitions of truth, beauty, and love are realized, and philosophical questions concerning the meaning of life can be answered. Lest the themes become too serious, a generous body of folklore has humor or nonsense as its theme.

Common folkloric elements include the following:

Magic objects (wands, staffs, a branch of rowan, everyday things invested with magical properties)

Mythical beasts (unicorns, dragons, satyrs, nymphs)

Spells of enchantment (turning a human into an animal, a fool, an inanimate object)

A long sleep (as in *Sleeping Beauty* and *Snow White*)

Transformations (from ugly to beautiful, from inanimate to real)

Groups of 3, 7, 12, or 4 (magic numbers probably coming from the natural world or symbols from early religious rituals)

Myths and Legends

When primitive people wanted to explain how the Earth began, or why the sun and the moon followed each other in the sky, they created stories. Prescientific explanations of the universe and its workings gave meaning and ritual to the lives of common people and the powerful alike. When the stories were prompted by questions of an afterlife, or an explanation of what happens after death, otherworlds were created with their own gods and goddesses, heroes, villains, and tricksters. Myths, unlike other stories, developed in relation to each other, so that we have a body of literature based on Greek myths, Roman myths, Scandinavian myths, and others. (The Greek word for "stories" was *mythos*.) Modern retellings, such as Jeanne Steig's *A Gift from Zeus* (2001) illustrated by William Steig, are still compelling.

Mythology is frequently broken into three broad types: creation myths; pourquoi tales (also called nature myths); and hero myths. *Creation myths,* sometimes called genesis myths, depict the struggle to form the Earth out of darkness, chaos, or the spirit world. For example, Genesis, the first book in the Bible, explains the origin of the Judeo–Christian heritage. Many cultures have an explanation of how the Earth began. In addition to those titles previously mentioned, see *The Four Corners of the Sky: Creation Stories and Cosmologies from Around the World* (Zeitlin, 2000).

Pourquoi stories, such as *Why Mosquitoes Buzz in People's Ears* (Aardema, 1975) and *How Chipmunk Got His Stripes* (Bruchac & Bruchac, 2001), are myths that explain why natural events occur. They offer explanations of the seasons, the placement of stars in the constellations, why thunder rolls in the sky, and the movements and behaviors of animals. Early societies created stories to rationalize the inexplicable, yet predictable, natural occurrences in the cycle of life.

As myths center on supernatural beings, set in otherworldly places and times, so legends bring mythical qualities to characters who perhaps could have lived in somewhat recognizable places, completing somewhat realistic tasks. A familiar hero myth, *The Wanderings of Odysseus: The Story of the Odyssey* (Sutcliff, 1996), gives life to a hero of ancient Greece.

Hero myths usually describe the exploits of people who begin life as orphans or people of very lowly status, then are elevated to high status through their good deeds or quests for greatness. Sometimes a miraculous event occurs to mark the potential hero, such as an initiation rite or a miraculous birth. The young person usually has a wise older mentor for guidance. The quest is entered with foreboding, because the future hero or heroine is acting against all odds of success. Finally, the climax proves that heroic qualities are within each person, that self-determination and a conscience can allow each of us to succeed. With these characteristics, heroic legends foreshadow the high fantasies of Chapter 8.

These hero stories reflect idealism through gentle, strong, and innocent characters who meet adversity with undaunted courage. Self-doubt is replaced by confidence, and the quests take on a dimension of self-discovery. *Sundiata, Lion King of*

From *The Wanderings of Odysseus* (Jacket Cover) by Rosemary Sutcliff. Artwork by Alan Lee. Used by permission of Dell Publishing, a division of Random House, Inc.

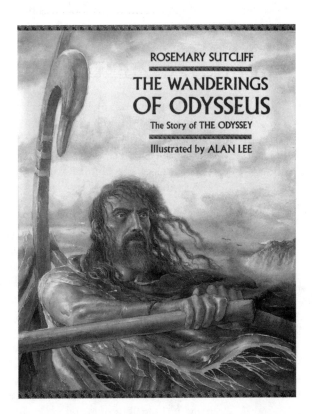

Mali (Wisniewski, 1992) is a heroic legend based on the powerful and benevolent Sundiata, who ruled Mali in the 14th century. His early life as a crippled and speech-less child was transformed by his bravery and intelligence with the help of an older mentor. David Wisniewski's cut-paper collage artwork adds a dimension of grandeur, projecting colors, symbols, and emotions of that legendary place and time.

Legends can elevate a common person into the realm of folklore through the exaggeration and enhancement of character traits. When the exaggeration reaches comic proportions, a tall tale is created. Examples of tall tales in U.S. folklore are stories about Paul Bunyan, the North American logger of tremendous size; Pecos Bill, a Southwestern cowboy; and John Henry, the African-American steel-driving man of early railroad-building fame. *Big Jabe* (Nolen, 2000) may enter the tall-tale pantheon as his exploits as a slave who helped others escape prior to the Civil War become known. Big Jabe, like the biblical Moses, was found floating down-river in a basket, and in a few months grew to supersize, foreshadowing his heroic feats of strength and goodness. Perhaps the next century will see legends from this century enter the pantheon of folklore.

REFLECTION   What modern myths and legends are being created today? Sensitive always to the demands of society's changing icons, what political, economic, sports, or musical heroes and heroines are being invented?

EVALUATING TRADITIONAL LITERATURE

Difficulty in evaluating traditional literature may stem from the fact that recently published works are retellings, adaptations, and translations of sometimes very old tales. Questions of authenticity arise, and because the old tales were oral and dynamic, not static artifacts, there is no first version to use as the "correct" or "pure" one. However, by becoming familiar with the classifications, definitions, and major characteristics of the subgenres presented in this chapter, you will be able to look for certain aspects unique to this genre: a linear or cumulative story structure; one-dimensional characters, with the exception of the hero; clean, spare language with occasional word play and stylistic patterns; and humorous or value-laden themes that speak to the truly important reasons for a society's existence.

Figure 4.4 outlines an evaluation scheme based on questions drawn from these salient characteristics of folklore. When selecting a book with audience and purpose in mind, ask questions like those in the outline. Also, check out a reliable review, one that you trust, for a knowledgeable person's opinion of the work. Following the evaluation scheme is another kind of evaluation model, a rubric based on a four-point scale. See which one works best for you and compare your results to those of your colleagues.

Following is an example of a four-point scale for evaluating the folk rhymes, songs, and proverbs of traditional literature. Using the questions in Figure 4.4, you also could create additional scales for fables, myths, and so on.

Figure 4.4
Evaluating traditional literature

Subgenre	My personal evaluation
Folk rhymes, songs, and proverbs	Are they memorable? Compelling? Is the vocabulary suitable, with interesting word play? Are the melodies tuneful and do they invite participation?
Fables and parables	Is the characterization one-dimensional? Is the plot succinct with an explicit moral lesson? Is the language appropriate? Does the moral teach a lesson I think is important?
Folktales and fairy tales	Is the language stylistic at appropriate times? Are there recognizable themes, interesting but not complex characters, and authentic cultural elements in the setting?
Myths and legends	Is the purpose clear (that is, creation, hero, or pourquoi myth)? Are the settings and characters authentic? Is there a compelling vision of human interaction in story form?

Four-Point Scale for Evaluating Folk Rhymes, Songs, and Proverbs

Name of Text: _____

Author and Illustrator: _____

When 1 stands for "very good," 2 is "good," 3 is "marginal," and 4 is "unsatisfactory," rate the book according to the following:

I. The rhyme/song/proverb is memorable and compelling.

1 _____ 2 _____ 3 _____ 4 _____

II. The vocabulary is suitable, with interesting word play.

1 _____ 2 _____ 3 _____ 4 _____

III. The story or song seems authentic, with conventional wisdom and a strong theme.

1 _____ 2 _____ 3 _____ 4 _____

IV. The song has a tuneful, easy-to-sing melody that invites participation.

1 _____ 2 _____ 3 _____ 4 _____

If folklore is presented in a picture-book format, as most is, the artwork also should be evaluated in relation to the text. See Chapters 5 and 6 for a discussion of evaluating artwork and text.

While there is latitude in accepting renditions of tales, it is wise to be alert to certain inappropriate practices. The most obvious errors occur when stories, movies, video games, or other examples stray from the flavor of the unadorned, sometimes earthy, oral tradition. Walt Disney's versions of the familiar stories *Cinderella, Beauty and the Beast,* and *Sleeping Beauty,* for example, are too pretty, too cute, and too fancy to be considered folklore—and inappropriate elements have been added. Chattering teacups, simpering heroes and heroines, and comic-book dragons and dwarfs are insulting to the genre. Controversies surrounding these adaptations began with the release of the movie *Snow White* in 1938, and continue today (Hearne, 1997). Hearne's major criticisms are that the folklore journey has been turned into a chase, heroines have been shaped like Barbie dolls, and commercialism has become rampant with fast-food restaurant toy tie-ins. At least Disney studios have grown more sensitive to issues of gender equity, as its *Pocahontas* and later films seem to show.

REFLECTION   Another criticism of the traditional folktales and fairy tales is that they are too violent for today's children. Do you agree?

THE WORLD'S TRADITIONAL LITERATURE

Increasing diversity in the number of cultural groups represented in the United States, as seen in the number of school-age children who do not speak English (Faltis, 1993), necessitates the inclusion of multicultural literature in every aspect of curricula. The value of literature to foster cognitive and affective development is well understood and, particularly for children who are sensitive to their own cultural differences, the comfort and delight that literature brings is a substantial addition to their well-being. This literature should include not just their own cultural literature; a variety that shows similarities and differences can be very important.

What follows is a short description of traditional stories from diverse cultural groups, as well as some information about related folklore and several exemplary works. The brevity allows you to search out those titles and authors that most represent what you need. Please note that many of these titles are considered picture books, but this should not lessen the appropriateness of these multicultural stories for a wide audience. Students of all ages will respond to the tales; the picture-book format often does not detract from the enjoyment of them by adolescents.

Traditional Literature from Africa and the Middle East

African folklore comes from many African countries and communities with distinct cultural references: Mali, Ashanti, Senegalese, Yoruba, Swahili, Zulu, and many more. When Africans were imported to the Americas as slaves, remnants of their folklore mixed with Caribbean stories, creating variations and adding new elements. These variations grew and flourished in the southern United States. Ananse, the trickster–spider of the Ashanti, became "Aunt Nancy" in some tales, and the Brer Rabbit stories, originally collected and retold by Joel Chandler Harris in the late 19th century, seem to have come from an African tradition of wily animal characters. As the characters in folklore are so often either good or evil, the ambiguity and enterprise of the trickster's role is especially compelling.

Rich language patterns; plots demonstrating wit and cunning, kindness and generosity; and values such as love of beauty, humor, and perseverance abound in African literature. Alan Shepard's retelling of *Master Man: A Tall Tale of Nigeria* (2001), illustrated by David Wisniewski, shows comically how a boastful man learns a lesson.

In addition to the books mentioned throughout this chapter, the following recent examples of African folklore may be consulted. To save space, the bibliographic information is given here and is not reproduced in the references at the end of this chapter. Please note that the (ad.) after the author's name signifies that the story is an adaptation.

Gershator, P. (ad.) (2000). *Only one cowry: A Dahomean tale.* New York: Orchard.

Hofmeyr, D. (ad.) (2001). *The Star-bearer: A creation myth from ancient Egypt.* New York: Farrar, Straus & Giroux.

MacDonald, M. R. (ad.) (2001). *Mabela the clever.* New York: Whitman. (Limba, Sierra Leone)

Mollel, T. M. (ad.) (2000). *Subira Subira.* New York: Clarion. (Tanzania)

Olaleye, I. O. (2000). *In the rainfield: Who is the greatest?* New York: Blue Sky/Scholastic. (Nigeria)

Traditional Literature from Asia

Folklore from Japan, Vietnam, China, the Philippines, and other Pacific Rim countries constitutes a varied and rich repository upon which some authors have based modern retellings and adaptations.

When compared to the pattern of story grammar that began our discussion of traditional literature, story grammar of traditional Asian folklore seems to exhibit an important difference. Often the main character seems to react to events rather than to cause them. Instead of a linear progression of mounting tension, the structure reflects an episodic movement in which there is no well-defined purpose or goal. In an analysis of Japanese folk tales, Matsuyama (1983) attributed this to values derived from Buddhist principles that deny aggression, competition, and individualism. A recent example is *Monkey King* (Young, 2001), in which the hero, trapped in Buddha's great hand, introduces a large cast of characters who are searching for enlightenment. Ed Young's carefully constructed and stunning artwork provides continuity in episode after episode.

Following are some recent and recommended examples of folklore from Asia. This bibliography is complete and is not reproduced at the end of this chapter.

Balouch, K. (ad.) (2000). *The king and three thieves: A Persian tale*. New York: Viking.

Casanova, M. (ad.) (2000). *The hunter: A Chinese folktale*. New York: Atheneum.

Kimmel, E. A. (ad.) (1999). *Sword of the Samurai: Adventure stories from Japan*. New York: Browndeer/Harcourt.

San Souci, D. (ad.) (1999). *In the moonlight mist: A Korean tale*. New York: Boyds Mills.

Sierra, J. (ad.) (1999). *The dancing pig*. New York: Gulliver/Harcourt. (Bali)

Souhami, J. (ad.) (2000). *No dinner! The story of the old woman and the pumpkin*. New York: Cavendish. (India)

Traditional Literature from the Americas

Because of the interest, availability, and sheer number of these examples, folklore representing the Americas will be split into three parts: (1) Native American, (2) Central and South America and the Caribbean, and (3) Rural America.

Native American Folklore

Analogous to the many distinct cultural groups in the African and Asian geographical areas, Native American cultures are heterogeneous, with features of the plains, the eastern woodlands, the southwestern deserts, and Canada all generating cultural differences expressed in ritual and mythology. It should be noted, however, that there are more similarities than differences, and four types, as identified by Bierhorst (1976), seem to be particularly noticeable in Native American folklore:

1. creation myths that depict an ordered world rising from the chaos of nature (Bierhorst, J. (ad.) (2000). *The people with 5 fingers: A Native California creation tale*. New York: Cavendish).

2. "family drama" or myths resulting from the closeness of people and families living together in kinship units (Running Wolf, M. B. (ad.) (2000). *On the trail of elder brother: Glous'gap stories of the Micmac Indians*. New York: Braziller/Persea.

3. hero myths in which the young hero is a trickster until he realizes the importance of social virtue, usually in a quest sequence (Goble, P. (ad.) (1998). *Iktomi and the coyote: A Plains Indian story*. New York: Orchard.

4. rites of passage, or crossing threshold myths, depicting passage in and out of a dream state or a parallel world (Vaughan, R. L. (ret.) (2001). *Eagle boy: A Pacific Northwest native tale*. Seattle, WA: Sasquatch.

In addition to the books just mentioned, following are additional recent and recommended books from Native American cultures. Native American legends, traditional ones and retellings, capture the imagination of many children.

The boy waited until day became night.

He shot an arrow into the falling star, pledging his love to the faithful maiden.

"Falling Star," a Native American Legend by Alyssa (7th grade).

Goble, P. (1992). *Love flute*. New York: Bradbury.

Norman, H. (comp. and ad.) (2000). *Trickster and the fainting birds*. New York: Gulliver/Harcourt. (Algonquin)

Van Laan, N. (1997). *Shingebiss: An Ojibwe legend*. Boston: Houghton Miffin.

Central and South America and the Caribbean

"Spanish-speaking children are the largest and fastest-growing school-age population of second-language learners in the United States" (Faltis, 1993, p. 7). Clearly this dictates a need to become aware of Hispanic and Latino/Latina folklore and explore possibilities of enjoying it in classrooms. From the island cultures of the Caribbean and Puerto Rico to the Southwest deserts, from the tip of South America to the southern United States, are vast differences in geography and culture. Also, ancient Mayan, Aztec, and Inca civilizations are evident in the folklore of this region.

Titles of the following books demonstrate the diversity of folktales with cultural roots in South and Central America.

Alvarez, J. (2000). *The secret footprints*. New York: Knopf. (Dominican Republic)

Ehlert, L. (1997). *Cuckoo: A Mexican folktale*. New York: Harcourt.

Hamilton, V. (2000). *The girl who spun gold*. New York: Scholastic. (West Indies)

Kimmel, E. A. (2000). *The two mountains: An Aztec legend*. New York: Holiday House.

Montes, M. (2000). *Juan Bobo goes to work: A Puerto Rican folktale*. New York: HarperCollins.

Pitcher, C. (2000). *Mariana and the merchild: A folktale from Chile*. New York: Eerdmans.

Rockwell, A. (2000). *The boy who wouldn't obey: A Mayan legend*. New York: Greenwillow.

Rural America

Titles of the following books demonstrate the diversity of folktales with cultural roots in rural America.

Aylesworth, J. (ad.) (2001). *The tale of Tricky Fox: A New England trickster tale*. New York: Scholastic.

Battle-Lavert, G. (2000). *The shaking bag*. New York: Whitman.

Johnson, P. B. (ad.) (2001). *Fearless Jack*. New York: McElderry.

Kimmel, E. A. (ad.) (2000). *The runaway tortilla*. New York: Winslow.

Sathre, V. (1999). *Slender Ella and her fairy hogfather*. New York: Yearling.

Washington, D. (ad.) (2000). *A big, spooky house*. New York: Jump at the Sun/Hyperion.

Traditional Literature from Europe

Folklore from Europe may be the most familiar of all, as it is the wellspring from which many of our early experiences derive. Greek gods and goddesses were perhaps among the first examples of mythology, providing common referents that we use often: Cupid, Narcissus, Aphrodite, Pandora, and Apollo. D'Aulaire and D'Aulaire's *Book of Greek Myths* (1962) is a classic in the genre. Another great family of mythology is represented in *Odin's Family: Myths of the Vikings* (Phillip, 1996). These are all collections, but many single-story picture books are available, too. Following are recent and recommended ones, and noted familiar authors, who are the retellers and adapters of these tales.

Climo, S. (ad.) (1999). *Magic and mischief: Tales from Cornwall*. New York: Clarion.

DeFelice, C. (ad.) (2000). *Cold feet*. New York: DK Inc. (Scotland)

Greene, E. (ad.) (2000). *The little golden lamb*. New York: Clarion. (Hungary)

Grimm, J. (2001) *The rabbit's bride* (adapted by Lucy Crane and Holly Meade), New York: Cavendish. (pan-European)

Huck, C. (2001). *The black bull of Norroway*. New York: Greenwillow. (Scotland)

San Souci, R. D. (ad.) (2000). *Peter and the blue witch baby*. New York: Doubleday. (Russia)

Sierra, J. (ad.) (2000). *The beautiful butterfly*. New York: Clarion (Spain)

RETELLINGS TOO GOOD TO MISS (FOR YOUNG AND OLD)

In a sense, all the folktales and fairy tales we have today are retellings of the ancient and not-so-old stories and poems. Modern writers adapt, collect, translate, and sometimes use fragments of stories to create literary fairy tales. When Hans Christian Andersen and others created their original stories in the 19th century, relying heavily on folktale elements, the genre expanded to include and embrace new tales as well as humorous, profound, and even shocking versions of the well-known. This bibliography is complete here and will not be referenced at chapter's end.

For Younger Readers

Bell, A. (2000). *Jack and the beanstalk: An English fairy tale*. New York: North-South.

Fearnley, J. (2000). *Mr. Wolf's pancakes*. Boston: Little/Tiger.

Moser, B. (ad.) (2001). *The three little pigs*. Boston: Little.

Osborne, M. P. (2000). *Kate and the beanstalk*. New York: Schwartz/Atheneum.

Wattenberg, J. (ad.) (2000). *Henny Penny*. New York: Scholastic.

Wiesner, D. (2001). *The three pigs*. New York: Clarion.

For Older Readers

Block, F. L. (2000). *The rose and the beast: Fairy tales retold*. New York: Cotler/HarperCollins.

Kindl, P. (2001). *Goose chase*. Boston: Houghton Mifflin.

McKinley, R. (2000). *Spindle's end*. New York: Putnam.

Napoli, D. (1999). *Spinners*. New York: Dutton.

Vande Velde, V. (2000). *The Rumpelstiltskin problem*. Boston: Houghton Mifflin.

Yolen, J. (comp.) (2000). *Sherwood: Original stories from the world of Robin Hood*. New York: Philomel.

SUMMARY

This chapter presented a story structure to initiate a discussion of traditional literature classified into four subgenres: folk songs, rhymes, and proverbs; fables and parables; folktales and fairy tales; and myths and legends. After a brief history of traditional literature, definitions, characteristics, common themes, characters, elements, and examples were given. Folktales, myths, and legends were especially detailed, as specific stories from collections of the Brothers Grimm, Greek myths, and other sources were summarized. Creation myths, nature myths, and hero myths were presented as three basic types of mythology, and legends were said to include stories of heroes and heroines and the exaggerations of tall tales.

Implicit in this chapter was the importance of traditional literature to provide a multicultural dimension to every child's experience. A variety of folklore, from many cultures and representing myriad themes, including humor, should permeate the curriculum, with special attention to the match between the ethnicity of children in a classroom and the multicultural literature presented.

Criteria for evaluation of traditional literature were suggested for all the subgenres, as well as a model of a rubric for evaluating folk rhymes and songs.

Concerns about stereotypical language and images and inappropriate retellings were raised, as well as concerns about the dearth of books reflecting some cultures. However, this decade is seeing a resurgence of interest in publishing folktales, and this speaks well for the availability of good books in the coming years. Picture books seem to be prolific, but well-written collections of stories for older readers are harder to find.

IMPLICATIONS FOR INSTRUCTION

Projects are outlined for scholars who want to explore additional topics, and activities are included for young readers and intermediate and middle school readers.

Projects

1. Stories in this chapter beg to be told. Become part of the oral tradition and learn to tell a story or polish your storytelling techniques. Many resources are available to help you; for example, see Appendix B.

2. Are you interested in finding folktales that feature girls and women in leading roles to contrast with passive, helpless heroines? Start with this one, and you'll be led to others: *Not One Damsel in Distress: World Folktales for Strong Girls* (Yolen, 2000) features talented, athletic and articulate girls.

3. A quick perusal of the *Horn Book Guide* will yield several retellings of standard Brothers Grimm tales and others. A perennial favorite, *Cinderella* has enjoyed recent popularity with *The Gift of the Crocodile: A Cinderella Story* (Sierra, 2000), *Cinderella Skeleton* (San Souci, 2000a),

Fair, Brown and Trembling: An Irish Cinderella Story (Daly, 2000), and *Little Gold Star: A Spanish American Cinderella Tale* (San Souci, 2000b). Compare these, or find a tale you enjoy and look for different versions that reflect multiple perspectives.

Activities for the Primary Level

1. In primary grades children can write or tell stories based on pourquoi tales. Think of intriguing topics and have the children generate questions, such as these: How did the triceratops get his horns? Why does snow fall from the sky? Who invented the first boat? Let imaginations have free rein.

2. Dramatizing folktales such as *The Three Billy Goats Gruff, The Three Pigs,* or *Sleeping Beauty* allows children to hear and speak predictable language patterns, to become a character, and thus move out of an egocentric perspective and into an empathic one, and to experience the pattern of events that leads to an internalization of story structure. All the following activities demonstrate the value of drama and movement, so organize some dramatic experiences for your children to enjoy. To increase language learning, introduce retellings (see "Too Good to Miss" and Margaret MacDonald's (2000) *Shake It Up Tales: Stories to Sing, Dance, Drum and Act Out*).

3. Retellings, such as the comical *The Stinky Cheese Man and Other Fairly Stupid Tales* (Scieszka, 1992), have delighted children and encouraged activities in writing, reading, and discussion. The two Jack-in-the-beanstalk stories mentioned in the Retellings "Too Good to Miss" section in this chapter have a male hero in one and a female in the other. The two "little pig" stories are also great to share.

Activities for the Intermediate and Middle Levels

1. Have children bring stories from home, stories about their own heritage, or those they have adapted from well-known stories. Collect stories from the community, and thus create your own folklore.

2. Children in middle grades enjoy myths, legends, fables, and tall tales and can be encouraged to create their own, either in written or oral form. After hearing some examples, they will enjoy writing or dramatizing some original stories. Exaggeration, characterization, story structure, and other elements can be taught, using the children's own work and relating it to the examples.

3. When studying folktales from different parts of the world, use a world map on the bulletin board to pinpoint origins of stories. If your curriculum unit distinguishes the types of folktales and myths, you can color-code them (e.g., blue for pourquoi tales, red for creation myths, and so on).

REFERENCES

Children's Works

Aardema, V. (1975). *Why mosquitoes buzz in people's ears.* New York: Dial.

Asbjornsen, P., & Moe, J. (1953). *East o' the sun and west o' the moon.* New York: Macmillan.

Bruchac, J., & Bruchac, J. (2001). *How chipmunk got his stripes.* New York: Dial.

Chang, M., & Chang, R. (1997). *The beggar's magic: A Chinese tale.* New York: McElderry.

Cohn, A. (1993). *From sea to shining sea: A treasury of American folklore and folk songs.* New York: Scholastic.

Collodi, C. (1996). *Pinocchio.* New York: Viking-Penguin.

Daly, J. (2000). *Fair, brown and trembling: An Irish Cinderella story.* New York: Farrar, Straus & Giroux.

D'Aulaire, I., & D'Aulaire, E. (1962). *Book of Greek myths.* Garden City, NY: Doubleday.

Demi. (1997). *Buddha stories.* New York: Holt.

Goble, P. (1992). *Love flute.* New York: Bradbury.

Higginsen, V. (1995). *This is my song: A collection of gospel music for the family.* New York: Crown.

Lang, A. (1889/1994). *The blue fairy book.* New York: Fine Communications.

Lang, A. (1890/1994). *The red fairy book.* New York: Fine Communications.

Nolen, J. (2000). *Big Jabe.* New York: Lothrop.

Opie, I. (1999). *Here comes Mother Goose.* Cambridge, MA: Candlewick.

Orgel, D. (2000). *The lion and the mouse and other Aesop's fables.* New York: DK Ink.

Phillip, N. (1996). *Odin's family: Myths of the Vikings.* New York: Orchard.

Pinkney, J. (2000). *Aesop's fables.* New York: North-South/SeaStar.

San Souci, R. D. (2000a). *Cinderella skeleton.* New York: Harcourt/Silver Whistle.

San Souci, R. D. (2000b). *Little gold star: A Spanish American Cinderella tale.* New York: HarperCollins.

Scieszka, J. (1992). *The stinky cheese man and other fairly stupid tales.* New York: Viking.

Shepard, A. (ad.) (2001). *Master man: A tall tale of Nigeria.* New York: HarperCollins.

Sierra, J. (ad.) (2000). *The gift of the crocodile: A Cinderella story.* New York: Simon.

Steig, J. (2001). *A gift from Zeus.* New York: HarperCollins.

Steig, W. (1990). *Shrek.* New York: Farrar, Straus & Giroux.

Sturges, P. (1999). *The little red hen (makes a pizza).* New York: Dutton.

Sutcliff, R. (1996). *The wanderings of Odysseus: The story of the Odyssey.* New York: Delacorte.

Thomas, G., & Crossley-Holland, K. (1985). *Tales from the Mabinogion.* Woodstock, NY: Overlook Press.

Wells, R. (1998). *The fisherman and his wife: A brand new version.* New York: Dial.

Winter, J. (2000). *The house that Jack built.* New York: Dial.

Wisniewski, D. (1992). *Sundiata, lion king of Mali.* New York: Clarion.

Yolen, J. (2000). *Not one damsel in distress: World folktales for strong girls.* New York: Harcourt/Silver Whistle.

Young, E. (2001). *Monkey king.* New York: HarperCollins.

Zeitlin, S. (2000). *The four corners of the sky: Creation stories and cosmologies from around the world.* New York: Holt.

Professional Works

Bettelheim, B. (1976). *The uses of enchantment.* New York: Knopf.

Bierhorst, J. (Ed.). (1976). *The red swan: Myths and tales of the American Indians.* New York: Farrar.

Campbell, J. (1968). *Hero with a thousand faces* (2nd ed.). Princeton, NJ: Princeton University Press.

Chukovsky, K. (1971). *From two to five* (rev. ed.). Berkeley: University of California Press.

Dundes, A. (Ed.). (1983). *Cinderella: A casebook.* New York: Wildman.

Faltis, C. (1993). *Joinfostering.* Upper Saddle River, NJ: Merrill/Prentice Hall.

Haugaard, E. (1983). *Hans Christian Andersen: The complete fairy tales and stories* (Trans.). Garden City, NY: Doubleday/Anchor Press.

Hearne, B. (1989). *Beauty and the beast.* Chicago: University of Chicago Press.

Hearne, B. (1997). Disney revisited, or, Jiminy Cricket, it's musty down here! *The Horn Book Magazine, 73*(2), 137–148.

Jung, C. (Ed.). (1964). *Man and his symbols.* Garden City, NY: Doubleday.

MacDonald, M. (2000). *Shake it up tales: Stories to sing, dance, drum, and act out.* New York: August House.

Manheim, R. (1983). *Grimm's tales for young and old* (Trans.). Garden City, NY: Doubleday/Anchor Press.

Matsuyama, U. (1983). Can story grammar speak Japanese? *The Reading Teacher, 36,* 666–669.

Mikkelsen, N. (2000). *Words and pictures: Lessons in children's literature and literacies.* Boston: McGraw-Hill.

Opie, I., & Opie, P. (Eds.). (1951). *Oxford dictionary of nursery rhymes.* Oxford: Oxford University Press.

Propp, V. (1968). *The Morphology of the folktale* (2nd ed.). Austin, TX: University of Texas Press.

Sutherland, Z. (1997). *Children and books* (9th ed.). New York: Longman.

Wrenn, D. (1976). *Welsh history makers.* Yorkshire, England: EP Publishing.

Additional Resources

Barchers, S. I. (2000). *Multicultural folktales: Readers theatre for elementary students.* Chicago: Teachers Ideas Press.
Barchers has assembled 40 story theatre scripts adapted from folktales. The reading levels are from grades 1 through 5.

DeVos, G., & Altmann, A. E. (1999). *New tales for old: Folktales as literary fiction for young adults.* Englewood, CO: Libraries Unlimited.
Classic western European folktales are retold and explained in this rich, well-organized book, along with Internet resources and suggested classroom projects.

Tomlinson, C. M. (Ed.) (1998). *Children's books from other countries.* Lanham, MD: Scarecrow Press.
This is an annotated bibliography of over 700 titles and includes translated books and winners of the Hans Christian Andersen and Margaret Batchelder Awards.

Zipes, J. (Ed.) (2000). *The great fairy tale tradition: From Straparola and Basile to the Brothers Grimm.* New York: Norton.
Fairy tales from Italy, France, and Germany are presented—116 in all—as well as 7 critical essays and 20 original illustrations in 38 thematic divisions.

Zipes, J. (2001). *Sticks and stones: The troublesome success of children's literature from Slovenly Peter to Harry Potter.* London: Routledge.
Nine essays by Zipes address topics in children's literature from a political and sociological perspective.

CHAPTER **5**

Picture Books for the Very Young

INTRODUCTION AND RESPONSE

Books for babies? Of course, because the importance of reading to children at an early age has long been touted as fundamental to school success. Literacy develops from early and frequent contact with language and story. Often, though, it is surprising to realize that infants and toddlers may benefit enormously from repeated exposure to children's books designed especially for them. Publishers and educationists have recognized this strong connection between babies and books, as revealed by sales figures and increased critical attention toward the content of books for the youngest (Giblin, 1996). Not only as a prelude to reading and writing, but also as an immediate cognitive and emotional experience, books bring delight, insight, and satisfaction to early learners.

This chapter explores the beginning of children's picture books, as well as the recent interest in and need for books for the very youngest audience—birth to about age 4. Questions from a newcomer in this area of children's literature might include these: What kinds of books are available and developmentally appropriate? How and why would one share a love of literature with an infant or a toddler? And how would one evaluate books written for this audience?

In order to begin thinking about these questions and others, recall now your earliest memory of being read to. Do you remember a parent or an older sibling reading to you? Can you recall the book and the feeling of satisfaction, belonging, and anticipation that this encounter (or others) generated? What book is at the beginning of your literary experience?

HISTORY OF THE CHILDREN'S PICTURE BOOK

Picture books are a fairly recent phenomenon in the literary tradition. Although Bishop Comenius produced *Orbis Pictus* in 1658, until the late 1800s the illustrated book was the usual type of book for children. Illustrations in books were either created singularly by hand (each picture or design was laboriously copied in each book) or, when books were printed on early printing presses, enmasse with woodcuts.

Woodblock illustrations (as in *Orbis Pictus*) were cheap and easily done. The artist drew a picture on a small block of wood (boxwood, for example) and then cut away everything that should not print. "The woodcut enabled many copies to be produced from the same block and. . .was a process particularly suited for combination with printing" (Whalley, 1975, p. 22). Many children were treated to woodcut images in early alphabet books, such as "D is for Duck" (see page 93). (For more early woodcut images, see www.sover.net/~oldlabel/woodcut_images.)

Another method, which was the opposite of raising the surface, was the **engraved plate.** In this method, the engraver drew the design on a metal plate (copper was used at first) and ink was forced into the design. This process was more expensive because of the metal plates used and required more artistry from the engraver. Also, because the surface to be printed was below the sheet of paper instead of above (as in woodblock printing), this method took longer and was thus more costly. However, the engraving (or **intaglio** process, as it is sometimes called) allowed for finer detail and was popular in the 1800s.

The third process that preceded modern printing of pictures was **lithography.** Actually, this process is still used in modern printing, but with different materials. In this method, based on the antipathy of oil and water, an oil-based chalk or paint was used to draw pictures on a limestone plate, which was then soaked in water. "After ink had passed over the stone, it would adhere where the chalk had marked the stone, and when a sheet of paper was placed under heavy pressure. . .the original design would print off" (Whalley, 1975, p. 23). Although this technique was cumbersome, it paved the way for future developments in printing and had the most important effect on the illustrations of children's books in the late 19th century (Meyer, 1983).

The industrial revolution of the 19th century spurred the invention of technology related to printing and reproducing illustrations. A pioneer in this field, Edmund Evans, can be credited with charting the course of modern book illustration because of his work in the late 1800s. He was an illustrator, an engraver, a printer, and a businessman, but his true genius seemed to be the recognition of artistic ability in others. His expertise allowed artists' visions to remain true in the mass production of

"D is for Duck"

book after book. Evans developed a full-color printing process, providing illustrators with the technology to realize images in a more consistent fashion. His artistry graces some early stories, but he was instrumental in encouraging and marketing the work of Walter Crane, Randolph Caldecott, and Kate Greenaway, the triumvirate of the best in early children's book artistry, who set standards for 20th-century work.

Arguably the most famous of the three is Randolph Caldecott, since the award for the most distinguished picture book published in the United States each year bears his name. The American Library Association awards this medal, and the list of honored books can be found in Appendix A. (The United Kingdom awards the Kate Greenaway medal yearly.)

Caldecott was born in 1846 and died just 39 years later. His art was humorous and whimsical, with rural scenes full of color and robust characters. The medal that bears his name depicts a man on horseback tearing through the countryside, and comes from a story entitled "John Gilpin's Ride" (Caldecott, 1977). Some of his illustrated stories have the distinction of having been continuously in print for over a hundred years. He worked for a bank and sketched, then ill health forced him to

Hey, diddle, diddle,
The Cat and the Fiddle,

retire. He died in the United States and was buried in St. Augustine, Florida. Maurice Sendak, a preeminent figure in children's literature, says of Caldecott's work:

> When I came to picture books, it was Randolph Caldecott who really put me where I wanted to be. Caldecott is an illustrator, he is a songwriter, he is a choreographer, he is a stage manager, he is a decorator, he is a theater person; he's superb, simply. He can take four lines of print that have very little meaning in themselves and stretch them into a book that has tremendous meaning—not overloaded, no sentimentality in it. (Billington, 1978, pp. 13–14)

Walter Crane flourished in early picture-book illustration and influenced many later artists. He was born in 1845, a year before Caldecott, and was the son of an artist. His work is characterized by well-defined forms, many profiles, and flat, bright colors because he thought children liked definite statements in design (Crane, 1981).

Kate Greenaway, also born in 1846, usually depicted many children in delicate settings or a rural, idyllic countryside. The children were serious but playful, and dressed in old-fashioned costumes.

These three artists worked in watercolor, paints, and ink (Caldecott preferred brown), and Evans' engraving and printing allowed the subtle differences of color and brushwork to initiate a new standard of book illustration. Each artist left a different legacy to picture-book illustration.

> Walter Crane was essentially a decorative artist who brought a lusty delight in design to the genre. Fey, theatrical Kate Greenaway was something like the Laura Ashley of her day and a fervent spear-carrier for the Victorian cult of innocent childhood. Caldecott's impact far exceeded that of his two rivals, was more in the nature of an explosion: an unhinging of the basic conventions of the illustrated book. (Marcus, 2001, p. 159)

Certainly other outstanding artists of the late 1880s and the 1900s pushed the boundaries of art and language, creating superb picture books. Beatrix Potter comes to mind as a foremost contributor to picture-book artistry. She left her unmistakable print on the children's book world with exquisitely detailed, pastel-tinted woodland animals: Peter Rabbit, Squirrel Nutkin, Benjamin Bunny. Arthur Rackham, Kay Neilson, and, in the 20th century, John Tenniel and N. C. Wyeth, and many others deserve recognition for their graceful artistry (Meyer, 1983).

England and the European continent continued to produce the best in children's book illustration until the chaos of World War I devastated industry and art (Bader, 1976). After that time, American assertiveness and expertise—as exemplified by the work of Ingri and Edgar D'Aulaire (*Ola,* 1932, and *George Washington,* 1936), Ludwig Bemelmans (*Hansi,* 1934, and *Madeline,* 1939), Marjorie Flack (*Angus and the Ducks,* 1930, and *The Story About Ping,* 1933), and Robert McCloskey (*Make Way for Ducklings,* 1940)—shifted preeminence in picture-book artistry to the United States. So many exceptional books continued to be produced that the American Library Association initiated the Caldecott Award in 1938, thus ensuring a legitimate place in children's literature for the picture book.

In the period between the world wars, sometimes called the second golden age of children's literature because of the output of outstanding books, American children's book publishing thrived. And, following the cataclysmic upheaval of World War II, the book industry again recovered to lead the world in picture-book production (Bader, 1976). Sadly, there are too many innovative and distinguished books to list here, but it is worthwhile to start with the Caldecott books listed in Appendix A and learn to recognize the many styles those illustrators and authors represent.

Before the close of this section on the history of picture books, I wish to acknowledge the contribution of Maurice Sendak to contemporary artistry. Winner of perhaps more prestigious awards in children's literature than anyone else, he has set the standard by which others judge themselves. For the last four decades, his body of work (over 80 books, set designs for opera, and collaboration on television programs and movies) has explored the meaning of modern childhood. He has become, as he himself said of Caldecott, a songwriter, a choreographer, a stage manager, and simply superb. Always empathetic to the inner child, he is probably best known for his trilogy beginning with *Where the Wild Things Are* (Sendak, 1963), continuing with *In the Night Kitchen* (1970), and culminating with the impressive and enigmatic *Outside Over There* (1981). John Rowe Townsend, respected critic and writer, says, "He is not merely a master but the one and only grandmaster of the picture book" (Townsend, 1992, p. 306). Picture books have evolved in the last century, and Maurice Sendak has been responsible for much of the sophistication, artistry, and childlike veracity found in the genre.

PRE-LITERACY AND CHILD DEVELOPMENT

Briefly, in Chapter 1, aspects of child development were related to psychosocial markers that indicated how young children were learning and growing. Behavioral markers such as acquiring language, forming attachments, mastering locomotor skills, beginning to learn autonomy, and enjoying parallel and pretend play were listed as typical psychological and social foci of children from birth to about 4 (see Figure 1.1). To these behavioral and emotional markers some additional cognitive aspects are now joined because babies are learning to comprehend and understand the world around them. Reading to infants and toddlers will spur cognitive processes such as organizing and differentiating information, recognizing symbolic representations of objects (the beginning of metaphorical thought), and relating thought (interior language) to expressive language. In Figure 5.1, psychosocial markers are

Figure 5.1
Suitable books related to psychosocial markers of early childhood

Psychosocial Marker	Suitable Books
Acquiring language	ABC books, counting books, nursery rhymes, and books in which objects are labeled.
Forming attachments	Concept books about emotions, bedtime books, human and animal stories about love and friendship.
Mastering locomotor skills	Interactive books with pointing, patting, finger plays (pat-a-cake), and physical movement (stepping, jumping, Mother-may-I, Simon says). Manipulative books (pop-up) and song books.
Beginning to learn autonomy	Concept books about learning to dress, toilet training, and self-esteem, for example. For infants, peekaboo books.
Enjoying parallel and pretend play	Concept books and simple story books about play (tea parties, playing house, imaginary gardening, or other activity, for example). Some wordless books may be appropriate to demonstrate the idea of pretend and parallel play.
Organizing and differentiating information	Concept books on clothes, trucks, food, pets, and many other topics.
Recognizing symbolic representation of objects	Same as above, as well as counting books, alphabet books, and simple stories.
Thought and language	All books can be used when interaction between adult and child extends beyond labeling to questions such as, for example, "What comes next?" "Do you remember this letter?" and "Is this like our ride to grandpa's house?"

listed with some suitable and developmentally appropriate kinds of books. Truly, many books will support the cognitive, emotional, and physical growth of a young child, but it is interesting and instructive to pinpoint special types that are specifically designed for infants through preschoolers. Following the chart, picture books for the very youngest are defined in more detail.

While the young child is acquiring language and beginning to understand the connection between language and thought (Vygotsky, 1962), **visual literacy** is also developing. During the first few months of life, "visual stimulation causes the visual cortex to organize and fine-tune itself in ways that are necessary for mature visual functioning" (Schickedanz, et al., 2001, p. 95). It seems natural, then, to promote the visual stimulation afforded by picture books. From newborns to infants and toddlers, visual sorting, organizing, depth perception, object constancy, and face perception are learned. These perceptual abilities are the foundation of further visual cognition, the understanding and interpretation of visual stimuli. Knowing how to read pictures (and television images, body language, billboards, computer graphics, and so on) is an invaluable skill, fostered by practice with lots of encounters. As humans develop, we not only learn to understand symbolic representation, but we learn to read the grammar of design as well (Nodelman, 1996).

◆ ◆ ◆

REFLECTION   Do you think we should pay more attention to visual literacy in schools? How is the concept related to media literacy?

Preschoolers learn to discriminate visually by looking at photographs of familiar objects.

DEFINITION OF PICTURE BOOKS FOR THE VERY YOUNG

The term *picture book* defines a particular kind of book in which the artwork is dominant. From cover to cover, on endpapers and every page, the first and most noticeable aspect of the book is its graphic display. Pictures, designs, abstract and representational art, in every *color* or shades of black and white, and employing unique arrangements of artistic elements (i.e., *line, shape, texture*) call out to the potential reader/listener. Imagine a shelf of picture books in a bookstore or in a child-care center: One's eye is immediately drawn to the riot of color, style, and design. A picture book is an invitation to a child to look, to hold, to flip pages, and—for very young children—sometimes to taste!

Picture book is really a genre classification denoting *format,* as content is not specified by the term at all. Content or subject matter may be fiction or nonfiction, realistic or fanciful, episodic or linear. In the picture-book format we find folktales, biographies, poetry, and other genres. The remarkable and absolute given is that whatever the content, illustrations gain ascendancy over the text. Particularly in picture books for very young children, the artwork carries the idea, conveying much more than the minimal text. The delicate balance between text and art mentioned in Chapter 6 tilts much more to art when the listener is a toddler. Uri Shulevitz, a renowned author and illustrator, says, "In a true picture book, words cannot stand on their own; without pictures, the meaning of the story will be unclear" (Shulevitz, 1996, p. 239). In his Caldecott honor book, *Snow* (1998), Shulevitz's few words begin to tell that *no* snow is forecast, while the pictures show an ever increasing snowfall. Young children can appreciate the humor of two stories unfolding (yes, it is; no, it isn't) and look for more and more snowflakes in the sky above a city scene. Finally, in the climax of this picture book, so much snow creates a fantasy world. Characters from the Mother Goose Book Store come alive and cavort with the boy in a grand snowfall. White rooftops are replaced on the next double-page spread by a completely white city, and then the satisfactory, confirming simple sentence on the last page pictures a happy child and his dog ready to play.

In Figure 5.1, certain kinds of books were listed in multiple categories: alphabet, or ABC books; counting, or number, or 123 books; nursery rhymes, or books written in rhyme; concept books; and some wordless books. These are appropriate for the youngest listener because of their brevity, their primarily episodic text, and their subject matter. Brevity and episodic text are important because of young listeners' short attention spans, and subject matter should fit the interests and needs of one's audience. Also, such books frequently appear in a hardy format so that babies and toddlers can chew on them, walk on them, throw them into the bathtub, and occasionally leave them outside in sandboxes and on swing sets. The books are often printed as board books (heavy cardboard pages) or on plastic or cloth pages. Printed in a wide variety of sizes and shapes, they are meant to last. Books that are meant to be patted, pulled, or manipulated in some way are called "toy" books (Kiefer, 1995).

SUBGENRES OF PICTURE BOOKS FOR YOUNG CHILDREN

Figure 5.2 provides definitions, examples, and curriculum values for the subgenres of picture books, though there are many more examples. A description of artwork follows.

Subgenre	Definition	Example	Curriculum Value
Alphabet (ABC) books	Books that present, in alphabetical order, objects linked by a unifying theme or idea.	*Chicka Chicka Boom Boom* by Bill Martin, Jr. and John Archambault, illustrated by Lois Ehlert.	These books teach the concepts of naming, alphabet recognition (visual discrimination), the sound of the initial consonant or vowel, and alphabetical order.
Counting (123) books	Books that present numerical order, sometimes with cardinal and/or ordinal numbers.	*Ten Red Apples,* written and illustrated by Pat Hutchins.	These books teach and reinforce numeral recognition, the concepts of number and quantity, and numerical order.
Mother Goose, nursery rhymes, and books written in rhyme	Books that present traditional rhymes as well as modern versions of short, pithy stories that rhyme.	*My Very First Mother Goose,* edited by Iona Opie and illustrated by Rosemary Wells.	Rhyming teaches auditory discrimination (the difference between sounds) such as "Hubbard" and "cupboard," "rye" and "pie," vocabulary development, and the beginning of the concept of story.
Concept books	Books that define a single thing or idea.	*My Colors/Mis Colores* by Rebecca Emberley.	These books help children develop concepts through language development. Words tell what something "is" in several different ways so that children develop an idea.
Wordless (pure) picture books	Books that contain little or no print; pictures tell the story.	*Cubes, Cones, Cylinders, and Spheres* by Tana Hoban.	Vocabulary is developed as children learn to tell a story or label objects.

Figure 5.2   Subgenres of picture books for young children

In addition to those listed in Figure 5.2, more examples of recent and recommended picture books for the very young follow.

Recent and Recommended Mother Goose and Nursery Rhyme Books

Park Beat: Rhymin' through the Seasons (London, 2001)
Off to the Sweet Shores of Africa: And Other Talking Drum Rhymes
    (Unobagha, 2000)
My First Nursery Rhymes (Whatley, 1999)
Willy Pogany's Mother Goose (2000)

Recent and Recommended Alphabet Books

Firefighters A to Z (Demarest, 2000)
ABC for You and Me (Girnis, 2000) (deserves a special look because of the
    photos of Down syndrome children used within the text)
Arf! Beg! Catch!: Dogs from A to Z (Horenstein, 1999)
ABC T-Rex (Most, 2000)
ABC Kids (Williams, 2000)

Recent and Recommended Counting Books

1 2 3 Pop! (Isadora, 2000)
Look Whooo's Counting (MacDonald, 2000)
10 Minutes till Bedtime (Rathmann, 1998)
One More Bunny: Adding from One to Ten (Walton, 2000)

Recent and Recommended Concept Books

You Go Away (Corey, 1976/1999)
What Is a Triangle? (Dotkich, 2000)
The Everything Book (Fleming, 2000)
Everywhere Babies (Meyers, 2001)

Recent and Recommended Wordless (or Nearly Wordless) Books

One Red Sun (Keats, 1999)
Ballerina! (Sis, 2001)
Ship Ahoy! (Sis, 1999)

REFLECTION What kinds of picture books are not appropriate for very young children? Are folktales and fairy tales suitable? Some experts suggest that 3- and 4-year-olds are not really ready for *Snow White, Cinderella,* and other well-known fairy tales. What do you think? Why would scholars suggest that?

Reprinted with the permission of Simon & Schuster for Young Readers, an imprint of Simon & Schuster Children's Publishing Division, from *CHICKA CHICKA BOOM BOOM* by Bill Martin Jr. and John Archambault, illustrated by Lois Ehlert. Illustrations copyright © 1989 by Lois Ehlert.

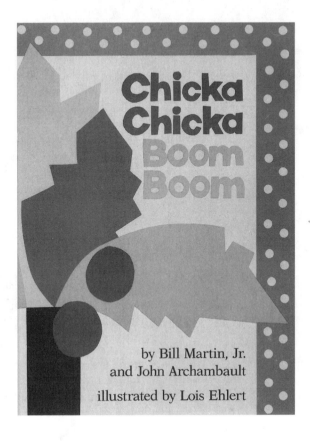

ARTISTIC ELEMENTS IN PICTURE BOOKS

Color, line, shape, format, texture—all these elements create the artwork in modern children's picture books. Color or the lack of it, bold line or faint, large shapes or small—these are all chosen by illustrators and arranged in a format to bring a text to life on the pages of a book and in the mind of the reader. These elements are joined with **media** and **style** to give us a full description of the indispensable art. Types of media include paints (watercolor and oil-based), chalk, charcoal, woodcuts and linoleum block prints, cloth, collage and montage, photographs, and anything else an artist uses to make the design. Style refers to the combination of every choice an artist makes as she or he creates the final book. It is the total effect of color, line, media, and shape. Terms for style can come from the art world, such as *impressionistic, surreal, expressionistic,* and *cartoon.* Style can be described more informally in adjectives such as "whimsical," "delicate," "vigorous," or "decorative." Publishers design the final "package," sometimes in collaboration with the artist, in a format they think will promote the book most successfully. Tall books, square books, books shaped in odd sizes, or tiny books for small hands are some of the format styles publishers choose. Publishers also determine the size of print, where the words appear on the page and the cover, the design or color of the end-papers, and many other aspects of how the book is put together.

The ABC book *Chicka Chicka Boom Boom* provides an excellent example of the artistic elements working together to create a coherent, pleasing, and suitable book for young readers. Here is an analysis of artistic elements:

- **Color**—What colors dominate? Is there visual contrast? Do the colors reflect the content? In *Chicka Chicka Boom Boom* the colors are bright, neon colors (bound to grab attention) offset with a lot of white space to influence the direction the eye moves down and across the page. Colors are harmonious with the same value in intensity.
- **Line**—Are characters/shapes outlined in black, or a contrasting color? Do the lines show movement? Is there a horizontal or vertical dimension to the lines? In *Chicka Chicka Boom Boom* the lines are straight, not outlined by a contrasting color, but very definite. The curve of the bending tree contrasts with the sharp edges of the letters and the border.
- **Shape**—What shape are the pictures on the page? Is there a uniform shape, or do characters change? Do the shapes relate to a perspective? In *Chicka Chicka Boom Boom* the silhouette of the tree in the middle of the double-page spread provides continuity and uniformity. Letters of the same size tumble about the edges and draw attention to the periphery, then back again. The border, alternating colors but framing every page, provides another pattern in this very patterned book. The shape of the letters is of crucial importance in an alphabet book; lowercase and uppercase letters are without adornment so that children can begin to recognize similarities and differences.
- **Format**—Is the book large, small, or the "right" size for the audience? What format features are important—endpapers? double-page spreads? In *Chicka Chicka Boom Boom* the large, easy-to-hold size is a fairly common one, with endpapers that echo the content or provide a graphic summary of the content. Format features determine where and how the words are placed on the page to generate excitement and anticipation for the page turn.
- **Texture**—How do the pictures convey smooth surfaces or rough ones? What technique has the illustrator used to give a textural effect? In *Chicka Chicka Boom Boom* the texture is smooth, with very little dimension to the pages. She has created a "flat" effect to draw attention to the letters. There is no background or foreground, just the tree, white space, and letters showing movement.

Visual elements such as these trigger our aesthetic response. We respond positively or negatively to the bright colors; the flat, cut-paper collage arrangement on each page; and the jaunty jumble of letters. The grammar of the design helps us to understand that this is an alphabet book, that all letters are equal, but that there is a certain order to follow. When the letters fall and get hurt, the visual information shows us how bad the wounds are! Media and style are superimposed on the grammar to create the overall effect. Lois Ehlert uses a collage of neon poster-paint letters and a green and brown tree on pure white for the mixed-media design, and the style could be described as "exuberant," "expressionistic," or perhaps even "rollicking."

REFLECTION Is this the way you would describe the style of *Chicka Chicka Boom Boom?* What is your aesthetic response to this book? What is your response to the content?

Recognizing Media and Style

As their technological skills and capabilities increase, illustrators are experimenting with new ways to combine paint, paper, clay, ink, wood, photos, and other materials. The goal is to render the artwork perfectly so that it depicts the action or the idea in a recognizable yet unique way. For young children, perhaps the art should be more realistic, so that understanding is more readily gained.

In most picture books specifically geared to babies and small children, the artwork dominates and is fairly representational. Designs are uncluttered with more white space providing a sharper contrast between image and background.

REFLECTION How simple and uncluttered should the artwork be for ages 1 to 4? Might the art be boring, or too stilted, if simple, representative pictures were found in most books?

Following are some examples of different media specifically for the very young. Notice the variety, and try to look at these books or others for this age to identify how artists construct art. In order to analyze and evaluate picture books, it is necessary to gain expertise in identifying media and style. Then we can better understand the choices artists make and respond to them aesthetically.

- *Collage—The Very Lonely Firefly* (Carle, 1999).
  In this reissued 1995 board book, Eric Carle uses his trademark medium of textured, vibrant collages, creating depth in the night sky. The last page includes a hidden tiny battery so the fireflies twinkle.
- *Photographs—Cubes, Cones, Cylinders and Spheres* (Hoban, 2000).
  A wordless, 24-page picture book in Tana Hoban's familiar medium, the colored photographs show everyday scenes in which one type of shape prevails.

- *Ink and gouache—Some Babies* (Schwartz, 2000).
  Delicate sketches in ink filled with the flat, bright colors of gouache (opaque watercolor) fit this bedtime story of a toddler who doesn't want to go to sleep.
- *Cut paper—My Colors/Mis Colores* (Emberley, 2000).
  Bright and bold cut-paper illustrations are the focal point of this bilingual concept book. One of a set of four, the others are *My Numbers/Mis Numeros; My Opposites/Mis Opuestos;* and *My Shapes/Mis Formas.*
- *Oil—Colors* (Diggory, 2000, illustrated by Svjetlan Junakovic)
  Rough-textured oil paintings in a vertical picture book show an object, then the design repeated with a fold-out flap forming an animal.
- *Watercolors—Toot and Puddle: Puddle's ABC* (Hobbie, 2000)
  Watercolors form scenes of each letter of the alphabet as Puddles teaches Otto, the turtle, to recognize the alphabet.
- *Mixed Media* (gouache, collage, colored pencil)—*Counting Kisses* (Katz, 2000)
  In this 26-page counting book, Karen Katz uses shades of pink and some contrasting colors to create a sweet and bouncy picture book.

These seven examples of media and style demonstrate the versatility of artists. Many more examples could point to trademark styles of well-known and highly successful artists such as Eric Carle and Tana Hoban, as well as to new artists experimenting with combinations of media and computer-generated graphics. As every book is unique, so is every reader/listener, and perhaps the true art is matching the perfect book with the child who needs and wants it at that time.

EVALUATING PICTURE BOOKS FOR THE VERY YOUNG

Because the artwork has such a crucial place in these picture books, as text is at a minimum in most instances, it is important to develop aesthetic criteria consistent with what is generally recognized as excellent, or valuable. However, one's responses to art and literature are also personal and idiosyncratic, so criteria for judging the work of others are not always slavishly adhered to. However, now that you know the basic artistic elements that can be used as a framework for judging design, and you have some knowledge of mixed media (including computer graphics) and styles, you have the tools to begin to separate the remarkable, truly fine books from others. Evaluation is a rigorous search for the best, whatever the age of the audience.

The following evaluation scheme (see Figure 5.3) is based on criteria that you may further develop and articulate according to your standards for art, for text, and for the purposes you have defined. Questions are listed that will help you to focus on certain aspects, and other questions may arise from your experience and expectations. Following the chart, a four-point scale is presented.

Components	Matching Book to Audience	Matching Book to Purpose
Art (What is my personal and professional response?)	Is the artwork unique? Original? Skillful? Are the pictures clear? Uncluttered? Does the artwork avoid stereotypes?	Does the artwork suit the developmental level of the audience? Will the artwork please my audience?
Text (What is my personal and professional response?)	Is the theme worthwhile? Is the language suitable (vocabulary, concept density, playful use of words)? Will the story or language appeal?	Will the subject matter interest my audience? Will it match curriculum objectives? Is the text (in theme and content) appropriate to the developmental age?
Combining art and text	Are the details in the art matched with the text details? Do the language and art complement each other in style, mood, and tone? Does the art achieve the proper balance with the text?	Does the book achieve a coherent, integrated wholeness? Is it something unique? If this is a personal gift for a child, is the book suitable? Are all parts ably crafted and handsomely presented?

Figure 5.3   Evaluating picture books for the very young

A Four-Point Scale for Evaluating Picture Books

Name of Text:_____

Author and illustrator:_____

When 1 stands for "very good," 2 is "good," 3 is "marginal," and 4 is "unsatisfactory," rate the book according to

    I. The theme and subject matter are appropriate for the developmental level of the audience.

        1 _____ 2 _____ 3 _____ 4 _____

    II. The language (words, sounds/phonemes, vocabulary, and sentence structure) is suitable.

        1 _____ 2 _____ 3 _____ 4 _____

    III. The artwork is successfully rendered, suitable, and aesthetically pleasing for the audience.

        1 _____ 2 _____ 3 _____ 4 _____

    IV. Art and text are integrated well and artwork is proportioned correctly for the text.

        1 _____ 2 _____ 3 _____ 4 _____

REFLECTION   After trying both of these methods, which seems better? Does it depend on the kind of book, or the purpose to which the book is put? Is it necessary for you to generate more than the four categories of content, language, artwork, and integration?

SUMMARY

This chapter defined picture books for the very young and provided criteria for a critical look at picture books. Books for babies, toddlers, and preschoolers were identified according to developmentally appropriate signposts. Picture books for this age were characterized by brief texts, dominance of pictures, and a simple arrangement on the page of text and artwork. Content was generally episodic rather than a story line, although as youngsters approach their third and fourth years, attention spans increase quickly to accommodate stories with simple plots and well-defined characters.

In this chapter, more than all the others in this text, the unique developmental needs of the audience are given full attention. Special consideration has been paid to content, format, and artwork based on psychological aspects of very young children. However, as precise as we try to be, it is impossible to predict what will captivate a busy toddler, or what will be the favorite bedtime story of a 3-year-old. Certain subgenres have stood the test of time and continue to delight and instruct, but young children should be given the opportunity to explore a wide range of styles and formats. Advantages of reading to this age group are that infants will listen to everything (e.g., you can read a newspaper, a novel, or the clues to a crossword puzzle) and busy toddlers will let you know very quickly if you have caught them in a listening mood. Therefore, alphabet and counting books, concept and some wordless books, and Mother Goose and rhymed text are especially appealing to this age group but should not be seen as the only kinds of books to explore.

A strong theme of this chapter was the importance of promoting reading to children as soon as possible. From the moment they are born, children are using their senses to learn about themselves and the world around them. As we know, this period of development, birth to about age 4, is crucial in perceptual, cognitive, social, emotional, physical, and language growth. It is seen as the time when human beings grow and learn at phenomenal rates, perhaps more than at any other time. The purposes for reading are many and all are important—and to establish a bond, to set an expectation for books in their lives, to form interests, to instigate curiosity, to establish patterns of listening, and to learn the intellectual habits of a lifetime are just some of the reasons given to support the role of literature in children's lives.

As the first of two chapters about art in children's books, artistic elements and how artists use them to create the story or enhance the text were defined and described. Color, line, shape, format, and texture all work together to form a memorable experience in early visual literacy for young children. Combined with media and style, the picture book is a collaborative art form unparalleled in literature.

IMPLICATIONS FOR INSTRUCTION

Throughout this chapter, sharing books with the very young has been suggested and activities have been implied. Following is a more explicit description of activities and hands-on projects.

Projects

1. Create a bibliography of "bedtime books" or think of another category that fulfills a need that you have in your work, such as bilingual books, manipulative books, or books that include songs. Following are some starters (all bibliographic information is given here and will not be repeated later):

Bedtime
Cowell, C. (2000). *What shall we do with the boo-hoo baby?* New York: Scholastic.
Kiesler, K. (Ill.) (1999). *Fishing for a dream: Ocean lullabies and night verses.* New York: Clarion.

Action
Appelt, K. (2000). *Toddler two-step.* New York: HarperFestival.
Chorao, K. (1999). *Knock at the door: and other baby action rhymes.* New York: Dutton.

Board Books
Walsh, M. (1999). *Do monkeys tweet?* Boston: Houghton Mifflin.

Singing Books and Toy Books
Hort, L. (2000). *The seals on the bus.* New York: Holt.

2. Keep a diary of the books you read to your infant/toddler/preschooler. It is fun to look back and see what was enjoyed at certain times in his or her development.
3. Try the evaluation schemes presented in this chapter. Select two or three random picture books for the very young from a library and apply the questions or the four-point scale (see page 105).

Activities for Very Young Children (ages 0–2)

1. Teach your infant and toddler the finger plays and physical movement in *Toddler Two-Step* and *Knock at the Door* (Appelt and Chorao, see page 107). Also, *Toddlerobics: Animal Fun* (Newcome, 1999) shows a group of energetic toddlers mimicking animal movements. The cultural diversity represented by the group of children adds to the energy and enthusiasm.

2. Reading nursery rhymes and poetry is most enjoyable and lays the foundation for auditory discrimination that is so necessary for future language and literacy development. You could begin with the following, but there are many books to choose from (see those mentioned earlier and also see Chapter 6): *I'm Small and Other Verses* (Moore, 2001) *Hippety Hop Hippety Hay: Growing with Rhymes from Birth to Age Three* (Dunn, 1999).

3. Singing and chanting are important for language development, also. In fact, recent research underscores the importance of music to cognitive development. Try speaking or singing the following rhymes:

    > Eensy weensy spider climbed up the water spout.
    > Down came the rain and washed the spider out.
    > Out came the sun and dried up all the rain,
    > So the eensy weensy spider climbed up the spout again.

    > This little piggie went to market.
    > This little piggie stayed home.
    > This little piggie had roast beef, but this little piggie had none.
    > And this little piggie went wee-wee-wee all the way home.
    > (To be chanted while holding toes one by one, from the big toe to the littlest.) (Yolen, 1992)

After a young child learns the chant, read this delightful picture book that elaborates on the chant, *Five Little Piggies* (Martin 1998).

Activities for Young Preschoolers (ages 2, 3, and 4)

1. Read, read, read—before naptime, after naptime, during meals, on the bus, always at bedtime, and on car trips. Encourage everyone to read to your child—aunts, uncles, grandparents, babysitters, spouses, and friends.

2. Collect several books by two or three well-known illustrators and see if your preschooler can point out similarities and differences.

3. Sing, dramatize, draw, write, hop, skip, and jump to the music and words. See Margaret MacDonald's *Shake it up Tales: Stories to Sing, Dance, Drum, and Act Out* (2000).

4. Encourage a response to the book or activity. Ask preschoolers questions, such as "What might happen next?" or "Did you like this story?" or "Why did you pick this one?" Modeling good questions teaches your preschooler to ask questions and to think critically.

REFERENCES

Children's Works

Ashbe, J. (2000). *What's inside*. New York: Kane/Miller.

Caldecott, R. (1977), *John Gilpin's ride and other stories*. New York: Warner.

Carle, E. (1999). *The very lonely firefly*. New York: Philomel.

Corey, D. (1976/1999). *You go away*. New York: Whitman.

Crane, W. (1981). *An alphabet of old friends and the absurd ABC*. New York: Metropolitan Museum of Art.

DeAngeli, M. G. (1953). *Book of nursery rhymes and Mother Goose*. Garden City, New York: Doubleday.

Demarest, C. L. (2000). *Firefighters A to Z*. New York: McElderry.

Dotkich, R. K. (2000). *What is a triangle?* New York: HarperFestival.

Dunn, O. (1999). *Hippety hop hippety hay: Growing with rhymes from birth to age three*. New York: Holt.

Emberley, R. (2000). *My colors/Mis colores*. Boston: Little Brown.

Fleming, D. (2000). *The everything book*. New York: Holt.

Girnis, M. (2000). *ABC for you and me*. New York: Whitman.

Hoban, T. (2000). *Cubes, cones, cylinders, and spheres*. New York: Greenwillow.

Hobbie, H. (2000). *Toot and puddle: Puddle's abc*. Boston: Little Brown.

Horenstein, H. (1999). *Arf! beg! catch!* New York: Scholastic.

Hutchins, P. (2000). *Ten red apples*. New York: Greenwillow.

Isadora, R. (2000). *1 2 3 pop!* New York: Viking.

Katz, K. (2001). *Counting kisses*. New York: McElderry.

Keats, E. J. (1999). *One red sun*. New York: Viking.

London, J. (2001). *Park beat: Rhymin' through the seasons*. New York: HarperCollins.

Long, S. (1999). *Sylvia Long's Mother Goose*. New York: Chronicle.

MacDonald, S. (2000). *Look whooo's counting*. New York: Scholastic.

Martin, B., Jr., & Archambault, J. (1989). *Chicka chicka boom boom*. New York: Simon & Schuster.

Martin, D. (1998). *Five little piggies*. Cambridge, MA: Candlewick.

Meyers, S. (2001). *Everywhere babies*. New York: Harcourt.

Moore, L. (2001). *I'm small and other verses*. Cambridge, MA: Candlewick.

Most, B. (2000). *ABC T-rex*. New York: Harcourt.

Murphy, M. (1999). *Please be quiet!* Boston: Houghton Mifflin.

Newcome, Z. (1999). *Toddlerobics: Animal fun*. Cambridge, MA: Candlewick.

Opie, I. (1996). *My very first Mother Goose*. Cambridge, MA: Candlewick.

Pogany, W. (2000). *Willy Pogany's Mother Goose*. New York: North-South/SeaStar.

Rathmann, P. (1998). *Ten minutes till bedtime*. New York: Putnam.

Schwartz, A. (2000). *Some babies*. New York: Orchard.

Sendak, M. (1963). *Where the wild things are*. New York: Harper & Row.

Sendak, M. (1970). *In the night kitchen*. New York: HarperCollins.

Sendak, M. (1981). *Outside over there*. New York: HarperCollins.

Shields, C. D. (2000). *Colors*. New York: Handprint.

Shulevitz, U. (1998). *Snow*. New York: Farrar, Straus & Giroux.

Sis, P. (1999). *Ship ahoy!* New York: Greenwillow.

Sis, P. (2001). *Ballerina!* New York: Greenwillow.

Unobagha, U. (2000). *Off to the sweet shores of Africa: And other talking drum rhymes*. New York: Chronicle.

Walsh, M. (1999). *Do monkeys tweet?* Boston: Houghton Mifflin.

Walton, R. (2000). *One more bunny: Adding from one to ten*. New York: Lothrop.

Whately, B. (Ill.). (1999). *My first nursery rhymes*. New York: HarperFestival.

Williams, L. (2000). *ABC kids*. New York: Philomel.

Yolen, J. (1992). *Jane Yolen's Mother Goose songbook*. New York: Caroline/Boyds Mill. Musical arrangements by Adam Stemple. Illustrations by Rosekrans Hoffman.

Professional Works

Bader, B. (1976). *American picture books from Noah's ark to the beast within*. New York: MacMillan.

Billington, E. (Ed.). (1978). *The Randolph Caldecott treasury*. New York: Frederick Warne.

Giblin, J. (1996). Trends in children's books today. In S. Egoff, G. Stubbs, R. Ashley, & W. Sutton (Eds.), *Only connect* (3rd ed., pp. 337–342). Toronto: Oxford University Press.

Kiefer, B. Z. (1995). *The potential of picturebooks*. Englewood Cliffs, NJ: Merrill/Prentice Hall.

MacDonald, M. R. (2000). *Shake it up tales: Stories to sing, dance, drum, and act out*. New York: August.

Marcus, L. (2001). Medal man: Randolph Caldecott and the art of the picture book. *Horn Book, 77* (2), 155–170.

Meyer, S. E. (1983). *A treasury of the great children's book illustrators*. New York: Harry N. Abrams.

Nodelman, P. (1996). *The pleasures of children's literature*. (2nd ed.). White Plains, NY: Longman.

Schickedanz, J. A., Schickedanz, D. I., Forsyth, P. D., & Forsyth, G. A. (2001). *Understanding children and adolescents*. (4th ed.). Needham Heights, MA: Allyn & Bacon.

Shulevitz, U. (1996). What is a picture book? In S. Egoff, G. Stubbs, R. Ashley, & W. Sutton (Eds.), *Only connect* (3rd ed., pp. 238–241). Toronto: Oxford University Press.

Townsend, J. R. (1992). *Written for children* (4th ed.). New York: HarperCollins.

Vygotsky, L. (1962). *Thought and language*. Cambridge, MA: MIT Press.

Whalley, J. I. (1975). *Cobwebs to catch flies: Illustrated books for the nursery and schoolroom 1700–1900* (pp. 22–23). Berkeley: University of California Press.

Additional Resources

Cullinan, B. E. (2000). *Read to me: Raising kids who love to read (rev. ed.)*. New York: Scholastic.
This small, paperback revision outlines ways and means adults can use to encourage and support young children in literacy development.

Lundin, A. (2001). *Victorian horizons: The reception of the picture books of Walter Crane, Randolph Caldecott, and Kate Greenaway*. (Published with the Children's Literature Association.) Lanham, MD: Scarecrow Press.
This is an historical account of the development and early technology of picture books in the late 1800s.

Marciano, J. B. (1999). *The life and art of Madeline's creator*. New York: Viking.
The grandson of Ludwig Bemelmans has written an affectionate biography of this influential author and illustrator.

McElmeel, S. L. (2000). *100 most popular picture book authors and illustrators: Biographical sketches and bibliographies*. Libraries Unlimited.
Illustrated with photographs, these 100 most popular were selected with adult and child input. More information on each is available through the many websites given.

CHAPTER 6

Picture Books for All

INTRODUCTION AND RESPONSE

Picture books for very young children were introduced in Chapter 5. Developmental aspects of infancy and toddlerhood, artistic elements, and the importance of reading to children provided the impetus for studying picture books as an art form and as a learning experience for the youngest audience. In this chapter, picture books continue to be the focus as this genre expands and diversifies in content, artistic expression, sophistication, and potential audience.

No longer the exclusive domain of babies and toddlers, picture books and illustrated books reach a wide audience. Children (about ages 4 through 8) in preschool and elementary school enjoy fiction, nonfiction, and poetry in a picture-book format, while children in middle grades (about ages 9 through 12) and into middle school (approximately ages 11 through 14) find that stories and information can be beautifully relayed visually. (Ages given are only rough guidelines of potential audience, as many other factors, such as content and purpose, more clearly determine suitability.) As children are emerging as readers, illustrations help to clarify and to extend comprehension. Pictures instigate early attempts to acquire visual literacy, so important in a society where some argue that visual transmitters have become the most pervasive bearers of ideas and information (Schwarcz & Schwarcz, 1991).

To continue our study of picture books in a more elaborated form, let's return to the artwork that makes this genre, in all its forms, truly unique. Select a contemporary picture book, such as *Under New York* (High, 2001), and analyze each of the basic artistic elements:

Color

Line

Shape

Texture

Format

Now, looking at style and media, how has the artist, Robert Rayevsky, conveyed the pace, emotional tone, and vibrancy of the city? His mixed-media illustrations combine paint, photo collage, and ink in a split perspective of above ground and below ground. Do these choices harmonize and balance with Linda Oatman High's text?

Under New York demonstrates sophistication in quality and quantity of detail, abstraction, theme, and content more appropriate for children of primary school age and older. The suggested audience is ages 5 through 8, but older children interested in architecture, archeology, city culture, or transportation would find the book informative. It is definitely not for the very young, but it is a picture book aimed at a school-age audience.

REFLECTION   If *Under New York* is unavailable to you, select a picture book that seems to be for the school-age audience and compare it to some of those mentioned in Chapter 5. Are there differences in tone, detail, subtlety, and perspective?

DEFINITION AND RATIONALE

Picture books use art and words to tell a story or describe an idea in relatively few pages. A picture book "is a unique art object, a combination of image and idea that allows the reader to come away with more than the sum of the parts" (Kiefer, 1995, p. 6). This interdependence of illustration and text, each relying on the other to create meaning, makes the picture book so unique. It is a delicate balance, and depending on the audience, the balance shifts toward words (for older children) or art (for younger children).

In her introduction to a seminal work, *American Picturebooks from Noah's Ark to the Beast Within* (1976), Barbara Bader defines and underscores the diverse role of picture books in our society: "A picture book is text, illustrations, total design; an item of manufacture and a commercial product; a social, cultural, historical document; and foremost an experience for a child" (p. 1). In this definition, picture books touch many aspects of society: commerce, history, art, sociology, and the child.

The term "picture book" denotes format, not content. It means simply that the text (expository, narrative, or poetic) is accompanied by many pictures or graphic designs. In picture story books, the usual 32-page format maintains a careful balance of art and text, with pictures taking up about half the space and text (meant to be read *to* a child) the other half. The story may be a traditional folktale, a modern folktale, contemporary or historical realism, a biography, or an informational book.

An illustrated book is one in which the artwork is still carefully balanced with the text, but the text is meant to be read *by* a child. Therefore, vocabulary is predictable, even controlled, sentences are shorter, and font size is larger than in picture storybooks. Sometimes these books are referred to as transitional books, easy readers, or beginning chapter books because they are a part of a literature-based reading program in a school setting. Illustrated books may be used as instructional texts in reading programs.

REFLECTION   What artist, in your estimation, has influenced picture books most?

GENRES, EXAMPLES, AND CURRICULUM VALUE OF PICTURE STORYBOOKS

Picture books are diverse in content. In addition to the subgenres mentioned in Chapter 5 (alphabet, counting, Mother Goose and nursery rhymes, concept, wordless), picture books comprise a part of familiar genres. That is, traditional literature, contemporary and historical realism, fantasy, poetry, biography, and information all include picture books. Figure 6.1 provides examples of picture books in genres defined and treated elsewhere in this text. However, because picture books cover a wide age range, and are usually directed toward a preschool- to school-aged audience, they are presented here.

Genres	Examples	Curriculum Value
Traditional literature (folktales and fairy tales, myths and legends, songs and rhymes, fables and parables)	*Mufaro's Beautiful Daughters* by John Steptoe	These stories define literature for young listeners and readers. The beginning of story, with character, plot, and setting, is internalized. Values, archetypes, metaphors, and other symbolic language is learned through story.
Contemporary and historical realism (school and family stories set in the present and past)	*Moses Goes to a Concert* by Isaac Millman (Moses is a hearing-impaired child who feels vibrations from the instruments.) *The Other Side* by Jacqueline Woodson (combating racial prejudice)	Realism also teaches story structure, with plot, characters, setting, figurative language, and theme. Children like to read about other children coping with problems, adventuring in exotic places, and having fun.
Fantasy (talking animals, science fiction, time fantasies, high fantasy, and extraordinary characters)	*Where the Wild Things Are* by Maurice Sendak	Fantasy teaches children to imagine, to solve problems, to enter an intellectual world of the author's creation.
Nonfiction (biography and information)	*Penguins!* by Gail Gibbons	Nonfiction books allow readers to delve into subjects of special interest that impart knowledge and encourage concept and vocabulary development.

Figure 6.1   Genres, examples, and curriculum value

Recent and recommended picture books in these genres may be found in other chapters: traditional literature, picture books for very young children, poetry, realism, fantasy, biography, and information. Also, the American Library Association's Randolph Caldecott award winners, Honor books, and Coretta Scott King Award and Honor books for illustration are listed in Appendix A. The accompanying CD-ROM lists many outstanding picture books in a variety of topics, and a section in the latter part of this chapter, Picture Books for Older Readers, contains complete bibliographic information for notable picture books.

RECOGNIZING MEDIA AND STYLE

As in chapter 5, mixed media is the rule rather than the exception in modern picture books. Tremendous advances in computerized-art software offer opportunities for increased versatility to artists willing to learn new techniques. Lolly Robinson, designer and production manager for the Horn Book, Inc., describes related developments in "The Newest Medium: Illustrating with Save and Undo" (Robinson, 2000). Learning to appreciate the different characteristics of media gives us insight into how picture books achieve the desired effect. For example, *Drummer Hoff* (Emberley, 1967), with its cumulative verse, strong alliterative consonant sounds, and militaristic theme, is appropriately illustrated with well-etched, sharp-edged woodcut designs in bold, bright colors. *Drummer Hoff* would not be as powerful in ephemeral watercolors or pen-and-ink sketches.

Whether painting, drawing, cutting or tearing paper, or clicking a mouse, artists assemble tools, paper, cloth, scratchboard, or photos to complement, extend, and enhance words. Sometimes it is difficult to determine the materials an artist uses. After the original artwork is photographed for the finished book, the appearance can change markedly. Also, many artists experiment with combinations of media, and "that also makes the detective task more difficult" (Stewig, 1995, p. 131). In addition, information about media is often not available on book jackets or within descriptive material provided by publishers. Following is a short list of well-known books whose illustrators employed recognizable media.

Type of Media	Example	Illustrator
Woodcuts	*Snowflake Bentley*	Mary Azarian
Collage/montage	*Smoky Night*	David Diaz
Drawings (carbon pencil)	*Jumanji*	Chris Van Allsburg
Watercolor	*Buttons*	Brock Cole
Scratchboard	*Cosmo and the Robot*	Brian Pinkney
Mixed media (watercolor, gouache, acrylics, and poster paint)	*Miss Rumphius*	Barbara Cooney
Computer-generated	*Little Miss Spider*	David Kirk

REFLECTION   Is there a medium you prefer, or find especially attractive?

As mentioned in the preceding chapter, **style** is the term that characterizes the total effect of a book's art: the elements of color, line, and so forth, as well as the media used and the emotional tone of the entire work. Terms for style may be associated with art theory and history: impressionistic, surrealistic, expressionistic, cartoon, and naïve. The term also has been associated with particular individuals (e.g.,

Jackson Pollock), as well as cultures ("Italianate") or eras ("baroque"). In children's books, it is defined most simply as the manner of expressing meaning (Kiefer, 1995). The meaning may be captured by words (whimsical, sweet, saccharine, dark, for example) or the meaning may be too complex to be stated with a singular adjective. In *Where the Wild Things Are* (Sendak, 1963), an unhappy little boy is being chastised by his mother (small pictures, line drawings), but as the fantasy develops the artwork becomes flamboyant, covers more and more of the page, and the little boy, Max, finally exults in an exuberant, wild rumpus. The satisfactory resolution shows a content little boy with a supper that is "still hot." The overall aesthetic experience includes a range of emotions triggered by perfectly balanced words and artwork. Much has been written about this modern classic of children's literature; more will be drawn from it. It is too complex to be described simply, as is true of the best books in children's literature.

CHARACTERS AND THEMES IN PICTURE STORYBOOKS

The kinds of characters often depicted in picture books include people disguised as animals, talking animals with human speech and emotions, personified objects, and human beings in realistic situations (Norton, 1999). Additionally, humans in fantasies—such as angels, aliens, and mythical creatures—could be added to this list. A favorite with illustrators seems to be anthropomorphized animals, as in *Olivia* (Falconer, 2000), which uses a childlike pig to confront the same daily situations most children face. Penguins, pigs, bears, birds, and even alligators have a special place as characters in children's literature.

REFLECTION   Do you have a special memory of an animal character from picture books? The mouse *Frederick* (Lionni, 1967) or *The Runaway Bunny* (Brown, 1942) may be important to you, or may trigger your memories.

Certain themes seem to dominate both realistic and fanciful picture books. Because the main character is often a small child or an animal, a theme of a small figure becoming powerful or maintaining power over bigger, adultlike characters is evident. Max in *Where the Wild Things Are* (Sendak, 1963) is a prime example.

In many modern stories, themes center on emotion—love, sadness, jealousy, friendship, fear, and so on. Themes also highlight lessons to learn, such as becoming independent, becoming skillful, building self-esteem, developing empathy, adjusting to change, and meeting new friends. Other themes echo values, such as patriotism, loyalty, and expressing individuality in a socially approved manner.

REFLECTION   Can you generate some examples of these themes in picture books?

EVALUATING PICTURE BOOKS

Evaluation is often subjective and personal. Both art and literature evoke idiosyncratic responses and, when they are combined in one work, the task becomes even more difficult to determine "good" or "beautiful." Also, evaluating two separate entities, art and language, plus the appropriate balance between them adds another dimension of judgment. Due to the three-pronged scope of this task, think of the evaluation as having three parts (see also Figure 6.2). (The three-part evaluation that follows takes the place of the four-point scale presented in other chapters. However, a scale could be constructed very easily; see pages 79 and 105.)

1. *First,* look carefully at the cover and predict what you think the illustrator is trying to say. What is the effect of the cover (on the dust jacket of the book)? Is the design of the jacket repeated on the cover of the book itself? If the art is important, it should carry over to the hard cover of the book. (Paperbacks are, of course, a different matter as there is no jacket to compare, but sometimes publishers will create a different cover for the paperback, and this begs for comparison.) Next, look at the endpapers: Are they plain or patterned? Are the colors and designs compatible with the cover? Is the visual story being told there?

Now, "read" the book, looking only at the art. (Begin with the title page, dedication, or whatever follows the endpapers.) Are the plot, character development, setting, and other literary elements obvious from the artistic elements used: color, line, shape, format, and texture? Ask "why" questions, as in "Why did the artist place the figure here?" or "Why was this color used?" Other important questions to ask are "Would I have done this?" and "What choices would I make to tell this story?" If you have really looked closely at the art, you will have an emotional and intellectual response to it. Keep this in mind as you evaluate the text.

2. *Second,* read the text and imagine what words of the story the art might depict or enhance. (Try not to be swayed by the art you have just seen, or look at the text first, then the art.) Again, the story or text should be compelling and provide a reason for turning each page. You should be engaged as a reader–listener even without the art to pull you into the story. The "why" questions work here, too: "Why did the author choose to do this?" and "Why do I like or not like this book?" Evaluation of text is influenced by its genre. Stories will be judged differently than information books because words and concepts are organized differently in each (story structure or expository text structure).

3. *Third,* think about how the art and text work together. You may want to read the book again, pausing at certain key points in the book (e.g., presentation of the problem, the climax, or some part of the rising action). The artwork must be an effective, collaborative entity, supporting and extending the key points of the story. Questions of balance arise here, too; neither art nor text should overwhelm unless there are reasons for it to do so.

Components	Matching Book to Audience	Matching Book to Purpose
Text (What is my professional and personal response?)	Are the theme, topic, and content appropriate to the listener's age? Is the language (vocabulary, concept density, playful and intelligent use of words) suitable? Will the plot or text appeal?	Will the subject interest or enlighten the intended audience? Will it hold their attention? Does it satisfy curriculum needs and plans?
Art (What is my professional and personal response?)	Is the artwork original? Unique? Skillful? Are the pictures clear? Does the artwork avoid stereotypes?	Will the artwork please my audience and teach my objectives? Does the art demonstrate techniques important to my needs and plans?
Combining art and text	Are the details in the art matched with the text? Do the language and art complement each other in mood, tone, and style? Does the art balance appropriately?	Does this book present something unique? If this is a personal gift for a child, is the book suitable? Will this book entertain and instruct my child(ren)?

Figure 6.2 Evaluating picture books

The following evaluation scheme is based on criteria that ask for a personal response, then guide your questioning about the appropriateness of the text and artwork for your intended audience and purpose (see Figure 6.2). This is very similar to the evaluation scheme in Chapter 5, and you might like to import some elements from Figure 5.3.

An evaluation is also swayed by opinions of experts and prevailing social and cultural attitudes. Do others like the book? Was it recommended by a friend, a colleague, or a good review in a reputable journal? In addition to your response, it is vital to seek out reviews of other respected scholars in the field. You can agree with them, or disagree, but your thoughts will be informed by the thoughts of others.

CONTROVERSIES, SENSITIVE ISSUES, AND CURRENT TRENDS

The evaluation process often reflects social and cultural attitudes and values. Children's literature is particularly susceptible to controversy and even censorship because of its socializing function in childhood. Children's books are used prolifically in schools to teach reading, science, social studies, and so on; therefore, many children are exposed to the messages in art and text. Some parents and organizations scrutinize reading material very carefully because it has the power to teach, to influence, and to affect us in subtle and overt ways. Several books are mentioned in this section as examples of particularly bitter controversies that led to censorship.

The Story of Little Black Sambo (Bannerman, 1899/1920) is such a story. No work of children's literature has been subjected to as much antipathy for quite so long. However, recent retellings by two major authors, coupled with new artwork, have resurrected this story and recovered its charm while eliminating its questionable parts. Written in India and published in 1899 in England, a series of misfortunes caused this little book to be reviled as the worst kind of racist writing perpetuated as children's literature.

Bader (1996) traced the acceptance, then rejection, of this story as social consciousness rose in the 20th century. Helen Bannerman, the wife of a British diplomat, wrote the story for her children. Because she sold her copyright in the beginning (against her wishes), different versions of *Little Black Sambo* (with horrific, caricatured artwork) reached the U.S. public. Not only were the pictures ugly, but the names—Sambo, Mambo, and Jumbo—were terms of disparagement in the African-American community and represented racist stereotyping for decades in the early 1900s. By the 1940s, reaction to this story ranged from indifference to active and vocal intolerance. In 1996, two new versions rescued this captivating story for a new generation of children. Julius Lester (1996) retold the tale of a strong, smart little boy who outwits five hungry tigers, cast it in an imaginary village (Sam-sam-sa-mara), and named everyone "Sam." *Sam and the Tigers,* illustrated by Jerry Pinkney in vibrant pencil and watercolor drawings, brought a wonderfully extravagant and rich dimension to the story.

In another version also published in 1996, using the original text by Bannerman, Fred Marcellino's artistry accurately placed the story in India, and used the names Babaji, Mamaji, and Papaji. *The Story of Little Babaji* (Bannerman, 1996) is a small book, close to the original in size, and Marcellino's watercolor renderings, sometimes ornate and lush, sometimes spare and focused, offer a memorable and honorable retelling to a new audience.

The rejuvenation and "sanitizing" of a story long held in disrepute raises questions for those who are interested in preserving the past but righting the wrongs of social injustice. Was it correct to censor *Little Black Sambo?* Is it correct to rewrite, change names and setting, and possibly destroy some of the integrity of the original tale? Has it been fair to besmirch Bannerman's name and story because of changing social values and other aspects over which she had no control? This experience has forced us to consider why we respond to books as we do, and what intelligent, enlightened evaluation should be. It also reminds us that not everyone sees a book as we do.

◆—◆—◆

REFLECTION   Try to find the three versions of *Little Black Sambo* and compare the original to Lester/Pinkney's retelling and Marcellino's *Little Babaji.* Which do you prefer? What is your response to these books and the controversy they represent?

Another controversy erupted over the use of *Nappy Hair* (Herron, 1997) in an elementary classroom in New York. The book was pulled from library and classroom when parents protested that it was derogatory to certain racial groups. A new teacher was attacked verbally and decided to leave the school. Children liked the book, and as is sometimes the case, a close reading of the text revealed that "nappy hair" was not a condemnation of a racial characteristic but a celebration of it.

Other books, *Jake and Honeybunch Go to Heaven* (Zemach, 1982) and *Five Chinese Brothers* (Bishop, 1938) have come under attack for portraying ugly racial stereotypes in text and art. Native Americans deplore the way they are sometimes pictured as warlike, inarticulate, and similar in look and manner when, as in all cultures, vast individual differences exist (Slapin & Seale, 1988). Clearly picture books allow us and force us to examine our perceptions and misperceptions about social and cultural attitudes.

◆

REFLECTION Are children seeing enough representations of their own cultural identities in the picture books of today? Are children with special needs represented frequently enough in picture books? (See additional books in Sensitive Issues, Special Needs, and Individual Differences in Chapter 12, as well as other books cited in this chapter.)

Today picture books continue to be shaped by the forces that have always affected literature and life. The economics of publishing, new technologies, and changing societal values all affect books for children. Trends have been identified in the last decade that will surely play out in the new century: increasing diversity in subject matter, and electronic artistry—such as Marc Brown's successful merchandising of his character, Arthur, on CD-ROM and on public television. The Marc Brown Arthur Chapter Book series, as *Arthur Makes the Team* (1998), was adapted successfully by Stephen Krensky for the Public Broadcasting System. Similar trends include internationalism and literacy efforts around the globe, as well as a marked emphasis in using picture books with older readers.

Trends that began in the 1960s, a decade of turbulent social change, continue to evolve and find expression in recent books. Subjects previously considered taboo or inappropriate for young children are available in picture-book format, such as homophobia, as in *Daddy's Roommate* (Wilhoite, 1990); living with AIDS, as in *Too Far Away to Touch* (Newman, 1995) and *Carmine's Story: A Book About a Boy Living with AIDS* (Schulman, 1997); and the Holocaust, as in *Elisabeth* (Nivola, 1997) and *Nine Spoons: A Chanukah Story* (Stillerman, 1998). Divorce is explained to a young child in *My Parents' Divorce* (Cole, 1998), and school violence is addressed in the picture book *Guns: What You Should Know* (Schulson, 1997). *Waiting to Sing* (Kaplan, 2000), an easy reader, is a story that deals with a child's reaction to his mother's death. Because of the sensitivity of the topics and the vulnerability of some children, the adult who reviews books and recommends or buys them has a responsibility to think carefully about the match between book and reader.

Internationalism in book publishing creates a wider market for children's books and draws attention to the need for books in Third World countries. Accompanying literacy efforts around the world are demands for stories that reflect diverse, multicultural perspectives. Picture books and easy readers fill a niche for beginning readers and also support such social concerns as stronger families, improved health conditions, and better economic opportunities for people in underdeveloped countries. Picture books today are most often printed outside the United States because labor and material costs are lower. Also on the rise is the formation of media conglomerates that include books, television, telephones, and Internet connections.

PICTURE BOOKS FOR OLDER READERS

Picture books are no longer the exclusive domain of young children. Teachers in fifth, sixth, and higher grades are using picture books when the subject matter and style are appropriate for their students and curricula. For educational and aesthetic purposes, picture books provide opportunities to study layout and design techniques, as well as artistic and symbolic language. Visual literacy, certainly a necessary component to intelligent television and website viewing, may be developed through picture books and other media. Clearly an enhancement to all facets of a curriculum, picture books are welcomed increasingly by upper-level teachers. Moreover, the readability levels of some picture books are suitable for middle-school readers (i.e. sixth, seventh, and eighth grades) because the books are not meant to be read *by* younger children, but *to* them.

Why has the audience for picture books so clearly expanded? Kiefer (1995) suggests that the visual depiction of such topics as homelessness, poverty, starvation, and war lead to credibility and an emotional understanding that can't happen in text alone. When visual and verbal are combined, the message is much more powerful and memorable. In an age attuned to acquiring information via television and computer screen, picture books are perceived as natural vehicles for transmitting knowledge.

Picture books dealing with historical, artistic, scientific, or literary elements become a welcome addition to curriculum planning. Moreover, with careful selection, the integrity of content-area knowledge is not compromised. Historical information and analysis gain a new dimension when high school students read *Faithful Elephants* (Tsuchiya, 1988). This poignant, factual account of elephants dying in the Ueno Zoo in Tokyo at the end of World War II brings a new understanding of war's consequences. In a high school English class, *The Bard of Avon: The Story of William Shakespeare* (Stanley & Vennema, 1992) gives students visual information about costumes, the construction of theaters, thatched-roof houses, and people's lives. *Love Flute* (Goble, 1992) and other folktales help teach seventh graders elements of plot, characterization, theme, and conflict in a multidisciplinary unit for middle school (Hillman, 1995). A wordless book, *A Day, a Dog* (Vincent, 2000) has a poignant message about cruelty and survival, a message for any age. The versatility of picture books, fiction and nonfiction, as well as the concentrated focus of subject matter encourage poor readers and good ones to explore topics in the content areas of middle school and beyond (Bishop & Hickman, 1992).

How would one select picture books for older readers? Depending on purpose, subject area, and audience, teachers should know enough about books and their students to make good matches. Generally though, the following guidelines could guide a decision:

- Artwork is appealing and accurate (especially in nonfiction), extending the textual information.
- Theme or concepts in the text are suitable for the intellectual level of the audience.
- There is no condescension in the language (vocabulary, tone, and so on).
- The purpose is clearly articulated; the teacher has modeled the effective use of picture books.

Following is a brief bibliography of picture books for older audiences. Many are older books published in years past, but they convey important messages. Chapters 4 and 7 highlight many picture books that are not addressed here. All bibliographic information is included and will not be referenced again at the end of this chapter. (More picture books for older readers may be found on the CD accompanying this text.)

Literary Elements
(Plot, characterization, irony, satire, point of view, tone, and so on)

French, F. (1986). *Snow White in New York*. Oxford, UK: Oxford University Press.

Hodges, M. (1993). *Don Quixote and Sancho Panza*. New York: Scribner's.

Macaulay, D. (1990). *Black and white*. Boston: Houghton Mifflin.

Price, L. (1990). *Aida*. New York: Harcourt.

Sendak, M. (1981). *Outside over there*. New York: HarperCollins.

Wiesner, D. (1999). *Sector 7*. New York: Clarion.

Young, E. (1997). *Voices of the heart*. New York: Scholastic.

(See also many of the rewritten folktales cited in Chapter 4.)

Social Issues

Burleigh, R. (2001). *Lookin' for bird in the big city*. San Diego, CA: Harcourt.

Gallaz, C., & Innocenti, R. (1980). *Rose Blanche*. Mandato, MN: Creative Education.

Lehn, B. (2000). *What is a teacher?* New York: Millbrook.

Maruki, T. (1980). *Hiroshima no pika*. New York: Lothrop.

Mochizuki, K. (1995). *Heroes*. New York: Lee.

Morrison, T. (1999). *The big box*. New York: Hyperion.

SUMMARY

It has been said that picture books are a 20th-century phenomenon. We have seen how Edmund Evans, Randolph Caldecott, and others set the stage for this rapid burst of expression in the late 19th century, and how U.S. creativity has since carried the genre forward with great virtuosity. As we enjoy the beginning of the 21st century, we see an increasing number of picture books available for a wider age range, ever more diverse subject matter, and artistic invention through technical wizardry.

This chapter presented picture books in a variety of media and styles, standards for evaluating them, and an artistic vocabulary with which to describe them. Controversies and current trends were given, and school use was the underlying rationale for an in-depth look. Visual literacy is a crucial skill in the new century, and picture books will help to develop it.

IMPLICATIONS FOR INSTRUCTION

Throughout this chapter, the use of picture books in primary and middle school classrooms has been encouraged. In this section, specific projects are outlined, along with ideas for a five-day unit on *Penguin Power!* in primary classrooms.

Projects

1. Describe the artwork and evaluate a number (five, for example) of picture books of your own choosing. Follow the criteria and methodology suggested earlier in this chapter, and then prioritize your list from best to worst. For more practice, have a friend evaluate the same five books and compare your final lists.

2. Write or make a picture book. Design the format, including cover and endpapers, dust jacket, size of print, size and placement of pictures, and so forth. Implement your decisions as to color, line, shape, medium, and style, and evaluate the final product.

3. Evaluate the use of art in some websites that are related to children's picture books. How does the art of a website compare to picture-book art? How do the website designers use color, line, shape, texture, and so on to tell a story or give information?

4. If your interest is in middle grades, high school, or beyond, continue to look for picture books in subject areas that would be helpful to you. For example, literature classes could use picture books to study literary elements, myths, biographies of authors, or poetry. In art classes, studying techniques, media, and style could be a part of a bookmaking unit.

A Unit for Primary Grades

Penguin Power!

Five days of a unit for grades 1 through 3 are outlined here. Within the outline are goals, purposes, activities, bibliography, and teaching suggestions for a heterogeneous classroom of about 20 children. National and state standards are not articulated because of the variance from region to region; however, the unit focuses on the reading, writing, listening, and speaking skills that are the basis of most reading and language arts standards. Included are familiar components of a literature-based unit that uses fiction and nonfiction to cross disciplinary lines. The outline is merely suggestive; ideas must be shaped to each classroom and the needs of the children within it. For example, the unit in a third-grade classroom would be somewhat different from the unit in a first-grade classroom. Nevertheless, principles and basic structure could remain the same.

Penguins are interesting and unique birds. Easily recognizable, yet somehow exotic, they seem to be inherently captivating to young readers and writers with their distinctive coloring and waddling locomotion.

The *purpose* of this unit is to study cold-sea and warm-sea penguins so that children are learning geographical facts about Antarctica and other regions of the Southern Hemisphere. In science, a study of physical and behavioral adaptations, diet, habitats, and predators gives children information with which to gain knowledge and to form values.

The *goals* of this unit include strategies and skills that permeate emergent literacy programs: phonic analysis, vocabulary development, alphabetizing, literal and inferential comprehension (critical thinking), outlining, and listening and reading for a purpose. Important goals of the unit are that children select penguin books for free reading and that they enjoy reading their books and books chosen to be read to them by teachers and parents.

Teaching Suggestions

Before the unit begins, it would be helpful to send a letter to parents or caregivers stating the goals of the unit and the bibliography and specifying the expectation that parents will read or listen to about 20 minutes of reading every night.

Creating an Alphabet Poem—Using letters of the alphabet, or the word P–E–N–G–U–I–N, have children find related words beginning with each letter and create a poem or journal entry. Younger children may find other activities more appropriate, such as "Say It and Write It," "Letter Search," or "Sorting by Letters" (Combs, 2002).

Penguin Journal—Cut several blank sheets of paper in the shape of a penguin and staple them together like a book.

Sharing Time/Brief Oral Report—Each day have some children share their new information from the previous day's reading (silent or being read to). This may be scheduled or done on an informal basis.

Partner Reading—Have children read to each other orally after they have read their passages silently. (*Buddy Reading* with older children may be organized, also.)

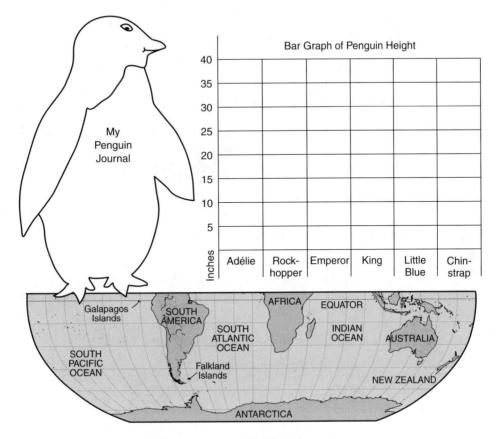

Figure 6.3 Penguin outline, graph, and bulletin board map

Public Reading—On the final day, have children prepare a paragraph or more to read aloud to the whole class (and parents and visitors, too). It could be a short selection from a book or a selection they have written.

A classic read-aloud to accompany the unit is *Mr. Popper's Penguins* by Richard and Florence Atwater, a Newbery Honor book first published in 1938 and available in paperback everywhere. As in previous units, square brackets ([ ]) denote what the teacher will do, and no brackets denotes what the teacher will say to the class. See Figure 6.3 for an outline of the Penguin Journal, the bar graph for the second day, and the map for the third day.

First Day: Today we're going to start our unit on penguins. How many of you have seen penguins? At the zoo? On television? Have you read books about penguins? Where do penguins live? How many kinds are there? [Some children will answer accurately; some may guess. Build on the answers and gently steer the discussion to the books displayed and the bulletin board showing the circle of the Southern Hemisphere, with Antarctica in the center.]

Let's listen for some of the answers to our questions: How many different kinds of penguins are there and where do they live? After we hear the book, we'll compare the characteristics of some penguins.

[Read-aloud: *Penguins!* (Gibbons, 1998). Multiple copies of this paperback would be helpful so that children may follow along; many third graders will read this fluently. Gibbons' picture book depicts 12 major species and lists the remaining 5 species at the end of the text. For this unit, we'll concentrate on the 12 species of penguins listed in Figure 6.4.] Lots of information in this book, right? Now, what did we learn? Yes, there are 17 different kinds of penguins, as most scientists agree [see also the authoritative guide *Penguins* (Peterson, 1979)]. [Adélie is pronounced uh–<u>day</u>–lee, with the accent on the middle syllable.]

Let's make a chart:

How are penguins like other birds?

_____

_____

[Penguins have feathers and wings, lay eggs in a nest, are warm-blooded, or keep themselves warm, for example.]

How are penguins different from most other birds?

_____

_____

_____

[They swim, they can't fly, they live on land near water, and so on]

[Children may volunteer other information that could be correct or questionable. Keep track of questions you're not sure about for later discussion.]

Let's review the answers to our first questions: There are 17 kinds of penguins, and they live in the Southern Hemisphere. Look at this bulletin board. If we were looking at the bottom of our globe, we would see this circle. [Demonstrate with a globe.] Do you recognize Antarctica? [Some children will know the continent at the "bottom of the world."] Do all penguins live in Antarctica? No? Do you remember from *Penguins!* which birds live there? Yes, the Emperor and Adélie penguins are there. [Have small construction paper replicas of the penguin species and place them on Antarctica.] Tomorrow, we're going to hear about Antarctica and Adélie penguins from a scientist who lived there and studied them.

To finish today, let's use our Penguin Journals to record some facts we know. Also, it is time to select a penguin book. Your book may be used for silent reading, and you may take it home to read and have your parents read to you. Your assignment, after you have selected your book, is to copy the chart we started in class, add to it, and begin to make an alphabet of penguin words [or spell penguin, or use another word activity].

Second Day: [Spend a few minutes talking about the book selections children made and what they learned from their books. You may want to call on five children every morning and schedule a brief oral report, making sure the children know what is expected (model it first). Or you may prefer a more informal "share time."] Today we're going to hear about one of the species of penguins that live in the Antarctic: the Adélies.

[Read-aloud: *My Season with Penguins: An Antarctic Journal* (Webb, 2000). Read page 3, "01 December. . ." and tell the children what the book is about. Show the pictures. Point out the map on page 4 and compare the perspective to the bulletin board. Remind the children that this is about Adélie penguins and they should listen for comparisons in size to Emperors and for three facts about the Adélies and their nesting behavior. Start reading page 11, "I walk to the colony," read through page 13, and show pictures. Start again on page 19, "Today two tall Emperors," and read through page 21.]

How do Adélies and Emperors compare in size? How do you know? [Have the children confirm their responses by citing the text.] Who can describe the Adélies? Who can mimic the "waddling gait?" Do Adélies often choose the same nest and the same mate? How do we know? How do scientists study animal and bird behavior? [If you choose to, read pp. 18, 23, and 43 about "banding" the penguins and also about attaching radio transmitters to mark penguin movements for nesting and feeding.] Now we are going to hear about the chicks (baby penguins). You have seen some pictures of the chicks. What color are they? What do they look like? How would you describe them? Are the chicks in any danger? How are they protected? Listen to this passage and think about the chicks, their size, their color, and their flippers. [Continue reading, pp. 27 and 28—"By now, almost all of the eggs are hatched"— and answer the questions above. You can also refer back to Gibbons' book to show a picture of a crèche of chicks.]

Assignment: Make a graph of the approximate height of these penguins: Adélie = 30 inches; Rockhopper = 25 inches; Emperor = 45 inches; Little Blue = 15 inches; Chinstrap = 30 inches; and King = 40 inches. [See also Figure 6.3.] Now write at least five to ten words in your Penguin Journal. We'll talk about the new words and your graph tomorrow. Don't forget silent reading here and at home.

Third Day: [Begin the period by sharing penguin facts and stories from the children's silent reading. Probably many children will be reading fiction, so ask about the differences between the Webb and Gibbons books and their stories. Elicit new words from their Penguin Journals. The glossary on page 48 of *My Season with Penguins* and words such as *crèche, fledgling, incubation, krill, Fahrenheit,* and *Celsius* will provide new words and clarify concepts.]

Today we're going to use our map of the Southern Hemisphere to plot where most penguin species live. If we went to Antarctica who would we find? That's right, Emperors and Adélies. And they're on our map. [Have a map prepared for each child. Also have paper cutouts of as many different species of penguins as the children in this class will need: perhaps 5 to 8 for younger children, as many as 12 for older children. In this group activity, model what to do by taking a penguin cutout, telling

Figure 6.4 This is where penguins live

Penguins	Homeland
Adélie, Emperor	Antarctica
African (also called Black-footed and Jackass)	Southern coast of Africa
Chinstrap	Islands between Antarctica and South America
Gentoo, King, Macaroni, and Rockhopper	Islands in the Indian, Atlantic, and Pacific Oceans (slightly warmer seas). Gentoo and Rockhopper live on the Falkland Islands, too.
Little-Blue, or Fairy and Yellow-Eyed, and Galagapos	Coasts of New Zealand and Australia, and the Galapagos Islands
Magellanic	Southern coast of South America. (They were named for the explorer, Ferdinand Magellan, who reported them in his voyage of 1519.)

where the species is found, and then placing it on the map. Children should be placing their penguin cutouts on their own maps. See Gail Gibbons' book for a good model. Because some penguins are found in several places, you may want to have several cutouts of those species. Figure 6.4 is a quick reference for penguin homes.]

What a great job you are doing! What is the weather like where these penguins live? Here is a book that answers some of our questions, *Do Penguins Get Frostbite? Questions and Answers about Polar Animals* by Berger and Berger. [This beautifully illustrated (by Higgins Bond) and fact-filled book answers over 70 questions about all polar animals. You may just pick out the questions about penguins, or include both Antarctic and Arctic animals.]

Assignment: In your Penguin Journal, write five questions that you have about penguins. One might be "Who are penguins' enemies and are they a protected or endangered species?" Today we'll continue with some partner reading when you've finished writing in your journal.

Fourth Day: [Begin by eliciting from the children what questions they have. Keep track of questions so that you can point individuals to resources. You may want to chart the most frequently asked questions on a chalkboard or easel and return to them later. Discuss what the children are reading and what their parents are reading to them.]

Today we're going to focus on the question "Who are penguins' enemies?" Do you remember what the book from the first day—*Penguins!*—said about the dangers penguins face? That's right, oil spills and overfishing. [Discuss what these mean and how they happen. Ask the children to listen for two more dangers and read pp. 22 and 39 in *My Season with Penguins* about skuas and leopard seals who prey on chicks. Show pictures of skuas and differentiate them from other birds in Antarctica that don't prey on penguin chicks, such as snowy petrels.]

Listen to this story about Adélies and Emperors, and see if you can tell what the danger is.

[Read-aloud: *Antarctica* by Helen Cowcher. This is a dramatic picture book with rich, full-color, double-page illustrations. It strongly suggests that human habitation and development are the major sources of danger to this continent. The last sentence is deliberately open-ended, however, and says that we don't know yet what the impact will be. Invite the children to share their views. Point to the penguin colonies as depicted on the map on the bulletin board and ask if the dangers would be the same in the Falklands or New Zealand. Some children will be interested in researching this topic on the Web or in texts.]

Assignment: Draw a picture of penguins and their enemies. Write a paragraph about what we can do to protect penguins and why we should protect them.

[After the assignment, give children a few minutes to read silently or with partners and, perhaps, to choose other penguin books.]

Fifth Day: [Explicit instructions to the children end here. What follows are ideas about this final day. As the unit has progressed, children have had opportunities to learn more and different information about penguins. Build on their interests and knowledge by suggesting additional activities, such as writing stories, poetry, letters to environmental agencies; creating artwork; or studying habitats and behavior. The unit could extend into individual or group projects, and this final day of group sharing could be a springboard into further study. Whether or not the unit concludes with this day, a 60-minute video from the public television series *Nature,* "The World of Penguins," would reinforce concepts. Other nonfiction books read aloud, such as *Penguins* (Resnick, 1997), would also reiterate basic ideas discussed in class and bring up others.

Another way to bring closure to the unit is through artwork. *Penguins* by Donald M. Silver and Patricia J. Wynne (1999), from the Scholastic Professional Book series, is full of "easy make and learn projects," such as Penguin Peek-Through Mask, Penguin Lift and Look Map, Penguin Parts Mini-Book, Off-to-the-Sea/To-the-Feeding-Grounds Dioramas, and many more. Construction-paper, egg-carton, and paper-plate penguins are easy and fun to make with relatively few parts to cut out and glue.

Finally, it would be educationally sound to have a public reading and invite parents and others to the reading class. Each child would have prepared a section of his or her favorite part, chapter, paragraph, or story to read aloud. The children could work together, or some pairs could be assigned to read chorally or to read alternating passages or sentences. With an appreciative audience, reading aloud builds confidence and is quite rewarding.

Ongoing assessment is a part of this unit, as it always is, through the children's writing, responses to questions, increased use of vocabulary, and interest in the material. A self-evaluation could be constructed so that each child evaluates his or her own learning, and an evaluation of the unit could be constructed so that children could give feedback to the teacher as to the organization and content covered.]

Bibliography for Penguin Power!

Children's Books:

Arrhenius, P. (1998). *The penguin quartet.* Minneapolis: Carolrhoda.

Atwater, R., & Atwater, F. (1988). *Mr. Popper's penguins.* Boston: Little Brown.

Berger, M., & Berger, G. (2001). *Do penguins get frostbite? Questions and answers about polar animals.* New York: Scholastic.

Cowcher, H. (1990). *Antarctica.* New York: Farrar, Straus & Giroux.

Gibbons, G. (1998). *Penguins!* New York: Holiday.

Jenkins, M. (1999). *The emperor's egg.* Cambridge: Candlewick.

Lester, H. (2000). *Tacky and the emperor.* Boston: Houghton Mifflin.

Murphy, M. (1999). *Please be quiet!* Boston: Houghton Mifflin.

Nixon, J. L. (2000). *Gus and Gertie and the missing pearl.* New York: North-South/SeaStar.

Resnick, J. P. (1997). *Penguins (Eyes on nature series).* Chicago: Kidsbooks.

Rey, M. (2000). *Whiteblack the penguin sees the world.* Boston: Houghton Mifflin.

Shields, C. D. (1999). *Martian rock.* Cambridge: Candlewick.

Sierra, J. (1998). *Antarctic antics: A book of penguin poems.* New York: Harcourt/Gulliver.

Stonehouse, B. (2000). *A visual introduction to penguins.* New York: Checkmark.

Webb, S. (2000). *My season with penguins: An Antarctic journal.* Boston: Houghton Mifflin.

Wiesmuller, D. (2000). *The adventures of Marco and Polo.* New York: Walker.

Resources for Adults:

Combs, M. (2002). *Readers and writers in primary grades.* Upper Saddle River, NJ: Merrill/Prentice Hall.

Peterson, R. T. (1979). *Penguins.* Boston: Houghton Mifflin.

Silver, D. M., & Wynne, P. J. (1999). *Penguins (Easy make and learn projects series).* New York: Scholastic Professional Books.

Websites and Videos:

New Zealand Penguins—www.penguin.net.nz/.

"Book Buddies" share a picture book.

"The World of Penguins" from public television's *Nature* series. Phone: 800–336–1917. Cost is approximately $19.95, plus shipping and handling.

Antarctic Antics (Sierra, 2001) is available in video, audio cassette, and 16 mm through Weston Woods, 265 Post Road West, Westport, Connecticut 06880.

Activities for the Intermediate and Middle Levels

1. Select an illustrator or have the children select one they would like to learn about. Have them imitate the illustrator's style.

2. Writing activities based on wordless picture books allow middle grade children to use their imaginations and their writing skills. For example, they could describe each page, tell the story, select and describe a character, write a play or poem that evokes a theme or character, recreate the artwork in a puppet show or diorama, or select music that relates to the book and write why the music "fits." A wordless book would make this assignment even more interesting.

3. If students are becoming enthusiastic and knowledgeable about picture books, organize a "Mock-Caldecott Committee" that selects a winner from a pile of newly published picture books. Students' critical thinking skills will be challenged as they analyze the books and defend their choices.

4. Assigning book buddies, or pairing older students and younger ones, enhances language-arts programs with all ages gaining facility in reading and enjoying books.

REFERENCES

Children's Works

Bannerman, H. (1899/1920). *The story of Little Black Sambo*. South Yarmouth, MA: A. D. Bragdon.

Bannerman, H. (1996). *The story of Little Babaji*. (Ill. by F. Marcellino). New York: HarperCollins.

Bemelmans, L. (1934). *Hansi*. New York: Viking.

Bemelmans, L. (1939). *Madeline*. New York: Puffin.

Bishop, C. (1938). *Five Chinese brothers*. New York: Putnam.

Briggs, J. (1998). *Snowflake Bentley*. (Ill. by M. Azarian). Boston: Houghton Mifflin.

Brown, M. (1998). *Arthur makes the team*. Boston: Little Brown.

Brown, M. W. (1942). *The runaway bunny*. (Ill. by C. Hurd). New York: Harper & Row.

Bunting, E. (1994). *Smoky night*. (Ill. by D. Diaz). New York: Harcourt.

Cole, B. (2000). *Buttons*. New York: Farrar, Straus & Giroux.

Cole, J. (1998). *My parents' divorce*. New York: Copper.

Cooney, B. (1982). *Miss Rumphius*. New York: Viking Penguin.

Emberley, B. (1967). *Drummer Hoff*. Upper Saddle River, NJ: Prentice Hall.

Falconer, I. (2000). *Olivia*. New York: Atheneum/Schwartz.

Gibbons, G. (1998). *Penguins!* New York: Holiday.

Goble, P. (1992). *Love flute*. New York: Bradbury.

Herron, C. (1997). *Nappy hair*. (Ill. by J. Cepeda). New York: Knopf.

High, L. O. (2001). *Under New York*. (Ill. by R. Rayevsky). New York: Holiday.

Kaplan, H. (2000). *Waiting to sing*. New York: DK Ink.

Kirk, D. (1999). *Little miss spider*. New York: Scholastic.

Lester, J. (1996). *Sam and the tigers*. (Ill. by J. Pinkney). New York: Dial.

Lionni, L. (1967). *Frederick*. New York: Pantheon.

Millman, I. (1998). *Moses goes to a concert*. New York: Farrar, Straus, & Giroux.

Newman, L. (1995). *Too far away to touch*. New York: Clarion.

Nivola, C. A. (1997). *Elisabeth*. New York: Farrar, Straus, & Giroux.

Pinkney, B. (2000). *Cosmo and the robot*. New York: Greenwillow.

Schulman, A. (1997). *Carmine's story: A book about a boy living with AIDS*. New York: Lerner.

Schulson, R. E. (1997). *Guns: What you should know*. New York: Whitman.

Sendak, M. (1963). *Where the wild things are*. New York: Harper & Row.

Sendak, M. (1981). *Outside over there*. New York: HarperCollins.

Stanley, D., & Vennema, P. (1992). *The bard of Avon: The story of William Shakespeare*. New York: Morrow.

Steptoe, J. (1985). *Mufaro's beautiful daughters*. New York: Lothrop.

Stillerman, M. (1998). *Nine spoons: A Chanukah story*. (Ill. by P. Gerber). New York: Hachai.

Tsuchiya, Y. (1988). *Faithful elephants*. Boston: Houghton Mifflin.

Van Allsburg, C. (1981). *Jumanji*. Boston: Houghton Mifflin.

Vincent, G. (2000). *A day, a dog*. Asheville, NC: Front Street.

Wilhoite, M. (1990). *Daddy's roommate*. Boston: Alyson.

Woodson, J. (2001). *The other side*. (Ill. by E. B. Lewis). New York: Putnam.

Zemach, M. (1982). *Jake and Honeybunch go to heaven*. New York: Farrar, Straus & Giroux.

Professional Works

Bader, B. (1976). *American picturebooks from Noah's ark to the beast within*. New York: Macmillan.

Bader, B. (1996). Sambo, Babaji, and Sam. *Horn Book, 72* (5), 536–547.

Benedict, S., & Carlisle, L. (Eds.). (1992). *Beyond words: Picture books for older readers and writers*. Portsmouth, NH: Heinemann.

Bishop, R. S., & Hickman, J. (1992). Four or fourteen or forty: Picture books are for everyone. In S. Benedict & L. Carlisle (Eds.), *Beyond words: Picture books for older readers and writers* (pp. 1–10). Portsmouth, NH: Heinemann.

Children's Books in Print. (1997). New York: Bowker, Reed, Elseviev, Inc.

Cianciolo, P. (1990). *Picture books for children*. Chicago: American Library Association.

Hillman, C. (1995, February). Struggling middle school readers and multicultural picture books. *Journal of Reading,* 387.

Kiefer, B. Z. (1995). *The potential of picture books: From visual literacy to aesthetic understanding*. Upper Saddle River, NJ: Merrill/Prentice Hall.

Norton, D. (1999). *Through the eyes of a child* (5th ed.). Upper Saddle River, NJ: Merrill/Prentice Hall.

Robinson, L. (2000). The newest medium: Illustrating with save and undo. *Horn Book, 76* (6), 667–680.

Schwarcz, J., & Schwarcz, C. (1991). *The picture book comes of age*. Chicago: American Library Association.

Slapin, B., & Seale, D. (Eds.). (1988). *Books without bias: Through Indian eyes*. Berkeley, CA: Oyate.

Stewig, J. W. (1995). *Looking at picture books*. Ft. Atkinson, WI: Highsmith.

Tompkins, G. E. (2001). *Literacy for the 21st century: A balanced approach* (2nd ed.). Upper Saddle River, NJ: Merrill/Prentice Hall.

Townsend, J. R. (1992). *Written for children* (4th ed.). New York: HarperCollins.

Additional Resources

Story-Huffman, R. (1999). *Caldecott on the Net: Reading and Internet activities*. Ft. Atkinson, WI: Alleyside Press.

Eighteen activities based on a theme, Learning Quests, are given. For example, photography is the theme of the learning quest based on the Caldecott winner Snowflake Bentley, *illustrated by Mary Azarian, written by Jacqueline Briggs Martin in 1999, and pub-lished by Houghton Mifflin. Some of the learning quests are suitable for middle grades.*

Tiedt, I. M. (2000). *Teaching with picture books in the middle school*. Newark, DE: International Reading Association.

This is an introduction to the topic of using picture books with older students. It includes nine chapters and lesson-plan outlines based on thematic divisions.

CHAPTER 7

The Pleasure and Power of Poetry

INTRODUCTION AND RESPONSE

In some classrooms, children are poets. Their work is visible on bulletin boards, on computer screens, and in poetry journals. They read poetry aloud, listen to other poets read, give suggestions to others about poem making, and seek out their favorite poets in anthologies and collections. Jack Prelutsky, Shel Silverstein, Gary Soto, Nikki Grimes, and many more poets are as familiar as authors Beverly Cleary, Katherine Paterson, and Maurice Sendak.

In other classrooms, the response to poetry is not so enthusiastic. In fact, poetry may not be evident, either visually or aurally. Some children (and adults) do not like poetry, do not choose to read or write it, and may disdain those who do. Why are there such wide-ranging differences in the response to this literary genre?

REFLECTION   Which classroom was more prevalent in your past: the one that stressed poetry or the one that ignored poetry?

There are probably as many reasons for differences in responses as there are people who respond to the quality of their poetry experiences in school. However, whatever the response, poetry deserves attention and acclamation because of its unique power to distill human emotion and thought into beautiful language. With its concentrated force, poetry can intensify experiences and involve our senses, emotions, and intellect. Myra Cohn Livingston, a superb poet, has suggested

Student teachers and a professor plan a poetry bulletin board for their classrooms.

that the point of poetry is not to classify, dissect, or analyze but "to arrive at an experience—to feel, to bring our emotions and sensitivities into play" (Livingston, 1996, p. 223).

By concentrating on the pleasure and power of poetry, readers can be awakened to the beauty and wonder that poets bring to everyday activities. Delight, humor, tragedy, joy—poems can convey all these feelings in words that sharpen our vision and bring new empathy and understanding to humdrum recollections.

This chapter focuses on the awesome ability of poetry to create meaning, to elicit an enthusiastic response, to satisfy deeply the need to express feelings and sensitivities. As the title of this chapter suggests, the dual emphasis is on discovering appropriate poems to read aloud in classrooms and other venues with children, and on encouraging children, adolescents, and adults to write poems. So begin this chapter by writing a poem, any kind, any length, any style. You may want to compose a haiku, cinquain, or ballad, or personify an inanimate object by giving it the human attributes of vision, hearing, and emotions. Whatever your choice, enjoy the creative—and challenging—task of discovering new poems and poets. (Refer to the Glossary for explanations of any terms you do not yet know.)

REFLECTION   What do you need to know about children's poetry to be successful in your role as teacher, librarian, parent, student, or administrator? What are your goals for this chapter?

DEFINING POETRY

Robert Frost, one of the premier poets of the 20th century, said a poem "begins in delight and ends in wisdom." Emily Dickinson, a notable poet of the 19th century, recognized and defined poetry through a physical sensation as she read a text. She said, "If I read a book and it makes my whole body so cold no fire can ever warm me, I know that it is poetry. If I feel physically as if the top of my head were taken off, I know that it is poetry." Poetry speaks to us, grabbing our attention immediately with an emotional and cognitive hook, or it is not poetry.

Poetry is a succinct expression that captures the essence of an idea or an object. The *sounds* of poetry come from the pulsating beat of the rhythm, repetition, and sometimes rhyme of the words. Poetry is meant to be spoken or read aloud. Often it tells a story, and sometimes the words are set to music. Because it suggests and hints at meanings, poetry seems more abstract, more symbolic than other writings. It is personal, concise, "imaginatively intense language, usually in verse" (Frye, Baker, & Perkins, 1985, p. 356).

Poets are often the most insightful users of language because they have the ability to distill human emotions and thought into a minimum number of words. They help us see familiar things in unique ways (Worth, 1992) and communicate what is sometimes impossible to explain. How do you describe the scent of a rose? The love for a child? The horror of a terrorist attack? Putting words around ideas or crystallizing emotions with symbols demands the most imaginative, yet practical, explanations of human and natural events.

Like other literary genres, poetry is difficult to define precisely. However, its qualities, or characteristics, have been described by many and a consensus emerges. Compared with prose, poetry is brief, intense, and patterned. Poetry has more intensity than prose, it uses more figurative language, and it sometimes follows rather strict structures. Structure refers to formulaic patterns that have evolved over time, such as those of sonnets, limericks, and haiku.

Defining poetry for children is not different from defining poetry for everyone. Simply put, there is no demarcation between "adult" poetry and "child" poetry (Clark, 1983). As in all literature, a sense of audience is intuited by the reader, so children's poetry is that which children read and enjoy.

REFLECTION   How would you characterize the differences between adult and children's poetry? How do you define poetry?

HISTORY OF POETRY FOR CHILDREN

Even before William Blake wrote and illustrated his poetry collection titled *Listen and Read: Songs of Innocence and Experience* (1789/1997), children's poetry was evident in nursery rhymes and Sunday school hymns. However, Blake's poems celebrated childhood rather than admonishing children, and for this reason his work changed perceptions of what poetry could and should be. The first line in this collection of 23 poems—*Piping down the valleys wild*—became a phrase associated with the joy and innocence of childhood. Much more than nursery rhymes or rhymed moral lessons, these poems capture a lyrical quality attuned to a child's understanding and expression (Carpenter & Prichard, 1984).

A harbinger of "nonsense" poetry was Edward Lear (1812–1888). With his whimsical limericks and celebrated poems (such as *The Owl and the Pussycat,* originally published in 1871) and the drawings and illustrations with which he accompanied them, Lear strove to amuse and entertain children with no condescension or sentimentality. His 1846 *Book of Nonsense* was immediately popular, and although he did not invent the limerick, it has come to be associated with his name (Hayward, 1996). As Lewis Carroll pushed boundaries in children's fantasy, so did Edward Lear give free rein to imaginary beasts and situations in verse, creating a foundation for broad humor and wit. A recent edition of *The Owl and the Pussycat* (1998), illustrated by James Marshall, captures the whimsy and playfulness of Lear's original as the Owl and his fiancée, an ultra fashion-conscious Pussycat, board a cruise ship in grand style.

One of the first story poems to captivate both adults and children, "The Pied Piper of Hamelin," was written by Robert Browning in 1842. This work popularized a form of poetry called *narrative poetry* and found its audience quickly and surely.

The Victorian and Edwardian periods in England, sometimes called the golden age of children's literature because of the classics for children produced in these periods, produced notable poetry for children (in addition to the novels mentioned in Chapter 2). Christina Rossetti, Robert Louis Stevenson, Walter de la Mare, and A. A. Milne set standards for children's poetry in the late 1800s and early 1900s.

In the United States, poetry for children began to flourish in the 1920s (Hopkins, 1993). The 20th century was a time of increasing diversity in poetic forms and subject matter (e.g., the work of poets such as Langston Hughes, who was the first to portray an African-American experience in poetry for children). The 1950s brought collections by John Ciardi and David McCord; the 1960s and 1970s saw efforts to bring a new realism to poetry. Humor from Shel Silverstein proved to be popular; his *Where the Sidewalk Ends* (1974) was on the *New York Times* bestseller list for three years. Jack Prelutsky's poems in *The New Kid on the Block* (1984) and *Something Big Has Been Here* (1990) captured the attention and interest of many elementary-school children.

Recent years have signaled a continuing and abiding interest in contemporary poets and their work. Awards now recognize significant contributions to this genre, and content is varied, reflecting the multiculturalism and realism in the lives of today's children. In the last two or three decades, rhyme is not as prevalent in poetry as it used to be. Increasingly, poems are written in *free verse,* which allows a freedom from metrical structures (Horning, 1997).

Following is a list of milestones in children's poetry. Perhaps you know some, most, or just a few of the works. Which ones would you keep in the canon of children's poetry, and which ones would you delete? Note that the decades between Langston Hughes and Nancy Willard have been left blank so that you can select your own poets and their collections.

1789	*Songs of Innocence,* William Blake
1822	*A Visit from St. Nicholas,* Clement Moore
1842	*The Pied Piper of Hamelin,* Robert Browning
1872	*Sing-Song,* Christina Rossetti
1885	*A Child's Garden of Verses,* Robert Louis Stevenson
1913	*Peacock Pie,* Walter de la Mare
1926	*When We Were Very Young,* A.A. Milne
1932	*The Dream Keeper and Other Poems,* Langston Hughes
*1981	*A Visit to William Blake's Inn,* Nancy Willard
*1988	*Joyful Noise,* Paul Fleischman

*Newbery Award winners

CHILDREN'S POETRY PREFERENCES

Research studies about children's preferences conducted several years ago (Terry, 1974; Fisher & Natarella, 1982; Kutiper, 1985) revealed the following trends:

- Most children prefer humorous, contemporary, and story poems that rhyme.
- An interest and enthusiasm for poetry declines as children advance through middle school, although that may be tempered somewhat when poetry is used productively by enthusiastic and knowledgeable teachers.
- Most children prefer literal poems that not only rhyme but have a strong sense of rhythm.
- Familiar and positive emotional experiences in poetry are more likely to be appreciated by children rather than abstract and self-expressive poems, at least until the upper middle school and high school years.
- Girls tend to like poetry better than boys do.

These preferences seem to have stood the test of time (Hillman, 1995). It is evident that if poetry appreciation is awakened early in a child's development and fostered throughout the elementary grades with a variety of poetic forms and topics, children and youth will likely enjoy poetry. Preferences can be stretched to include the linguistic diversity and the cognitive growth that poems offer. The teacher's role in fostering a desire for poetry and knowledge about this literary genre is crucial and difficult, but rewarding. Also, because of the strong infusion of the writing process into school language arts programs in the last two decades, new methodologies in teaching poetry through writing have been successful (Hillman, 1995; Marcus, 1992; Schneider, 2001).

REFLECTION   Is poetry, like other literature, supposed to instruct *and* entertain equally? Can poetry become too didactic? Or too fluffy, without substance?

EVALUATING POETRY

Given the characteristics of poetry that speak to its emotional intensity, rhythmic and figurative language, and compactness, it stands to reason that poetry is evaluated by the presence or absence of those characteristics. In other words, the degree of compactness, emotional intensity, or rhythmic language determines a poem's success or failure. A poem is as compact as it needs to be and, similarly, as intense and as rhythmically appealing. The rhyme should not have a "singsongy regularity that deadens the senses. . . . Writers can easily become so bound to rhyme that it dictates the word choice, and the words lose their power and meaning" (Horning, 1997, pp. 70–71).

Choosing among "good" poems is difficult, but having a purpose helps us make the right choice. However, there are qualities that are common in mediocre poems that are never acceptable in poetry for children: the negative qualities of sentimentality, didacticism, condescension, and nostalgia.

Sentimentality is a shallow or false emotion that masks or tries to manipulate a heartfelt response. Poetry of the 19th century is sometimes seen as sentimental, like the overstated verses of romance on greeting cards.

When the message of poetry or prose tends to educate or instruct the reader in a heavy-handed way, we call the poem **didactic.** Much of children's literature over the years has been considered didactic.

Condescension is a matter of tone; it creates a patronizing air of treating the child/reader/listener as someone of little knowledge or experience. No dignity is afforded to the audience.

Nostalgia is also a matter of tone, and appears when the poet writes with a backward view toward childhood, creating a childhood that should have been instead of recognizing what has been. Simply stated, sentimentality, didacticism, condescension, and nostalgia have no place in poetry.

Evaluation leads some critics to distinguish between poetry and verse (Lukens, 1999). Poetry is seen as the better of the two, as it represents a loftier, rarer, and finer expression of distilled thought and emotion. Verse, however, can be pleasant and entertaining, but it is occasionally contrived and awkwardly written. Greeting

Criteria	My Personal Response	Matching Poem to Purpose, Audience
Emotional intensity	Does the poem capture my attention immediately? Do I feel wonder? Delight? Excitement? Sadness? Is the poem sentimental, nostalgic, or condescending?	Does it stretch my audience's imagination and empathy? Will my audience understand the humor? Is the subject appropriate?
Rhythmic and figurative language	Are images vivid? Are the word choices appropriate? Is the rhyme forced or natural?	Will the images provoke recognition? Will the poem support "teachable moments" for alliteration, onomatopoeia, rhyme scheme, and other poetic elements?
Brevity	Is a unique view expressed in an economy of words? Does the form or shape contribute to its meaning?	Does it fit into the time limits of my curriculum? Will the poem sustain attention?

Figure 7.1 Evaluating poetry

cards, commercial slogans, rap and other song lyrics, and the rhymed couplets in some picture books (Dr. Seuss, for example) are viewed as verse but not true poetry. This distinction, if we find truth in it, colors our evaluation of a written work. When verse is trite and commonplace, it becomes doggerel.

In the evaluation scheme in Figure 7.1, criteria in the form of questions are posed so that you can evaluate a poem or a group of poems for your own use. Read the poem aloud, read it silently, and study what the poet does to achieve a certain tone and effect. The four-point scale below demonstrates how a rubric could be constructed to evaluate certain poems or groups of poems. The four-point scale is useful when a more objective evaluation is needed.

Four-Point Scale for Evaluating Poetry

Name of Poem (or Collection or Anthology): _____

Poet (and Illustrator): _____

When 1 stands for "very good," 2 is "good," 3 is "marginal," and 4 is "unsatisfactory," rate the poem (or group of poems) according to:

Emotional Intensity

    I. The emotions I feel as I read the poem strongly resonate with my approval.

        1 _____ 2 _____ 3 _____ 4 _____

    II. The poem captures my interest immediately in an intriguing way.

        1 _____ 2 _____ 3 _____ 4 _____

Rhythmic and Figurative Language

    III. The words create images in my mind.

        1 _____ 2 _____ 3 _____ 4 _____

    IV. The poem would be fun to read aloud.

        1 _____ 2 _____ 3 _____ 4 _____

Brevity

    V. Each word contributes to the success of the overall effect.

        1 _____ 2 _____ 3 _____ 4 _____

    VI. The poem leaves the reader wanting more.

        1 _____ 2 _____ 3 _____ 4 _____

SUBGENRES OF POETRY

Poems take many forms and, indeed, poets are continually experimenting with new forms. This section presents prevalent forms of children's poetry while acknowledging that others are possible. As in other genres, it is impossible to categorize everything neatly. In an effort to standardize terminology, these forms are analogous to subgenres. They represent the ways the poetry genre can be categorized. However, because they are commonly called *forms* in most other studies, they will be called forms here. Next, **ballads, narrative poetry, lyrical poetry, free verse, haiku, limerick, concrete poetry,** and prescriptive forms such as **cinquain** and **diamante** are defined and exemplified.

REFLECTION   How important is it to correctly categorize the form of a poem? Can one appreciate the poem without recognizing the form? Would the recognition help in appreciating the poet's craft?

Ballads

Ballads originally were narrative poems composed in short stanzas—or verses—for singing. Troubadours in medieval times sang of heroes and happenings, unrequited love, revenge, and work. Frequently, refrains were repeated between stanzas that usually had four lines. Familiar examples of ballads such as *On Top of Old Smoky* and *Blowin' in the Wind* are found in the Kennedys' *Knock at a Star* (1999, pp. 127, 129). Another example, *Drill, Ye Tarriers, Drill,* is an American ballad of the 19th century (Cooper et al., 1959). This work song refers to the immigrant workers (mostly Irish men) who used steam drills to dig down into the deep

bedrock of Manhattan island to lay the foundation for some of the early skyscrapers. Tarriers were unskilled laborers stationed beside the steam drills to remove the loosened rock.

Drill, Ye Tarriers, Drill

(Verse)
Early in the morning, the boss comes round
To chase the gang to the quarry ground,
For hard work Johnny is a driving lad,
And if we don't hustle we get in bad
(Refrain)
So it's drill ye tarriers drill,
Then drill ye tarriers drill.
So we work all day no sugar in our tay,
Oh eight long stretches and six hours' pay
So drill ye tarriers drill. (Repeat line twice.)

Narrative Poetry

Like ballads, narrative poems tell a story, but the verses are longer and typically there is no refrain. Well-known classics—such as *Twas the Night Before Christmas,* also titled *A Visit from St. Nicholas* (Moore, 1822/1990), *The Pied Piper of Hamelin* by Robert Browning (1842/1999), and *The Highwayman* by Alfred Noyes (1913/1990)—exemplify narrative poetry at its best. *The Cremation of Sam McGee* (Service, 1987) tells a great story about the frozen north and Sam McGee who foiled death.

Narrative poetry of Henry Wadsworth Longfellow told the story of Paul Revere's ride (*The Midnight Ride of Paul Revere,* illustrated by Jeffrey Thompson, 2000) and personalized a native American childhood in *Song of Hiawatha,* (Longfellow, 1983) among many others. Ann Whitford Paul's narrative poetry, *All by Herself: 14 Girls Who Made a Difference* (1999) is for fourth- through sixth-graders and recounts the courage of girls—some who are well-known and some who are unknown—who performed courageous acts.

Lyrical Poetry

Lyrical poetry is personal and descriptive with no prescribed length or structure. It typically captures an imaginary moment or reveals a feeling. Like narrative poetry, lyrical poetry lends itself well to music, as the poem's lyrics could be the words to a song.

Who Has Seen the Wind?

Who has seen the wind?
  Neither I nor you:
But when the leaves hang trembling,
  The wind is passing through.
Who has seen the wind?
  Neither you nor I:
But when the trees bow down their heads,
  The wind is passing by.

Christina Rossetti

Christina Rossetti's poetry is sublimely lyrical, and sets a high standard for modern poets. Two who meet the challenge are Dennis Lee (*Bubblegum Delicious,* illustrated by David McPhail, 2001), for primary-age children, and Alice Schertle (*A Lucky Thing,* illustrated by Wendell Minor, 1999), for fourth- through sixth-graders. Humorous, lively, and fun to read aloud, these poems describe delicious moments, either real or imagined.

Free Verse

Free verse is poetry that has no discernible pattern or form. It depends on the natural rhythm of language to provide a structure. Quite often free verse does not rhyme, but the words portray images, feelings, and thought in a unique way. *Poem* by Langston Hughes (1932/1994a), expresses a poignant moment in brief, delicate sentences.

Poem

I loved my friend.
He went away from me.
There's nothing more to say.
The poem ends,
Soft as it began—
I loved my friend.

Langston Hughes

A recent trend in novels has been to tell the story in free verse. *Out of the Dust* (Hesse, 1997), a Newbery award winner written in free verse, is a heart-rending story of a girl's maturation on an Oklahoma dust bowl farm in the 1930s. Similarly, Virginia Wolff's *True Believer* (2001) and Ron Koertge's *The Brimstone Journals* (2001) use free verse to reveal the innermost thoughts of their protagonists. In *Carver: A Life in Poems* (2001), Marilyn Nelson wrote a biography of George Washington Carver in free verse.

Haiku

Haiku is an ancient Japanese form of three-line poetry. It is a sophisticated expression in which the meaning is often elusive. Haiku seems simple because of the poem's brevity, but its structure of a five-syllable first line, seven-syllable second line, and five-syllable third line is more complex than it seems because of the limited text. Also, haiku focuses on an immediate occurrence, often something in nature—not something that happened in the past (Esbensen, 1975).

"Stars," by Emily, a fourth-grader, captures the immediacy of the night but also hints at eons of brightness in the galaxy.

A fourth-grader writes her poem in haiku form, celebrating the natural world.

Stars

A beautiful star
So bright in the night, shining
In the galaxy.

by
Emily Hillman

The well-known poet, Paul Janeczko has selected haiku from ancient Japanese poets to modern ones in his *Stone Bench in an Empty Park* (2000), illustrated with photographs by Henri Silberman. Janeczko's aim was to show that poetry and nature can be found in the city as well as suburbs or country.

From the same tradition as haiku, **tanka** is a poetic form in which two seven-syllable lines are added to the three-line haiku. It allows the poet to expand the immediate occurrence just a bit.

Limericks

Limericks are five-line poems in which the **rhyme scheme** is a, a, b, b, a (the first, second, and fifth lines and the third and fourth lines rhyme). There is a definite, rollicking rhythm in the flow of the lines. Limericks are often funny when they describe something or compare elements out of the ordinary. Edward Lear wrote many limericks, and his style in many of them was to use the same word at the end of the first line and the last line.

There Was a Young Lady Whose Nose

There was a young lady, whose nose
Continually prospers and grows;
When it grew out of sight,
She exclaimed in a fright,
"Oh! Farewell to the end of my Nose!"

Edward Lear

Knock at a Star (Kennedy & Kennedy, 1999) contains many great examples of limericks, from Edward Lear and "Anonymous" to recent ones by John Ciardi and William Jay Smith. Smith's collection, *Around My Room* (2000), illustrated by Erik Blegvad, is a rollicking collection that includes limericks for very young children. Bill Grossman writes for elementary children in *Timothy Tunny Swallowed a Bunny* (2001), illustrated by Kevin Hawkes. His 18 "modified" limericks are droll and provide good models for writing.

Concrete Poetry

A poem written in the shape of a tree, an ice-cream cone, an animal, or something that visually reinforces the meaning of the whole is called a concrete poem. By arranging the words, and even the punctuation marks, as a picture, the poet creates a new form that is unique to a specific poem. In a collection of concrete poems called *A Poke in the I* (2001), Paul Janeczko and Chris Raschka team up to create and pay homage to humorous, witty, and quite lovely poems suggested for fourth- through seventh-graders. A poetry collection that celebrates light in its many apparitions is *Flicker Flash* (Graham, 1999). With concrete poetry in the forms of candles, a flashlight, lightning bolt, refrigerator light, and so on, Graham and Nancy Davis's illustrations would enhance any poetry collection.

A POKE IN THE I. This Collection Copyright © 2001 Paul B. Janeczko; Illustrations Copyright © 2001 Chris Raschka. Reproduced by permission of the publisher Candlewick Press, Inc., Cambridge MA.

Arnold Adoff, a consistently well-respected poet for many years, experiments with free verse and concrete poetry in *Touch the Poem* (2000) for grades 2 through 5. His poetry allows readers to explore the sense of touch, sight (with Lisa Desimini's illustrations), and hearing (when the poems are read aloud).

Cinquain, Diamante, and Other Forms

A cinquain is a five-line poem that follows this pattern:

first line	two syllables
second line	four syllables
third line	six syllables
fourth line	eight syllables
fifth line	two syllables

Influenced by Japanese haiku and tanka (Esbensen, 1975), a cinquain magnifies the importance of finding the perfect match between word and meaning. A derivative form of cinquain doesn't count syllables but uses words instead.

first line	one word (giving the title)
second line	two words (describing the title)
third line	three words (expressing an action of the title)
fourth line	four words (expressing a feeling of the title)
fifth line	one word (a synonym of the title)

Following is a cinquain written by a third-grader.

My Dog

black
shaggy hair
cold wet nose
lying by my bed
Shauna

By Jessica

A diamante is a seven-line poem that forms a diamond shape.

first line	one word (subject, a noun)
second line	two words (adjectives)
third line	three words (verbs or verb forms)
fourth line	four or five words (a phrase related to the subject)
fifth line	three words (verbs or verb forms)

sixth line	two words (adjectives)
seventh line	one word (an antonym of the subject)

Diamantes are interesting because they can begin with one topic and end with its opposite. The shift occurs in the fourth line, which should be pertinent to both topics. The following example, written by a sixth-grader, demonstrates the shift:

Diamond
brilliant, expensive,
sparkling, glittering, polishing,
Mined under the Earth's soil
digging, chipping, working
cheap, dark
Coal.

Cinquains and diamantes represent poetic forms that do not depend on rhyme but still rely on crucial knowledge of word choice to convey a thought. Because of their "rules," children treat these forms as word puzzles and find them challenging and satisfying—as both readers and writers.

ELEMENTS OF POETRY

Poets, teachers, and critics use language—the "tools of the trade"—to talk about poetry and prose. As mentioned in Chapter 3, the aspects of analysis provide all who study literature a vocabulary to discuss and evaluate it. Many of the terms in Chapter 3, especially in the figurative language section, are pertinent to poetry. Terms such as **alliteration, metaphor, simile, symbol, personification, assonance, consonance,** and **allusion** bring an understanding to the richness of a poem's meaning(s). Other elements in that section can be applied to poetry to allow us to appreciate the complexity of a poet's work.

This section extends those literary elements by adding three more terms necessary to poetic analysis: **onomatopoeia, internal rhyme,** and **rhyme scheme.** These three seem to be essential to understanding poetry in the beginning of an analysis. Because poetry is complex, especially when rhythm and stress are studied, you are encouraged to continue beyond what this text provides. A good resource is *An Introduction to Poetry* (Kennedy, 1990).

Onomatopoeia, that wonderful word that looks like a mouthful of vowels with an occasional consonant thrown in, refers to words that sound like their meanings. The "meow" of a cat, the "sizzle" of a hamburger frying in a pan, the "oomph" of someone sitting on a soft sofa—all these words sound like the action itself. Of course poetry, with its emphasis on just the right word for the precise movement, uses onomatopoeia. Sometimes onomatopoeic words are coined for just the right phrase, as in *Jabberwocky,* Lewis Carroll's famous nonsense poem. A verse of Eve Merriam's *What in the World?* also demonstrates onomatopoeia. The animals are aptly described by the sounds they make and the rhyming that captures exactly their appearance and demeanor.

What in the World?

What in the world
  goes whiskery friskery
    meowling and prowling
      napping and lapping
        at silky milk?
Psst,
What is it?
What in the world
  goes leaping and beeping
    onto a lily pad onto a log
      onto a tree stump or down to the bog?
Splash, blurp,
Kerchurp!

Eve Merriam

This excerpt from Eve Merriam's poem also shows internal rhyming. *Leaping* and *beeping* are chosen to give the line rhythm; because the words sound alike, the line picks up speed as well. Thus movement is conveyed through internal rhymes.

Rhyme scheme has been described in the section about limericks, and it refers to a pattern created at the end of lines by the rhyming words. For example, the limerick is a, a, b, b, a. A couplet, or two lines that rhyme, is a, a.

REFLECTION   What is the rhyme scheme of the previously mentioned ballad *Drill, Ye Tarriers, Drill*?

CONTEMPORARY POETS

There are many outstanding 20th-century poets who weave word magic in their contributions to literature for children. In 1977 the National Council of Teachers of English (NCTE) initiated an Award for Excellence in Poetry for Children, which is given for the body of a poet's work. Some of those who have received this honor are David McCord, Aileen Fisher, Karla Kuskin, Myra Cohn Livingston, Eve Merriam, John Ciardi, Lilian Moore, Arnold Adoff, Valerie Worth, Barbara Esbensen, and Eloise Greenfield. The works of these prolific poets appear in many anthologies and in their own collections.

To honor a promising children's poet, the International Reading Association bestows a Lee Bennett Hopkins Promising Poet award every third year. In 2001, the award went to Craig Crist-Evans for his book, *Moon Over Tennessee: A Boy's Civil War Journal,* written in free verse. A 13-year-old boy leaves his farm in northeastern Tennessee to accompany his father, who is a confederate soldier, and eventually witnesses his father's death at Gettysburg. Woodcut illustrations by Bonnie Christensen match the drama and emotion of the vivid poetry.

In addition to the significant poets and their collections mentioned in this chapter, following are some recent multicultural and general collections that will help you discover contemporary poetry for children. There are many new, exciting collections organized by topic, as well. Consult reviewing sources such as *Horn Book Magazine* or the *Bulletin of the Center for Children's Books* for outstanding poetry written for children and adolescents and, in some cases, by children and adolescents.

RECENT ANTHOLOGIES AND COLLECTIONS: A BIBLIOGRAPHY

A bibliography of recent and recommended poetry anthologies (a volume of several poets' work) and collections (a volume of several poems by the same poet) are presented here. Titles and subtitles give an indication of the theme or content of the volume. Some of the collections have been placed under a multicultural heading, such as African-American, Native American, and so forth, to help you find poems of a particular theme or content. Because poetry anthologies and collections are so diverse, headings such as "animals," "sports," "humor," and others are also included. The "YA" designation refers to volumes especially appropriate for young adults. This list should help you select some poetry for classrooms and other venues. Perhaps your school or public library would like to augment its poetry collection: this list would be a place to start. All bibliographic information is included, and is not repeated in the references at the end of this chapter.

Anthologies

Franco, B. (Ed.) (2001). *Things I have to tell you: Poems and writing by teenage girls.* Cambridge: Candlewick. YA

Hopkins, L. B. (Ed.) (2000). *My America: A poetry atlas of the United States.* New York: Simon & Schuster.

Johnson, D. (Ed.) (2000). *Movin': Teen poets take voice.* New York: Orchard. YA

Lindbergh, R. (Ed.) (2000). *In every tiny grain of sand: A child's book of prayers.* Cambridge: Candlewick.

Nye, N. S. (Sel.) (2000). *Salting the ocean: 100 poems by young poets.* New York: Greenwillow.

Prelutsky, J. (Sel.) (1999). *The 20th century children's poetry treasury.* New York: Knopf.

Themed Collections and Anthologies

Animals, Birds, and Insects

Florian, D. (2000). *Mammalabilia.* New York: Harcourt.

McKelvey, D. K. (2001). *Locust pocus! A book to bug you.* New York: Philomel.

Schertle, A. (1999). *I am the cat.* New York: Lothrop.

Willard, N. (2001). *The moon and riddles diner and the sunnyside café.* New York: Harcourt.

Humor

Bush, T. (2000). *Ferocious girls, steamroller boys, and other poems in between.* New York: Orchard.

Dakos, K. (1999). *The bug in teacher's coffee: And other school poems.* New York: HarperCollins.

Florian, D. (1999). *Laugh-eteria.* New York: Harcourt.

Hort, L. (2000). *Tie your socks and clap your feet: Mixed-up poems.* New York: Atheneum.

Kennedy, X. J. (1999). *Elympics.* New York: Philomel.

Prelutsky, J. (2000). *It's raining pigs and noodles.* New York: Greenwillow.

Prelutsky, J. (2001). *Awful ogre's awful day.* New York: HarperCollins.

Sports

Adoff, A. (2000). *The basket counts.* New York: Simon & Schuster.

Hopkins, L. B. (1999). *Sports! Sports! Sports!: A poetry collection.* New York: HarperCollins.

Smith, C. R. (1999). *Rimshots: Basketball pix, rolls, and rhythm.* New York: Dutton.

Miscellaneous

Florian, D. (1999). *Winter eyes.* New York: Greenwillow.

George, K. O. (2001). *Toasting marshmallows: Camping poems.* New York: Clarion.

Hines, A. G. (2001). *Pieces: A year in poems and quilts.* New York: Greenwillow.

Hughes, T. (2000). *The mermaid's purse.* New York: Knopf.

McNaughton, C. (2000). *Wish you were here (and I wasn't): A book of poems and pictures for globe trotters.* Cambridge: Candlewick.

Nordine, K. (2000). *Colors.* New York: Harcourt.

Nye, N. S. (2000). *Come with me: Poems for a journey.* New York: Greenwillow.

Philip, N. (Ed.) (1998). *War and the pity of war.* New York: Clarion.

Rogasky, B. (Comp.) (2001). *Leaf by leaf: Autumn poems.* New York: Scholastic.

Singer, M. (2000). *On the same day in March: A tour of the world's weather.* New York: HarperCollins.

Stevenson, J. (1999). *Candy corn.* New York: Greenwillow.

Updike, J. (1999). *A child's calendar.* New York: Holiday House.

Wong, J. (1999a). *Behind the wheel: Poems about driving*. New York: McElderry. YA

Wong, J. (1999b). *The rainbow hand: Poems about mothers and children*. New York: McElderry.

African and African-American Collections and Anthologies

Dunbar, P. L. (2000). *Jump back honey: The poems of Paul Lawrence Dunbar* (Comp. by Ashley Bryan & Andrea Davis Pinkney). New York: Jump at the Sun/Hyperion.

Lewis, J. P. (2000). *Freedom like sunlight: Praisesongs for Black Americans*. New York: Creative Editions.

Rochelle, B. (Comp.) (2001). *Words with wings: A treasury of African American poetry and art*. New York: Amistad/HarperCollins.

Steptoe, J. (Ill.) (1998). *In daddy's arms I am tall: African Americans celebrating fathers*. New York: Lee & Low.

Unobagha, U. (2000). *Off to the sweet shores of Africa and other talking drum rhymes*. New York: Chronicle.

Asian and Asian-American Collections and Anthologies

Ho, M. (1996). *Maples in the mist: Children's poems from the Tang dynasty*. New York: Lothrop.

Wong, J. S. (1996). *A suitcase of seaweed and other poems*. New York: McElderry/Simon.

Wong, J. S. (2000). *Night garden: Poems from the world of dreams*. New York: McElderry.

Hispanic and Caribbean Collections and Anthologies

Berry, J. (1999). *Isn't my name magical: Sister and brother poems*. New York: Simon & Schuster.

Medina, J. (1999). *My name is Jorge: On both sides of the river*. New York: Wordsong.

Mora, P. (Ed.) (2001). *Love to Mama: A tribute to mothers*. New York: Lee & Low.

Native American Collections and Anthologies

Bruchac, J. (1996). *The circle of thanks: Native American poems and songs of thanksgiving*. New York: BridgeWater.

Castillo, A. (2000). *My daughter, my son, the eagle, the dove: An Aztec chant*. New York: Dutton.

When the rain sings: Poems by young Native Americans. (1999). (Comp. by the National Museum of the American Indian). New York: Simon & Schuster.

— ◆ —

REFLECTION   How could you celebrate National Poetry Month (every April) this year? For more information, contact the Academy of American Poets, 548 Broadway, Suite 1208, New York, NY 10012–3250.

SUMMARY

Poetry, at the heart of literature for children, beats strongly in our contemporary lives. A great variety of subject matter for all ages, from the youngest listeners to the most sophisticated readers, can be found in many excellent collections and anthologies. The writings of modern poets, coming from urban and rural multicultural perspectives, are easily accessed in libraries, schools, and bookstores.

This chapter presented a wide range of children's poetry and identified notable poets and some of their well-known works. A brief look at the beginnings of modern poetry began this discussion, followed by an attempt to define poetry or at least—because a precise definition proved to be elusive—to provide a recounting of characteristics of poetry.

Poetry is characterized by qualities of brevity, emotional intensity, rhythmic and figurative language, and a structure that marks its difference from prose. An analogy might be "Poetry is to language as ballet is to dance." That is, poetry is language at its most precise, at its most controlled, sophisticated, symbolic, and intense. Ballet, of all the dance forms, also seems to be very controlled, precise, sophisticated, and intense. Both demand a willingness to soar beyond the usual and the easy, with great rewards possible at the end.

Subgenres of poetry described and exemplified in this chapter were ballads, narrative poetry, lyrical poetry, free verse, haiku and tanka, limericks, concrete poetry, cinquain, diamante, and formulaic patterns. Many of the examples were drawn from notable contemporary poets' work, and these poets, many of whom have won awards, were listed so that their contributions can be studied and appreciated.

IMPLICATIONS FOR INSTRUCTION

In this section, you have a chance to reflect on the ideas, definitions, and examples presented in this chapter. In addition, projects and activities with children are described, and you are encouraged to try them.

Projects

1. Check out websites related to children's poetry. Use your favorite poet's name as a key word and see if he/she has a web page. If possible, create a web page for your favorite poet(s). Write a short biography and include a

list of poetry, with clip art, that you think is appropriate. Incorporate this web page into your own personal web page if you have one.

2. Begin your own poetry file. Collect poems that appeal to you, and categorize them into topics that are relevant to your use. You may want to collect "weather" poems, "animal" poems, "peace" poems, or "Vermont" poems. Whatever you choose, an important criterion for selection is your own satisfaction with the poem for your own needs.

3. Organize a poetry-reading session with colleagues or friends. Rehearse, then read aloud some of your favorite poems, or write some of your own. Add a musical background or combine your talents with another performance artist.

4. Find out if your state arts council, humanities council, or another group will help sponsor a poet in the school or classroom. Many states offer opportunities for "artists in residence" at elementary schools, middle schools, high schools, or community centers, and many poets, artists, dancers, and musicians are eager to share their talents with children.

5. What kind of poems do children prefer? Conduct an experiment with a group of children by selecting some poems and judging the group's response to them. See Children's Poetry Preferences, earlier in this chapter, for studies that demonstrate a methodology to measure preferences.

6. Poetry for and by children with special learning or physical difficulties is sadly lacking. Could you find suitable poetry for some special children you know? This is a delicate task. You should know the child very well because you don't want to be too obvious with some, nor too indirect with others. See Activity 5 for the Primary level for one example of matching a book about a special learner to a poem.

Activities for the Primary Level

1. Do some "word gathering" poetry. Elicit from a group of young children "snow" words or "green" words, or pick another topic. You may be surprised at the variety you hear. When many words have been gathered and listed, you and the children can categorize them. The natural rhythm of language will be apparent when the categories are read aloud. The topic word becomes the title of the poem, and the last line can be anything to summarize the activity.

2. Read a poem aloud every day to young children. Don't isolate poetry into a certain time period or subject area, but instead draw from your poetry file favorite poems that fit into every subject or celebration.

3. Find poems that can be illustrated, or set some to music, drums, or movement. If you read Douglas Florian's *Mammalabilia*, what kind of music or accompaniment would complement each animal? Or, make a scrapbook with each page including the poem and artwork about the poem.

4. Encourage your children to write cinquains, diamantes, or "I wish . . ." poems. Young children often believe that poetry must rhyme, so the structure

of these forms allows them to see poetry in a new way. Playing with word poems can begin by finding words (adjectives) that use the letters of a person's first name to describe that person and then combining the result with the person's self-portrait:

V   vivacious

A   alert

L   lanky

E   easy

R   running

I   inspiring

E   ecstatic

5. Combine poetry and prose. For example, if you are reading aloud *Crow Boy* (Yashima, 1955), a book about a special learner, also present a poem that expresses what the main character might feel. *Crows,* by David McCord (Dunning, Lueders, & Smith, 1966), is a poem that Chibi would like. For character development in a novel, consider with children which poem might describe a character, or might have been written by a character, or might express what the main character is feeling. This activity works well in the middle grades, too. Can you think of some examples?

Activities for the Intermediate and Middle Levels

1. *Word Dance* is a nonprofit quarterly magazine that spotlights poetry, short stories, haiku, and other writing by students. Write for a submission form and deadlines: Playful Productions, Inc., PO Box 10804, Wilmington, DE 19850, USA, or check out www.worddance.com. Encourage elementary, middle school, and high school students to write, and help them submit their poems.

2. Children are using the Internet to write and send poems. Pen pal relationships may be forged across great distances with electronic communication, and the Internet makes it more exciting.

3. Following is an example of a class poem in free verse in which children described a raindrop:

Poetry Splash

> What is a raindrop?
>   A raindrop is . . .
>   wet water,
>   cold, maybe warm,
>   a signal to put on your raincoat,
>   a drink to a butterfly.

Everyone contributes an idea, and a class poem emerges.

4. Alfred Noyes' dramatic poem, *The Highwayman,* has inspired artwork in three different styles. With your students, compare the illustrations of Charles Keeping, which won the Kate Greenaway Medal in Britain (Noyes, 1981), Charles Mikolaycak (Noyes, 1983), and Neil Waldman (Noyes, 1990). Which do you prefer? Which do your students prefer? How do you describe the styles?

5. What music would you choose to accompany one of the poems found in this chapter, such as *Who Has Seen the Wind?* or *The Pied Piper of Hamelin,* or another of your choice? Performance possibilities abound with poems from Arnold Adoff's *Touch the Poem* (2000).

6. Choral reading is another way to enjoy poetry with a class. Two-by-two oral reading is another. If your students are new to it, *Joyful Noise: Poems for Two Voices* (Fleischman, 1988) provides a great introduction to two-by-two oral reading. Fleischman's more recent book, *Big Talk: Poems for Four Voices* (2000), illustrated by Beppe Giacobbe, features choral reading in four parts. A color-coded staff directs the voices to a particular line, and the result is a great read-aloud!

REFERENCES

Poetry and Children's Works

Adoff, A. (2000). *Touch the poem.* (Ill. by Lisa Desimini). New York: Blue Sky/Scholastic.

Blake, W. (1789/1997). *Listen and read: Songs of innocence and experience.* New York: Dover.

Browning, R. (1842/1999). *The pied piper of Hamelin.* (Ill. by Bud Peen). New York: Abrams.

Carroll, L. (1871/1977). *Through the looking glass.* New York: St. Martin's.

Cooper, I., Freeburg, R. E., Imig, W., Nordholm, H., Rhea, R., & Serposs, E. H. (1959). *Music in our life.* Morristown, NJ: Silver Burdett Co.

Crist-Evans, C. (2000). *Moon over Tennessee: A boy's Civil War journal.* (Ill. by Bonnie Christensen). Boston: Houghton Mifflin.

de la Mare, W. (1913/1989). *Peacock pie.* New York: Holt.

Dunning, S., Lueders, E., & Smith, H. (Eds.). (1966). *Reflections on a gift of watermelon pickle.* Glenview, IL: Scott, Foresman.

Fleischman, P. (1988). *Joyful noise: Poems for two voices.* New York: Harper.

Fleischman, P. (2000). *Big talk: Poems for four voices.* (Ill. by Beppe Giacobbe). Cambridge, MA: Candlewick.

Florian, D. (2000). *Mammalabilia.* New York: Harcourt.

Graham, J. B. (1999). *Flicker flash.* (Ill. by Nancy Davis). Boston: Houghton Mifflin.

Grossman, B. (2001). *Timothy Tunny swallowed a bunny.* (Ill. by Kevin Hawkes). New York: Geringer/HarperCollins.

Hesse, K. (1997). *Out of the dust.* New York: Scholastic.

Hughes, L. (1994a). *The collected poems of Langston Hughes.* New York: Knopf.

Hughes, L. (1994b). *The dream keeper and other poems.* New York: Knopf.

Janeczko, P. B. (Sel.) (2000). *Stone bench in an empty park.* (Photography by Henri Silberman). New York: Orchard.

Janeczko, P. B. (Comp.) (2001). *A poke in the I: A collection of concrete poems.* (Ill. by Chris Raschka). Cambridge: Candlewick.

Kennedy, X. J., & Kennedy, D. (1999). *Knock at a star* (rev. ed.). (Ill. by Andrew Portwood). Boston: Little, Brown.

Koertge, R. (2001). *The brimstone journals.* Cambridge, MA: Candlewick.

Lear, E. (1871/1998). *The owl and the pussycat.* New York: HarperCollins.

Lear, E. (1846/1991). *Nonsense poems of Edward Lear.* (Ill. by Leslie Brook). New York: Clarion.

Lee, D. (2001). *Bubblegum delicious.* (Ill. by David McPhail). New York: HarperCollins.

Longfellow, H. W. (1983). *Hiawatha.* (Ill. by Susan Jeffers). New York: Dial.

Longfellow, H. W. (2000). *The midnight ride of Paul Revere.* (Ill. by Jeffrey Thompson). New York: National.

Merriam, E. (1962). *There is no rhyme for silver.* New York: Atheneum.

Milne, A. A. (1982). *When we were very young.* New York: Yearling.

Moore, C. (1822/1990). *Twas the night before Christmas*. New York: Clarion.

Nelson, M. (2001). *Carver: A life in poems*. New York: Front Street.

Noyes, A. (1913/1981). *The highwayman*. (Ill. by Charles Keeping). London: Oxford.

Noyes, A. (1913/1983). *The highwayman*. (Ill. by Charles Mikolaycak). New York: Lothrop, Lee, & Shepard.

Noyes, A. (1913/1990). *The highwayman*. (Ill. by Neil Waldman). New York: Harcourt Brace Jovanovich.

Paul, A. W. (1999). *All by herself: 14 girls who made a difference*. New York: Harcourt/Browndeer.

Prelutsky, J. (1984). *The new kid on the block*. New York: Greenwillow.

Prelutsky, J. (1990). *Something big has been here*. New York: Greenwillow.

Rossetti, C. (1952). *Sing song*. New York: Macmillan.

Schertle, A. (1999). *A lucky thing*. (Ill. by Wendell Minor). New York: Browndeer.

Service, R. W. (1987). *The cremation of Sam McGee*. New York: Greenwillow.

Siegmeister, E. (arr.) (1964). *The Joan Baez songbook*. New York: Ryerson Music Publishers.

Silverstein, S. (1974). *Where the sidewalk ends*. New York: Harper & Row.

Silverstein, S. (1996). *Falling up*. New York: HarperCollins.

Smith, W. J. (2000). *Around my room*. (Ill. by Erik Blegvad). New York: Farrar, Straus & Giroux.

Stevenson, R. L. (1997). *A child's garden of verse*. New York: Victor Gollancz.

Willard, N. (1981). *A visit to William Blake's inn*. New York: Harcourt Brace Jovanovich.

Wolff, V. E. (2001). *True believer*. New York: Atheneum.

Yashima, T. (1955). *Crow boy*. New York: Viking.

Professional Works

Carpenter, H., & Prichard, M. (1984). *The Oxford companion to children's literature*. New York: Oxford University Press.

Clark, L. (1983). Poetry unfettered. In J. May (Ed.), *Children and their literature: A readings book* (pp. 133–137). West Lafayette, IN: Children's Literature Association.

Esbensen, B. (1975). *A celebration of bees*. Minneapolis, MN: Winston.

Fisher, C., & Natarella, M. A. (1982). Young children's preferences in poetry: A national survey of first, second, and third graders. *Research in the Teaching of English, 16,* 339–353.

Frye, N., Baker, S., & Perkins, G. (1985). *The Harper handbook to literature*. New York: Harper & Row.

Hayward, C. (1996, May). Lear's nonsense. *Book Links, 5,* 43–50.

Hillman, C. (1995). *Poetry instruction and assessment in the middle grades*. Unpublished thesis for Master of Arts in Education, Saint Michael's College, Vermont.

Hopkins, L. B. (1993). American poetry for children: The 20th century. *Fanfare, 1,* 75–82.

Horning, K. T. (1997). *From cover to cover: Evaluating and reviewing children's books*. New York: HarperCollins.

Kennedy, X. J. (1990). *An introduction to poetry* (7th ed.). New York: HarperCollins.

Koch, K. (1970). *Wishes, lies, and dreams*. New York: Chelsea.

Kutiper, K. S. (1985). *A survey of the adolescent poetry preferences of seventh, eighth, and ninth graders*. Unpublished Ed.D. dissertation, University of Houston, Texas.

Livingston, M. C. (1996). The poem on page 81. In S. Egoff, G. Stubbs, R. Ashley, & W. Sutton (Eds.), *Only Connect* (3rd ed., pp. 214–224). Toronto: Oxford University Press.

Lukens, R. (1999). *A critical handbook of children's literature* (6th ed.). New York: Longman.

Marcus, S. (1992). Machinery for the muse: Computers and poetry. In Duke, C., & Jacobsen, S. (Eds.), *Poets' perspectives: Reading, writing and teaching poetry* (pp. 179–202). Portsmouth, NH: Boynton/Cook.

Schneider, D. (2001). Something beautiful: Reading picture books, writing poetry. *Book Links, 10* (5) (April/May), 50–55.

Terry, A. (1974). *Children's poetry preferences*. Urbana, IL: National Council of Teachers of English.

Worth, V. (1992). Capturing objects in words. *The Horn Book, LXVIII,* 568–569.

Additional Resources

Cullinan, B. E., Scala, M. C., & Shroeder, V. C. (1995). *Three voices: An invitation to poetry across the curriculum*. Portland, ME: Stenhouse.

Thirty-three proven strategies are presented here for grades K–8, along with hundreds of brief suggestions.

Grimes, N. (2000). The power of poetry. *Book Links, 9 (4),* (March 2000), 38–40.

Excerpts from Grimes's talk at the Center for the Book in the Library of Congress address the importance of poetry and the need to include it in our lives.

Taachi, M. J. (2000). Teens movin' with poetry. In *Book Links, 9 (4),* (March 2000), 38–40.

In New York City, workshops at the public library attract teens, and their language turns into poetry.

CHAPTER 8

Imaginary Worlds of Fantasy

INTRODUCTION AND RESPONSE

In fantasy, authors draw their inspiration and creative impulses from the real world, referred to as the *primary world,* or they imagine a secondary world in which fantastic characters appear or events occur. Children's literature features some well-known secondary worlds: Oz, Wonderland, Redwall, Narnia, dollhouses, gardens, and so on. Lloyd Alexander, a well-known author of children's fantasy, says, "Fantasy deals with the impossible, not the illogical. Creating a secondary world where the impossible becomes ordinary does not carry with it a license to do as one pleases. In its conception and in its deep substructures, the fantasy world must, if anything, be more carefully rationalized than the real world", (Alexander, 1987, p. 196). The secondary world must be logical, even recognizable, with an inner consistency to its natural laws.

Sometimes the primary and secondary worlds coexist, side by side, with the fantasy world intersecting occasionally with the real world. This coexistence is fully realized in J. K. Rowling's chronicle of Harry Potter. Hogwarts—the magical school and seat of power, illusion, sorcery, and learning—is a part of the British countryside. It appears in another form, possibly a castle ruin, to "muggles" (i.e., non-magical people), but to Harry and other wizards, Hogwarts is real, tangible, and connected to places we can recognize.

A writer's work is considered to be within the fantasy genre if at least one element is outside the realm of possibility (Cameron, 1962). Fantasy is a careful blend of realism and impossibility, with fantasy elements closely related to natural occurrences, but with a unique aspect of their own. In animal fantasies such as *Fire*

Bringer (Clement-Davies, 2000), the fantastic element is the humanized deer. Rannoch, Willow, Thistle, Sgorr, and other woodland animals speak, share their feelings, plan for the future, and solve problems like human beings. However, they retain most of the characteristics of their species—size, shape, instinct, and habitat—in the primary world.

In the well-known fantasies for children listed in Figure 8.1, consider the fantastic element present in each that allows the story to fit into the genre of modern fantasy. Why are these works considered to be fantasies?

Understanding and anticipating unique aspects of fantasy will help readers comprehend and enjoy this sometimes abstract genre. By definition, fantasy is more abstract than realistic fiction. All fiction requires a suspension of disbelief to enter the time, place, and circumstances that an author creates. However, fantasy pushes the boundaries of realism, as it invents and constructs metaphors for the real world. Fantasy demands more from readers—more attention, more suspension of disbelief, and more imagination.

Figure 8.1
Identifying elements
of fantasy

Title	**Fantasy Element**
Tuck Everlasting	
Harry Potter and the Sorcerer's Stone	
Charlotte's Web	

This chapter describes modern fantasy as it has evolved from traditional literature. Its characters, themes, plots, and settings enrich children's literature and delight children, showing them the empowerment of imagination and story. After a brief look at the development of modern fantasy in the last century, the chapter continues with a closer look at each of the subgenres of fantasy, followed by an evaluation scheme and notable authors.

REFLECTION   If you were creating a fantasy world, what would it be like? What kinds of creatures or characters would populate the world? Who or what would run the world? What logic, or illogic, would characterize it?

HISTORY OF MODERN FANTASY

Fantasy for children has its roots in traditional literature. From the talking animals of fables to spells of magic and incantation, traditional literature provides imaginary settings and events that are recalled in modern fantasy. Likewise, characters from traditional literature, such as fairies, ogres, mermaids, and giants, appear in modern fantasy. Folktales, anonymous and deeply rooted in a folk culture, preceded and gave impetus to modern fantasy.

In the 19th century, a transition between the shorter fairy tale and modern novels of fantasy can be seen in two major contributions to children's literature. First, *The Three Bears* by Robert Southey (1837/1998) was so similar to folktales that its origin continues to be in doubt. However, in Southey's version, which immediately popularized the story, an old woman trespasses into the bears' house; later versions substituted a young girl named Silver-Hair, who finally became Goldilocks by the turn of the 20th century (Opie & Opie, 1974).

Second, Hans Christian Andersen's poetic, ephemeral stories blended successfully the two strains of modern fantasy and traditional folklore. Translated into English and published in 1846 under the title *Wonderful Stories for Children* (now *Andersen's Fairy Tales,* 1957), these modern, literary fairy tales evoked contemporary issues as well as timeless ones. "The Little Mermaid," "The Ugly Duckling," and "The Emperor's New Clothes" are examples of the many classics by Andersen.

The true beginning of modern fantasy in children's literature coincided with the publication in the early 1860s of Lewis Carroll's *Alice's Adventures in Wonderland* and Charles Kingsley's *Water Babies* (Townsend, 1987). Their appearance ushered in a remarkable period in which children's books began to achieve a certain status in the literary world and grew more plentiful to serve a rising middle class. As the better-known of the two, *Alice,* with its absurdist logic, created a compelling secondary world, a "wonderland" in which the succession of fantastic creatures provided a counterpoint to the always practical and forthright Alice. The Rev. Charles Dodgson, better known as Lewis Carroll, a shy professor of mathematics at Oxford University, wrote *Alice* and its sequel, *Through the Looking Glass* (1871), for the daughter of a dean at the college.

Another minister, George MacDonald, also had a profound effect on modern fantasy. In his allegorical quest–romances, which included *At the Back of the North Wind* (1871) and *The Princess and the Goblin* (1872), MacDonald helped to establish the modern tradition known as sacred or ethical fantasy (Moss & Stott, 1986), in which themes of eternal goodness and truth prevail. The high fantasies of C. S. Lewis and J. R. R. Tolkien, with their strong themes of goodness overpowering evil, owe a debt to MacDonald's fantastic stories of quest–romance.

"By the end of the nineteenth century fantasy as a literary genre had gained full acceptance" (Levin, 1987, p. 167). E. Nesbit's richly textured fantasies, such as *The Enchanted Castle* (1907/1992) and Rudyard Kipling's animal fantasies were immensely popular on both sides of the Atlantic. Carlo Collodi created *Pinocchio* (1889/1987), an animated toy fantasy, while folklore from Russia, Eastern Europe, Scandinavia, the British Isles, Asia, and other parts of the world was collected and retold in updated publications (see Chapter 4).

Considered to be the first modern fantasy in the United States, *The Wonderful Wizard of Oz* (Baum, 1900/1998) achieved popularity but no critical acclaim. When compared with other famous fantasies of the time, such as *The Wind in the Willows* (Grahame, 1908/1984) and *Peter Pan* (Barrie, 1904/1991), Baum's work was thought to lack coherence, but subsequent years have softened that judgment.

No history of modern fantasy would be complete without acknowledging the huge influence of J. K. Rowling's *Harry Potter* series at the end of the 20th century. It is truly a phenomenon in the publishing industry to have a "children's" fantasy hero, Harry Potter, grace the covers of *Time* (September 20, 1999, vol. 154, no. 12) and *Newsweek* (July 17, 2000, vol. 136, no. 3), as well as articles in major newspapers and scholarly journals all over the English-speaking world, and top the bestseller list. Adults as well as children embrace this unlikely lad and his friends and thrill to the extraordinary ability of Rowling to conceptualize and write a humorous, spine-tingling, and poignant series of possibly seven books.

How do the *Harry Potter* books strike such emotional depth in the reading public? First, Rowling is a gifted writer who writes from a deeply formed knowledge of the fantasy genre. She knows the works of the important authors: Lewis, Tolkien, Cooper, MacDonald, Andersen, and others who have used imaginative literature to invoke our sense of justice and goodness. She writes unerringly of bad forces, bad people and bad wizards, and is not afraid to present terror and then hold it in check.

Drawing by J. R. (9th grade) "The Whomping Willow" from *Harry Potter and the Chamber of Secrets.*

Rowling knows just when to add a light touch, and how long to push the brutality before Percy, or Mrs. Weasley, Albus Dumbledore, Hagrid, or even Aunt Marge diverts us from the abyss of hopelessness and evil. The balance of good and evil has to be constantly monitored, and in her books it is.

Second, Rowling's creativity, invention, and linguistic word play are quite beyond anything published in children's literature since *Alice in Wonderland* (and perhaps these books surpass even that). Examples can be found on every page of the series: portraits with moving and speaking characters, the cover of the *Book of Monsters* with real monsters, Peeves the Poltergeist, the Whomping Willow, Blast-ended Skrewts, and more. Rowling has invented new species and memorable words: muggles; Diagon Alley; floo-powder; quidditch; the monetary system of galleons, silver sickles, and knuts; squibs; portkey; and parselmouth. These terms are picturesque, as J. R. demonstrates in his drawing of the anthropomorphic Whomping Willow.

Rowling has a clear sense of audience. It is interesting that she uses adolescent language—along with an adolescent sense of humor, code of honor, and the loyalties and motivations of children—while paradoxically the books have been found to be appealing to adults.

Last, the buoyancy and humor, and sheer likeability of the characters—Harry, Ron, Hermione, and others—creates a bond with readers who want to know Harry Potter and his world. We care about him; we sense his purpose and make it our own. His enemies are our enemies.

The *Harry Potter* books could be considered high fantasy because of characteristics described relative to that subgenre. Harry is an orphan, he has a mission/quest to rid the world of evil, he has a wise mentor, and his world has the medieval trappings of heraldic crests, castles, chivalric codes of honor, and ancient magic. However, sometimes classification systems do not do justice to the complex nature of fantastic literature, and Rowling's books transcend easy classification because of their complex and compelling nature. To date, five books, plus movie and other accompanying marketable items, are available. The books are *Harry Potter and the Sorcerer's Stone* (1997), *Harry Potter and the Chamber of Secrets* (1999a), *Harry Potter and the Prisoner of Azkaban* (1999b), *Harry Potter and the Goblet of Fire* (2000), and possibly, *Harry Potter and the Order of the Phoenix* in 2002 or 2003.

REFLECTION Are you aware of the controversies surrounding the *Harry Potter* series? If so, do you agree or disagree with the accusations? If not, what would you predict they are?

Some Classics of Modern Fantasy

The Wonderful Wizard of Oz, L. F. Baum (1900)

Peter Pan, J. Barrie (1904)

The Wind in the Willows, K. Grahame (1908)

**The Voyages of Dr. Dolittle,* H. Lofting (1922)

Winnie-the-Pooh, A. A. Milne (1926)

Mary Poppins, P. L. Travers (1934)

The Hobbit, J. R. R. Tolkien (1937)

Pippi Longstocking, A. Lindgren (1950)

The Lion, the Witch and the Wardrobe, C. S. Lewis (1950)

Charlotte's Web, E. B. White (1952)

The Borrowers, M. Norton (1953)

**A Wrinkle in Time,* M. L'Engle (1962)

**The High King,* L. Alexander (1968)

A Wizard of Earthsea, U. Le Guin (1968)

**The Grey King,* S. Cooper (1975)

Eva, P. Dickinson (1988)

**The Ear, the Eye, and the Arm,* N. Farmer (1994)

Harry Potter and the Goblet of Fire, J. K. Rowling (2000)

*Newbery Award winner or honor book

REFLECTION   Is modern fantasy a popular genre today? Do some children prefer it? What kind of children are drawn to fantasy and when? Did you enjoy fantasy as a child?

SUBGENRES OF MODERN FANTASY

Modern fantasy consists of a great variety of stories, a variety that begs for some kind of classification. Subgenres form naturally around common characteristics in this diverse genre. High fantasy, time fantasy, and science-fiction fantasy seem clear-cut, with common aspects, usually relating to a secondary world, uniting each of them. Animal fantasies have as their common aspect and fantasy element the **personification,** or anthropomorphizing, of animals. Extraordinary characters and inventions is a subgenre that includes people who can perform impossible feats, inventions imbued with magical power, animated toys, tiny people (leprechauns, sprites, and others), large people (giants), and others whose appearance marks them as mystics. Extraordinary characters could also include ghosts, vampires, ghouls, mermaids, the "faery folk," and other terrible and wonderful beings.

Although categories will help in classifying literature, some stories may overlap into two subgenres, and some into no subgenre at all. Categorization should not become the purpose of studying literature, but a means of studying, comparing, and enjoying (see Figure 8.2).

Animal Fantasies

Animal fantasies come from one of the oldest forms of literature, the beast tales (Swinfen, 1984). Fables, folktales, and other forms of traditional literature showed human affinity to animals in the many depictions of anthropomorphism. In traditional literature, animals were often seen as guardians of a secret wisdom, the wisdom of Earth in its natural state.

In modern fantasy, the best examples of children's literature show a careful blend of human characteristics with animal qualities. It has been said that E. B. White

Figure 8.2
Subgenres of
modern fantasy

Subgenres of Modern Fantasy
Animal fantasies
High fantasies
Time fantasies
Science-fiction fantasies
Extraordinary characters and inventions

studied spiders for three years before he wrote *Charlotte's Web,* which could account for his finding the perfect balance of Charlotte's ruthlessness in some things and compassion in others.

Modern animal fantasies are most often set in the primary world and show animals in a quest for a better life. Sometimes the quest entails a band of small animals seeking to overpower larger, evil adversaries and to restore, or create, a more just society. Thus animal fantasies satirize modern predicaments today, such as our political struggles to reach an ideal state. *Mrs. Frisby and the Rats of NIMH* (O'Brien, 1971), an animal fantasy awarded the Newbery Medal, is such a story. The astounding intelligence mistakenly given to the rats while they were subjects of scientific experiments at the National Institutes of Mental Health gave them delusional ideas about their self-worth and power.

Brian Jacques, popular author of the *Redwall* fantasies, has recently published the thirteenth in that series, *Lord Brocktree* (2000), which retains the energy and coy cleverness of the others. Illustrated by Fangorn, the book's many characters, plot, setting, and theme (vanquishing evil), as well as foods and various British accents, form a coherent whole and a ripping good story. The badger Lord Brocktree and Dottie, a beautiful and courageous hare, journey to Salamandastron to free Stonepaw and his band of warriors entrapped by Ungatt Trunn. As usual, several subplots are woven into the story, with Lord Brocktree, Dottie, and Stonepaw clearly victorious at the end.

REFLECTION   The *Redwall* series, *Mrs. Frisby and the Rats of NIMH* (the movie version is *Mrs. Brisby and the Rats of NIMH*), and *Fire Bringer* each contain bloody battles in the final climax, as do many animal fantasies. Similarly, *Charlotte's Web* is sometimes criticized for its theme of death and resurrection. Do you think animal fantasies contain more violence than other fantasy forms? Do animal characters seem to be more ruthless than humans?

In addition to the all-animal fantasy are stories in which human beings and animals interact. *Stuart Little* (White, 1945) gained renewed popularity with a recent movie. Stuart, a mouse, becomes part of a human family and convincingly melds fantasy and reality in his escapades. In *I Was a Third Grade Spy* (Auch, 2001), the spy is Arful, a dog who speaks. Arful spies on the girls for his owner, Brian, and Brian's friends, Josh and Dougie. Chapters alternate between Arful's reporting on the girls' talent-show entry and Josh's view of events. These books illustrate humorous and positive relationships between animals and humans.

Animal fantasies, whether they are set in the real world or in a secondary world, allow us to regard history or contemporary life through the eyes of a being similar to us, yet distinctively different. This perspective—from an animal's point of view—challenges our prejudices and causes us to reexamine our relationships with the animal kingdom. After knowing Wilbur from *Charlotte's Web* or *Babe* (King-Smith, 1985), the gallant pig who fulfilled his destiny as a sheepdog, do we not regard pigs as smarter, more caring, and more interesting? Whimsical, realistic, or allegorical, the best animal fantasies combine humanitarian ideals with a good story.

Recent and Recommended Animal Fantasies

Ereth's Birthday, Avi (2000)

The Mouse and His Child, R. Hoban (1967/2001)

The Dark Portal, R. Jarvis (2000)

Sunwing, K. Oppel (2000)

The High Rise Private Eyes: The Case of the Puzzling Possum, C. Rylant (2001)

High Fantasy

The term *high fantasy* has been coined fairly recently. Although we don't know who first combined the words *high* and *fantasy,* we do know that this subgenre evolved from an old form of literature, the medieval romance of the 11th and 12th centuries. In this form, legendary exploits of King Arthur and his knights heroically questing for the Holy Grail are given shape in a literary world. *High* has come to signify a fantasy that resides in a secondary world marked by a medieval ethos of chivalry, honor, and codes of behavior. Perhaps it also refers to the seriousness of purpose and lofty idealism of the hero's quest, which is essentially to restore the world to its innocent, Garden-of-Eden state. This secondary world, magical and at risk, propels theme, characters' actions, and outcomes. It is sometimes called a *perilous realm* because of the danger and suspense. Unicorns, dragons, potions, runes, and magical swords are common in this realm.

Secondary worlds are crucial aspects of high fantasy; indeed most of the great fantasies are named after their worlds—Narnia, Middle-Earth, Earthsea, and Prydain, to mention a few. Each is the central symbol of the fantasy and, to encourage a reader to step into the world, these secondary worlds must have logic and an inner consistency that permits belief. They are close enough to the primary world to allow identification, yet far enough away to allow the creation of fantastic creatures and unlikely occurrences.

Because modern high fantasy relates to an older form, the romance, certain characteristics prevail:

- The hero or heroine is an orphan, or of lowly status.
- A destiny is placed on the hero or heroine by a wise, older mentor or an enigmatic character.
- The destiny takes the form of a quest in which the hero or heroine must find something or do something involving danger and hardship, usually at great cost and personal sacrifice.
- The destiny, after it is accepted by the hero or heroine, is imbued with great moral fervor, because a clear distinction exists between right and wrong, good and evil.

- The secondary world in which this happens is a medieval world, marked by medieval dress and weaponry, castles, a "simple" way of life, and no technology.
- The climax of the quest is an apocalyptic battle between a small number of "good" forces led by the hero or heroine and a huge army of evil forces.
- Characters are flat (except for the hero or heroine); personalities are not developed because action and theme are most important.

High fantasy is by its nature philosophical, allowing an author to define and separate goodness and evil. Moral dimensions of high fantasy build on ethical and sacred foundations. The main character is a common person who is called on to perform beyond his or her capabilities and somehow summons the strength to do it. Invited by a herald to do a task that is seemingly impossible, the main character often is persuaded by a bit of magic. High fantasy gives us all hope that we, too, can rise beyond our capabilities to achieve our hopes and expectations.

The works of MacDonald, Lewis, and Tolkien defined and heavily influenced this subgenre. As a medieval scholar and a Christian, C. S. Lewis drew especially

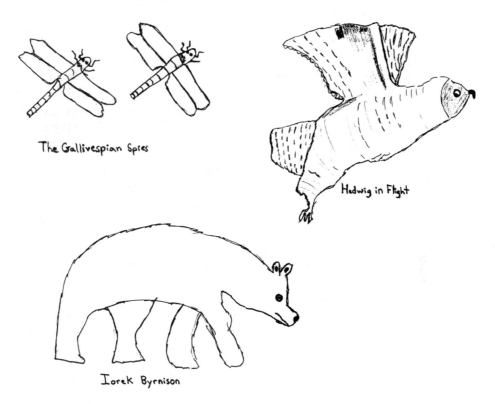

The Gallivespian Spies

Hedwig in Flight

Iorek Byrnison

Drawings by John William (8th grade):
The Gallivespian Spies from *The Amber Spyglass*
Iorek Byrnison from *The Golden Compass*
Hedwig in Flight From the *Harry Potter books.*

evocative imagery from biblical and literary sources for his *Narnian Chronicles,* of which *The Lion, the Witch and the Wardrobe* (1950/1988) is first in a series of seven.

Philip Pullman created the most complex, daunting, and ultimately rewarding high fantasies of the previous ten years with *His Dark Materials* series—*The Golden Compass* (1996), *The Subtle Knife* (1997), and the breathtaking *The Amber Spyglass* (2000). These books lead us into parallel worlds inhabited by people and their animal familiars: flying witches, talking–thinking animals, tiny creatures (Gallivespians), horrible monsters (cliffghasts), bear-Kings, spectors, mulefa, and many more. These fantastic creatures stimulate the imagination, as student John William demonstrates in his drawings of Iorek Byrnison and the Gallivespians, as well as Hedwig from *Harry Potter.*

Pullman's first book focuses on Lyra Belacqua, a feisty streetwise (and presumably parentless, although when we find out who her parents are, it would be better not to have any) young girl who lives with scholars in a pseudo–Oxford College. Lyra has a "daemon," as does everyone in her world, who can mirror her thoughts and emotions and act as her conscience on occasion. Before Lyra's puberty, the daemon can change shape and form, assuming an animal form such as a moth or an ermine. Lyra becomes the possessor of the golden compass and realizes its value but doesn't know how to read it. Powerful forces are determined to gain control of the compass and eventually subjugate the world, but Lyra escapes to the North. She is searching for her father, a scientist–philosopher who is seeking to understand elementary particles called "dust." She is running from her mother who represents an inquisition-like arm of the Church. The first book ends as Lyra watches a city form in the sky behind the aurora borealis. Her father climbs toward the sunlit city of another world, and Lyra follows him.

In the second book, Will Parry is pursued by sinister government agents because of the work his father has done with dust and parapsychology among arctic tribes. Will's world is much like ours, until he gains possession of a knife that cuts through the boundaries between worlds. When he meets Lyra, they search for his father and find him dying. His father articulates the series theme of the battle between good and evil, between reason and ignorance: "'There are two great powers . . . and they've been fighting ever since time began. . . . Every little increase in human freedom has been fought over ferociously between those who want us to know more and be wiser and stronger, and those who want us to obey and be humble and submit'" (Pullman, *The Subtle Knife,* 1997, p. 321).

The third book, eagerly awaited by Pullman fans, finds Lyra and Will battling the forces of evil led by the rebel angel Metatron. Meanwhile, in a seemingly unimportant subplot, scientist Dr. Mary Malone uses an amber spyglass to discern the properties of dust. After the apocalyptic battle with rogue angels and assorted renegades, Will and Lyra go back to the worlds they know best. Reuniting many characters from the first two books, and creating new scenarios, Pullman combines elements of science-fiction fantasy, time fantasy, and high fantasy. Like the *Harry Potter* series, these books are too complex and far-ranging to categorize easily. However, Lyra and Will share the characteristics of a high fantasy hero and heroine.

Also, theological questions arise in this fantasy series, as the three novels spark thought and discussion about the "meaning of God in an apparently godless world. Pullman confronts serious social issues with a humanistic perspective and imaginatively extends the assumptions and arguments of traditional theology" (Zipes, 2001, p. 5). In a featured review, Gregory Maguire acknowledges the connection between Pullman's series and the moral ferocity of C. S. Lewis, even when the stories seem to be satirizing organized religion (Maguire, 2000). Maguire comments on the breathtaking narrative force, sensuous description, and "counterpoints and overtones in this massive symphonic accomplishment" (Maguire, 2000, p. 737). It is a demanding, engrossing, not-for-the-faint-hearted trilogy that represents what literature for children, adolescents, *and* adults should be—thought-provoking, emotion-inducing, and unforgettable.

High fantasy includes other stories set in secondary worlds, with heroes and heroines, journeys, battles between good and evil, and magic as key ingredients. Another ingredient often employed, coming from folklore, is that inherent in each person and object is a true, secret name. Knowing the true name either gives one control over a person or object, or makes one responsible for that person or object.

Recent and Recommended High Fantasies

The Hidden Arrow of Maether, A. Beaverson (2000)

Island of the Aunts, E. Ibbotson (2000)

Parsifal's Page, G. Morris (2001)

Lirael, G. Nix (2001)

Squire: Protector of the Small, T. Pierce (2001)

Rowan of Rin, E. Rodda (2001)

I Am Morgan le Fay: A Tale from Camelot, N. Springer (2001)

Time Fantasy

The notion that time runs in several directions has long fascinated authors, scientists, and philosophers. Is time cyclical, or is it linear? Do other worlds exist in different time schemes? In time fantasies, authors construct *parallel worlds* that touch our primary world in magical places, allowing time travel back and forth. Another world existing simultaneously with ours presents all sorts of possibilities in literary invention. In addition, there are historical time fantasies, or time-warp fantasies, in which a character from the present can go back in time, or a character from long ago can come to the present. The author of such a fantasy must create an accurate historical period, as well as a logical method of transportation. An example of a humorous, popular time fantasy is the latest in the *Time Warp Trio* series by Jon Scieszka, *See You Later, Gladiator* (2000), illustrated by Adam McCauley. Its trio of three boys appeals to young readers in the second and third grades who find humor in these zany trips to the past.

Natalie Babbitt plays with the notion of time in *Tuck Everlasting* (1975/2000), in which members of the Tuck family gain immortality by drinking water from a spring in the woods near Winnie Foster's house. The story is told from Winnie's point of view and presents her thought that the absence of time in one's life is a burden too heavy to bear. At the end she chooses to forego an immortal life. Was her choice the better one?

Arguably one of the best time fantasies and the one against which others are invariably judged is *Tom's Midnight Garden* (Pearce, 1958). When his brother contracts measles, Tom is sent to live with a boring aunt and uncle. One sleepless night a clock in the hall strikes 13, and Tom slips out into the backyard, which has become a garden. He meets a little girl, Hatty, whose age changes in subsequent meetings in a changing garden. Puzzled, he finally solves the mystery with the help of an elderly woman who lives upstairs. Winner of the Carnegie Medal, this book will cause a reader to regard time differently ever after. As time shifts, its fluidity suggests to us thoughts of actions and consequences, growing older and younger, the way we use time in our lives, and time's relativity.

Recent and Recommended Time Fantasies

Babe and Me: A Baseball Card Adventure, D. Gutman (2000)

The Grave, J. Heneghan (2000)

Civil War on Sunday, M. P. Osborne (2000)

Be First in the Universe, S. Spinner (2000)

Roughing It on the Oregon Trail, D. Stanley (2000)

REFLECTION   If you were writing a time fantasy, would you create a parallel world, or would you go back into the past? What would be the problems inherent in each case?

Science-Fiction Fantasy

Science-fiction fantasy's secondary world is the future. More speculative and more fantastic than other subgenres, it has evolved from science fiction, itself a fairly recent subgenre in literature.

Science fiction as a literary form began with the publication of Mary Shelley's *Frankenstein* in 1817 (Carpenter & Prichard, 1984). By introducing medical technology with the transplanting of a human brain, Mary Shelley explored futuristic social ramifications of such science. Jules Verne launched this subgenre firmly with his fantastic and stunning predictions of future technology in *Voyage to the Center of the Earth* (1864/1978) and other books.

Science fiction, a blend of rational technological explanations and a literary form called **story,** seems a paradox. Can an author mix cold, hard facts and futuristic machinery into a compelling narrative with interesting characters? If the story contains too much science, it suffers; however, the story must accommodate scientific information unobtrusively. The best science fiction not only balances science and fiction but also provides a vision of the future. It can cause us to rethink gender roles, to plan for a just society, and to reshape institutions—and it can warn us what might happen if we do not change our habits.

Just such a story is *The Giver* (Lowry, 1993), a Newbery award winner set in a futuristic place, yet very realistic. The main character is selected to be the repository of memories for his community. Telepathically, this adolescent receives visions and narrations from an elder, the "Giver" of these memories, in this very controlled, close-knit society. Through these glimpses of time past, Jonah realizes the danger that the amoral values in his society represent. A chilling look at the future, written by a superb author well-known in children's literature, this book is popular and thought-provoking. The ambiguous ending raises questions, gives some people hope, and leads us to contemplate the decisions we make today. Lowry continues her speculation into the future with *Gathering Blue* (2000).

The distinction between science fiction and science-fiction fantasy is none too clear, but the latter is a more accessible, less hard-core version of science fiction. In science-fiction fantasy, less attention is paid to the accurate scientific explanation of phenomena and more attention is paid to the literary balance of story and phenomena. Whether a story is considered science fiction or science-fiction fantasy depends on the degree to which scientific data are based on fact or fiction. When the story is much more important than the science, it is appropriately called science-fiction fantasy. In most examples of this subgenre for children, the term *science-fiction fantasy* or simply *science fantasy* is used.

Technological invention attracts children who have grown up with Nintendo, Gameboys, the Internet, cell phones, and Palm Pilots, and who have understood almost from conception how to program a VCR. Recent books of science-fiction fantasy capitalize on interests of children and encourage them to think about solutions to today's problems, using technology as well as human creativity and intelligence. William Sleator is a popular and inventive author who specializes in technological fantasies drawing from science, mathematics, and physics. His recent *Marco's Millions* (2001) appeals to science-fiction enthusiasts.

John Marsden, an Australian author, has created a science-fiction fantasy for older readers with *Darkness Be My Friend* (1999). In this action-packed adventure, teenagers fight for survival in the outback after a foreign enemy has taken over the government and cities in Australia. Using subterfuge and placing characters in extreme danger again and again, this novel shows what a future world can resemble. Also warning readers about the future (a common theme in science-fiction fantasy) is Rodman Philbrick's *The Last Book in the Universe* (2000). This is a post-apocalyptic saga in which the "normals" live in gang-dominated "urbs" (urban and suburban areas) and genetically improved "proves" are the favored ruling class. Spaz, a "defective" because he is epilepctic and has seizures, receives a message from his sister who is ill. He must break rules to journey to see her. Accompanied by other "defectives" and a "prove," he makes the harrowing journey to personal freedom.

Science-fiction fantasies are apt to be dark, pessimistic, a dystopian view of a future world that doesn't quite work because of our excesses in the present. However, there are some humorous and lighthearted science-fiction fantasies, and these are usually for younger readers.

Recent and Recommended Science-Fiction Fantasy

Starbright and Dream Eater, J. Cowley (2000)

Enchantress from the Stars, S. Engdahl (1970/2001)

Hole in the Sky, P. Hautman (2001)

Keeper of the Isis Light, M. Hughes (1980)

Floodland, M. Sedgewick (2001)

First Day on a Strange New Planet, D. Yaccarino (2000)

Extraordinary Characters and Inventions

Children's literature is replete with extraordinary characters drawn from the experiences of childhood. Nannies who turn common outings into adventures, toys that come to life, tiny people who live in familiar nooks and crannies—all are easily imagined by most children. Characters like Mary Poppins and Pippi Longstocking have long delighted children with their superhuman feats. Many modern fantasies contain make-believe characters who act in realistic situations. Superman and other comic-book heroes and heroines come from a tradition of magical characters in folklore and myth.

Special powers of all these characters lift the stories into the fantasy realm. Dav Pilkey's *Captain Underpants and the Perilous Plot of Professor Poopypants* (2000) is a funny send-off of the Superman mystique and enjoys great appeal with young readers.

The Moorchild (McGraw, 1996), a recent Newbery honor book, is an outstanding example of a fantastic character who speaks to our human condition in a powerful way. The moorchild is Saaski, a half-human, half-moorfolk changeling who is exiled from the moors and left with human parents. As she grows she is ridiculed, then persecuted for being different. A sprightly, sympathetic creature, with parents who love her very much, she returns their love by rescuing their daughter. As she restores the human child to her family, Saaski gains her own freedom.

A contemporary story with mythlike dimensions is *Maniac Magee* (Spinelli, 1990). Maniac is truly an extraordinary character with superhuman attributes, but the story is so realistic that some might argue it is not a fantasy at all. However, Maniac's extraordinary ability to run, the depth of his compassion, and his other unique qualities—even his heroic separation from other characters—create a fantasy. Jerry Spinelli, the author, calls him a legendary hero drawn from common childhood memories and myths (Spinelli, 1991). Stanley Yelnats, the hero of *Holes* (1999), a Newbery award winner by Louis Sachar, is also a character who is mythical and "larger than life" in this tall tale about being falsely accused and gaining redemption. In *Night Flying* (Murphy, 2000), Georgia Louisa Hansen celebrates her sixteenth birthday by flying; in fact, all the Hansen women can fly in an otherwise realistic story of family secrets and coming-of-age.

REFLECTION   Are there other characters in your reading who seem realistic, yet are strange enough to qualify for superhuman status? This could be someone who seems perfectly ordinary, yet who has a talent or a quirk that makes him or her fantastic.

Since Lilliput in *Gulliver's Travels* delighted readers, miniature worlds and tiny people have held a special fascination for those who appreciate fantasy. While *The Borrowers* (Norton, 1953) created their own tiny quarters in a real house, other tiny people have lived in nooks and crannies elsewhere. Personified dolls and toys represent an obvious magical element in children's books. Memorable toys, like those in *Winnie-the-Pooh* (Milne, 1926/1988) and in the sentimental *The Velveteen Rabbit* (Williams, 1922/1991), become real as they move and act in the primary world.

A note of caution: The popular book, *The Indian in the Cupboard* (Banks, 1980), has been criticized because of the stereotypical treatment of Little Bear. As a Native American fantasy character, he speaks with an unlikely guttural syntax and is savage and naïve (Slapin & Seale, 1988).

REFLECTION   Could fantasy characters stereotype a cultural group in a harmful way?

Recent and Recommended Extraordinary Characters

The Stones Are Hatching, G. McCaughrean (2000)

The Leprechaun Who Wished He Wasn't, S. Parkinson (2000)

I Was a Rat, P. Pullman (2000)

Queen of Atolia, M. W. Turner (2000)

Magic Can Be Murder, V. Vande Velde (2000)

The Magic Paintbrush, L. Yep (2000)

EVALUATING FANTASY

Good fantasy has to be compelling and well written, with action and some well-developed characters, hallmarks of all literature. Because of the particularly fanciful nature of this genre, attention must be paid to fantasy elements and how they are used. Fantasy elements could be a secondary or parallel world as the setting, a bit of magic, a personified animal or toy, or an extraordinary character who is good or evil. These elements must be a convincing part of the plot, rising from an inner coherence of the entire story. Logic and consistency have an important part in fantasy, as they help a reader cross the threshold into a secondary world; we must believe in the fantasy, understanding and enjoying the transformation of truth in another dimension.

In addition to these general elements, some particular questions related to each of the subgenres are listed in Figure 8.3. As in other chapters, a four-point scale,

Figure 8.3
Evaluating modern fantasy

Subgenre	My Personal Response
Animal fantasy	How believable are the anthropomorphic animals? Which animal characteristics do they retain while adding human ones?
High fantasy	Is the main character heroic enough? How believable is the secondary world? Is the quest dramatic and purposeful? What philosophical truths underlie the heroic quest?
Time fantasy	Is the passage between times convincing? If two time periods are shown (e.g., historical and modern), are they both authentic? Are characters compelling and is the plot well paced?
Science-fiction fantasy	Does the technology seem too contrived? What does the human dimension add? In what way does the story raise questions about the future? Are the characters stereotypical?
Extraordinary characters and inventions	Are characters stereotypical? How plausible is the relationship between extraordinary and ordinary?

similar to a rubric, is given after the personal response is evaluated. (In this chapter, the scale is for one of the subgenres: animal fantasy).

Four-Point Scale for Evaluating Animal Fantasy

Name of Text: _____

Author (and illustrator): _____

1 stands for "very good," 2 is "good," 3 is "marginal," and 4 is "unsatisfactory." Rate the book according to the following:

I. The anthropomorphic animals are believable and exhibit human traits as well as animal ones.

1 _____ 2 _____ 3 _____ 4 _____

II. The habitat of the animals retains characteristics of the natural world.

1 _____ 2 _____ 3 _____ 4 _____

III. The plot and subplots unfold quickly; characters are motivated by events occurring within the plot.

1 _____ 2 _____ 3 _____ 4 _____

IV. Animals speak in individual voices; dialogue is used effectively, as is description.

1 _____ 2 _____ 3 _____ 4 _____

REFLECTION   Do you think censorship is as much of a threat to fantasy as it is to realism? What might people find objectionable about the fantasies we have discussed in this chapter? How would that affect an evaluation of a particular book?

SUMMARY

In the mid-1800s, modern fantasy developed from fairy tales, myths, legends, fables, and other narratives of traditional literature. By the end of the 19th century, a recognized genre had been established. Extraordinary characters, secondary worlds, at least one touch of the impossible—all these fantasy elements and more found their way into remarkable and compelling books for children.

More abstract than other genres, fantasy requires a willing suspension of disbelief. Like poetry, fantasy explains universal truths through metaphor. Fantasy is serious, with profound issues of good and evil, mortality and immortality, compassion and revenge inherent in stories. Fantasy is also humorous, poking fun at our eccentricities and revealing human nature from a different point of view.

The importance of reading fantasy was implicit in each section. Fantasy liberates the imagination as it suggests alternatives in a secondary (or primary) world and encourages divergent thinking. Often it depicts moral and ethical dimensions in characters and actions. Fantasy challenges the status quo in ways that realistic fiction cannot. Each of the subgenres—animal fantasy, high fantasy, time fantasy, science-fiction fantasy, and extraordinary characters and inventions—allows readers to create solutions and imagine a better world for the future.

IMPLICATIONS FOR INSTRUCTION

First, the Projects section will encourage your direct involvement with the material, then the Activities section offers suggestions for bringing fantasy and children together in a classroom or similar setting.

Projects

1. Try some classifying by subgenre to see if the categories work for you. For example, take the three titles found in Figure 8.1 and categorize them according to what you now know about the classification system. Also, try some evaluation by applying the response questions or the four-point scale on the books you select.

2. How many modern fantasies have been made into movies? Go to the video-rental store or library and make a list of some prominent fantasy movies. Better yet, rent or check out some and compare them to the book. In addition, Harry Potter websites related to the movie and books are numerous and can be accessed easily with a search. Try www.harrypotter.ws.

3. Write a short story related to one of the subgenres. What if you wanted to create a character who traveled back in time to another period—the Revolutionary War, for example? Why would a character want to do that, and how could she? Explore some of the intricacies of writing fantasy.

4. This chapter barely touched on the dark side of fantasy: gothic horror stories, vampirism, malevolent ghosts, and goblins. Find some popular vampire books or ghost stories and evaluate them according to the criteria.

Activities for the Primary Level

1. Children will enjoy bringing a toy or a stuffed animal to school and writing stories about it. Personifying beloved toys will lead to further animal fantasies. Or how about dressing up as a favorite fantasy character?

2. Time travel in the easy reader *Dinosaurs Before Dark* (Osborne, 1992) takes two children back to when dinosaurs lived. Their travel is generated by a wish as they hold a book with a scene pictured on the book's jacket. Many primary children can read this fantasy, make a wish, and then describe their imaginary visits. (Have some colorful book jackets on hand depicting interesting places that would encourage children to write or speak of imaginary adventures.)

Also, Random House is launching a set of nonfiction books that correspond to the *Magic Tree House* series, of which *Dinosaurs: Magic Tree House Research Guide #1* (Osborne & Osborne, 2000) is available.

3. Films, videotapes, and audiotapes provide fantasy experiences for children, and often can be related to books or characters already known. Explore resources—in video stores, the Weston Woods catalog, or libraries—for connections to books, and compare versions of fantasies.

4. *The High Rise Private Eyes* (Rylant, 2001), an animal fantasy–mystery for young readers, offers opportunities to delve into a mystery unit that combines fantasy and realistic characters. Focus on characters first: Find similarities and differences between the animal detectives and the human detectives.

Activities for the Intermediate and Middle Levels

1. Following are four "fast finger" questions about the *Harry Potter* books that fifth- and sixth-graders enjoy. After these, children can make up their own questions. (If the "fast finger" questions initiate too much competition in a classroom, these questions simply could be part of a study guide.)

   - From *Harry Potter and the Sorcerer's Stone,* order these events from first to last:

     a. Harry Potter proves to be a natural "seeker" in a midnight duel with Malfoy.

     b. Harry Potter and Ron Weasley take Norbert the Norwegian Ridgerunner to the top of the tower under the Invisibility Cloak.

     c. Harry is "sorted" into Gryffindor House by the Sorting Hat.

     d. Harry goes to the zoo and the Brazilian boa constrictor escapes.

   - Place these "Defense of the Dark Arts" teachers in the *reverse* order (from Harry Potter's fourth year at Hogwarts to the first):

     a. Lockhart   b. Mad Eye Moody   c. Quirrell   d. Lupin

   - Animals!!!! Arrange these animals from *largest* to *smallest:*

     a. Aragog   b. Mrs. Norris   c. Buckbeak   d. Scabbers

   - In *Harry Potter and the Sorcerer's Stone,* who did Harry meet first, then second, then third and fourth?

     a. Hermione   b. Ron   c. Firenze   d. Hagrid

2. Work with children to organize a scavenger hunt through several high fantasies to find swords, chalices, runes, potions, medieval customs and food, real animals, imaginary animals, real people, imaginary people, symbols of evil, symbols of good, and so on.

3. Have an art show with drawings of fantasy characters and scenes. The two that are pictured in this chapter are indicative of adolescent boys who enjoy fantasy.

4. Retellings of common fairy tales written for older readers are appealing to this age group. *Beast* (Napoli, 2000), *Beauty* (McKinley, 1978), and *The Rose and the Beast* (Block, 2000) are "Beauty and the Beast" from different points of view. Reading groups or individuals could compare these stories along several dimensions: characters, plot, setting, point of view, symbols, figurative language, and surprises. See other retellings for older readers in Chapter 4.

REFERENCES

Children's Works

Alexander, L. (1968). *The high king*. New York: Holt.

Andersen, H. C. (1846/1957). *Andersen's fairy tales*. Philadelphia: John C. Winston.

Auch, M. J. (2001). *I was a third grade spy*. New York: Holiday House.

Avi. (2000). *Ereth's birthday*. New York: HarperCollins.

Babbitt, N. (1975/2000). *Tuck everlasting*. New York: Farrar, Straus & Giroux.

Banks, L. (1980). *The Indian in the cupboard*. New York: Doubleday.

Barrie, J. (1904/1991). *Peter Pan*. New York: Viking.

Baum, L. F. (1900/1998). *The wonderful wizard of Oz*. New York: Morrow.

Beaverson, A. (2000). *The hidden arrow of Maether*. New York: Delacorte.

Block, F. L. (2000). *The rose and the beast*. New York: Cotler/HarperCollins.

Carroll, L. (1871/1998). *Alice's adventures in wonderland and through the looking glass*. New York: Putnam.

Clement-Davies, D. (2000). *Fire Bringer*. New York: Dutton.

Collodi, C. (1889/1987). *Pinocchio*. New York: Putnam.

Cooper, S. (1975). *The grey king*. New York: Atheneum.

Cowley, J. (2000). *Starbright and Dream Eater*. New York: HarperCollins.

Dickinson, P. (1988). *Eva*. New York: Delacorte.

Engdahl, S. (1970/2001). *Enchantress from the stars*. New York: Atheneum.

Farmer, N. (1994). *The ear, the eye, and the arm*. New York: Orchard.

Grahame, K. (1908/1984). *The wind in the willows*. New York: Penguin.

Gutman, D. (2000). *Babe and me: A baseball card adventure*. New York: Avon.

Hautman, P. (2001). *Hole in the sky*. New York: Simon & Schuster.

Heneghan, J. (2000). *The grave*. New York: Farrar/Foster.

Hoban, R. (1967/2001). *The mouse and his child*. New York: Harper & Row.

Hughes, M. (1980). *Keeper of the isis light*. New York: Simon & Schuster.

Ibbotson, E. (2000). *Island of the aunts*. New York: Dutton.

Jacques, B. (2000). (Ill. by Fangorn). *Lord Brocktree*. New York: Philomel.

Jarvis, R. (2000). *The dark portal*. New York: North-South.

Kindl, P. (1993). *Owl in love*. Boston: Houghton Mifflin.

Kindl, P. (2001). *Goose Girl*. Boston: Houghton Mifflin.

Kingsley, C. (1997). *Water babies*. New York: Morrow.

King-Smith, D. (1985). *Babe*. New York: Random House.

Le Guin, U. (1968). *A wizard of earthsea*. New York: Parnassus.

L'Engle, M. (1962). *A wrinkle in time*. New York: Farrar, Straus, & Giroux.

Lewis, C. S. (1950/1988). *The lion, the witch and the wardrobe*. New York: Macmillan.

Lindgren, A. (1950). *Pippi Longstocking*. New York: Viking Press.

Lofting, H. (1922/1988). *The voyages of Dr. Dolittle*. New York: Delacorte.

Lowry, L. (1993). *The giver*. Boston: Houghton Mifflin.

Lowry, L. (2000). *Gathering blue*. Boston: Houghton Mifflin.

MacDonald, G. (1871/1992). *At the back of the north wind*. New York: Troll.

MacDonald, G. (1872/1993). *The Princess and the goblin: With colour plates*. London: Johannesen.

Marsden, J. (1999). *Darkness be my friend*. Boston: Houghton Mifflin.

McCaughrean, G. (2000). *The stones are hatching*. New York: HarperCollins.

McGraw, E. (1996). *The moorchild*. New York: Simon & Schuster/McElderry.

McKinley, R. (1978). *Beauty*. New York: Harper & Row.

Milne, A. A. (1926/1988). *Winnie-the-Pooh*. New York: Dutton.

Morris, G. (2001). *Parsifal's page*. Boston: Houghton Mifflin.

Murphy, R. (2000). *Night flying*. New York: Delacorde.

Napoli, D. (2000). *Beast*. New York: Atheneum.

Nesbit, E. (1907/1992). *The enchanted castle*. New York: Morrow Books of Wonder.

Nix, G. (2001). *Lirael: Daughter of the clayr*. New York: HarperCollins.

Norton, M. (1953). *The borrowers*. New York: Harcourt.

O'Brien, R. (1971). *Mrs. Frisby and the rats of NIMH*. New York: Atheneum.

Oppel, K. (2000). *Sunwing*. New York: Simon & Schuster.

Osborne, M. P. (1992). *Dinosaurs before dark*. New York: Random.

Osborne, M. P. (2000). *Civil war on Sunday*. New York: Random.

Osborne, M. P., & Osborne, D. (2000). *Dinosaurs: Magic tree house research guide #1*. New York: Random House.

Parkinson, S. (2000). *The leprechaun who wished he wasn't*. Dublin: The O'Brien Press.

Pattison, D. (2000). *The wayfinder*. New York: Greenwillow.

Pearce, P. (1958). *Tom's midnight garden*. Philadelphia: Lippincott.

Philbrick, R. (2000). *The last book in the universe*. New York: Scholastic/Blue Sky.

Pierce, T. (2001). *Squire: Protector of the small*. New York: Random House.

Pilkey, D. (2000). *Captain Underpants and the perilous plot of Professor Poopypants*. New York: Scholastic/Blue Sky.

Pullman, P. (1996). *His dark materials: Book one: Northern lights* (known as *The Golden Compass* in the United States). New York: Knopf.

Pullman, P. (1997). *His dark materials: Book two: The subtle knife*. New York: Knopf.

Pullman, P. (2000a). *His dark materials: Book three: The amber spyglass*. New York: Knopf.

Pullman, P. (2000b). *I was a rat*. New York: Knopf.

Rodda, E. (2001). *Rowan of rin*. New York: Greenwillow.

Rowling, J. K. (1997). *Harry Potter and the sorcerer's stone* (published as *The philosopher's stone* in England). New York: Scholastic.

Rowling, J. K. (1999a). *Harry Potter and the chamber of secrets*. New York: Scholastic.

Rowling, J. K. (1999b). *Harry Potter and the prisoner of Azkaban*. New York: Scholastic.

Rowling, J. K. (2000). *Harry Potter and the goblet of fire*. New York: Scholastic.

Rowling, J. K. (In Press). *Harry Potter and the Order of the Phoenix*. New York: Scholastic.

Rylant, C. (2001). *The high rise private eyes: The case of the puzzling possum*. New York: Greenwillow.

Sachar, L. (1999). *Holes*. New York: Farrar/Foster.

Scieszka, J. (2000). (Ill. by Adam McCauley). *See you later, gladiator*. New York: Viking.

Sedgewick, M. (2001). *Floodland*. New York: Delacorte.

Shelley, M. (1817/1995). *Frankenstein*. New York: St. Martin's Press.

Sleator, W. (2001). *Marco's millions*. New York: Dutton.

Southey, R. (1837/1998). *The three bears*. New York: Dorling Kindersley.

Spinelli, J. (1990). *Maniac Magee*. Boston: Little, Brown.

Spinner, S. (2000). *Be first in the universe*. New York: Delacorte.

Springer, N. (2001). *I am Morgan le Fay: A tale from Camelot*. New York: Philomel.

Stanley, D. (2000). *Roughing it on the Oregon trail*. New York: Cotler/HarperCollins.

Swift, J. (1726/1995). *Gulliver's travels*. New York: Gramercy.

Tolkien, J. R. R. (1937). *The hobbit: Or, there and back again*. London: G. Allen & Unwin.

Travers, P. L. (1934). *Mary Poppins*. New York: Harcourt.

Turner, M. W. (2000). *Queen of Atolia*. New York: Greenwillow.

Vande Velde, V. (2000). *Magic can be murder*. New York: Harcourt.

Verne, J. (1978). *The annotated Jules Verne: From the Earth to the moon*. Trans. by Walter J. Miller. New York: Crowell.

White, E. B. (1945). *Stuart Little*. New York: Harper & Row.

White, E. B. (1952). *Charlotte's web*. New York: Harper & Row.

Williams, M. (1922/1991). *The velveteen rabbit*. New York: Doubleday.

Yaccarino, D. (2000). *First day on a strange new planet*. New York: Hyperion.

Yep, L. (2000). *The magic paintbrush*. New York: HarperCollins.

Professional Works

Alexander, L. (1987). Opening statement to "The perilous realms: A colloquy." In B. Harrison & G. Maguire (Eds.), *Innocence and experience* (p. 196). New York: Lothrop, Lee & Shepard.

Cameron, E. (1962). *The green and burning tree*. Boston: Little, Brown.

Carpenter, H., & Prichard, M. (1984). *The Oxford companion to children's literature*. New York: Oxford University Press.

Levin, B. (1987). Introduction to fantasy: The perilous realms. In B. Harrison & G. Maguire (Eds.), *Innocence and experience*. New York: Lothrop, Lee & Shepard.

Maguire, G. (2000). The amber spyglass. *The Horn Book Magazine, LXXVI*, (6), 735–738.

Moss, A., & Stott, J. (1986). *The family of stories*. New York: Holt, Rinehart & Winston.

Newsweek. July 17, 2000, vol. 136, no. 3.

Opie, I., & Opie, P. (1974). *The classic fairy tales*. London: Oxford University Press.

Slapin, B., & Seale, D. (Eds.). (1988). *Books without bias: Through Indian eyes*. Berkeley, CA: Oyate.

Spinelli, J. (1991). Maniac Magee: Homer on George Street. *Horn Book, LXVII*(1), 40–41.

Swinfen, A. (1984). *In defence of fantasy*. London: Routledge & Kegan Paul.

Time. September 20, 1999, vol. 154, no. 12.

Townsend, J. R. (1987). *Written for children* (3rd rev. ed.). Philadelphia: Lippincott.

Zipes, J. (2001). Philip Pullman's quest. *Riverbank Review*, Winter, 2000–2001.

Additional Resources

Nikolajeva, M. (2000). *From mythic to linear: Time in children's literature*. Lanham, MD: Scarecrow.
This analysis of many children's books focuses primarily on fantasy.

Yolen, J. (2000). *Touch magic: Fantasy, faerie, & folklore in the literature of childhood*. New York: August House.
This is a collection of 16 essays, as 6 have been added to the original 10.

CHAPTER 9

Realism in the Here and Now

INTRODUCTION AND RESPONSE

What do Nancy Drew, Harriet the Spy, Tom Sawyer, and Holden Caulfield have in common? They are characters most of us know, characters who seem to be parts of our lives if we read about them in childhood or adolescence. Characters like these are real in our imaginations because their lives, problems, families (or lack of them), and communities are familiar to us. Even when we are reading a book about characters and situations in a part of the world we've never seen or know very little about, we can enter the story vicariously, knowing that it could really happen. Events, emotions, setting, and characters mirror life as we understand it to be. Such is the essence of realistic fiction: stories that *could happen,* that seem to be real.

Contemporary realistic fiction is the most popular genre of children's fiction. Many children want to read about characters just like themselves in situations they recognize. Common experiences, from the joy of achieving a goal to the pain of losing a friend, are described in fiction. Characters like Sophie in *The Wanderer* (Creech, 2000), seem as real as the girl next door, except that Sophie, spun into the wonder of fiction, achieves immortality as a 12-year-old sailing with her uncles and cousins on a voyage of discovery. *Wanderer* is the 45-foot ship crossing the Atlantic Ocean in a terrible storm, and "Wanderer" is also Sophie, an adopted child who wants to stop wandering and become a part of her new family.

Because this is a popular genre, with many different kinds of stories, this chapter will no doubt trigger memories of reading experiences from your childhood. To begin thinking about these stories, recall now some realistic books and characters from your memories of early reading. If you were asked to name a character you liked or admired, a character you wanted to be, whom would you name?

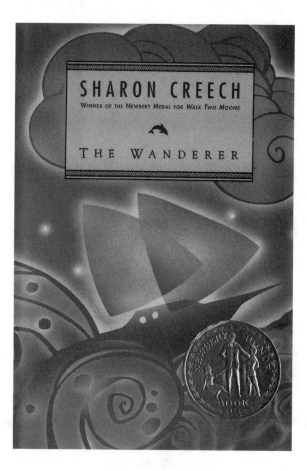

Perhaps your character and book will be mentioned in the discussion of realistic fiction that follows. Because this genre has been controversial in its realistic portrayal of problems that children and adults face, several books have been hallmarks of change. These books will be highlighted in a brief history of realistic fiction.

Next, subgenres of contemporary fiction will be presented, with examples of recent mainstream and multicultural stories. Because there are so many types of realistic fiction, the subgenres are grouped into "focus on character" and "focus on plot" themes. An evaluation scheme for realistic fiction is presented, along with bibliographies focusing on diversity.

Controversies inherent in a graphic depiction of realism are highlighted in the summary of this chapter. How "real" can literature for children be? Controversies frequently center on elements of violence, profanity, sexuality, and other aspects of reality found in children's books. These aspects often invite censorship, but if censorship is applied, what is an intelligent response? A special section, Combating Censorship, suggests a mechanism for dealing with this sometimes explosive situation.

Most of the books mentioned in this chapter are written for an audience of third- or fourth-graders and beyond. There are many "young adult" titles, or books appropriate for seventh grade through high school. No books that could be considered picture books are mentioned, although there are picture books appropriate for children in these grades (see Chapter 6). However, books are included in this chapter that are considered "transitional books" and "easy readers" for those children who are beginning to read in first grade and beyond. These easy books are very important to introduce young readers to the joy of reading and to help them achieve independence as fluent readers.

REFLECTION   Censorship seems to be immutably drawn to this genre because of the nature of people's attitudes about what children should and should not be reading. Do you know of any realistic fiction that critics have censored or attempted to censor? Can you think of any titles that seem controversial?

DEFINING CONTEMPORARY REALISM

Fiction is the organization of a series of patterns we call story (Nodelman, 1996). Fiction is the most common mode of children's literature; it is what we generally think of first when we define literature for children. *Realistic fiction,* then, is the "real" story; it is what we perceive reality to be, filtered through the literary devices of story. What we perceive reality to be, or the "real world," is slightly different for each of us, because our individual perceptions come from a composite of psychological and physical attributes. When our unique perceptions as readers and authors enter the fictional world of literature with its demands of plot, theme, setting, character, and so forth, realism is subjective and abstract. Thus it becomes fiction—which is a metaphor for truth. Jill Paton Walsh, a writer and critic, points out the dual nature of *real* and *imaginary* when she says, "Realistic fiction is about imaginary people, living in imagined contexts, doing what was never done, saying what was never said" (Walsh, 1981, pp. 35–36). Realism, then, is fiction, the product of an author's fertile imagination.

As authors draw stories from the real world, they fictionalize as they create scenarios and characters and invent plots and points of view. This is the art of telling a story. Nevertheless, the story is grounded in common perceptions of what life is like. Realistic fiction must be believable when tested against our perceptions of reality, and good writers can help readers see common and familiar things in a new way. Conversely, good writers also help us see uncommon and unfamiliar things in situations that seem real, helping us learn from vicarious experience just as we learn from actual experience. Thus, the adjective *realistic* refers to the common perceptions that we share with others about the nature of reality.

Contemporary, of course, refers to the here and now. It is a word for describing the setting—the time and place. One tricky aspect of determining whether a story is contemporary is the age of the reader. What is contemporary for an adult may not necessarily be contemporary for a child. A story set in Detroit in the late 1960s is likely to be in the distant past for a child but may seem contemporary to an adult. Another aspect of contemporary comes into play when reading old books. When *Little Women* by Louisa May Alcott was written in 1868, it was a contemporary story; now it is considered historical. Thus, the division between contemporary and historical is largely arbitrary. In this textbook, the timeline dividing historical and contemporary occurs after the 1960s—that is, stories about ancient times through World War II and continuing into the civil rights era are considered historical fiction, which will be discussed in Chapter 10, and stories set in the 1970s to the present are considered contemporary fiction.

REFLECTION   Given the parallels between realistic fiction and societal concerns, what do you predict will occur in children's books of the next decade? Will there be noticeable trends in publishing books about certain topics related to children's and adolescents' issues?

VALUE OF CONTEMPORARY REALISM

Children and adolescents learn about themselves, their peers, and a wider span of relationships, problems, and ideas through literature that reflects reality. Even when stories are far removed from a child's point of reference, realism is the bridge that often carries readers into the unknown. Thus, literature extends the range of life experiences, as it allows a safe exploration of human relations and geography through the imagination of the reading process. Through imagination, readers can live vicariously anywhere from a Somali village to an urban apartment. Also, characters who are, for example, solving problems, building self-esteem, and learning to cope with disabilities serve as models for living in our contemporary world.

HISTORY OF CONTEMPORARY REALISM

Realistic fiction began with *Robinson Crusoe* (Defoe, 1719/1965), which was published in 1719. Although not written principally for children, it proved to be popular with a wide audience and encouraged many other writers to experiment with a realistic, though fictionalized, story. A few years later, in 1744, John Newbery began publishing realistic and didactic stories such as *A Little Pretty Pocket-Book* (1744/1967) for children.

Examples of outstanding realism from the 19th and early 20th centuries are captured in the following list. (Note how many of the books have been made into movies. Realism seems easier to adapt than other genres.)

1826	*The Last of the Mohicans,* James Fenimore Cooper
1865	*Hans Brinker, or the Silver Skates: A Story of Life in Holland,* Mary Mapes Dodge
1868	*Little Women,* Louisa May Alcott
1876	*The Adventures of Tom Sawyer,* Mark Twain
1884	*Heidi,* Johanna Spyri
1911	*The Secret Garden,* Frances Hodgson Burnett
1938	*The Yearling,* Marjorie Kinnan Rawlings
1944	*The Black Stallion,* Walter Farley
1948	*King of the Wind,* Marguerite Henry

Great adventures, as in *Tom Sawyer,* unforgettable characters *(Heidi),* and depth of emotional intensity *(The Secret Garden)* have rendered these stories classics. Other books portraying families in crisis, children coping with adversity, adventure, and mystery have been written by such authors as Juliana Horatia Ewing, Charlotte Yonge, Charles Dickens, O. Henry, Sir Arthur Conan Doyle, and Kate Douglas Wiggin, to name just a few.

One has only to look at the list of early Newbery winners, beginning in 1922, as well as awards in other countries to note the prevalence of realistic fiction, both contemporary and historical. Many outstanding books enabled children to read stories about their own communities and the wider world. The period from 1925 through 1940 was called a golden age of children's literature in the United States (Smith, 1963) because of the high quality of many books. Laura Ingalls Wilder's seven *Little House* books typified this productive period (see Chapter 10), as did the poignant realistic animal story *The Yearling* by Marjorie Kinnan Rawlings. Realistic animal stories, such as *Where the Red Fern Grows* (Rawls, 1961), continue to captivate children today.

After World War II, realistic fiction in the United States began to show more diversity in character and conflict. An early coming-of-age novel that set the stage for a new realism was *Catcher in the Rye* (Salinger, 1951). Teenage Holden Caulfield's language, behavior, and alienation are still controversial and the book is sometimes the target of censorship even today.

Family stories continued to be the norm, but a new kind of family story, *Harriet the Spy* (Fitzhugh, 1964/2000), proved to be prophetic in its more realistic depiction of children. Harriet was a strong-willed, intelligent, somewhat disobedient, humorous, and curious girl, and the novel revealed a psychological and philosophical depth new to children's realistic fiction (Wolf, 1975).

As society moved through the turbulent 1960s, children's literature also mirrored the clash of different values. What had been considered inappropriate as reading material for children was questioned, as authors wrote books that actually reflected the lives children were leading. The young author S. E. Hinton wrote about violence between socioeconomic classes and an unconventional family headed by an older brother in *The Outsiders* (1967). Other groundbreaking books of the 1960s broke taboos in children's literature when they dealt with controversial topics such as sexuality, death, dysfunctional families, alcoholism, drugs, eating disorders, and abuse. Paul Zindel, M. E. Kerr, Norma Klein, and other authors wrote to a young adult audience, embracing issues that were new. *Are You There, God? It's Me, Margaret* (Blume, 1968) was tamer than most, speaking frankly about menstruation. By the 1980s, there seemed to be no topic that was not tackled within the context of fiction for young people. Book after book cast a juvenile protagonist into lifelike circumstances. Some were well written, but more often than not they were didactic, shallow, and narrow stories, usually written in first person to convey personal alienation and hostility (Egoff, 1980, pp. 356–369). When the shock value of some of the more lurid stories, such as the anonymous *Go Ask Alice* (1971), had run its course, a more evenhanded, balanced story resulted.

In the last decade and a half, writers have moved from a restrictive focus on a problem to a more inclusive view, balancing all elements of story. No longer is a novel defined by its problem; the condition is part of characters' lives. Examples bringing about this change to a fuller treatment of realism were Newbery award winners *Bridge to Terabithia* (Paterson, 1977), *Jacob Have I Loved* (Paterson, 1980), and *Dear Mr. Henshaw* (Cleary, 1983).

REFLECTION   *Bibliotherapy* is the practice of addressing an emotional problem by reading books in which a character with the same problem as the reader finds a solution. For example, if a reader is coping with a death in the family, the reader is directed toward a book in which a character is coping with a death. Are you aware of instances when bibliotherapy was used, or warranted?

In addition to the new realism, contemporary realistic fiction broke barriers of other kinds. African-American characters slowly became more obvious in important roles, though until the 1970s they were not necessarily more frequently portrayed (Carlson, 1970). *Zeely* (Hamilton, 1967) was one of the first books that was not self-conscious about the tensions of racism or integration; it simply told a riveting story about a young girl in the South. Gender differences also were downplayed in many stories as women and girl characters assumed more significant and independent roles.

Each first in making children's fiction more realistic could no doubt be documented, and the resulting list would illustrate parallels between literature and society's changing attitudes that are mirrored in fiction. Because there are more elderly people in society today, books with intergenerational stories are more numerous. An emphasis on diversity pays heed to the many schoolchildren who come from Europe, Asia, and other parts of the world. Stories of homeless families and children proliferate as economic conditions force that reality on many. Books reflect changing gender-role identities, and families are defined in many ways: single parent, double parent (sometimes of the same sex), grandparent, foster parent, stepparent, and any combination. Although there is much to be done to make minority cultures more significant in children's literature, some progress has been evident.

EVALUATION OF CONTEMPORARY REALISM

Contemporary realistic fiction must resonate with realistic situations, problems, and characters. Realism mirrors life as we believe it to be, and in fiction that mirror sometimes turns into a window, a telescope, or a magnifying glass. Nevertheless, the reflection of the image is faithful to our perception of reality.

In evaluating realistic fiction for your personal reading, or for school, home, or library, certain questions are sure to surface:

- How graphically can writers describe violence or sexuality?
- What kind of language is appropriate? Or inappropriate?
- Are there topics or themes that are not suitable?

With these three questions and your personal responses in mind, consider the additional questions in Figure 9.1.

Figure 9.1
Evaluating realistic fiction

Subgenres	My Personal Response
Stories of survival, family, and school, and animal realism (Focus on character)	How do the main characters grow and learn about the world and themselves? Is character development consistent with the theme? Do the characters act, react, and speak realistically? Are the characters interesting?
Stories of sports, mystery and adventure, humor, and series books (Focus on plot)	Is the plot fresh and new (not contrived and predictable)? How has the author used language effectively? Is the theme worthwhile? Does the theme subvert the story?

• ◆ •

REFLECTION How "real" do you want children's books to be? Are you shocked by some of the stories published today? Given that children and adults see virtually any kind of topic realistically programmed on television (even with the "V" chip), does it even matter what our standards are?

SUBGENRES OF CONTEMPORARY REALISM

Because life is complex and multifaceted, realistic fiction, which mirrors life, has myriad subjects and themes. Writers of realistic fiction use the whole scope of conflicts—person against self, person against other, person against nature, and person against society—sometimes in the same book. Writers use flashbacks, different points of view, and stylistic devices such as dialects to a greater extent in realistic fiction than in other genres. Instead of the predictable happy ending, realistic fiction experiments with open-ended stories. Due to wide-ranging subjects and forms in realistic fiction, subgenres are not as clear-cut as they are in fantasy, for example, or in poetry.

Typically, realistic fiction has been categorized as animal realism, survival stories, mystery and adventure, sports, humor, series books, family and school stories, and what used to be called "problem novels." (Problem novels, a subgenre created by the new realism of previous decades, have been subsumed under family and school stories because the emphasis is no longer so blatantly on a medical or societal problem—drugs, death, suicide, rage, incest, and so on.) All these categories can be cumbersome because rarely is a book just a "horse story" or just a "sports story." Relationships between characters, interactions among literary elements, and fully developed characters ensure that books cannot be easily pigeonholed. Therefore, a more sensible method might be to look for another way of dividing the genre into manageable parts. For purposes of discussion, the typical subgenres mentioned here will be grouped into two supercategories: focus on **character** and focus on **plot.**

In the focus on character, survival stories, animal realism, and family and school stories are grouped together because the main character or characters assume primary importance in the novel. Their actions, relationships, and introspections take precedence over other story elements. Character development drives the action instead of simply being a part of it. In the focus on plot, action and events seem more prominent and characters are not so individualistic. Sometimes they exist merely to serve the plot and push it forward. Focus on plot includes sports, mystery and adventure, humor, and series books (see Figure 9.1).

Focus on Character

In books that focus on character, the protagonist makes self-discoveries and develops as a more knowledgeable and compassionate person, whether alone or as part of a family group. In such coming-of-age novels, themes are often articulated as follows:

- forming one's own identity; gaining independence
- reconciling personal goals with broader family, societal, and peer goals
- proving competence and building self-esteem
- learning to take care of others
- overcoming prejudice

These themes are also seen as rites of passage as the characters grow, experience change, and become more compassionate, knowledgeable adults. Change occurs when characters interact with each other and with situations within the novel. The three subgenres of survival, family and school, and animal stories illustrate these themes as each focuses on young people growing into greater responsibility and awareness of themselves and the world around them.

Evaluating realistic fiction with some objectivity is difficult. The following four-point scale helps, in addition to the personal response questions given earlier. The following statements, focusing on character development, may help to provide insight into a novel. Read the novel, then—alone or with colleagues—mark your evaluation on the sliding scale. It can be informative to share responses or to use the statements as discussion points.

Four-Point Scale for Evaluating Character Focus in Realism

Name of Text:_____

Author:_____

Illustrator:_____

1 stands for "very good," 2 is "good," 3 is "marginal," and 4 is "unsatisfactory." Rate the book according to the following:

I. The main character develops insight into the causes of his/her own behavior.

   1 _____ 2 _____ 3 _____ 4 _____

II. Characters change and grow; their dynamism gives energy to the novel.

   1 _____ 2 _____ 3 _____ 4 _____

III. There is a balance between fully developed characters (round) and minor characters (flat).

   1 _____ 2 _____ 3 _____ 4 _____

IV. Minor characters contribute to the plot and theme in significant ways.

   1 _____ 2 _____ 3 _____ 4 _____

V. Characters are interesting and realistic.

   1 _____ 2 _____ 3 _____ 4 _____

Survival Stories

Typically, survival stories pit protagonist against nature, with nature becoming a symbolic antagonist. Proving competence in physical and psychological terms is always at the heart of these stories. *Hatchet* (Paulsen, 1987) is a quintessential survival story, with a preadolescent boy Brian marooned in the Canadian wilderness. First surviving a plane crash, then an exhausting fight for physical survival with few tools, he becomes emotionally healed. In a "what if" sequel, Paulsen casts Brian into a new and even more difficult season: *Brian's Winter* (1996). Relying on skills he learned in the summer and his few tools, Brian again proves his resourcefulness in an inhospitable environment. Jean Craighead George's popular *My Side of the Mountain Trilogy* (1959/2000) about Sam Gribley and his survival in the wilderness is now available to new readers.

Urban survival stories also show protagonists battling against an uncaring environment. *The Goats* (Cole, 1987) pits two children, scapegoats of their summer camp, against the rural and urban challenges of surviving uncaring adults as they run away and try to survive with no food, money, clothes, or self-esteem. Survival stories depend on a careful description of the rural or urban setting to challenge the main character and dramatize the danger. Urban/suburban survival stories are more numerous now because such communities are much more prevalent now than they were in the past. There are no longer as many wilderness and low population centers as there were in previous times.

Recent and Recommended Survival Stories

A Face First, P. Cummings (2001)

Stranger in Dadland, A. Koss (2001)

Pondfire, B. Maynard (2000)

Seek, P. Fleischman, (2001)

Family and School Stories

Whether overcoming problems at school or at home, child and adolescent characters are depicted with a wide range of experiences that reflect reality in the present time. The following notable books have been published recently and deserve mention in this large genre. If you are looking for new examples of fine writing, compelling characters, and stories that move you to laughter and tears, try these. As in other chapters, all bibliographical information is included here and is not repeated at the end of this chapter. A number of books deserve recognition, so national and international contemporary realism can be found later in this chapter, as well as on the companion CD.

Bauer, J. (2000). *Hope was here.* New York: Putnam. When 16-year-old Hope and her aunt move to Wisconsin to work as a waitress and cook, they become involved in a campaign to oust the town's corrupt mayor.

Coman, C. (2000). *Many stones.* New York: Front Street. Berry accompanies her father to South Africa to attend the funeral of her murdered older sister. Her deep anger toward her father for leaving the family and the violence against her sister results in a conflicted and taut drama of family relationships.

Couloumbis, A. (1999). *Getting near to baby*. New York: Putnam. Living with bossy Aunt Patty, 12-year-old Willa Jo narrates this story about the sadness in her family after her baby sister dies.

Gantos, J. (2000). *Joey Pizga loses control*. New York: Farrar, Straus & Giroux. Joey, much calmer since starting his medicine, spends his summer with his father and eccentric grandmother. His father tells him to stop the medicine as Joey is trying to pitch his father's baseball team into the championships.

Holt, K. W. (1999). *When Zachary Beaver came to town*. New York: Holt. During the summer of 1971 in a small Texas town, 13-year-old Tyler and his best friend Cal meet the star of a sideshow, 600-pound Zachary Beaver, the fattest boy in the world.

Lester, J. (2001). *When Dad killed Mom*. New York: Silver Whistle/Harcourt. In a California setting, a psychologist shoots his wife, an artist, on the street. Their daughter and son uncover motives and events prior to the infamous trial.

Lynch, C. (2001). *Freewill*. New York: HarperCollins. A complex, layered novel for older readers, *Freewill* is the struggle of Will to find his place in a world of grief, rage, pain, and woodworking.

Spinelli, J. (2000). *Stargirl*. New York: Knopf. In a story about the perils of popularity, the courage of nonconformity, the thrill of first love, and attitudes about physical beauty, Stargirl raises questions and changes beliefs at Mica High School

Trueman, T. (2000). *Stuck in neutral*. New York: HarperCollins. Shawn's cerebral palsy keeps him from communicating, but his thoughts are lively, intelligent, and occasionally sarcastic. He is threatened by his father, who is intent upon a mercy killing.

Wolff, V. E. (2001). *True believer*. New York: Atheneum. LaVaughn is committed to learning and leaving her neighborhood to go to college. Her plans are derailed when she falls in unreciprocated love with a boy and her mother begins dating.

Wynne-Jones, T. (2001). *The boy in the burning house*. New York: Kroupa/Farrar. A mystery, a suicide, a villainous minister, and blackmail make this an exceptionally dramatic novel.

Animal Realism

Contrasted with animal fantasy, in which animals are personified, these stories treat animals realistically. Horses, dogs, mountain lions, and coyotes are characters through which the balance between the natural world and human beings is shown. Relating to animals reveals character development, as animals frequently seem to affect a special bond of friendship with children. The growing relationship between a child and an animal unfolds as each learns to trust the other. Newbery winner *Shiloh* (Naylor, 1991), which is set in West Virginia, exemplifies the unique love between a boy and his dog. Marty loves and feeds a scared, starved animal and protects it from its abusive owner. The very popular *Shiloh Season* (Naylor, 1996) continues this story.

Recent and Recommended Realistic Animal Stories

Notes from a Liar and Her Dog, G. Choldenko (2001)

Absolutely Lucy, I. Cooper (2000)

Because of Winn-Dixie, K. DiCamillo (2000)

Runaway Radish, J. Haas (2001)

Focus on Plot

Many stories of contemporary realistic fiction focus on an action-packed plot that propels characters through a series of exciting events. In contrast to books mentioned in the previous section, character development is minimal in these stories, and setting is simply described. Emphasis is on the topic that defines these subgenres: sports, mystery and adventure, humor, and a large category called series books.

Books in these subgenres sometimes constitute light reading, as they tend to be less profound, less challenging, and more entertaining. These books are accessible to many readers and often lure an unmotivated reader into the pages of the most current popular fiction. This is not to say that thoughtful, even provocative books are not found in these subgenres, as the recommended books that follow demonstrate, but the vast majority of these stories are amusing, fast-paced, and undemanding.

Four-Point Scale for Evaluating Plot Focus in Contemporary Realism

Name of Text:_____

Author:_____

Illustrator:_____

1 stands for "very good," 2 is "good," 3 is "marginal," and 4 is "unsatisfactory." Rate the book according to the following:

    I. The plot moves forward briskly with plenty of action.

       1 _____ 2 _____ 3 _____ 4 _____

    II. The subplots contribute significantly to the ultimate resolution of the novel.

       1 _____ 2 _____ 3 _____ 4 _____

    III. The plot is neither too predictable nor too contrived.

       1 _____ 2 _____ 3 _____ 4 _____

    IV. Interaction among plot, characters, and theme (and other literary elements) results in a well-written novel.

       1 _____ 2 _____ 3 _____ 4 _____

V. This is an interesting (and/or nail-biting, laughing-out-loud, crying-at-the-end) page turner that will please my students.

1 _____ 2 _____ 3 _____ 4 _____

Sports Stories

Sports stories use the vehicle of fiction to explain the rules of the sport and to initiate the beginner into its demands and rewards. Sports stories are sometimes seen as metaphors for fostering an American way of life—urging competition, winning, and achieving a tangible goal. In the best sports stories, competitors view the outcome with grace, realizing "Winning isn't everything" or learning the hard lessons of loss. Baseball, basketball, hockey, soccer, skiing—contemporary realistic fiction includes stories about these sports and many more. Male and female characters are found in title roles, although males dominate.

Night Hoops (Deuker, 2000) is another contemporary basketball book with two well-drawn characters and plenty of sports action. Nick Abbot, a high school sophomore, is determined to star as point guard for his varsity team this year. However, parental pressure, plummeting grades, and his own cockiness consign him to the bench. Meanwhile, Trent, the juvenile delinquent next door, begins to use Nick's backyard court. As the boys shoot hoops together, they form an uneasy duo. Basketball draws them together and is the catalyst for redemption and growth.

Recent and Recommended Sports Stories

Soccer Duel, M. Christopher (2000)

Tennis Ace, M. Christopher (2000)

Whale Talk, C. Crutcher (2001) (swimming)

Gold Dust, C. Lynch (2000) (baseball)

Girls Got Game: Sports Stories and Poems, S. Macy (ed.) (2001)

Tall Tales: Six Amazing Basketball Dreams, C. R. Smith, Jr. (2000)

Fighting Ruben Wolfe, M. Zusak (2001) (boxing)

Mystery and Adventure

Suspense, danger, and drama permeate stories that keep readers turning pages. We read with a flashlight under the covers when we were young; now some of us have "graduated" to P. D. James, Tony Hillerman, and Tom Clancy, ensuring that mysteries will always be a part of our reading repertoire. For children today, good contemporary mysteries and adventures are exciting and full of interesting plot twists and vicarious thrills.

For older readers, *The Body of Christopher Creed* (Plum-Ucci, 2000), a nominee for the 2001 Edgar Award from the Mystery Writers of America (see www.mystery writers.org), is a mesmerizing tale of two high school students trying to solve the disappearance of a harassed student. When they find a body in the woods, more suspense follows. Also on the short list for the award was *Silent to the Bone* (Konigsburg, 2000), a book in which an older brother is accused by a British au pair of shaking and dropping his baby sister. The winner of the award was *Counterfeit Son* (Alphin, 2000), about a boy who assumes the identity of one of his serial-killer father's victims. For avid mystery readers, these are some of the best.

For younger readers, the Encyclopedia Brown books, such as *Encyclopedia Brown and the Case of the Slippery Salamander* (Sobol, 1999), include ten short mysteries that are complete in a few pages. Encyclopedia, a fifth-grade student in Idaville, is so named because of his quick thinking and the logic he brings to bear on the cases his father, the chief of police, brings home.

Recent and Recommended Mysteries and Adventures

Dark Secrets, E. Chandler (2000)

Who's In the Hall? A Mystery in Four Chapters, B. Hearne (2000)

Sammy Keyes and the Hollywood Mummy, W. Van Draanen (2001)

Humor

Writing really funny books takes a great sense of humor, a command of language, and knowledge of children. Humor is a special gift that can easily slip into sarcasm or satire and cease to be funny. Events that may be funny to one person are not necessarily funny to another. Thankfully there are writers who bring a comedic touch to fiction and entertain while causing us to regard the world with more insight.

Lois Lowry is well known for her funny books about Anastasia Krupnik and her little brother, Sam. In one of these, *Zooman Sam* (1999), Sam's role as zooman at his nursery school's Future Job Day leads to exciting activities with animals and people. His irrepressible good humor keeps the story eventful and lighthearted. Stories like these are humorous and celebrate generally good children doing ordinary activities. Another ordinary, delightfully funny child is Ramona from *Ramona's World* and other books in the series by Beverly Cleary (1999 and others).

For older students (middle school and beyond), British author Louise Rennison writes with biting wit *On the Bright Side, I'm Now the Girlfriend of a Sex God: Further Confessions of Georgia Nicolson* (2001) and *Angus, Thongs, and Full Frontal Snogging: Confessions of Georgia Nicolson* (2000). These are confessional stories of a young teen.

Recent and Recommended Humorous Books

Everything on a Waffle, Polly Horvath (2001)

Trial by Jury/Journal, K. Klise (2001)

Lizzie at Last, C. Mills (2000)

A Book of Coupons, S. Morgenstern (2001)

Fat Camp Commandos, D. Pinkwater (2001)

Series Books

There are many kinds of series books in juvenile literature. Nonfiction series in biography, science, history, and other subject areas are numerous. (Chapters 11 and

12 contain references to series books in curriculum areas.) Series books in fiction are very noticeable in bookstores: *American Girl, Animorphs, Thoroughbreds,* and *Sweet Valley University* (developing from *Sweet Valley Twins* and *Sweet Valley High*) are among the many series published to appeal to the mass-market audience. Available now are many series related to television programs—*Buffy the Vampire Slayer* and *Dark Angel,* among others.

For adults, we have romance novels, westerns, a good deal of science fiction, and some of the popular reading on best-seller lists; these books are not considered literature, and they are not reviewed by standard reviewing sources. Nonfiction series have slightly more credibility than fiction, but usually the term connotes books that are not to be taken seriously as literature for young readers or adults.

Historically, the term *series books* denotes a group of cheaply produced mass-marketed books dating from the early 1900s and centering on the adventures of upwardly mobile U.S. youths. Action-packed series—*The Rover Boys, The Bobbsey Twins, The Hardy Boys, Tom Swift,* and the most popular of all, *Nancy Drew*—actually were written by the Stratemeyer Syndicate, a "literary machine." At the turn of the 19th century, Edward Stratemeyer was a successful author of dime novels, which were popular fiction aimed toward adolescents. He concocted a plan that would make money, produce a handsome product, employ writers, and provide fiction for this segment of the population, who now had some leisure time to read. Stratemeyer fashioned story ideas into three-page outlines, and then sent these sketches to aspiring writers who had answered classified ads in New York newspapers (Watson, 1991). Books were churned out monthly under fictitious names according to a formula devised by Stratemeyer. He controlled the editing, publishing, and distribution. When he died in 1930, his daughter, Harriet Stratemeyer Adams, took over the empire and continued the formulaic tradition, even writing some of the Nancy Drews herself. Edward Stratemeyer was a genius at mass-marketing and, even though the books were cheap, predictable, poorly written, and stereotypical, he should be recognized for providing reading material to immigrants who wanted to learn the English language and to many rural and urban people who couldn't afford anything else. (See http://stratemeyer.net for more information.)

Series books were criticized as vulgar, tawdry, and even "subliterature," and many libraries refused to buy them (Soderburgh, 1980). However, as attitudes changed toward appropriateness and suitability in children's books, and the sustained popularity of these series continued to drive this phenomenon in the publishing industry, controversy faded. Yet modern series books still tend to perpetuate a somewhat negative tone, "focusing on wealth, materialism and appearance rather than the inner qualities of character" (Jordan, 1996, p. 22). They are still formulaic, often stereotypical (minorities are rarely included), and inevitably shallow.

Even though series books are not considered quite the harbingers of moral decay they once were, the dilemma of popularity versus quality remains. Teachers want children to select books that are entertaining and enlightening, and often series books only entertain. Susceptible to the latest fad, they have a short demand period in libraries and schools that must always spend wisely for lasting value. For example, the *Goosebump* series by R. L. Stine, popular just a few years ago, is no longer in demand. Although callous, chilling, horrific, and predictable, the series enjoyed the spotlight briefly and then swept into oblivion.

REFLECTION   Did you read any series books when you were in elementary school? What were the popular series?

COMBATING CENSORSHIP

According to *Reading Today* (Micklos, 2001), the newspaper of the International Reading Association, book challenges remain frequent. During the 1990s, the Office for Intellectual Freedom of the American Library Association received reports of more than 5,000 challenges to books in libraries and schools. Frequently challenged titles were from the *Goosebumps* series, but other authors—Maya Angelou, Judy Blume, Katherine Paterson, Robert Cormier, and J. D. Salinger, for example—were also subject to many censorship challenges. Schools and libraries must be proactive in assuaging would-be censors from limiting children's choices and the intellectual freedom that comes from a wide range of literature.

The American Library Association, in its material on preserving intellectual freedom, outlines a procedure to combat censorship (American Library Association, 1996). Essentially, the procedure suggests that libraries, schools, and other groups promoting literature establish written criteria for selection of books and materials. Then, when anyone challenges a certain book, criteria can demonstrate the worth of its inclusion. If questions are still raised, the procedure suggests that libraries offer a form to be filled out by the challenger. After having read the entire work, the challenger must specify, in writing, why a book should be removed from circulation. (Too often passages are taken out of context and their "unsavory" features are magnified.) Then a panel of people—librarians, the challenger, and perhaps others—can decide if the judgment to remove the book is warranted. The procedure is important because it allows libraries and schools to establish criteria for all selections and to remove some of the emotionalism when charges are raised. Standards of community tolerance can be applied by the panel. Guidelines for teachers and school library media specialists and a list of related websites should be available and easily accessible in every school and library (Simmons & Dresang, 2001).

Censorship is sometimes used as a weapon and it never achieves its goal (McClure, 1995). It polarizes a community, gains notoriety for books that sometimes don't deserve the attention (and some that do), and suppresses ideas that need to be analyzed and debated in a democratic society. With adequate selection and evaluation procedures, this threat to intellectual freedom can be minimized.

NATIONAL DIVERSITY: BIBLIOGRAPHY

To conclude this chapter, two bibliographies are presented. The first, a bibliography of national diversity, lists books that are set in the United States, but depict people from the diverse cultures that are politically set apart from the mainstream. The bibliography focuses especially on books about African-Americans, Native Americans, Hispanics, European-Americans, Asian-Americans, and the Gay and Lesbian community. The second bibliography, a bibliography of international diversity, deals with international settings such as Africa, Asia, the Pacific Islands, Australia and New Zealand, the Caribbean, and Europe.

The following books are recent and recommended, and you can look for more on the companion CD-ROM. As literature, their stories move us to regard the world and its diversity in positive ways and create understandings where little existed before. (All bibliographical information is included here and will not be repeated at the end of the chapter.) Some books are designated "YA," as suitable for young adults. (Note that there are analogous bibliographies in Chapter 10 related to historical realism.)

African-American

Williams, L. A. (2000). *When Kambia Elaine flew in from Neptune*. New York: Simon.

Williams-Garcia, R. (2001). *Every time a rainbow dies*. New York: HarperCollins.

Woodson, J. (2000). *Miracle's boys*. New York: Putnam.

Asian-American

Lee, M. (1999). *F is for fabuloso*. New York: Avon.

Na, A. (2001). *A step from heaven*. New York: Front Street.

European-American

Snell, G. (Ed.). (2001). *Thicker than water: Coming of age stories by Irish and Irish American Writers*. New York: Delacorte.

Hispanic

Rice, D. (2001). *Crazy loco*. New York: Dial.

Saldaña, R., Jr. (2001). *The jumping tree: A novel*. New York: Delacorte.

Skarmeta, A. (2000). *The composition*. Toronto: Groundwood.

Native American

Bruchac, J. (2001). *Skeleton man*. New York: HarperCollins.

Little, K. G. (1999). *Enchanted runner*. New York: Avon.

Gay and Lesbian

Ferris, J. (2000). *Eight seconds*. New York: Harcourt. YA

Ryan, S. (2001). *Empress of the world*. New York: Viking. YA

Sanchez, A. (2001). *Rainbow boys*. New York: Simon. YA

Taylor, W. (1999). *The blue lawn*. New York: Alyson. YA

INTERNATIONAL DIVERSITY: BIBLIOGRAPHY

Almond, D. (2000). *Kit's wilderness*. New York: Delacorte. (England)

Bjork, C. (1999). *Vendela in Venice*. New York: Farrar, Straus & Giroux. (Sweden/Italy)

Carmi, D. (2000). *Samir and Yonatan*. New York: Scholastic. (Israel/Palestine)

Clarke, J. (2000). *Night train*. New York: Holt. (Australia)

Ellis, D. (2001). *The breadwinner*. Toronto: Groundwood. (Afghanistan)

Hicyilmaz, G. (2000). *Smiling for strangers*. New York: Farrar, Straus & Giroux. (Yugoslavia/England)

Holzworth, W. (1999). *I'm José and I'm okay: Three stories from Bolivia*. New York: Kane. (Bolivia)

Honey, E. (2001). *Fiddleback*. New York: Knopf. (Australia)

Joseph, L. (2000). *The color of my words*. New York: HarperCollins. (Caribbean)

Kessler, C. (2000). *No condition is permanent*. New York: Philomel. (Sierra Leone)

Kurtz, J. (2001). *Jakarta missing*. New York: Greenwillow. (Kenya)

Mahy, M. (2000). *24 hours*. New York: Hamilton/McElderry. (Australia)

Naidoo, B. (2001). *The other side of truth*. New York: HarperCollins. (Nigeria)

Salisbury, G. (2001). *Lord of the deep*. New York: Delacorte. (Hawaii)

Soto, G. (2000 reissue). *Baseball in April and other stories*. New York: Harcourt. (Caribbean)

Staples, S. F. (2000). *Shiva's fire*. New York: Farrar, Straus & Giroux. (India)

Watson, K. (2000). *Juice*. Sydney: Freemantle Arts Center. (Australia)

Whelan, G. (2000). *Homeless Bird*. New York: HarperCollins. (India)

SUMMARY

Contemporary realistic fiction, a very popular genre, draws its power from lifelike characters, setting, and conflict. Characters remind us of people we know; setting evokes emotional ties to times and places sometimes remembered and clearly recognized. Plots must be plausible, describing the unfolding of possible events.

Subgenres of contemporary realism were first divided into focus on character and focus on plot. Modern books with a focus on character include survival stories, animal realism, and family and school stories. Focus on plot includes mystery–adventure, sports, humor, and series books.

The very nature of realistic fiction raises questions about how much reality or what kind of reality should be contained in children's books. Should children be exposed to the sordid, very desperate reality that some people confront daily? Life is hard; it destroys innocence and causes despair. Does that kind of realism have a place in children's literature?

There are no easy answers to what is appropriate for today's child. What is appropriate is the freedom for authors to create and for readers to select the books that enlighten and enrich our understanding of our lives. Each book, if controversial or subject to censorship, must be evaluated as a total work according to the purpose and audience for whom it is intended. Parents have a responsibility to monitor the reading of their children; they alone can restrict it, but only for their own children and not for others.

IMPLICATIONS FOR INSTRUCTION

First, projects are suggested that will allow you to become more familiar with contemporary realism. Next, activities to do with children in primary, intermediate, and middle level classrooms are listed. Feel free to create your own projects and activities as well. If you are already working in a classroom, you will be able to adapt some of the activities here to your group of children.

Projects

1. Compare a series book—a *Nancy Drew,* for example, to *The Wanderer* (Creech, 2000) or *Because of Winn-Dixie* (DiCamillo, 2000). Note differences in tone, style, structure, depth of emotional realism, and any other important factors. Use the four-point scale for focus on character and focus on plot, and see what happens.

2. From books published in the past several years, select ones that include characters representing diverse cultures. Do you find portrayals of Native Americans and/or African-Americans changing from early time periods to the current decade? Sex-role stereotyping is a similar issue, as is the fact of aged characters. Are the elderly always pictured as doddering, forgetful, or maudlin?

3. The website for the Mystery Writers of America organization contains a page called "Kids Love a Mystery." Check out www.mysterywriters.org to find out if this would be interesting to you and also to see the Edgar Award winners for children and adults.

4. The website of the American Library Association that focuses on censorship is www.ala.org/bbooks/index/html. Consult it to find out what kinds of challenges people bring to books, and what books are listed. See if your favorite book is listed!

Activities for the Primary Level

1. Ramona Quimby is a funny, sweet character in several Beverly Cleary novels appropriate for independent reading in second and third grades. A recent public television series has also depicted Ramona's escapades. The latest, and last, book of Ramona is *Ramona's World* (Cleary, 1999). After children have read some of the books, or, in the case of kindergarten and first grade, listened to read-alouds, create a character cluster of Ramona.

2. You might use the following transitional books of contemporary realism to encourage independent silent reading by primary children. Each author has many titles, so explore your library for more.

   David Adler, *Cam Jansen*
   Betsy Byars, *Herculeah Jones*
   Ann Cameron, *Julian, Huey, and Gloria*
   Paula Danziger, *Amber Brown*
   Suzy Kline, *Horrible Harry*
   Peggy Parrish, *Amelia Bedelia*
   Cynthia Rylant, *Henry and Mudge*
   Louis Sachar, *Marvin Redpost*
   Marjorie Weinman Sharmat, *Nate the Great*

3. Step into the shoes of your favorite character, and for discussions, bulletin boards, and art activities, have your children think of their favorite characters (see Figure 9.2). It may be someone in a story you are reading aloud, or one of the characters from book groups going on at the present time. With a large shoeprint (at least one for each child), children could do the following:

   (1) Write three facts about the character on the cut-out.

   (2) Get three to five shoeprints and write one event from the story on each one. Arrange the shoeprints in order to create a sequence of events.

   (3) Illustrate one or more events on the shoeprints. The following books may help to focus this activity, and you may find more: *Shoes* (Nichelason, 1997) and *Shoeshine Whittaker* (Ketteman, 1999).

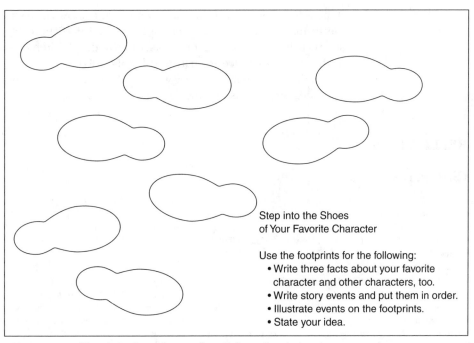

Step into the Shoes
of Your Favorite Character

Use the footprints for the following:
• Write three facts about your favorite
  character and other characters, too.
• Write story events and put them in order.
• Illustrate events on the footprints.
• State your idea.

Figure 9.2 Step into the shoes of your favorite character

Activities for the Intermediate and Middle Levels

1. Try the "Step into a Character's Shoes" activity just described in the previous section (see Figure 9.2).

2. Children can become aware of censorship and the political ramifications of such a process if discussions are launched or the ALA website is accessed. If there is a controversial book, or an issue that children in a middle level classroom are reading about, encourage the children to find out what censorship is, who has the right to censor, and what our obligations are to protect intellectual freedom in a democratic society.

3. Many children in intermediate and middle schools are beginning to learn instruments in school music programs. Following are some books that display the courage and perseverance it takes to learn to play an instrument well. (See activity 3 in Chapter 10 for historical realism with the same theme—a young musician compelled to make music.)

The Sandy Bottom Orchestra, G. Keillor & J. L. Nilsson (1996)

Becoming Felix, N. H. Wilson (1996)

The Mozart Season, V. E. Wolff (1991)

The Facts and Fictions of Minna Pratt, P. MacLachlan (1988)

4. If there is interest in quiz and reality television shows in your classroom, use the format to incorporate contemporary realistic fiction. Plan a "Survivor" skit by using characters from books, or have the children generate questions in the multiple-choice format used by *Who Wants to be a Millionaire?* The *Jeopardy* game board with answers, with "contestants" generating the correct question, is a useful and fun-filled activity, too.

REFERENCES

Children's Works

Alcott, L. M. (1868/1987). *Little women*. New York: Dell Yearling Classics.

Alphin, E. (2000). *Counterfeit son*. New York: Harcourt.

Anonymous. (1971). *Go ask Alice*. New York: Macmillan.

Blume, J. (1968). *Are you there, God? It's me, Margaret*. New York: Bradbury.

Burnett, F. H. (1911/1987). *The secret garden*. New York: Dell Yearling Classics.

Burnford, S. (1961). *The incredible journey*. Boston: Little, Brown.

Chandler, E. (2000). *Dark secrets*. New York: Archway.

Choldenko, G. (2001). *Notes from a liar and her dog*. New York: Putnam.

Christopher, M. (2000a). *Soccer duel*. Boston: Little, Brown.

Christopher, M. (2000b). *Tennis ace*. Boston: Little, Brown.

Cleary, B. (1983). *Dear Mr. Henshaw*. New York: Morrow.

Cleary, B. (1999). *Ramona's world*. New York: Morrow.

Cole, B. (1987). *The goats*. New York: Farrar, Straus & Giroux.

Cooper, I. (2000). *Absolutely Lucy*. New York: Golden Books.

Cooper, J. F. (1826/1898). *Cooper's the last of the Mohicans: A narrative of 1757*. Boston: Ginn & Company.

Creech, S. (1994). *Walk two moons*. New York: Harper-Collins.

Creech, S. (2000). *The wanderer*. New York: Cotler/HarperCollins.

Crutcher, C. (2001). *Whale talk*. New York: Greenwillow.

Cummings, P. (2001). *A face first*. New York: Dutton.

Defoe, D. (1719/1965). *The life and adventures of Robinson Crusoe*. Baltimore: Penguin Books.

Deuker, C. (2000). *Night hoops*. Boston: Houghton Mifflin.

DiCamillo, K. (2000). *Because of Winn-Dixie*. Boston: Candlewick.

Dodge, M. M. (1865/2001). *Hans Brinker, or the silver skates: A story of life in Holland*. New York. Presbyterian & Reformed Pub. Co.

Farley, W. (1944). *The black stallion*. New York: Random House.

Fitzhugh, L. (1964/2000). *Harriet the spy*. New York: Delacorte.

Fleischman, P. (2001). *Seek*. New York: Marcato/Cricket.

George, J. C. (1959/2000). *My side of the mountain trilogy*. New York: Dutton.

Haas, J. (2001). *Runaway radish*. New York: Greenwillow.

Hamilton, V. (1967). *Zeely*. New York: Macmillan.

Hearne, B. (2000). *Who's in the hall? A mystery in four chapters*. New York: Greenwillow.

Henry, M. (1948). *King of the wind*. New York: Rand McNally.

Hinton, S. E. (1967). *The outsiders*. New York: Viking.

Horvath, P. (2001). *Everything on a waffle*. New York: Farrar, Straus & Giroux.

Keillor, G., & Nilsson, J. L. (1996). *The sandy bottom orchestra*. New York: Hyperion.

Ketteman, H. (1999). *Shoeshine Whittaker*. New York: Walker.

Klise, K. (2001). *Trial by jury/journal*. New York: HarperCollins.

Konigsburg, E. L. (2000). *Silent to the bone*. New York: Atheneum.

Koss, A. (2001). *Stranger in Dadland*. New York: Dial.

Lowry, L. (1999). *Zooman Sam*. Boston: Houghton Mifflin.

Lynch, C. (2000). *Gold dust*. New York: HarperCollins.

MacLachlan, P. (1988). *The facts and fictions of Minna Pratt*. New York: Harper.

Macy, S. (ed.) (2001). *Girls got game: Sports stories and poems*. New York: Holt.

Maynard, B. (2000). *Pondfire*. New York: Putnam.

Mills, C. (2000). *Lizzie at last*. New York: Farrar, Straus & Giroux.

Morgenstern, S. (2001). (Trans. by G. Rosner, ill. by S. Bloch). *A book of coupons*. New York: Viking.

Naylor, P. R. (1991). *Shiloh*. New York: Atheneum.

Naylor, P. R. (1996). *Shiloh season*. New York: Atheneum.

Newbery, J. (1744/1967). *A Little pretty pocket-book: Milestones in children's literature*. New York: Harcourt, Brace & World.

Nichelason, M. G. (1997). *Shoes*. New York: Carolrhoda.

Paterson, K. (1977). *Bridge to Terabithia*. New York: Crowell.

Paterson, K. (1980). *Jacob have I loved*. New York: Crowell.

Paulsen, G. (1987). *Hatchet*. New York: Bradbury.

Paulsen, G. (1996). *Brian's winter*. New York: Bradbury.

Pinkwater, D. (2001). *Fat camp commandos*. New York: Scholastic.

Plum-Ucci, C. (2000). *The body of Christopher Creed*. New York: Harcourt.

Rawlings, M. K. (1938/1966). *The Yearling*. New York: C. Scribner's sons.

Rawls, W. (1961). *Where the red fern grows*. New York: Doubleday.

Rennison, L. (2000). *Angus, thongs, and full frontal snogging: Confessions of Georgia Nicolson*. New York: HarperCollins.

Rennison, L. (2001). *On the bright side, I'm now the girlfriend of a sex god: Further confessions of Georgia Nicolson*. New York: HarperCollins.

Salinger, J. D. (1951). *Catcher in the rye*. Boston: Little, Brown.

Smith, C. R., Jr. (2000). *Tall tales: Six amazing basketball dreams*. New York: Dutton.

Sobol, D. (1999). *Encyclopedia Brown and the case of the slippery salamander*. New York: Delacorte.

Spyri, J. (1884/1986). *Heidi*. Stamford, CT: Longmeadow Press.

Twain, M. (1876/1989). *The adventures of Tom Sawyer*. New York: Penguin.

Van Draanen, W. (2001). *Sammy Keyes and the Hollywood mummy*. New York: Knopf.

Wilder, L. I. (1932). *Little house in the big woods*. New York: Harper & Row.

Wilson, N. H. (1996). *Becoming Felix*. New York: Farrar, Straus & Giroux.

Wolff, V. E. (1991). *The Mozart season*. New York: Holt.

Zusak, M. (2001). *Fighting Ruben Wolfe*. New York: Levine/Scholastic.

Professional Works

American Library Association. (1996). *Intellectual freedom manual* (5th ed.). Chicago: Author.

Carlson, J. (1970). *A comparison of the treatment of the Negro in children's literature in the periods 1929–1938 and 1959–1968*. Unpublished dissertation. Ann Arbor, MI: University Microfilms.

Egoff, S. (1980). The problem novel. In S. Egoff, G. T. Stubbs, & L. F. Ashley (Eds.), *Only Connect* (2nd ed.). Toronto: Oxford University Press.

Jordan, A. D. (1996). Bathtub reading: Series books. *Teaching and Learning Literature, 5,* 14–22.

McClure, A. (1995). Censorship of children's books. In S. Lehr (Ed.), *Battling dragons* (pp. 3–30). Portsmouth, NH: Heinemann.

Micklos, J. (Ed.). (2001). Banned books week invites readers to celebrate the freedom to read. *Reading Today, 19*(1).

Nodelman, P. (1996). *The pleasures of children's literature* (2nd ed.). New York: Longman.

Simmons, J. S., & Dresang, E. T. (2001). *School censorship in the 21st century: A guide for teachers and school library media specialists*. Newark, DE: International Reading Association.

Smith, D. (1963). *Fifty years of children's books*. Champaign, IL: National Council of Teachers of English.

Soderburgh, P. (1980). The Stratemeyer strain: Educators and the juvenile series book, 1900–1980. In S. Egoff, G. T. Stubbs, & L. F. Ashley (Eds.), *Only Connect* (2nd ed., pp. 63–73). Toronto: Oxford University Press.

Walsh, J. P. (1981). The art of realism. In B. Hearne & M. Kaye (Eds.), *Celebrating children's books*. New York: Lothrop, Lee & Shepard.

Watson, B. (1991, Fall). Tom Swift, Nancy Drew and pals all had the same dad. *The Smithsonian,* 50–61.

Wolf, V. (1975). Harriet the spy: Milestone, masterpiece? In F. Butler (Ed.), *Children's Literature Annual, 4* (pp. 120–126). Philadelphia: Temple University Press.

Additional Resources

Hogan, W. (2001). *The agony and the eggplant: Daniel Pinkwater's heroic struggle in the name of y a literature*. Lanham, MD: Scarecrow Press.
A profile of this humorous author, this critique of his work is insightful and filled with his quotes.

Lehr, S. (Ed.) (2001). *Beauty, brains, & brawn: The construction of gender in children's literature*. Portsmouth, NH: Heinemann.
Fourteen essays discuss gender in many children's books, Harry Potter among them. The need for politically aware pedagogy is stressed.

Scales, P. R. (2001). *Teaching banned books: 12 guides for young readers.* Chicago, IL: American Library Association.
   Scales takes 12 challenged novels (e.g., The Goats and Roll of Thunder, Hear My Cry), and develops 12 teaching units related to first amendment rights.

Children's Book Clubs

Scholastic (P.O. Box 7502, Jefferson City, MO 65102).
Troll (2 Lethbridge Plaza, Mahwah, NJ 07430).
Trumpet (P.O. Box 604, Holmes, PA 19043).
   These book clubs provide inexpensive, popular paperback books to children in elementary schools.

CHAPTER 10

Realism in the Past

INTRODUCTION AND RESPONSE

Reading in novels of historical realism about the horror of war, hardship and humor on the Oregon Trail, and Viking ships plundering early English villages gives children and adolescents spectacular insight into human history as it unfolded. Such stories—set in the past, evoking castles and kings, prairies and pioneers—allow readers to enter vicariously an historical period and learn from it. Our understanding of today's world is enhanced by historical realism with its glimpses into the past.

The term *realism* denotes a particular kind of fiction. The emphasis in Chapter 9 was on contemporary realistic fiction, or stories that could actually happen. In this chapter, historical fiction is the focus, or realistic stories that *could have happened* in a previous time. When done well, historical realism re-creates the past with attention to an accurate representation of what we know to be factual. A noted writer of historical realism, Joan Aiken, says, "Only fiction, or a truly perceptive biography, can communicate this real appreciation of how the past looked, sounded, felt and smelt" (Aiken, 1996, p. 67). Although the story is fiction, made up of characters who may or may not have lived, the important element is the historical context of time and place interacting with personal and societal attitudes. Historical fiction dramatizes and humanizes the sterile facts of history.

In this chapter, many children's books of historical fiction are described and listed according to five subgenres that are based roughly on a chronology of civilization. Criteria for evaluation are proposed, and an extensive bibliography of historical realism is presented. Ideas for a thematic unit entitled "When Children Went to War" are included prior to the Implications for Instruction section.

To recall this genre, historical realism, or historical fiction as it is sometimes called, study the photo of the cover of *Bud, Not Buddy* (Curtis, 1999). This important book received the Newbery Medal and the Coretta Scott King Award in 2000, the first book to win both prestigious awards simultaneously. The cover photo

From BUD, NOT BUDDY by
Christopher Paul Curtis,
copyright © 1999 by
Christopher Paul Curtis. Used
by permission of Random
House Children's Books, a
division of Random House, Inc.

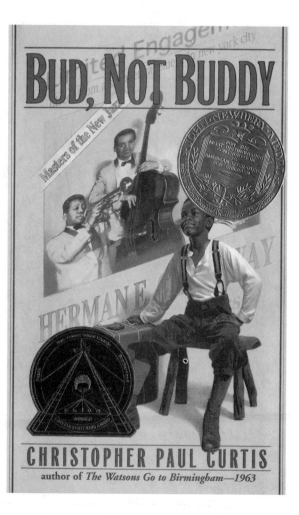

reveals key elements in the story that have historical significance: the child's dress, music denoting the "new jazz" of the 1930s, and the name, Herman E. Calloway (partially obscured by the boy's figure). The boy's facial expression and tilt of his head show a guarded optimism, and the assertiveness of the title seconds this interpretation. What do you notice about the cover? How does this scene evoke a realistic glimpse of the past, a past that we have never experienced? Does your response lead you to remember other books that are deeply embedded in your reading experience? This chapter should trigger memories of well-known, emotionally satisfying and cognitively rewarding books and should lead you to discover many more.

DEFINING HISTORICAL FICTION

The term *historical fiction* implies that an author has created a story set in the past. The story is realistic: It could have happened and it coincides with what we know to be true in a previous time. Nevertheless, it is still a story with imaginary characters and plot. The distinguishing feature of this genre is that the term *historical* connotes some measure of truth. There is an authenticity in the setting, as the time and place reflect a veracity that can be judged by other historical documents. Thus, authors of historical fiction are concerned with accuracy of detail. Through research into primary documents and secondary sources, they re-create as realistic a world as possible.

REFLECTION   How possible is it to be completely authentic in a work of fiction? How important is it? Don't we always distort history when we combine fiction and fact?

While the term *historical* connotes some measure of truth, it is still an arbitrary term with respect to a time period. As mentioned in Chapter 8, the timeline of history is divided into "historical" time, from ancient times to the late 1960s, and "contemporary" times, from the 1970s to the present. Books in this chapter will cover time periods from the beginning of recorded time to the Civil Rights era. However, discrepancies exist among scholars of children's literature as to what constitutes "historical." Some now consider not only the aftermath of World War II, but also the period of the "Cold War" and the conflict in Southeast Asia as properly historical (Galda & Cullinan, 2002). Clearly, in the minds of children today, what happened before the 1980s could be considered history. A case in point is a previous book written by the Newbery/King winner Christopher Paul Curtis, *The Watsons Go to Birmingham—1963* (1995). In the summer of 1963, the Watsons, an African-American family from Flint, Michigan, go to Birmingham, Alabama, to visit their Grandma. This Newbery honor book captures a specific time in history dramatically and poignantly. Told from the point of view of the young son, humor turns to horror on September 15, 1963, when a bomb kills four little girls in the Sixteenth Avenue Baptist Church. As this event was a catalyst in the Civil Rights movement, this book is tied to a past specific time in history, and it is deemed historical realism.

Historical realism is the most common mode of historical fiction for children and adults. However, historical fantasy (see Chapter 8), which is also historical fiction, is another creative example of using an historical setting in stories. "Time fantasies" often contrast a past time and the present, and some fantasies, such as *A Proud Taste for Scarlet and Miniver* (Konigsburg, 1973) are completely set in a past time (and in a fantasy world: the afterlife). *Roughing It on the Oregon Trail* (Stanley, 2000), another time fantasy, involves twins who travel back in time to 1843 and experience the trials and vicissitudes of trail life. Because fantasy has been discussed, this chapter examines only books of historical realism.

HISTORY OF HISTORICAL FICTION

In the 19th century, when children's literature blossomed into various genres, stories with historical settings gained wide popularity and brought a new dimension to readers. Robert Louis Stevenson's *Treasure Island* (1883/1996) and Howard Pyle's *Otto of the Silver Hand* (1888/1967) immediately set the stage for high adventure, and slightly romanticized the past. Sir Walter Scott's *Ivanhoe* (1819/1994), legends of King Arthur, Robin Hood, and others had previously found their way into mainstream fiction.

In 1929, the Newbery medal was awarded to *The Trumpeter of Krakow* by Eric Kelly (1928/1966). This was a complex story of a 15th-century Polish boy who, at risk of his life, bravely played a hymn in the cathedral tower, signaling the villagers of danger. Recognition from the prestigious Newbery committee brought attention to the genre of historical fiction.

Significant books in the development of historical realism must include the *Little House* series by Laura Ingalls Wilder. Published from 1932 to 1943—beginning with *Little House in the Big Woods* (1932)—these well-loved stories, almost autobiographical, describe the pioneer ethos in flowing, but unadorned prose. Placed in the top echelon of historical fiction, the *Little House* books are valued for their literary quality and are a "superb example of the mythology of the American frontier and are worthy of study as such" (Fellman, 1996, p. 114). Other hallmarks of this genre include *Johnny Tremain* (Forbes, 1943), which captures the spirit of the colonists in the American Revolution, and *The Door in the Wall* (de Angeli, 1949), a touching, timeless story of a crippled boy in 14th-century England struggling with his handicap while striving to become a knight's page. Elizabeth George Speare's two Newbery winners—*The Witch of Blackbird Pond* (1958/2001) and *The Bronze Bow* (1961)—were touchstones for carefully researched, compelling stories about characters interacting with society's pressures to conform.

The establishment of the Laura Ingalls Wilder Award in 1954 (from the American Library Association) and the Scott O'Dell Award (www.scottodell.com/sosoaward.html) in 1981 also added stature to the place of historical fiction in the world of children's literature by honoring authors for their work.

REFLECTION What would you add to the list? Has your touchstone for historical fiction been included?

In addition to the books just mentioned, the following outstanding books of historical realism bring a period of history into the lives of children today. Others are described in the sections that follow.

*Caddie Woodlawn, C. R. Brink (1935)

All-of-a-Kind Family, S. Taylor (1951)

*Island of the Blue Dolphins, S. O'Dell (1960)

*Across Five Aprils, I. Hunt (1964)

*A Gathering of Days, J. Blos (1979)

*Catherine, Called Birdy, K. Cushman (1994)

*A Year Down Yonder, R. Peck (2000)

*A Newbery Award Winner or Honor Book

VALUE OF HISTORICAL REALISM

Children relive the past through historical realism. They can gain an understanding of their own heritage or someone else's in books that portray the human condition with dignity. By looking at the past through a compelling story, readers see interrelationships of past and present—how the past influences the present and predicts the future. Historical realism helps children see and judge the mistakes of the past. Because change is a constant condition of life, historical fiction helps readers realize that change is essential, that growth and development depend on change. Very often the main character is a catalyst for change, and tension arises in the story when old attitudes clash with new.

Themes in historical realism echo themes in contemporary works: gaining independence, becoming more sensitive to the needs of others, broadening one's world view, coping with life's problems, and proving competence. When Jill Paton Walsh writes of a village isolating itself to prevent the spread of the plague in the early 1600s (*A Parcel of Patterns,* 1983), parallels can be drawn to contemporary problems, such as the Ebola virus and AIDS. Characters display the many responses that people would show today: fear, anger, fortitude, courage, even apathy, thus making this work of historical realism relevant and compelling.

Other themes specific to historical fiction are listed below. As you think about these themes, generate examples in your own mind of actual stories, or ask others for examples from their childhood reading. Examples from recently published books are given.

- *Clash between indigenous peoples and invaders, or clash between old and new ideas*

  Raven of the Waves (Cadnum, 2001)
  Witness (Hesse, 2001)
  The Sketchbook of Thomas Blue Eagle (Matthaei & Grutman, 2001)

- *Love of the land or the sea*

  A Year Without Rain (Love, 2000)
  Storm Warriors (Carbone, 2001)
  The Land (Taylor, 2001)

- *Upholding loyalty and honor*

  Dream Soul (Yep, 2000)
  The Executioner's Daughter (Williams, 2000)

- *Cruelty and futility of war* (also see bibliography in When Children Went to War at the end of this chapter)

  Forgotten Fire (Bagdasarian, 2001)

- *Movement and change to better conditions*

  Nory Ryan's Song (Giff, 2000)
  Stick and Whittle (Hite, 2000)
  Oranges on Golden Mountain (Partridge, 2001)

EVALUATING HISTORICAL FICTION

Like contemporary fiction, historical fiction must resonate with realistic situations, problems, and believable characters. In evaluating a work of historical fiction, certain criteria are applied that pertain to all literature. A good story, well told, that enlightens as well as entertains is key to our enjoyment. Our intellect is engaged, and we empathize with characters, even identify with some of them. As with other realism, we have questions about too much violence, blatant sexuality, and inappropriate language.

Certain criteria pertain specifically to historical fiction. The authenticity of the story must ring true. Characters must act in accordance with the spirit of the times. One would not judge historical times with a 20th-century viewpoint. However, one should not judge the past too harshly, or too stereotypically. In *At the Sign of the Star* (Sturtevant, 2000), set in London in the 1600s, a young woman takes charge of her family's printing business. While women's roles were narrowly defined in the past, there were still women and circumstances that could realistically allow that to happen. So, a criticism that "women were never allowed to be in business" would not be justified. The past should not be romanticized, nor all awful things overlooked; nor should the past necessarily be held up to the enlightened social consciousness of the late 20th century.

In historical fiction, accurate historical settings must be created from facts gleaned from research. Such research, from primary sources when possible, manifests details that are indispensable to a high quality of realism. Authors are prepared to reveal how their research was conducted. Readers should be aware of the need to represent the past accurately, and develop a critical reading stance when judging historical fiction. The evaluation scheme in Figure 10.1 poses criteria in the form of questions so that you can evaluate aspects of historical realism.

Figure 10.1
Evaluating historical realism

Criteria	My Personal Response
Authenticity in Setting Plot Character Development Theme Language	Are the time and place vividly described and historically accurate? Is what happens in the story consistent with what could happen (and still fresh and new)? Do characters grow and change in keeping with the time period? How does the theme permeate the story? Is the theme familiar? Does the language give a flavor of the period without overwhelming it?
Research Notes from the author	Are sources evident? Do facts overpower the story? Does the story help the reader regard a past time in a new, more informed, light?

As in other chapters, a four-point scale is given here in order to make the evaluation more objective for those who find this easier. Questions pertaining to authenticity and research force the evaluator to circle a number; then the values may be added to produce a total score, or the values may be discussed individually to score certain aspects of the book.

Four-Point Scale for Evaluating Historical Realism

Name of Text: _____

Author (and illustrator and translator, in some cases): _____

1 stands for "very good," 2 is "good," 3 is "marginal," and 4 is "unsatisfactory." Rate the book according to the following:

Authenticity

    I. The setting is vividly described and realistic for the time and place.

       1 _____ 2 _____ 3 _____ 4 _____

    II. The plot moves ahead with suspense.

       1 _____ 2 _____ 3 _____ 4 _____

    III. The characters change, grow, interact, and behave realistically.

       1 _____ 2 _____ 3 _____ 4 _____

    IV. The theme is worthwhile.

       1 _____ 2 _____ 3 _____ 4 _____

    V. Language patterns (dialect, usage) contribute to the historical feeling of the story without overwhelming it.

       1 _____ 2 _____ 3 _____ 4 _____

Research

    VI. Research is evident (e.g., author's notes, bibliography, or suggested readings).

       1 _____ 2 _____ 3 _____ 4 _____

    VII. The research contributes to the story without overwhelming it.

       1 _____ 2 _____ 3 _____ 4 _____

REFLECTION Is it possible to judge the past by today's standards? Should characters in historical fiction, for example, be free of sexist attitudes, or evidence more accepting standards of violent behavior?

SUBGENRES OF HISTORICAL FICTION

In five chronological categories, beginning with ancient times and continuing through the first half of the 20th century, historical fiction for children demonstrates

Figure 10.2
Subgenres of
historical realism

Approximate Dates	Subgenre
Beginning of recorded time to A.D. 400	The Ancient World
A.D. 400 to A.D. 1500	The Medieval and Renaissance Worlds
A.D. 1500 to A.D. 1800	Exploration and Colonization
A.D. 1800 to A.D. 1900	Western Expansion and Industrialization
A.D. 1900 to A.D. 1960	The Early and Mid-20th Century

powerful themes in a realistic world. Broad historical eras outlining the categories, or subgenres, have been arbitrarily chosen for this book:

The Ancient World

The Medieval and Renaissance Worlds

Exploration and Colonization

Westward Expansion and Industrialization

The Early and Mid-20th Century

In the subgenres of historical realism that follow, a brief explanation hits the high points of each era (see Figure 10.2). Descriptions of some novels are followed by a recommended list. Many of the authors have several noteworthy books to their credit, so if a particular book is unavailable, try another. You are encouraged to add your preferred historical realism titles and to continue to look in libraries, schools, and bookstores for additional worthy books.

The Ancient World

Stories set in this period, from earliest recorded time to the fall of the Roman Empire (about A.D. 400), seem almost mythlike in their antiquity. However, using careful research to uncover the few facts available, gifted authors re-create life and times in ancient cultures.

Rosemary Sutcliff is unsurpassed for her ability to bring contemporary relevancy to stories of ancient times in Britain. Her *Song for a Dark Queen* (1978) describes a female warrior, Queen Boudicca, as she leads her people in eastern England against Roman invaders about A.D. 50. It is a sad story because the Dark Queen is doomed to fail; nevertheless, her personal courage and intelligence light this shadowed period.

Recent and Recommended Books About the Ancient World

Shiva: An Adventure of the Ice Age, J. H. Brennan (1989) (Europe)

Troy, A. Geras (2001) (Greece)

Pharaoh's Daughter: A Novel of Ancient Egypt, Lester (2000)

The Wadjet Eye, J. Rubalcaba (2000) (Egypt and Mediterranean area)

The Medieval and Renaissance Worlds

Beginning with the Dark Ages and continuing into the Renaissance, this period covers more than a thousand years, from A.D. 400 to about A.D. 1500. In Europe, as well as in Asia, Africa, and the Americas, certain cultures ruled through conquest and subjugation. Roman Catholicism permeated much of Europe, providing a political structure for future nation-states to emerge. In Asia, the Byzantine Empire flourished.

Other great civilizations in the Americas (the Aztecs and the Mayas, for example), Africa (the Mali), and Asia (dynasties in China and Japan) rose and fell in cycles of historical importance.

Human drama set on these historical stages portrays tales of chivalrous knights, feudal wars, and the bravery of individual men and women. In a Newbery Honor book, *The Striped Ships* (McGraw, 1991) carried William the Conqueror to England's shore in 1066. A young Saxon, Juliana, saw the ships in the distance and then lived through the turmoil that followed the Norman victory at the Battle of Hastings. Juliana's persistence and love for her family proved key to her survival.

Recent and Recommended Books About the Medieval and Renaissance Worlds

Shakespeare's Scribe, G. Blackwood (2000) (Britain)

The Fated Sky, H. Branford (1999) (Viking Norway)

The Book of the Lion, M. Cadnum (2000) (England & the Holy Land – Crusades)

Matilda Bone, K. Cushman (2000) (Britain)

The Devil and His Boy, A. Horowitz (2000) (England)

Nzingha: Warrior Queen of Matamba, P. McKissack (2000) (Africa)

Marguerite Makes a Book, B. Robertson (1999) (France)

Exploration and Colonization

Columbus's expedition of 1492, extending the voyages of discovery that preceded it, metaphorically and literally opened up a new world. Adventures on land and sea recounted the perils of the unknown and the courage of those who risked lives and fortunes to discover uncharted territory. Celebrating the restless human spirit, stories of exploration sometimes demonstrate a devaluation and callousness to indigenous people and their cultures.

Colonies in the New World led to the formation of new nation-states. As the American colonies moved inexorably to the break with their parent country, so did other colonies in South America, led by Simón Bolivar. In Europe, winds of democracy were fanned by the French Revolution. Further exploration in the East began to reveal political structures and cultures in China, Japan, and other Asian areas of significance.

Significant books of this period include *Johnny Tremain* (Forbes, 1943), *The Witch of Blackbird Pond* (Speare, 1958/2001), and *The Sign of the Beaver* (Speare, 1983). Mary Jane Auch's *The Road to Home* (2000), the third book in a trilogy of pioneer life, presents the poignant story of a family that was shattered by the hard life of building a home in the wilderness; a different perspective is voiced by the eldest daughter who returns East.

Recent and Recommended Books of Exploration and Colonization

Fever 1793, L. H. Anderson (2000)

Sleds on Boston Common: A Story from the American Revolution, L. Borden (2000)

The Weaver's Daughter, K. B. Bradley (2000)

Waiting for Deliverance, B. Urban (2000)

Hannah's Winter of Hope, J. Van Leeuwen (2000)

Western Expansion and Industrialization

In the United States, the 19th century saw the population expand toward western agricultural land while filling up eastern cities. Pioneers and immigrants demonstrated a love for personal freedom and a willingness to brave unfamiliar territory. A conviction that freedom was a right for every person led to the Civil War and the final abolition of slavery.

Advances in medicine, technology, communications, and transportation led to a better quality of life for many people. Education became possible for a greater percentage of the population.

The quintessential pioneer story depicting the American dream and spirit was told in the *Little House* books by Laura Ingalls Wilder. She was more than 60 years old when she wrote these seven books about her childhood and her family as they moved from territory to homestead in the years from 1860 to 1880. Each book is a separate adventure, but together they present a coherent portrait of pioneer life in slow-paced plots full of details of everyday life. The books begin with *Little House in the Big Woods* (1932) and continue through *These Happy Golden Years* (1943).

Versatile author Avi explored historical realism in his outstanding *Beyond the Western Sea* books: *The Escape from Home* (1996) and *Lord Kirkle's Money* (1996). The sweeping, larger-than-life characters and well-plotted, fast-paced adventure mesmerize readers.

Recent and Recommended Books of Westward Expansion and Industrialization

Bluestem, F. Arrington (2000)

Nory Ryan's Song, P. R. Giff (2000)

Skullduggery, K. Karr (2000)

Hannah's Journal: The Story of an Immigrant Girl, M. Moss (2000)

Lyddie, K. Paterson (1991) (Vermont, Massachusetts)

Jip His Story, K. Paterson (1996) (Vermont, Massachusetts)

Soon Be Free, L. Ruby (2000)

The Midnight Train Home, E. Tamar (2000)

The Early and Mid-20th Century

The world was caught up in two wars during the first half of the 20th century. Global conflict replaced regional conflicts of previous eras. The literature of historical realism became the lens through which we saw scenes of combat, displacement of persons, and horrendous atrocities inflicted upon men, women, and children.

Other economic and social events included the collapse of world markets, known as the stock-market crash of 1929, and the resulting Great Depression of the 1930s. Society became more mobile, as people immigrated from country to country and, in the United States, from state to state. The advent of television hastened a consciousness of a new world order.

(All the books listed in the text set compiled for When Children Went to War at the end of this chapter are recent and recommended historical realism of this century.)

Recent and Recommended Books of the Early and Mid-20th Century

Brooklyn, Bugsy, and Me, L. Bowdish (2000) (New York)

Jake's Orphan, P. Brooke (2000) (North Dakota)

What Happened on Planet Kid, J. Conly (2000) (Virginia)

The Hero of Ticonderoga, G. Gauthier (2001) (New York)

Esperanza Rising, P. M. Ryan (2000) (Mexico/U.S.)

Roll of Thunder, Hear My Cry, M. Taylor (1976/2001) (Arkansas)

REFLECTION   What are the effects of censorship on historical realism? Are there certain books that have been threatened with censorship?

DIVERSITY IN HISTORICAL REALISM: A BIBLIOGRAPHY

In an effort to be comprehensive, the following bibliography highlights recent historical fiction with diverse settings and characters. Because literature allows, in fact demands, that we consider different points of view, our reading and learning are richer when they include vicarious journeys into the past and into other lives, to other continents, and beyond the mainstream of U.S. life.

The following bibliography of historical fiction is based upon the cultures of African-Americans, Asian-Americans, Native Americans, and so on. These stories take place in the United States, but they focus on people of color or people considered disenfranchised politically. The details of publication are not repeated in the end-of-chapter references.

African-American

Lyons, M. E., & Branch, M. M. (2000). *Dear Ellen Bee: A Civil War scrapbook of two Union spies*. New York: Atheneum.

McKissack, P. (2000). *Color me dark: The diary of Nellie Lee Love—the great migration north*. New York: Scholastic.

Myers, W. D. (2001). *The journal of Biddy Owens: The Negro leagues*. New York: Scholastic.

Schwartz, V. F. (2000). *Send one angel down*. New York: Holiday.

Sigelson, K. (2000). *Escape south*. New York: Golden.

Taylor, M. (1995). *The well*. New York: Dial.

Warner, S. (2001). *Finding Hattie*. New York: HarperCollins.

Asian-American

Gilmore, R. (2001). *A group of one*. New York: Holt (Indian-Canadian)

Na, A. (2001). *A step from heaven*. New York: Front Street.

Yep, L. (2000a). *Dream soul*. New York: HarperCollins.

Yep, L. (2000b). *The Journal of Wong Ming Chung: A Chinese miner*. New York: Scholastic.

Native American and Creole

Dadey, D. (2000). *Cherokee sister*. New York: Delacorte.

Doucet, S. A. (2000). *Fiddle fever*. New York: Clarion (Creole)

Jacobs, P. S. (1997). *James Printer: A novel of rebellion*. New York: Scholastic. (Nipmuc)

Osborne, M. P. (2000). *Adaline Falling Star*. New York: Scholastic.

(See also *The Sketchbook of Thomas Blue Eagle* by Matthaei and Grutman, 2001)

Gay and Lesbian

Larson, R. (1997). *What I know now*. New York: Holt.

SUMMARY

Historical realistic fiction, a popular genre, draws its power from lifelike characters, setting, and conflict in times past. Characters remind us of people we know; setting evokes emotional ties to times and places sometimes remembered and clearly recognized. Plots must be plausible, describing the unfolding of possible events. When the story is well told, with characters interacting with each other and a society re-created from the past, we can compare the past with the present and understand our world a little better. The value of historical realism lies in the window to the past it gives us; readers see changes and the effects of change. Books of historical realism allow us to view change as positive and inevitable.

In this chapter, historical fiction was defined and discussed, and many exemplary books were listed to illustrate the subgenres of historical realistic fiction, as represented in five historical eras: (1) the Ancient World, (2) the Medieval and Renaissance Worlds, (3) Exploration and Colonization, (4) Westward Expansion and Industrialization, and (5) the early and mid-20th Century. Stories from these eras exemplified the authenticity so necessary in evaluating historical realism. An evaluation scheme was presented in which authenticity and research were key features.

To complete the chapter, a bibliography was presented that is suitable for readers in elementary and middle grades. The bibliography focused on multicultural books in the United States, critically acclaimed stories featuring African-Americans, European-Americans, Hispanic-Americans, Native Americans, and gay and lesbian characters. Realism, as a literary genre, embraces every cultural group and helps readers to understand those who are different and similar, whether in contemporary times or times past.

To summarize this chapter, the following unit outline composed of a text set and teaching suggestions demonstrates how historical realism can be used pedagogically in a reading program.

When Children Went to War: Text Set and Teaching Suggestions

Based on the theme *the cruelty and futility of war,* books and teaching suggestions appropriate for a classroom of intermediate and middle school children are presented here. The theme relates specifically to World War II and historical realism that depicts children's roles in the United States and abroad as they coped with the horrific actions of humankind in their individual lives. Through literature, readers can learn about the heroic struggle, sacrifice, and courage others have made to ensure peace and prosperity for future generations. Wide-ranging discussions are possible through literature circles and grand conversations described in the teaching suggestions.

Text Set: When Children Went to War

The following books, either some or all, are the reading list for silent reading and the teaching suggestions that follow. Some take place overseas (Europe and Japan), while some are set in the United States. (All bibliographic information is here, rather than at the end of this chapter.) The books represent a variety of reading levels for grades 4 through 7. For more ideas, see the text set Holocaust in Chapter 1.

Cutler, J. (1999). *The Cello of Mr. O.* New York: Dutton.
> *An old man refuses to be daunted by the war and plays his cello in the bombed-out village center, thus giving courage to listeners. (A picture book, this could be used to introduce the unit.) (Easy)*

Gaeddert, L. (2000). *Friends and enemies*. New York: Atheneum.

> *Two boys in the Midwest, one the son of a Methodist minister and the other a conscientious objector, find themselves on opposite sides of the conflict about how best to be a patriot. (Moderate)*

Giff, P. R. (1998). *Lily's crossing*. New York: Delacorte.

> *Lily, living with her grandmother on Long Island, waits for her father to return. (Easy)*

Harrison, B. (1999). *Theo*. New York: Clarion.

> *The younger brother of a Greek resistance fighter becomes drawn into the war. (Easy)*

Hertenstein, J. (1999). *Beyond Paradise*. New York: Morrow.

> *Two teenage girls, daughters of missionary parents in China, are captured by the Japanese and sent to a POW camp in the Pacific. (Difficult)*

Isaacs, A. (2000). *Torn thread*. New York: Scholastic.

> *Two sisters in a Nazi labor camp in Czechoslovakia try to retain happy memories of parents and family. (Moderate)*

Lisle, J. T. (2000). *The art of keeping cool*. New York: Jackson/Atheneum.

> *Two 13-year-old boys, Robert and Elliot, witness the anti-German fervor in Sachem, Rhode Island, while the community fears a submarine invasion. (Moderate)*

Lowry, L. (1989). *Number the stars*. Boston: Houghton Mifflin.

> *Two girls protect a Jewish family from the Gestapo in Denmark. (Easy)*

Myers, W. D. (1999). *Journal of Scott Pendleton Collins*. New York: Scholastic.

> *A young African-American soldier writes of his part in the Normandy invasion. (Moderate)*

Vaugelade, A. (2001). *The war: A fable*. Minneapolis, MN: Carolrhoda.

> *A picture book, with animals representing characters, this story could also be used to introduce the unit by a read-aloud in a whole group setting. (Easy)*

Walters, E. (2000). *Caged eagles*. Vancouver: Orca.

> *In a Canadian internment camp, two Japanese boys struggle with injustice, physical hardship, and misunderstanding. (Moderate)*

Wulffson, D. (2001). *Soldier X*. New York: Viking.

> *A young German soldier is captured by Russians and assumes the identity of a Russian soldier. (Difficult)*

Teaching Suggestions

Journaling   Journal questions should be prepared in advance, and carefully constructed to elicit critical responses from readers as they progress through the story. For each day, at the beginning of literacy, the groups of students can formulate their own questions based on their own reading from the previous day or night, and the teacher can give three or four of the prepared questions to the group. The kind of questions that might be used include questions like "How has _____ (a character) changed in this chapter?" "What did he/she/they learn about their past?" "How do they describe the enemy?" "What is _____ afraid of most?" and "What would you do if you were _____ ?"

Literature Circles   Literature circles, popularized by Harvey Daniels in his seminal work, *Literature Circles: Voice and Choice in the Student-Centered Classroom* (1994), are excellent organizational tools that allow students to generate and maintain a book discussion. Within the circle (from four to eight students), each child has an assigned role: discussion-leader, summarizer, travel-tracer, illustrator, vocabulary-enhancer, and so on. The roles rotate around the group so that each child experiences a different purpose as the discussions continue daily, biweekly, or whenever the literature circle meets.

DRTA   A directed reading thinking activity (DRTA) helps children predict (or set purposes for reading aloud or silently) and then read to confirm or reject their predictions. It is a very focused, teacher-directed instructional technique that teachers use to teach and evaluate the reading strategies and skills employed by their students. In a unit such as this one, the teacher would schedule her/his time with small groups or individual children. Then, sitting down with the group, the teacher would model his or her own prediction. With the children taking turns, they would predict, read, and prove. This cycle is continued. An excellent source for a further explanation of the DRTA method is *Literacy for the 21st Century: A Balanced Approach* (Tompkins, 2001).

A Grand Conversation   As a culminating activity, a "grand conversation" with some (but not all) questions prepared by the teacher is a successful way to bring closure to this unit. The common theme of all the books selected for this text set is the "cruelty and futility of war," so this is the time to look at the big picture of these books and how they manifest the theme. The whole class could meet to discuss similarities and differences in character, setting, plot, and tone and how the books made them feel about war. A grand conversation is not based on specific factual information from books as much as an after-dinner conversation among friends. However, in *Effective Literacy Instruction* (Leu & Kinzer, 1999), guidelines are suggested so that the conversation proceeds smoothly and effectively.

Other Ideas   Depending upon how long the unit should last, the reading capabilities of the students, opportunities for homework or longer periods of literacy time during the school day, and the willingness and enthusiasm of the students, many activities could be added to the enrichment of the literary experience. Following are some ideas that permit readers to think about the novel in depth: story maps, character maps, writing dialogue and plays, dramatizing key scenes, and, especially, making connections to nonfiction.

In conclusion, this is a heavy topic for elementary and middle school children. The harsh reality of wartime conditions, probably foreign to almost all children in the United States, is evident in these powerful, humbling, and scary stories. The seriousness of this theme will shock some children and parents, but it is a worthwhile theme to be explored, and literature allows us to explore it with empathy and understanding.

IMPLICATIONS FOR INSTRUCTION

First, projects will encourage your active involvement with the material. Reading, analyzing, creating bibliographies, evaluating, and discussing with others are examples of projects. Next, activities for primary as well as intermediate and middle levels are described. Many of these activities have been classroom-tested. Try them in your classroom or with your children.

Projects

1. A timeline of historical fiction would be fitting. Review the History of Historical Fiction section earlier in this chapter and create a timeline, or at least a chronological list of the books discussed in that section, adding your own favorites.

2. Create a list of books of historical realism that have been filmed or televised—for example, *Sarah, Plain and Tall; Treasure Island;* and *Heidi.*

3. Evaluate one of your historical novels according to the criteria given in Figure 10.1. Do the criteria work for you?

4. To find a list of the Scott O'Dell winners, see the March issues of *The Bulletin of the Center for Children's Books,* published by the University of Illinois Press. Also, find out the criteria for the award. For example, are international books eligible? (See www.scottodell.com/sosoaward.html.)

Activities for the Primary Level

1. To a class of second- or third-graders, read aloud *Bud, Not Buddy* (Curtis, 1999) and have the children write or discuss their "rules for living" as Bud did.

2. *Roughing It on the Oregon Trail* (Stanley, 2000) is a story written for 6- to 9-year-olds in which twins find themselves transported with their grandmother to the Oregon Trail in 1843. As a class reading, this book could be used to develop projects in drama, art, music, geography, nutrition, and many other topics. Read the book and see what creative projects would interest your students.

3. Two very moving stories to listen to, to dramatize, to illustrate, and to appreciate are *Stone Fox* (Gardiner, 1980) and *Red-Dirt Jessie* (Myers, 1992). Good readers in the third and fourth grades can read them independently, and older, reluctant readers will find them interesting. Both have young characters bent on saving the family farm despite hardships while pulling a father or grandfather out of a severe depression. Both characters love a dog: Willy and the noble Searchlight; Jessie and the semiwild Ring. The story of Jessie and her family is continued in *Spotting the Leopard* (Myers, 1996).

4. In the past, animals were treated differently and were a much more vital part of the economy and family life. Horses and dogs, for example, were not just

pets but had vital roles in helping people live. In a unit about animals, discuss the differences in how people treated animals and why. In *Gib and the Grey Ghost* (Snyder, 2000), the young girl's relationship with a horse, the Grey Ghost, helps her to explore the events in the novel. Similarly, *Star in the Storm* (Harlow, 2000) is about a Newfoundland dog that proves his worth with the family.

Activities for Intermediate and Middle Levels

1. *A Bone from a Dry Sea* (Dickinson, 1992) is a great read-aloud or silent read that alternates past and present chapters. Two stories, one told by Li in ancient times and the other by Vinny on an archeology dig in Africa in the present, use *place* as a unifying element. In writing exercises, children could use place to imagine "What it was like here 3,000 years ago, or 300 years ago" and contrast stories of their own lives with the past.

2. After reading *The Sign of the Beaver* (Speare, 1983) and *Across Five Aprils* (Hunt, 1964), ask children to write simulated diary entries from Attean's point of view and from Jenny's. Using a minor character to reflect in a diary entry helps to learn about another point of view, since the main character's point of view is often expressed literally.

3. Young musicians sometimes have to demonstrate courage and persistence, in spite of family censure, to become skillful. For great historical realism about a boy wanting to play the cornet in 1930s Chicago, see *The Jazz Kid* (Collier, 1994); about a boy in Louisiana who wants to play Cajun music, see *Fiddle Fever* (Doucet, 2000); and about a young girl who wants to sing, see *The Midnight Train Home* (Tamar, 2000).

4. Family history is revealed by grandmothers in *My Daniel* (Conrad, 1989) and *The Night Journey* (Lasky, 1981). After children hear or read these books, they could collect oral stories from their grandparents or write a story about themselves and put it in a time capsule for a future reader. In addition, both books alternate past and present, Lasky's more obviously than Conrad's, thus providing an interesting format for children to try in their own writing. Janet Hickman's *Jericho* (1994) is also a compelling story that alternates chapters between great-granddaughter and great-grandmother while revealing four generations of family history.

5. For older students, a unit on the Holocaust can be successful for teaching empathy, historical accuracy, and the critical skills of reading, speaking, listening, and writing. Following are three well-acclaimed books and a film receiving the ALA Notable distinction for 1996. It is wise to read or preview these first, however, to find out if the emotional content is right for your group. (Also see the text sets in this chapter and Chapter 1.)

Four Perfect Pebbles: A Holocaust Story, by L. Perl and M. B. Lazen (1996)

Nightfather, by C. Friedman (translated from Dutch) (1994)

The Final Journey, by G. Pausewang (1996)

Children Remember the Holocaust (1996) (film, 46 minutes), Society of Visual Education, 6677 N. Northwest Hwy., Chicago, IL 60631–1304. (Appropriate for ages 12 and older)

6. The newspaper format used by Paul Fleischman in *Dateline: Troy* (1996) tells the story of the Trojan War using a collage of newspaper clippings from modern events (World War I through the Persian Gulf War). Children would enjoy this visual, artistic way to tell a story in history related to their studies. How about creating a newspaper about the building of the transcontinental railroad or searching for gold in California? Students will generate many ideas and gain knowledge about the period they're studying.

REFERENCES

Children's Works

Anderson, L. H. (2000). *Fever 1793.* New York: Simon & Schuster.

Arrington, F. (2000). *Bluestem.* New York: Philomel.

Auch, M. J. (2000). *The road to home.* New York: Holt.

Avi. (1996a). *Beyond the western sea—Book one: The escape from home.* New York: Orchard.

Avi. (1996b). *Beyond the western sea—Book two: Lord Kirkle's money.* New York: Orchard.

Bagdasarian, A. (2001). *Forgotten fire.* New York: Kroupa/DK Ink.

Blackwood, G. (2000). *Shakespeare's scribe.* New York: Dutton.

Blos, J. (1979). *A gathering of days.* New York: Scribner.

Borden, L. (2000). *Sleds on Boston Common: A story from the American Revolution.* New York: McElderry.

Bowdish, L. (2000). *Brooklyn, Bugsy, and Me.* New York: Farrar.

Bradley, K. B. (2000). *The weaver's daughter.* New York: Delacorte.

Branford, H. (1999). *The fated sky.* Boston: Candlewick.

Brennan, J. H. (1989). *Shiva: An adventure of the ice age.* New York: Lippincott.

Brink, C. (1935). *Caddie Woodlawn.* New York: Macmillan.

Brooke, P. (2000). *Jake's orphan.* Toronto: DKInk/Kroupa.

Cadnum, M. (2000). *The book of the lion.* New York: Viking.

Cadnum, M. (2001). *Raven of the waves.* New York: Orchard.

Carbone, E. (2001). *Storm warriors.* New York: Knopf.

Children Remember the Holocaust. (1996). Chicago, IL: Society of Visual Education.

Collier, J. (1994). *The jazz kid.* New York: Holt.

Conly, J. (2000). *What happened on planet kid.* New York: Holt.

Conrad, P. (1989). *My Daniel.* New York: Harper.

Curtis, C. P. (1995). *The Watsons go to Birmingham—1963.* New York: Delacorte.

Curtis, C. P. (1999). *Bud, not Buddy.* New York: Delacorte.

Cushman, K. (1994). *Catherine, called Birdy.* New York: Clarion.

Cushman, K. (2000). *Matilda Bone.* New York: Clarion.

de Angeli, M. (1949). *The door in the wall.* New York: Doubleday.

Dickinson, P. (1992). *A bone from a dry sea.* New York: Delacorte.

Dorris, M. (1992). *Morning girl.* New York: Hyperion.

Doucet, S. A. (2000). *Fiddle fever.* New York: Clarion.

Fleischman, P. (1996). *Dateline: Troy.* New York: Candlewick.

Forbes, E. (1943). *Johnny Tremain.* Boston: Houghton Mifflin.

Friedman, C. (1994). *Nightfather.* New York: Persea Books.

Gardiner, J. (1980). *Stone fox.* New York: Crowell.

Gauthier, G. (2001). *The hero of Ticonderoga.* New York: Putnam.

Geras, A. (2001). *Troy.* New York: Harcourt.

Giff, P. R. (2000). *Nory Ryan's song.* New York: Delacorte.

Harlow, J. H. (2000). *Star in the storm.* New York: McElderry.

Hesse, K. (2001). *Witness.* New York: Scholastic.

Hickman, J. (1994). *Jericho.* New York: Greenwillow.

Hite, S. (2000). *Stick and Whittle.* New York: Scholastic.

Horowitz, A. (2000). *The devil and his boy.* New York: Philomel.

Hunt, I. (1964). *Across five Aprils.* New York: Follett.

Karr, K. (2000). *Skullduggery.* New York: Hyperion.

Kelly, E. P. (1928/1966). *The trumpeter of Krakow* (rev. ed.). New York: Macmillan.

Konigsburg, E. L. (1973). *A proud taste for Scarlet and Miniver*. New York: Atheneum.

Lasky, K. (1981). *The night journey*. New York: Warner.

Lester, J. (2000). *Pharaoh's daughter: A novel of ancient Egypt*. San Diego: Silver Whistle/Harcourt.

Love, D. A. (2000). *A year without rain*. New York: Holiday.

Matthaei, G., & Grutman, J. (2001). *The sketchbook of Thomas Blue Eagle*. San Francisco: Chronicle.

MacLachlan, P. (1985). *Sarah, plain and tall*. New York: Harper & Row.

McGraw, E. (1991). *The striped ships*. New York: McElderry.

McKissack, P. (2000). *Nzingha: Warrior queen of Matamba*. New York: Scholastic.

Moss, M. (2000). *Hannah's journal: The story of an immigrant girl*. New York: Harcourt/Silver Whistle.

Myers, A. (1992). *Red-dirt Jessie*. New York: Walker.

Myers, A. (1996). *Spotting the leopard*. New York: Walker.

O'Dell, S. (1960). *Island of the blue dolphins*. Boston: Houghton Mifflin.

Partridge, E. (2001). *Oranges on Golden Mountain*. New York: Dutton.

Paterson, K. (1991). *Lyddie*. New York: Dutton.

Paterson, K. (1996). *Jip his story*. New York: Dutton.

Pausewang, G. (1996). *The final journey*. New York: Viking.

Peck, R. (2000). *A year down yonder*. New York: Dial.

Perl, L., & Lazen, M. B. (1996). *Four perfect pebbles: A Holocaust story*. New York: Greenwillow.

Pyle, H. (1888/1967). *Otto of the silver hand*. New York: Dover.

Robertson, B. (1999). *Marguerite makes a book*. San Francisco: Getty.

Rubalcaba, J. (2000). *The wadjet eye*. New York: Clarion.

Ruby, L. (2000). *Soon be free*. New York: Simon & Schuster.

Ryan, P. M. (2000). *Esperanza rising*. New York: Scholastic.

Scott, W. (1819/1994). *Ivanhoe*. New York: American Guidance.

Snyder, Z. K. (2000). *Gib and the Grey Ghost*. New York: Delacorte.

Speare, E. G. (1958/2001). *The witch of blackbird pond*. Boston: Houghton Mifflin.

Speare, E. G. (1961). *The bronze bow*. Boston: Houghton Mifflin.

Speare, E. G. (1983). *The sign of the beaver*. Boston: Houghton Mifflin.

Spyri, J. (1884/1986). *Heidi*. Stamford, CT: Longmeadow Press.

Stanley, D. (2000). *Roughing it on the Oregon Trail*. New York: HarperCollins/Cotler.

Stevenson, D. (Ed.). *Bulletin of the center of children's books*. Champaign, IL: University of Illinois Press.

Stevenson, R. L. (1883/1996). *Treasure Island*. London: Longman.

Sturtevant, K. (2000). *At the sign of the star*. New York: Farrar, Straus & Giroux.

Sutcliff, R. (1978). *Song for a dark queen*. New York: Crowell.

Sutcliff, R. (1990). *The shining company*. New York: Farrar, Straus & Giroux.

Tamar, E. (2000). *The midnight train home*. New York: Knopf.

Taylor, M. (1976/2001). *Roll of thunder, hear my cry*. New York: Fogelman.

Taylor. M. (2001). *The land*. New York: Fogelman.

Taylor, S. (1951). *All-of-a-kind family*. Chicago, IL: Follett.

Urban, B. (2000). *Waiting for deliverance*. New York: Orchard.

Van Leeuwen, J. (2000). *Hannah's winter of hope*. New York: Fogelman.

Walsh, J. P. (1983). *A parcel of patterns*. New York: Farrar, Straus & Giroux.

Wilder, L. I. (1932). *Little house in the big woods*. New York: Harper & Row.

Wilder, L. I. (1943). *These happy golden years*. New York: Harper & Row.

Williams, L. E. (2000). *The executioner's daughter*. New York: Holt.

Yep, L. (2000). *Dream soul*. New York: HarperCollins.

Professional Works

Aiken, J. (1996). Interpreting the past: Reflections of an historical novelist. In Egoff, Stubbs, Ashley, and Sutton (Eds.), *Only connect*. Toronto: Oxford University Press.

Daniels, H. (1994). *Literature circles: Voice and choice in the student-centered classroom*. York, ME: Stenhouse.

Fellman, A. C. (1996). Don't expect to depend on anybody else . . .: The frontier as portrayed in the Little House books. In F. Butler, R. H. W. Dillard, & E. L. Keyser (Eds.), *Children's literature annual, 24*. New Haven, CT: Yale University Press.

Galda, L., & Cullinan, B. (2002). *Literature and the child* (5th ed.). Belmont, CA: Wadsworth/Thomson Learning.

Leu, D., & Kinzer, D. (1999). *Effective literacy instruction* (4th edition). Upper Saddle River, NJ: Prentice Hall.

Tompkins, G. (2001). *Literacy for the 21st century: A balanced approach*. Upper Saddle River, NJ: Prentice Hall.

Additional Resources

Anderson, A. W. (1999). *Medieval knight—read me a book.* Lanham, MD: Scarecrow.

For upper elementary and middle grades, this gives programming ideas presented in clear, easy-to-follow plans.

Bosmajian, H. (1996). Mildred Taylor's story of Cassie Logan: A search for law and justice in a racist society. In F. Butler, R. H. W. Dillard, & E. L. Keyser (Eds.), *Children's Literature Annual, 24,* 141–160. New Haven, CT: Yale University Press.

Bosmajian comments on an unusual theme in historical realism for young people—law and justice—and relates characters and plot to other works.

Delta Education Media Treasures, Nashua, New Hampshire.

A catalog of videos, audiocassettes, CD-ROMs, and additional material is available. Titles mentioned in this chapter include Laura Ingalls Wilder videos, Meet the Author videos (Lucy Maud Montgomery, Scott O'Dell, Elizabeth George Speare, Lois Lowry, Avi, for example), videos of books (Hatchet, The House of Dies Drear, Island of the Blue Dolphins), and other pedagogical aids.

CHAPTER 11

Biography: The Story of a Life

INTRODUCTION AND RESPONSE

A fascination with real people and their life stories draws us toward biography. "Bio," meaning life, and "graph," referring to writing, aptly name this genre of literature. Good biographers—writing about people's lives, the rich and famous and the ordinary and everyday—weave facts into a striking pattern of purpose, achievement, and insight.

Biographical writing is also a bridge between fact and fiction. When facts are unknown, or obscured by the passage of time, biographers must balance what they know to be true with a careful interpretation of what might be true. As in historical realism (see Chapter 10), factual accuracy is critically important. We depend on biography for children and adults to have authenticity; we must rely on the truthful retelling of the story.

Biography is nonfiction, and a well-established genre of literature. Quite frequently, biography and autobiography appear on best-seller lists, thus indicating popularity with the reading public. Children, too, are sometimes drawn to the romance and charisma of a well-written account of a person's life. The drama of living day to day and meeting challenges, solving problems, and becoming enmeshed in social relationships may be a compelling story from the pen of a good biographer. This chapter explores how biography became well-established and why this genre is important in children's literature. Notable biographers are listed among the recent and recommended examples. Marc Aronson's exciting *Sir Walter Ralegh and the Quest for El Dorado* (2000) is such an example. A winner of many awards, this biography is a careful blend of research and fine writing. Documentation is evident in the use of graphics, including artwork from the period. The "cast of characters" is

Cover from SIR WALTER
RALEGH AND THE QUEST
FOR EL DORADO by Marc
Aronson. Cover art Copyright ©
2000 by Kayley LeFaiver. Used
by permission.

given at the book's beginning so that the reader is prepared for the full and exciting life Sir Walter Ralegh experienced. At the conclusion, Aronson provides endnotes, a bibliography, a timeline, and an index to give further credence to the authenticity of this biography.

As we focus on truth, on the accurate depiction of a person's life, begin to sift fact from fiction in your own life. Do you keep a personal journal? If so, read a few entries and then, for an audience of friends, write an episode based on those entries. If not, recall something that happened to you, an event that comes back to you with clarity, and write about it for an audience. As you compose your autobiographical sketch, think about the decisions you are making. Selecting facts, putting them in some order, and making the finished product interesting and readable is no easy task. How much invention is allowable? In your writing, will you make up dialogue or enhance a scene with added description? A biographer walks a tightrope between fact and fiction to tell a truthful story. Enjoy your dilemma on the tightrope, and share your story and insight with friends.

REFLECTION   What is difficult about writing your autobiography? What is easy? You know the "story," so what are the stumbling blocks? How is writing biography different from other kinds of writing?

HISTORY OF BIOGRAPHY AND AUTOBIOGRAPHY FOR CHILDREN

Biography, as a genre, gained recognition in the 18th century and developed into an art form epitomized by James Boswell's *Life of Samuel Johnson*. This period of literary history was an age attuned to self-revelation, gossip, and confession, and everyone— actresses, murderers, statesmen, evangelists, and businessmen—wrote autobiographies (Stauffer, 1941). However, these books were not written for children, nor considered appropriate for them, since the style was to recount every fact, every conversation, and every act with pedantic precision. Those children who could read were expected to admire biographical accounts of the exemplary lives of saints and martyrs. Most biographies were wordy, repetitive, and didactic.

It is puzzling, though, why the outpouring of notable children's books in the next century, considered the golden age of children's literature, did not include significant biographies and other nonfiction. Because of the lack of good nonfiction, children's literature grew to be closely associated with fiction, and imaginative stories (fantasy and realism) were much more likely to be considered literature of high quality.

In the midst of many lackluster biographies, though, a few examples are considered classics in the world of children's literature. The first Newbery prize awarded to a biography, *Invincible Louisa* (Meigs, 1933), presented to children a contemporary and realistic view of a well-known person, Louisa May Alcott. The word "invincible" gives a clue to how Cornelia Meigs, the biographer, selected facts to support her theme of Louisa's indomitable spirit in spite of grinding poverty and heavy family responsibilities. Instead of the usual children's biography in which all controversial and unpleasant facts were omitted, Cornelia Meigs chose to include material that depicted the Alcott family in truthful, if sometimes harsh, circumstances.

The next important biography, a Newbery winner in 1940, was *Daniel Boone* (Daugherty, 1939). Although well-written and realistic, it gave a sentimental portrait of the U.S. frontiersman and has been justly criticized for romanticizing the past and glorifying the settlers' point of view at the expense of Native Americans.

Anne Frank's deeply moving autobiography, *Diary of a Young Girl* (1952), brought her story and the tragedy of the Holocaust to readers in a way no other form could match. Similarly, in *Through My Eyes* (Bridges, 1999), Ruby Bridges tells her own story as a 6-year-old desegregating a public elementary school in New Orleans. Her courage and tenacity, and that of her family, are portrayed searingly through archival photos and news accounts. As literature moves minds and hearts, these autobiographies gave evil a human face and still offered hope for the human ability to rise above it.

Mary Mehlman Burns (1995) summarized the dearth of good biographies for children as she stated, "Until the mid-nineteen seventies, biography was the step-child among the genres of children's literature. Not that there were too few but rather that there were too few that qualified as literature, let along good biography" (p. 60). Too many biographies were dull, as writers tended to treat subjects as objects of hero worship and neglected to present facts that would contradict a wholesome image. Children's literature was particularly susceptible to the idea that children should only be exposed to a narrow range of behaviors and attitudes. In the 1970s, as in other genres, many taboos were broken and biographical subjects were seen with both positive and negative qualities.

REFLECTION Is it important for children to read about flaws in someone who is or was an important person?

A milestone in biography was Russell Freedman's *Lincoln: A Photobiography* (1987). Its spectacular use of archival photographs, integrated with thoughtful text, brought this man and this era to life in the reader's mind. The popular and meritorious *Lincoln* won the Newbery award, even though biographies had been forgotten for several years. Russell Freedman continues to be a significant voice in biography for children and adolescents. In 1998 he was honored with the Laura Ingalls Wilder Award from the American Library Association. The award is given every three years to an author or illustrator who has made a substantial and lasting contribution to literature for children.

Milton Meltzer (1976), a prominent biographer and historian, decried the lack of attention paid to nonfiction in prizes designed to honor literary work. He also lamented the poor effort of reviewers evaluating nonfiction in major journals, a thought seconded by Seymour Simon, a prolific and well-respected writer of science books for children (DeLuca & Natov, 1982). Perhaps due in part to prominent authors calling for more attention to biography and informational books, two prestigious awards for nonfiction were established: the Boston Globe–Horn Book Award and the Orbis Pictus, both given by the National Council of Teachers of English. A recent Orbis Pictus winner, *Leonardo da Vinci* (Stanley, 1996), and an honor book, *The Life and Death of Crazy Horse* (Freedman, 1996), demonstrate the best in biography for children—fully researched, compelling life stories with a foundation of truth and accuracy. In this tradition, the 2001 Orbis Pictus award was presented to Jerry Stanley for *Hurry Freedom: African Americans in Gold Rush California* (2000), another sterling example of the best of biography.

While there is a richness that is fairly new in biography, there is still a lot of shoddy writing, lack of research, and mass-market proliferation. Ann Flowers, a former editor of *The Horn Book Guide,* warned several years ago that there was also "a horrid proliferation of ill-conceived, poorly edited, and shoddily produced series books—usually but not always nonfiction" (Flowers, 1990, p. 19). A common occurrence in publishing, series of biographies or informational books around a theme—women scientists of the 20th century, for example—seem to generate a cookie-cutter approach to producing mass-market biographies. Nonfiction is particularly susceptible to superficial scholarship and uninspired writing. Probably because of the added demands of factual accuracy and verifiable authenticity, books that present facts must be carefully evaluated and selected. In particular, biographies of sports and entertainment figures are apt to be glamorized and presented in sensationalized prose. Biographies of the singer or athlete of the moment are rushed to press.

Milestones in Biography for Children

Invincible Louisa, C. Meigs (1933)

Diary of a Young Girl, A. Frank (1952)

Lincoln: A Photobiography, R. Freedman (1987)

Leonardo da Vinci, D. Stanley (1996)

Hurry Freedom: African Americans in Gold Rush California, J. Stanley (2000)

REFLECTION How popular is biography? Do children seek out biographies? Were you an avid reader of biographies as a child? As an adult? At what age do children begin to choose biographies for independent reading?

DEFINING BIOGRAPHY

Biography is the written record of an individual's life. It is a record of events, conversations, and inferred thoughts and motives of a person interacting with circumstances in the world. An *autobiography* is a record of a person's life written by that person. Lives of people—famous or common—may become interesting stories in the hands of a competent biographer who can sift through the minutiae of daily living, find the essence of a life, and record it with imagination and wit. *Memoirs* are personal accounts, often written from a subjective point of view about a specific period. Few memoirs exist for children.

Biography, as a genre, stands between the fiction of historical and contemporary realism and the facts of information books. Not altogether factual, but borrowing from allusion and inference, biographies are creative attempts to bring a person to life in literature. Philip Guedalla, a prominent biographer, said the biography is a region bounded on the north by history, on the south by fiction, on the east by obituary, and on the west by tedium (Boorstin, 1986).

Biographers must explore every known detail (somewhat tedious in practice, no doubt) and decide what is important and what can be tossed aside. Imposing a narrative structure on all these details gives shape to a biography, while the selection and integration of detail give theme and point of view. A person's life is a story, but it takes a talented, meticulous writer with knowledge of history and an interest in detective work to write a biography of candor and worth.

Some biographies are based largely on fiction, and other biographies are based mostly, if not totally, on well-documented facts. When writing for children, biographers have often felt the need to fictionalize. Facts that were not known were made up; facts thought to be unsuitable for children were changed. The amount of fiction included in biographies for children gives rise to terms that refer to this orientation: **authentic biography, fictionalized biography,** and **biographical fiction** (Huck, Hepler, Hickman, & Kiefer, 1997).

Authentic biography is a term for carefully researched histories about people in which almost everything can be substantiated in fact. Authors do not create conversations, events, or scenes. Jean Fritz (1989, 1999) is well-known for the authenticity of her biographies for children. Others are mentioned in subgenres that follow.

Fictionalized biography is a term for biography that includes aspects of invention, supposition, and inference. By necessity or to tell a good story, facts are omitted, not known, or embroidered to make a point. *Minty: A Story of Young Harriet Tubman* (Schroeder, 1996)—written for young children, and a recent Coretta Scott King Award winner for illustration—is an example of a fine fictionalized biography. (A list of Coretta Scott King Award books appears in Appendix A.)

Biographical fiction is, as the term infers, fiction with a brief bow to accuracy. Many stories classified as historical fiction can be considered biographical fiction if an historical person figures prominently or even incidentally. Such stories are really not biographies and should not be evaluated as such. They can be excellent stories, but their purpose is not to impart an accurate biographical sketch of someone. Quite often, historical realism nods to biography when the story includes characterizations of real people. An example of this is Paul Samuel Jacobs' *James Printer: A Novel of Rebellion* (1997). Jacobs elaborates on the life of James Printer, a Nipmuc Indian in 17th-century New England who is apprenticed to Samuel Green, a printer and bookmaker. Educated and converted by the English, James Printer is caught in the struggle among King Philip, the Pokanet chief who leads the Native American forces, and the colonists, who represent his new identity.

Another example of biographical fiction is *Cleopatra VII: Daughter of the Nile* (Gregory, 1999) in the Scholastic *Royal Diaries* series. Drawing from the few facts that were known, Kristiana Gregory created a diary for 12-year-old Cleopatra. While the main events were historically accurate, Gregory added details to make Cleopatra believable and charismatic.

In the last few years, a healthy trend toward authentic biographies for young people has been evident. As in other genres of children's literature, the new realism of the 1960s permeated biography. Facts that had been considered inappropriate, too adult, or unsuitable became acceptable and contributed their truth to more life-like depictions of notable figures. Biographies now may portray people who grapple with life, make mistakes, and fall short of perfection. Critics insist that biographers strive for and maintain the same scholarly rigor when writing for children as when writing for adults. Authentic biographies for young children, such as *Abigail Adams* (Wallner, 2001) and *Heroine of the Titanic: The Real Unsinkable Molly Brown* (Landau, 2001), show a careful regard for facts and the integrity of the subject of the biography.

VALUE OF BIOGRAPHY FOR CHILDREN

Biographies present models of achievement, compassion, and heroism—people who have worked under difficult circumstances to create lives worth living and telling about. Historical biographies provide glimpses into the past, where one can observe the realism of living conditions and childhood in a different time and place. Contemporary biographies show possible actions and attitudes in our world today, and tell of decisions that people made to better themselves. When the story of one person's life is written with magnetism, it can enhance the drama and purpose of all of our lives.

REFLECTION   Generate the names of five people who should be the subjects of biography. They can be historical or contemporary. Who would you write about first? Someone famous? Or someone not as well-known?

EVALUATING BIOGRAPHY

Contemporary biographies, like other genres of children's literature, must combine a well-written story with a thorough foundation of authentic detail. Nonfiction writing based on research has four basic criteria for excellence:

- accuracy
- judicious selectivity
- organization
- imaginative and lively use of facts (Haviland, 1973)

To judge the worth of a particular book, begin with the questions listed in Figure 11.1, then add the questions in the four-point scale.

Figure 11.1
Evaluating biography

Criteria	My Personal Response
Accuracy	Is scholarship or research evident? What are the biographer's credentials?
Selection of facts	How were the facts selected? Why did the biographer choose this subject?
Organization of facts	How well are facts integrated into the theme? Do the facts support the theme and style? What was the biographer's point of view?
Imaginative and lively use of facts	Does the work hold your attention? Does it have insights and revelations? How does it challenge you to consider the subject differently?

Four-Point Scale for Evaluating Biographies

Name of Text: _____

Author (illustrator, translator): _____

    1 stands for "very good" or yes, 2 is "good," 3 is "marginal," and 4 is "unsatis-factory" or no. Rate the book according to the following:

    I. The biographer's credentials show that he/she is knowledgeable and skillful.

        1 _____ 2 _____ 3 _____ 4 _____

   II. There are no obvious gaps or errors in the facts.

        1 _____ 2 _____ 3 _____ 4 _____

  III. The point of view is neither too laudatory nor too derisive.

        1 _____ 2 _____ 3 _____ 4 _____

  IV. The facts support the style and theme of the biography.

        1 _____ 2 _____ 3 _____ 4 _____

    Further selection criteria depend on your purpose and audience. Is the subject of this biography of interest to the children with whom you work? Does it fit into thematic units you envision in your curriculum planning? Are you going to read this biography aloud? Is the subject sufficiently meritorious or provocative to devote class time to reading and discussion? These evaluative questions should guide your selection as well.

    One important clue leading to a judgment about selection and organization of facts often lies in the subtitle of the biography. Because biographies frequently include subtitles, we can use the phrase to predict theme, style, or author's point of view. For example, Julius Lester's *The Blues Singers: Ten Who Rocked the World* (2001) is very similar to Roxane Orgill's *Shout, Sister, Shout! Ten Girl Singers Who Shaped a Century* (2001), except when a careful look at the title and subtitle reveals subtle differences. The blues singers are men and women, while the shout sisters are all female. The scope of each book is large, covering ten singers and many decades, but Lester confines his biographies to blues singers and Orgill implies that several styles are included.

* ◆ *

REFLECTION Should biographers like or admire their subjects? Or should there be some emotional distance, or even antipathy between them? How does the biographer's admiration of a subject affect the point of view?

SUBGENRES OF BIOGRAPHY

In this section, biography is divided into two subgenres: historical and contemporary. Biographies of historical figures are discussed first, and examples are drawn from books for older readers and books for younger readers (picture books and transitional books). Similarly, biographies of contemporary figures are presented with examples of collections and autobiographies, including books about people of color, women, and sports and entertainment figures. This section is meant to be a quick introduction to the range of biography available to children.

Biographies of Historical Figures

Jean Fritz, a premier example of a biographer, does not invent dialogue or idealize her subjects. Winner of the first Orbis Pictus award for nonfiction in 1990 for *The Great Little Madison* (1989), she writes with a sense of humor and breathes life into her historical subjects. As she states, "We cannot afford to forget the past is not just a series of events; it is *people* doing things" (Fritz, 1981, p. 86.). Written for a wide range of readers, Fritz's many biographies attest to her interest and ability to captivate young readers. *Why Not, Lafayette?* (1999) is one of her recent ones.

Russell Freedman also has a well-deserved reputation for writing outstanding biographies for children, often using photographs, paintings, and pictures of archival material. *Babe Didrikson Maharius: The Making of a Champion* (1999) is one of his biographies in which middle-level readers will find a compelling story presented in an inviting format. Using the pictorial interest of readers to entice them into biography is a hallmark of Diane Stanley, whose *Leonardo da Vinci* (1996) was cited in previous sections of this chapter. She continues to write excellent authentic biographies, often in picture book form. Her *Michelangelo* (2000) is an Orbis Pictus honor book.

REFLECTION What are the additional factors involved in evaluating picture-book biographies? How much is the artwork an important aspect to evaluate as well as the text?

Recent and Recommended Biographies of Historical Figures

America's Champion Swimmer: Gertrude Ederle, D. Adler (2000)

Shipwrecked! The True Adventures of a Japanese Boy, R. Blumberg (2001)

Uncommon Traveler: Mary Kingsley in Africa, D. Brown (2000)

Frank O. Gehry: Outside In, J. Greenberg & S. Jordan (2000)

George Washington & the Founding of a Nation, A. Marrin (2001)

**The Holy Twins: Benedict and Scholastica,* K. Norris (2001)

In the Time of the Knights, S. Tanaka (2000) (biography of William Marshall)

*Picture book or transitional book

Biographies of Contemporary Figures

From sports figures to political activists, subjects in contemporary biographies should be realistically depicted, including positive and negative facets of their lives. Note that good contemporary biographies are less numerous than historical ones. Perhaps the list of notable subjects to choose from is shorter, or perhaps it is more difficult to write critically about someone who is still alive. Whatever the case, contemporary biographies are more apt to be written with less attention to analysis and a careful weighing of facts, especially those of sports and entertainment figures.

Recent and Recommended Biographies of Contemporary Figures

Talking with Artists, vol. 3, P. Cummings (Ed.), (1999)

*Here We All Are, T. de Paola (2000)

*Toni Morrison: The Magic of Words, J. Haskins (2001)

Carter G. Woodson: The Man Who Put "Black" in American History, J. Haskins & K. Benson (2000)

Uncommon Champions: Fifteen Athletes Who Battled Back, M. Kaminsky (2000)

The Greatest: Muhammed Ali, W. D. Myers (2001)

Sammy Sosa: Héroe do los jonromes, J. Savage (2000)

In Real Life: Six Women Photographers, L. Sills (2000)

*Picture book or transitional book

RECENT BIOGRAPHIES TOO GOOD TO MISS

Following is an extra bibliography (complete here and not referenced later) of excellent biographies of people of diversity in the United States and the World. It includes contemporary and historical subjects.

Coburn, B. (2000). *The triumph of Everest: A photobiography of Sir Edmund Hillary.* New York: National.

Dash, J. (2001). *The world at her fingertips: The story of Helen Keller.* New York: Scholastic.

Demi. (2001). *Gandhi.* New York: McElderry.

*de Paola, T. (2001). *On my way.* New York: Putnam.

Gold, A. L. (2000). *A special fate: Chiune Sugihara, Hero of the Holocaust.* New York: Scholastic.

Gorrell, G. K. (2000). *Heart and soul: The story of Florence Nightingale.* Plattsburgh, NY: Tundra.

*Herrera, J. F. (2000). *The upside down boy/El Niño de cabeza.* New York: Children's.

Kozar, R. (2000). *Michael J. Fox*. New York: Chelsea.

Krull, K. (2000). *Lives of extraordinary women: Rulers, rebels (and what the neighbors thought)*. New York: Harcourt.

Left Hand Bull, J., & Haldane, S. (1999). *Lakota hoop dancer*. New York: Dutton.

Marrin, A. (2000). *Sitting Bull and his world*. New York: Dutton.

Murphy, J. (2000). *Pick and shovel poet: The journeys of Pascal D'Angelo*. New York: Clarion.

Reef, C. (2001). *Sigmund Freud: Pioneer of the mind*. New York: Clarion.

Rockwell, A. (2000). *Only passing through: The story of Sojourner Truth*. New York: Knopf.

Soto, G. (2000). *Jessie DeLaCruz: A profile of a United Farm Worker*. New York: Braziller/Persea.

*Winter, J. (2001). *Once upon a time: The story of Benny Goodman*. New York: Hyperion.

*Picture book or transitional book

SUMMARY

Biography and its related forms (autobiography and memoir) are fairly recent additions to the serious study of children's literature. Until the 20th century, biography was virtually ignored by scholars who defined and evaluated children's books. Adult biographies were often romanticized, often overfictionalized accounts of famous people. They were read for instructional purposes rather than as examples of literary works.

When the new realism permeated children's literature in the 1960s, biographies also showed changing attitudes. No longer were historical and contemporary figures pictured so heroically or so romantically. A more balanced account of a life story, combined with verifiable authenticity, began to appear in biography for children. Jean Fritz, Milton Meltzer, David Adler, Russell Freedman, Albert Marrin, and a few others raised standards with authentic biographies based on fact.

In this chapter, biography was divided into historical and contemporary periods, based on when the subject (person) of the biography lived. A brief history of biography was included, as well as evaluative criteria with which to judge these books. Many books were listed, and notable authors were mentioned.

This clearly is a genre that makes a great contribution to children's lives. Children are drawn to good stories about people they admire and want to emulate. Many opportunities exist within school curricula to use biographies effectively. The growing frequency of examples of biography among notable and award-winning books attests to its growing popularity and abundance. Therefore, the responsibility for choosing the best of biography, for determining the appropriate balance between fact and fiction, rests with us.

REFLECTION   Has your view of the purpose or the scope of biography changed as a result of reading this chapter and some of the examples given? How do you view children's biographies differently now, if you do?

IMPLICATIONS FOR INSTRUCTION

In this section, projects and activities are described that show some of the issues in an active way, such as finding out about authors, comparing books, and applying criteria for evaluation. Activities for the primary level and activities for the intermediate and middle levels are suggested so that you can test some of your theories with children in classrooms.

Projects

1. Compare several biographies about the same person so that different themes, points of view, and styles are obvious. Also look for discrepancies. A text set of biographies about a single subject could be created to use in a classroom. See the four biographies of Joan of Arc on the CD-ROM accompanying this text, for example.

2. Many children's authors have written autobiographies or have been featured in biographies. See if any of your favorite authors have written about themselves or have been the subject of a biography. Following is a brief list to get you started:

   Here we all are, T. de Paola (2000)

   Guts: The true stories behind Hatchet *and* The Brian Books, G. Paulsen (2001)

   Beatrix Potter, J. Malam (1998)

   Roald Dahl, C. Powling (1998)

3. Practice applying the criteria for evaluation of biography by choosing some books, then answering the questions in Figure 11.1. How do the criteria help you make judgments?

4. How are you doing on your own autobiography (suggested in the beginning of this chapter)? Have you written a vignette and read it to anyone? Do you have a relative—grandmother or great-grandmother, for example—who has family history that you want to record? Start now!

5. For interesting and pertinent subjects, check out the *Biography* television program on the Arts and Entertainment cable channel. For critical television viewing, become familiar with the program and evaluate the content and style of a particular biography that interests you.

Activities for the Primary Level

1. Many biographies are now written for beginning readers (some have been asterisked in this chapter as picture or transitional books). Use these books to elicit drama (acting out some scenes), to initiate writing exercises (for example, "What would you do if . . .?"), or to discuss why this person is important. It would be interesting to start with *Fannie in the Kitchen* (Hopkinson, 2001), a biography of Fannie Farmer, or *Our Neighbor Is a Strange, Strange Man* (Seymour, 1999), the biography of Melville Murrell, the eccentric inventor of the first glider.

2. Primary-level children can write their life stories. One way to begin is to create a timeline for the children. When were they born? Where did they live? What significant events have happened to them? Perhaps a baby brother or sister has come, or family changes have occurred. After enough events are placed on a timeline, connect them in an autobiography. Parents can help find pictures for a photobiography.

3. Biographies can fit into themes chosen for primary classrooms: Biographies of scientists, musicians, politicians, and so forth will fit into units on ecology, social history, or animals, for example. Take some of the units you have been developing and think of people who have contributed to that field. Maybe you can find biographies of those people. Biographies can be read aloud, to complement the theme of the unit, or for independent reading.

4. Easy-reader biographies published by Carolrhoda Press (Minneapolis, MN) in the *Tell Me About* series are *Beatrix Potter* (Malam, 1998) and *Roald Dahl* (Powling, 1998). Each has 24 pages and should please the emerging reader. Combine these with Tomie de Paola's *On My Way* (2001), the last of his autobiographical trilogy.

Activities for the Intermediate and Middle Levels

1. When a group or individual is reading a book by Walter Dean Myers (see text set in Chapter 1), read also his memoir *Bad Boy: A Memoir* (2001a) to see if there are events in fiction that can be related to nonfiction. The question "Where does an author get his or her ideas?" may be answered in the biography of that author.

2. Biographies of the same person are rich in comparisons. Information can be collected and then compared on a character chart or a semantic web. For example, Albert Marrin's treatment of *George Washington & the Founding of a Nation* (2001) could be compared to many biographies of George Washington, or biographies of George Washington and Benjamin Franklin could be cross-referenced. James C. Giblin's *The Amazing Life of Benjamin Franklin* (2000) is an excellent source of information on Franklin and the colonial period.

3. Dramatic scenes flourish in well-written biographies, and middle-level readers enjoy acting out a "You are there" scenario. What would it be like to create a scene where Cornwallis surrenders to George Washington at Yorktown, or one in which Madame Curie presents her findings to skeptical scientists?

4. Encourage children to create their own photobiographies. Most will have pictures from home and other "archival" material to add. Children may want to write about themselves; some may want to write about each other. This is a good way to discuss the importance of primary sources when gathering information and selecting and organizing facts.

REFERENCES

Children's Works

Adler, D. (2000). *America's champion swimmer: Gertrude Ederle*. New York: Harcourt.

Aronson, M. (2000). *Sir Walter Ralegh and the quest for El Dorado*. New York: Clarion.

Blumberg, R. (2001). *Shipwrecked! The true adventures of a Japanese boy*. New York: HarperCollins.

Bortz, F. (1997). *To the young scientist: Reflections on doing and living science*. New York: Watts.

Bridges, R. (1999). *Through my eyes*. New York: Scholastic.

Brown, D. (2000). *Uncommon traveler: Mary Kingsley in Africa*. Boston: Houghton Mifflin.

Cummings, P. (Ed.). (1999). *Talking with artists,* vol. 3. New York: Clarion.

Daugherty, J. (1939). *Daniel Boone*. New York: Viking.

de Paola, T. (2000). *Here we all are*. New York: Putnam.

de Paola, T. (2001). *On my way*. New York: Putnam.

Frank, A. (1952). *The diary of a young girl*. New York: Doubleday.

Freedman, R. (1987). *Lincoln: A photobiography*. New York: Clarion.

Freedman, R. (1996). *The life and death of Crazy Horse*. New York: Holiday.

Freedman, R. (1999). *Babe Didrikson Zaharias: The making of a champion*. New York: Clarion.

Fritz, J. (1989). *The great little Madison*. New York: Putnam.

Fritz, J. (1999). *Why not, Lafayette?* New York: Putnam.

Giblin, J. C. (2000). *The amazing life of Benjamin Franklin*. New York: Scholastic.

Greenberg, J., & Jordan, S. (2000). *Frank O. Gehry: Outside in*. New York: DKInk.

Gregory, K. (1999). *Cleopatra VII: Daughter of the Nile*. New York: Scholastic.

Haskins, J. (2001). *Toni Morrison: The magic of words*. New York: Millbrook.

Haskins, J., & Benson, K. (2000). *Carter G. Woodson: The man who put "black" in American history*. New York: Millbrook.

Hopkinson, D. (2001). *Fannie in the kitchen*. New York: Schwartz/Atheneum.

Jacobs, P. S. (1997). *James Printer: A novel of rebellion*. New York: Scholastic.

Kaminsky, M. (2000). *Uncommon champions: Fifteen athletes who battled back*. New York: Boyds Mills.

Landau, E. (2001). *Heroine of the Titanic: The real unsinkable Molly Brown*. New York: Clarion.

Lester, J. (2001). *The blues singers: Ten who rocked the world*. New York: Jump at the SunHyperion.

Malam, J. (1998). *Beatrix Potter*. New York: Carolrhoda.

Marrin, A. (2001). *George Washington & the founding of a nation*. New York: Dutton.

Meigs, C. (1933). *Invincible Louisa: The story of the author of "Little Women."* Boston: Little, Brown.

Myers, W. D. (2001a). *Bad boy: A memoir*. New York: HarperCollins.

Myers, W. D. (2001b). *The greatest: Muhammed Ali*. New York: Scholastic.

Norris, K. (2001). *The holy twins: Benedict and Scholastica*. New York: Putnam.

Orgill, R. (2001). *Shout, sister, shout! Ten girl singers who shaped a century*. New York: McElderry.

Paulsen, G. (2001). *Guts: The true stories behind* Hatchet *and* The Brian *books*. New York: Delacorte.

Powling, C. (1998). *Roald Dahl*. New York: Carolrhoda.

Savage, J. (2000). *Sammy Sosa: Héroe do los jonromes*. New York: Lerner Sports.

Schroeder, A. (1996). *Minty: A story of young Harriet Tubman*. New York: Dial.

Seymour, T. (1999). *Our neighbor is a strange, strange man*. New York: Orchard.

Sills, L. (2000). *In real life: Six women photographers*. New York: Holiday.

Stanley, D. (1996). *Leonardo da Vinci*. New York: Morrow.

Stanley, D. (2000). *Michelangelo*. New York: Harper-Collins.

Stanley, J. (2000). *Hurry freedom: African Americans in gold rush California*. New York: Crown.

Tanaka, S. (2000). *In the time of the knights*. New York: Hyperion.

Wallner, A. (2001). *Abigail Adams*. New York: Holiday.

Professional Works

Boorstin, D. (1986). Welcome. In J. Y. Cole (Ed.), *Biography and books*. Washington, DC: Library of Congress.

Burns, M. M. (1995). Biography. In A. Silvey (Ed.), *Children's books and their creators*. Boston: Houghton Mifflin.

DeLuca, G., & Natov, R. (1982). Who's afraid of science books? An interview with Seymour Simon. *The Lion and the Unicorn, 6,* 10–27, Brooklyn, NY: Brooklyn College, Department of English.

Flowers, A. (Ed.). (1990). Silver lining in a big, black cloud. *The Horn Book Guide, 2* (1). Boston: Horn Book, Inc.

Fritz, J. (1981). The very truth. In B. Hearne & M. Kaye (Eds.), *Celebrating children's books*. New York: Lothrop, Lee and Shepard.

Haviland, V. (1973). *Children and literature: Views and reviews*. Glenview, IL: Scott Foresman.

Huck, C., Hepler, S., Hickman, J., & Kiefer, B. (1997). *Children's literature in the elementary school* (6th ed.). Madison, WI: Brown & Benchmark.

Meltzer, M. (1976). Where do all the prizes go? The case for nonfiction. *The Horn Book, LII,* 17–23.

Stauffer, D. (1941). *The art of biography in eighteenth-century England*. Princeton, NJ: Princeton University Press.

Additional Resources

Biography today: Profiles of people of interest to young readers. Omnigraphics, Inc. Penobscot Building, Detroit, MI 48226.

A monthly magazine for middle readers, Biography Today includes timely, short articles about people in the news, as well as historical figures.

Author Information

Biographical information about authors and illustrators is presented here. Chances are, the biography you are looking for will be included in one of these resources.

Buzzeo, T., & Kurtz, J. (1999). *Terrific connections with authors, illustrators, and storytellers: Real space and virtual links*. Chicago, IL: Libraries Unlimited.
Connecting kids to "book people" is the aim, and the authors explore classroom visits, mail (electronic and snail), and websites.

Feldman, R. H. (1998). Children's book authors and illustrators on the web. In *Book Links, 8,* 1 (September 1998), 51–54.
Authors and illustrators are listed with the web addresses.

Jones, R. E., & Stott, J. C. (2000). *Canadian children's books: A critical guide to authors and illustrators*. Toronto: Oxford University Press.

Over 100 Canadian authors and illustrators including French-Canadian are profiled. Canadian awards and winners are listed.

McElmeel, S. L. (2000). *100 most popular picture book authors and illustrators: Biographical sketches and bibliographies*. Chicago, IL: Libraries Unlimited.
These 100 most popular were selected with adult and child input. More information is available through the websites given.

Weiss, J. S. (2001). *Profiles in children's literature: Discussions with authors, illustrators, and editors*. Lanham, MD: Scarecrow.
This book summarizes and quotes from information derived from personal interviews in Dr. Weiss' video series.

CHAPTER 12

Books of Information

INTRODUCTION AND RESPONSE

Facts, knowledge, information—children read books to learn about the world they inhabit and the solar systems beyond. So much information is available through print and electronic media that this genre has seen remarkable growth in the last two decades. Nonfiction, or books of factual content, along with encyclopedias, textbooks, and other works written to inform, proliferate in school libraries, public libraries, and homes. As a genre of children's literature, books of information are characterized by absolute authenticity, factual accuracy, and up-to-date knowledge.

In this chapter, books of nonfiction, or **information,** as the genre is more apt to be called, gain center stage in our exploration of children's literature. Informational books are defined, and the phenomenon of their rapid rise in importance is discussed. An evaluative scale is presented, and several subgenres are listed. As you begin this phase of discovery, visit a school or public library and take note of the kinds of books in this genre. What topics are represented? How much space in the library is devoted to nonfiction (and how much to fiction)? How are the books categorized? Do you recognize authors' names or a familiar book? What questions do you have about nonfiction?

REFLECTION   What do you remember about information books from your childhood? Do any stand out? Were you, and are you still, an avid reader of nonfiction?

HISTORY OF INFORMATION BOOKS FOR CHILDREN

The history of informational books for children began with *Orbis Pictus, or the World Illustrated,* although "courtesy books," from as early as the 15th century, imparted information about manners. Historically, children and adults read religious books and scientific books for information throughout the centuries. When one considers the type of reading matter available to children and adults before the 18th century, much of it seems informative and heavily didactic.

It wasn't until this century that nonfiction gained its literary place in the world of children's books. When the first Newbery award was given to *The Story of Mankind* by Dr. Hendrik Van Loon (1922), informational books gained credibility. Even this informational book is a "story," thus capitalizing on a sense that fiction, or at least the narrative form, is more closely aligned to what we think literature should be. A respected scholar of children's literature, Lillian Smith, expressed the point of view of many when she said, "Informational books are infrequently literature and seldom do they survive the generation for which they are written" (1953, p. 180). The short period of up-to-date information, because knowledge was changing and expanding, worked against this genre establishing a foothold in literature for children.

When David Macaulay's superb books *Cathedral: The Story of Its Construction* (1973) and *Castle* (1977) won awards (see Caldecott Honor books in Appendix A), it was recognized that information could be presented and critiqued as literature. Honored for their artwork, these books and others by Macaulay demonstrated a successful blend of art and text that represented milestones in nonfiction for children. Biographies had been recognized before this time, but information seemed to confront a prejudice. Happily, many informational books have overcome this prejudice with good writing, attractive formats, artful uses of graphic material, and a clear sense of direction and structure.

Because of the growing importance of nonfiction, its increased quantity and quality in book production, and a demand from school and public libraries for good biographies and current knowledge, these genres have become major forces in children's literature. School curricula, planned by teachers who value literature-based instruction, use informational books in all subject areas—science, social studies, literature, mathematics, music, and more.

As mentioned in Chapter 11, many informational books are published for children. Ann Flowers, former editor of *The Horn Book Guide,* warned about the proliferation of shoddy books and hasty writing that marked many of the "series" books that publishers crank out for the school market. It is especially important to be vigilant about books of information.

REFLECTION   Do you think a bias exists against nonfiction in children's literature? Several years ago, Jo Carr (1982, p. ix) said there is a "consistent, if unconscious denigration of nonfiction for children," which "contrasts sharply with serious treatment of nonfiction for adults." Do you think this is still true?

DEFINING INFORMATIONAL BOOKS

Informational books for children (and adults) cover almost every conceivable topic. An explosion of knowledge, increased use of informational books in schools, and a higher quality of book production push this genre to the top when one looks at the number of books published each year. One can see the results of this proliferation in schools and public libraries. Although fiction usually gains the most attention from specialists in literature, nonfiction has equal if not more stature in the marketplace and in the classroom.

Books of information supplement and, in some cases, provide the basis for curricula in science and social studies. Teachers using topical approaches, thematic units, and innovative organizational structures (such as cooperative grouping, multiage classrooms, and so on) find that trade books offer the necessary variety and versatility to sustain these innovations and satisfy pedagogical demands.

The touchstone book pictured for this chapter is the award-winning *My Season with Penguins* (Webb, 2000). Written in a journalistic style by Sophie Webb, a research scientist who studied Adélie penguins in the Antarctic, the most recent knowledge is shared with readers from early elementary through middle school. Webb's

Cover, from MY SEASON WITH PENGUINS by Sophie Webb. Jacket art © 2000 by Sophie Webb. Reprinted by permission of Houghton Mifflin Company. All rights reserved.

intimate, first-person journal and watercolor, gouache, and graphite drawings make this science book especially appealing to children and adults. Content is fact filled, and the purpose of the National Science Foundation–funded study is very clear. As mentioned in Chapter 6, text and art provide a solid foundation for a unit on penguins, the Antarctic, oceanography, methods of research, and other areas.

In the past few years, books of information have appeared in increased quantity and, more importantly, in improved quality (Bamford & Kristo, 2000). Books are designed to invite the reader in, to make knowledge as accessible as possible. In keeping with the idea that visual literacy is a crucial skill for the television-reared child, much attention is paid to the careful preparation of graphic elements accompanying the text (Kerper, 1998). In subject areas, graphic elements enhance the story line, such as the photographs used in *Orphan Train Rider* (Warren, 1996). It is interesting to note that the photograph on the cover is not the main character in the book. However, the photographs throughout help to tell a compelling, authentic story of young children abandoned then accepted into loving or punitive homes. The ordeal of the main character, Lee Nailling, who is separated from his brothers in the 1920s, is told in this book, an honored informational book in 1997.

In a critical evaluation of nonfiction for children, Margery Fisher (1972) pointed out that informational books may be used as propaganda. Information may be selectively offered, and it might reflect a tendency to persuade. Objectivity is essential, she asserted, to guard against an unhealthy use of selective information. The temptation to use information as propaganda was valid in 1972, and is still valid today.

REFLECTION   Even nonfiction can distort the truth in its necessary reorganizing of reality. The writing process ensures that facts are selected and interpreted as concepts are developed. Is there some potential for the misuse of facts or the selection of certain facts and the exclusion of others, as Fisher asserts?

Types of Information Books

Informational books transmit knowledge. They do not simply describe what happens, but explain why and how. They are usually written in an expository style, as contrasted with the narrative style associated with fiction (see Structures of Expository Writing following this section). Many types of informational books exist; the most common ones are described here.

1. *Nonfiction chapter books:* Books in which most of the information is organized into chapters and graphic material is included when necessary. Knowledge is primarily conveyed through the printed word. The intended audience is literate.

2. *Illustrated informational books:* Books that show and tell. Many scientific books are illustrated lavishly with diagrams, photos, charts, reproductions of computer screens, and so forth. Text and graphics are about equally important in conveying information.

3. *Concept books:* Books that explain a concept (see the picture-book description of concept books in Chapter 5). For young readers and listeners, concept books are picture books to be read to an audience. Usually the text is minimal.

4. *Photo essays:* Much like illustrated information books, except that photo essays use photos almost exclusively. There is about an equal balance between photos and text.

5. *Fact books:* These are books of text and minimal graphics, organized around topics such as those found in an encyclopedia, or "how-to" manuals such as those found with computers or for driver's education. *The Guinness Book of World Records*, a popular book with most children, published annually by the Sterling Publishing Company, is an example.

REFLECTION   Can you think of an example in each of the previous categories? Are there adult books that come to mind, or other children's books that fit the types listed above?

STRUCTURES OF EXPOSITORY WRITING

Just as knowledge of narrative structure enhances reading comprehension (see Chapter 3 for a discussion of how important an internalized narrative structure is to beginning and proficient readers), knowledge of expository structure is similarly helpful to readers. As we are familiar with story elements—character, plot, and setting—so do we need to be familiar with elements of expository text—enumeration, sequence, cause/effect, and compare/contrast, among others. Unlike narrative structure, expository writing does not tell a story with a beginning, middle, and end; instead it explains, describes, compares, and sometimes enumerates. Expository discourse is more complex and difficult to read, as it usually contains more concepts, more details, and more specialized vocabulary.

When the discourse of expository writing is analyzed, the *paragraph* is usually the unit of analysis (instead of a larger unit, such as the story), although occasionally in children's books, several paragraphs, or even a chapter, may be combined to show a discernible pattern. So we find in expository writing several kinds of paragraphs that reflect different organizational patterns. According to literacy specialists, if readers are anticipating these patterns or structures, comprehension comes more easily (Leu & Kinzer, 1999; Richardson & Morgan, 1997; Tompkins, 2001).

Definitions and Examples of Patterns in Expository Writing

Organizational patterns, or expository structures, are found in factual writing. When readers are aware of the patterns, content is mastered more quickly. To demonstrate the prevalence of these structures, following are first the definitions, then some excerpts taken from *My Season with Penguins* (Webb, 2000) and *Blizzard* (Murphy, 2000).

Description   The most frequently used pattern in expository writing, it is most often a paragraph with a main idea and subordinate details. The main idea may be at the beginning, embedded in the middle, or at the end.

Description example

On Monday, March 12, people from Delaware on up to Maine, and inland as far as the Mississippi River, woke to discover a white and hostile visitor lurking outside. A blizzard was rattling their windowpanes and piling up snow against their doors. (*Blizzard*, p. 25)

Time Sequence   This is a narrative order in which events happen sequentially, in order. Sometimes key words, such as *next, then,* and *last* are used to signal the reader that the structure is a sequence.

Time sequence example

Sue bends over, grabs an incubating penguin, and maneuvers the bird's body and flippers under her arm so its head peeks out behind, much like a large football. She places my wool hat over the eggs to keep them warm. Then she holds the bird while I put on the metal flipper band and attach a PIT tag. . . . After banding, Sue places the penguin gently next to its nest and releases it. It fusses a bit, then sits back on its nest. (*My Season with Penguins*, p. 18)

Compare/Contrast   This is a paragraph in which usually two major concepts, or things, are compared. Differences and similarities are mentioned to give the reader a clear understanding.

Compare/contrast example

Today two tall Emperor penguins are on the fast ice, dwarfing the Adélies. They have blackish feet that they stare at periodically. One Emperor lifts his head and lets out a trumpet. They breed on an ice tongue off Beaufort Island which is about thirty miles (fifty kilometers) to the north of Cape Royds. (*My Season with Penguins*, p. 19)

Enumeration   This is a paragraph in which numerous "things" are listed. Key words are *first, second,* and so on. Math books and cookbooks usually have good examples of enumeration structure.

Enumeration example

During the winter of 1880–1881, the Plains were hit by a series of particularly fierce blizzards—one a week, each lasting three or more days, from January through April. These storms stopped railroad service for seventy-nine straight days and dumped eleven feet of snow in the Dakota territory. (*Blizzard,* p. 113)

Cause/Effect   Paragraphs in which relationships are explored, where events happen because of other events, show a cause-and-effect structure. Sometimes the paragraph can have the effect first, as the main idea, then give the causes. Historical writing frequently employs cause/effect structure.

Cause/effect example

The penguins are increasingly aggressive, frequently charging us with their hard, paddle-like wings. Sometimes they just run up to us, raise their neck ruffs, and growl—a throaty noise that leaves nothing misunderstood: "GET OUT!" Not only the breeders behave this way but also the nonbreeders. All the penguins are excited by the activity of rearing chicks. (*My Season with Penguins,* p. 31)

These organizational patterns seem to be related to content areas in a general way. In mathematics, for example, enumeration, time sequence, and description are apt to be more predominant than the others because of the nature of math textbooks and trade books. In social studies, cause/effect, description, and time sequence are common. Science books also use cause/effect, description, and compare/contrast quite frequently. Description seems to be a common denominator in all nonfiction, and because of this it is necessary to teach how to find the main idea and how to distinguish the main idea from the subordinate details.

Teaching Suggestion: The use of graphic overviews as readers are introduced to the material has been shown to be very helpful (Allan & Miller, 2000). When the graphic overview gives the readers clues as to what to expect, and how to organize the material, the material is easier and more inviting to the reader. For some graphic overviews related to each of the patterns listed above, see Figure 12.1. As you introduce the topic and the reading assignment, you can demonstrate in these pictorial charts how the facts are related to each other and thus are easier to remember and think about as students read.

EVALUATING INFORMATIONAL BOOKS

Writing in informational books should be clear, concise, and compelling. Graphics must also be clear, labeled properly, and balanced with text. Facts should be organized so that information is easily accessible and understandable. Generally, information should proceed from simple to complex, from general to specific.

In selecting nonfiction, two things should be avoided. First, objects should not be personified. When a human characteristic is imposed on a nonliving element, accuracy is compromised. For example, to give human emotions to a planet or a tree would be misleading and would move the information from the realm of science into

Figure 12.1 Graphic overviews related to expository text

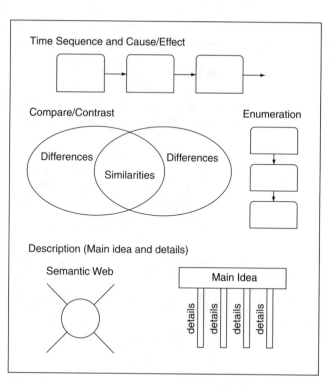

mythology. It is perfectly fine to mythologize trees or planets, but not under the guise of scientific information. Second, if opinions are given as facts, readers are again misled. Look for clear statements of conjecture, or theory, or to note the use of words like "may be" or "could be" instead of the emphatic "is."

Figure 12.2 presents questions to ask while evaluating a work of nonfiction.

REFLECTION Could these criteria be applied to electronic texts as well? If you or your students are reading factual material from the Internet, would these questions help you to think critically?

Four-Point Scale for Evaluating Informational Books

Name of Text: _____

Author (and Illustrator): _____

1 stands for "very good," 2 is "good," 3 is "marginal," and 4 is "unsatisfactory." Rate the book according to the following:

Figure 12.2
Evaluating
information books

Criteria	My Personal Response
Accuracy of facts	What are the author's credentials? What evidence is there of scholarship and research? How are opinions differentiated from facts?
Selection of facts	Are childlike analogies used to explain difficult concepts? Are concepts developed convincingly?
Organization of facts	Is the format attractive? Are graphics clear and labeled? Is there a framework, or overview, into which specifics fit?
Imaginative and lively use of facts	Does the writing challenge and stimulate the reader? What is the author's attitude toward the information?

Accuracy of facts

    I. The author's credentials and reputation are explicitly presented.

        1 _____ 2 _____ 3 _____ 4 _____

   II. It is easy to differentiate the author's opinions from substantiated facts.

        1 _____ 2 _____ 3 _____ 4 _____

Selection of facts

   III. Concepts and analogies or metaphors used to explain and demonstrate concepts are clear and age appropriate.

        1 _____ 2 _____ 3 _____ 4 _____

   IV. If facts support several points of view, the reader is made aware of the arguments for all sides.

        1 _____ 2 _____ 3_____ 4 _____

Organization of facts

    V. The format is attractive, with a clear font for text and graphic elements interspersed and labeled.

        1 _____ 2 _____ 3 _____ 4 _____

   VI. The table of contents and chapter organization are clearly represented with an inherent, understandable order.

        1 _____ 2 _____ 3 _____ 4 _____

  VII. The organization includes additional bibliographies, an index, and other helpful material.

        1 _____ 2_____ 3 _____ 4 _____

Imaginative and lively use of facts

VIII. The writing is interesting, compelling, and stimulating.

1 _____ 2 _____ 3 _____ 4 _____

IX. The author respects the content and the reader.

1 _____ 2 _____ 3 _____ 4 _____

SUBGENRES OF NONFICTION

To give some structure to our discovery of nonfiction, school subject areas are used in this section to differentiate the subgenres listed. Note that, as in other chapters, the subgenres may also be divided into different areas within the content. Therefore, the following subgenres are used:

Humanities (art, music, dance)

Math and Technology (number theory, algebra, mathematical computation, and so on)

Science (biological, physical, and Earth sciences)

Social Studies (history, economics, cultures, psychology)

Some divisions of school curricula are not included. They have either been included in previous chapters (such as folktales and nursery rhymes, literature, poetry, and biography) or have been subsumed into the subgenres listed above. The subgenres listed above relate to curriculum planning as well. Each is described briefly, followed with a list of recommended books. (Note authors and subjects for future reference.) These subgenres are meant to suggest divisions among all available information, but not to be rigid and mutually exclusive. Some categories may overlap, because knowledge among content areas is interrelated and multifaceted in many cases. Also, only recent books are recommended to ensure up-to-date knowledge. Books for beginning readers are generally mentioned first in the following lists.

Humanities (The Arts)

Music, the visual and performing arts, architecture, and even crafts, games, and hobbies are included in this subgenre. Other humanities, specifically modern and traditional literature and poetry, have been treated in previous chapters. History, often considered part of the humanities, is in Social Studies in this text, as it is in school curricula. The following books, outstanding among the many that are available, are listed with books appropriate for younger readers first, then increasing in difficulty.

Recent and Recommended Books of the Humanities

Hush, Little Baby: A Folk Song with Pictures, M. Frazee (1999)

The Story of the Incredible Orchestra, B. Koscielniak (2000)

What Do Illustrators Do? E. Christelow (1999)

Welcome to the Globe: The Story of Shakespeare's Theatre, P. Chrisp (2000)

The Round Book: Rounds Kids Love to Sing, M. R. MacDonald and W. Jaeger (1999)

Dance! E. Cooper (2001)

The Renaissance, R. Mathews (2000)

Lucky 13: Solitaire Games for Kids, M. Street (2001)

Building Big, D. Macaulay (2000)

Mathematics and Technology

Nonfiction trade books with mathematics content are not plentiful. There seems to be a heavy reliance on math textbooks used for instruction and a paucity of literary writing in fields related to math. When children outgrow counting books and picture story books containing mathematical concepts, the availability of interesting, thought-provoking informational books is low. Literary writing contrasts sharply with technical writing, and manuals accompanying computers, Palm Pilots, digital cameras, and so forth contain technical explanations.

Therefore, the following is a small list of recommended books related to mathematics and technology. Teachers should continue to search for high-quality writing in this area by consulting other teachers and librarians, perusing trusted book review sources, using magazine articles judiciously, and encouraging fine mathematicians who are writers to write for children and youth. The following books are listed in order of difficulty, with the first ones appropriate for young readers.

Recent and Recommended Books of Mathematics and Technology

Subtraction Action, L. Leedy (2000)

The Grapes of Math, G. Tang (2001)

Ten Times Better, R. Michelson (2000) (This includes poetry)

G Is for Googol: A Math Alphabet Book, D. Schwartz (1998)

Tiger Math: Learning to Graph from a Baby Tiger, A. W. Nagda & C. Bickel (2000)

The History of Counting, D. Schmandt-Besserat (1999)

The Clock, T. Duffy (2000)

Teaching suggestion: (for all expository text patterns) A K-W-L chart is an introductory activity that continues as children read and find out about their topic. A blank three-column chart headed with "K" (on the left), "W" (in the middle), and "L" (on the right) is presented to the class. In the K column, children say what they already *K*now about the topic. (Teacher or another child records the information.) At the same time, or immediately after, children generate questions that they *W*ant to answer. This raises purpose-setting questions for their silent reading. After a period of reading, the class comes together again and addresses the third column, "What I've *L*earned about _____." Thus the K-W-L chart is a reference for children and teachers as the unit progresses.

Science

From physical sciences to natural sciences, from medical technology to astronomy, books in this subgenre provide current information to children and adults. It is important to check the copyright so that information in this fast-growing field of knowledge is recent. Science books for children and youth are plentiful, and many good scientists write well in their fields. For example, Seymour Simon (1987/2000), Sally Ride (1999), and Franklyn Branley (2000), are scientists who are respected, influential, and prolific writers.

The following books are grouped into three levels according to difficulty: younger readers (first grade through third); middle readers (fourth grade through seventh); and older readers (seventh through high school). Topics in the first two lists are similar (space, time, dinosaurs, rocks, and animals, in order), and there is some similarity between the second list and the third. This is to demonstrate that if a classroom is studying a topic such as space exploration, there are books available at different reading levels so that children can find a comfortable book at their instructional level.

Recent and Recommended Books of Science (for young readers)

Destination: Mars, S. Simon (1987/2000)

Telling Time, J. Older (2000)

Dinosaurs at the Ends of the Earth: The Story of the Central Asiatic Expedition, B. Floca (2000)

The Best Book of Fossils, Rocks, and Minerals, C. Pellant (2000)

Making Animal Babies, S. B. Collard III (2000)

Recent and Recommended Books of Science (for middle readers)

The Mystery of Mars, S. Ride & T. O'Shaughnessy (1999)

On Time: From Seasons to Split Seconds, G. Skurzynski (2000)

Digging for Bird-Dinosaurs: An Expedition to Madagascar, N. Bishop (2000)

Shaping the Earth, D. H. Patent (2000)

New Animal Discoveries, R. Orenstein (2001)

It's So Amazing! A Book About Eggs, Sperm, Birth, Babies, and Families, R. H. Harris (1999)

No Sweat Projects: Hairy Science and *No Sweat Projects: Thumbs Up Science,* J. Brallier (2001)

Recent and Recommended Books of Science (for older readers)

It's Perfectly Normal: Changing Bodies, Growing Up, Sex and Sexual Health,
    R. H. Harris (1994)

Twin Tales: The Magic and Mystery of Multiple Birth, D. Jackson (2001)

Science Projects About Solids, Liquids, and Gases, and *Science Projects About*
    Sound, and *Science Projects about the Physics of Toys and Games,* R.
    Gardner (2000)

Epidemics, L. Yount (2000)

Cloning, J. DuPrau (2000)

Teaching suggestion: (For all types of expository text patterns) Two-column note taking is a useful technique to practice when children are reading nonfiction to gather information for reports, research projects, or writing assignments. In this technique, the notebook page is divided into one-third (left side) and two-thirds (right side). On the right side, students write direct information from the text, on the left their personal response. The response may be as short as an exclamation point if they are surprised by any fact or as detailed as paraphrasing the information and analyzing it. Two column note taking is especially effective when children are reading science books with lots of new information to categorize, remember, and apply. This technique is also called a double-entry journal.

Social Studies

Families, occupations, government, economics, social problems, customs, and holidays are some of the topics found in this subgenre. Added to this already weighty list is history, because history constitutes a large part of the social studies curricula. Under the Social Studies umbrella we find the disciplines of anthropology, economics, political science, geography, and even philosophy and psychology. This is a large category, with many excellent informational books. Also, many books are multidisciplinary, with social, scientific, political, and economic information embedded with themes and topics. Note how many of the Orbis Pictus award winners and honor books fit into the Social Studies subgenre (see Figure 12.3). As in previous lists, books for young readers are listed first, then more difficult ones.

Recent and Recommended Books of Social Studies

Throw Your Tooth on the Roof: Tooth Traditions from Around the World, S.
    Beeler (1998)

One Day at the Wood Green Animal Shelter, P. Casey (2001)

So You Want to be President? J. St. George (2000)

Give Me Liberty! The Story of the Declaration of Independence, R. Freedman
  (2000)
Bound for the North Star: True Stories of Fugitive Slaves, D. B. Fradin (2000)
The Wigwam and the Longhouse, C. Yue & D. Yue (2000)
What's Cooking: The History of American Food, S. Whitman (2001)
Fire in Their Eyes: Wildfires and the People Who Fight Them, K. M. Beil (1999)
Terrorism, A. G. Gaines (1998)

Orbis Pictus Award Winner—2000	*Through My Eyes* (R. Bridges, 1999, Scholastic)
Honor Books—2000	*At Her Majesty's Request: An African Princess in Victorian England* (W. D. Myers, 1999, Scholastic)
	Clara Schumann: Piano Virtuoso (S. Reich, 1999, Clarion)
	Mapping the World (S. A. Johnson, 1999, Atheneum)
	The Snake Scientist (S. Montgomery, 1999, Houghton Mifflin)
	The Top of the World: Climbing Mount Everest (S. Jenkins, 1999, Houghton Mifflin)
Orbis Pictus Award Winner—2001	*Hurry Freedom: African Americans in Gold Rush California* (J. Stanley, 2000, Crown)
Honor Books—2001	*American's Champion Swimmer: Gertrude Ederle* (Adler, 2000, Gulliver Books)
	The Amazing Life of Benjamin Franklin (Giblin, 2000, Scholastic)
	Michelangelo (D. Stanley, 2000, HarperCollins)
	Wild and Swampy: Exploring with Jim Arnosky (Arnosky, 2000, HarperCollins)
	Osceola: Memories of a Sharecropper's Daughter (A. Govenar, Ed., 2000, Jump at the Sun/Hyperion)
Orbis Pictus Award Winner—2002	*Black Potatoes: The Story of the Great Irish Famine, 1845–1850* (S.C. Bartoletti, 2001, Houghton Mifflin)
Honor Books—2002	*The Cod's Tale* (M. Kurlansky, 2001, Penguin Putnam Books)
	The Dinosaurs of Waterhouse Hawkins: An Illuminating History of Mr. Waterhouse Hawkins, Artist and Lecturer (B. Kerley, 2001, Scholastic Press)
	Martin's Big Words: The Life of Dr. Martin Luther King, Jr. (D. Rappaport, 2001, Hyperion Books for Children)

Figure 12.3 Orbis Pictus awards: outstanding nonfiction for children and youth

Teaching suggestion: (For all types of expository text patterns) A cube that children construct can be used to explore six dimensions or viewpoints of a topic (Tompkins, 2001). The instructional procedure introduces these six steps: (1) describe the topic; (2) compare the topic to something else; (3) associate the topic with something else; (4) analyze the topic; (5) apply the topic; and (6) argue for or against the topic. Each side of the cube will address one of these steps. Students can construct a cube, then cut six pieces of paper that may be glued on each side. Or students can write directly on one of the squares and then fasten the cube together. (For a larger cube, use a 17" by 11" sheet.)

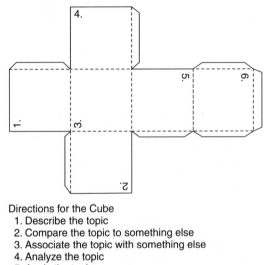

Directions for the Cube
1. Describe the topic
2. Compare the topic to something else
3. Associate the topic with something else
4. Analyze the topic
5. Apply the topic
6. Argue for or against the topic

AWARD-WINNING NONFICTION FOR CHILDREN

The Orbis Pictus Award from the National Council of Teachers of English is bestowed upon an outstanding children's informational book or biography each year. The committee also designates honor books. Each year's list highlights worthy nonfiction and calls attention to this important genre of children's literature. Figure 12.3 is a composite of the Orbis Pictus Award winners and honor books for the last three years. Most are social studies and science books, and some were mentioned in Chapter 11. (All bibliographic material is included; the books will not be referenced at the end of the chapter.)

The American Library Association, promoting children's literature with Notable Lists and the Newbery, Caldecott, Coretta Scott King, Batchhelder, Printz, and other awards, has also started to recognize an outstanding work of nonfiction with the Robert F. Sibert Award. The first recipient of this new award, first given in 2001, was *Sir Walter Ralegh and the Quest for El Dorado* by Marc Aronson (see Chapter 11) and honor books were *The Longitude Prize* (Dash, 2000), *Blizzard!* (Murphy, 2000), *My Season with Penguins* (Webb, 2000), and *Pedro and Me: Friendship, Loss, and What I Learned* (Winick, 2000).

SENSITIVE ISSUES, SPECIAL NEEDS, AND INDIVIDUAL DIFFERENCES

Informational books often illuminate topics that are difficult to discuss. Illness, coping with stress, loss, learning differences, and other topics are treated sensitively in nonfiction. Biography, contemporary and historical realism, and poetry may also give information to a curious and needy reader. Following is a summary of books that address these issues; some have been mentioned previously in chapters. Controversies, Sensitive Issues, and Trends in Chapter 6 also contains books in these categories. This is a complete bibliography, and titles are not referenced at the end of this chapter.

> Alexander, S. H. (2000). *Do you remember the color blue? And other questions kids ask about blindness.* New York: Viking.
>
> Bradley, K. B. (2000). *Weaver's daughter.* New York: Delacorte. (asthma)
>
> Freymann, S., & Elffers, J. (1999). *How are you peeling? Foods with moods.* New York: Scholastic. (emotions)
>
> Gantos, J. (2000). *Joey Pigza loses control.* New York: Farrar. (attention-deficit-hyperactivity-disorder)
>
> Girnis, M. (2000). *A B C for you and me.* Morton Grove, IL: Whitman. (Down syndrome children are pictured)
>
> Kaplan, H. (2000). *Waiting to sing.* New York: DKInk. (death)
>
> Millman, I. (1998). *Moses goes to a concert.* New York: Farrar. (hearing-impaired)
>
> Rodowsky, C. (2001). *Clay.* New York: Farrar, Straus & Giroux. (autism)
>
> Rogers, F. (2000). *Extraordinary friends.* New York: Putnam. (cerebral palsy, Down syndrome children are pictured)
>
> Weaver, B. N. (2001). *Rooster.* New York: Winslow. (mentally disabled neighbor)

SUMMARY

As the focus of this chapter, informational books were defined and the types were described. Evaluative criteria for evaluating books could also be applied to text found on the Internet: accuracy of data, wise selection and organization of data, and an attractive format to appeal to children. Usually more specific and up-to-date than textbooks, these trade books are used extensively in school classrooms.

The best informational books, perhaps competing with television and the Internet, are colorful, well-organized, pertinent, and well-written. They are based on content from science, history, technology, the social sciences, religion, psychology, the fine arts, and mathematics. The last decade has seen unprecedented quality and quantity in these books.

As knowledge explodes exponentially, literature of fact is more and more necessary to fill gaps in school curricula. Accurate information is crucial to living responsibly and well. With more than half of the children's books published annually today considered to be nonfiction, the popularity and the need for factual books seems firmly entrenched. However, with the popularity and sizable number of books produced comes the added responsibility of selecting the best for schools, homes, and libraries. Nonfiction, with its foundation of accuracy and authenticity, must be judged by the strictest criteria for excellence. This is difficult to do, because those of us who know literature and children do not always have the knowledge that must be conveyed. Similarly, people who do have the knowledge—in scientific fields, for example—do not always understand the audience for whom they are writing, nor do they have the talent for writing literate prose. The challenge of nonfiction is to combine the art of literature with the science of knowledge, a challenge that continually intrigues and entertains us as we enter the 21st century.

IMPLICATIONS FOR INSTRUCTION

After some projects are suggested, activities for young readers and intermediate and middle readers are suggested.

Projects

1. Select a topic that interests you and see how it is presented in some informational books. For example, if you like space, dinosaurs, Wales, or pioneers, there are books for you. You can go to the library to survey the collection, surf the Internet to gather resources, and consult reviewing sources to find nonfiction (as well as fiction).

2. Practice applying the criteria for evaluation of informational books by choosing some books, then answering the questions in Figure 12.2. How do the criteria and the four-point scale help you to make judgments?

3. How many works of nonfiction are presented among the Newbery Award winners and honor books? In the Coretta Scott King Award books? (See Appendix A for a list of awards.) Is nonfiction represented in the Caldecott list? Estimate a number or percentage, then find out how accurate your estimation is.

4. Find some examples of the structures of expository writing, like those presented in this chapter, in the informational books you are reading. Are the structures of description, time order, and so forth readily apparent in your trade books? Develop a lesson plan from the teaching suggestions and graphic overviews.

Activities for the Primary Level

1. From common classroom thematic units on subjects related to ecology, the human body, the ocean, and many other topics, children can create alphabet books. If you are studying the ocean, for example, an alphabet book might start like this: A Anemone, B Barracuda, and so on. Children would learn these words from the informational books read to them and by them. They will want to illustrate their books, too.

2. Children can learn to compare two information books on the same topic. The two books about Mars (see recommended Science books)—*The Mystery of Mars* (Ride & O'Shaughnessy, 1999) and *Destination: Mars* (Simon, 1987/2000)—will have similar information yet include different facts. A graphic overview of two overlapping circles (see Figure 12.1 for compare/contrast) will help to start the discussion or support the discussion as the books are read. For two books on the theatre, see *Welcome to the Globe: The Story of Shakespeare's Theatre* (Chrisp, 2000) and Aliki's *William Shakespeare and the Globe* (1999).

3. Singing from some of the outstanding music information books is always a great activity for young children. *The Round Book* (MacDonald & Jaeger, 1999) has some great rounds to sing, and some of the rounds include recorder melodies, too.

4. *Throw Your Tooth on the Roof: Tooth Traditions from Around the World* (Beeler, 1998) is a delightful cross-cultural book ready to encourage global understanding. The universal process of losing teeth through the childhood years unites rather than divides us. After hearing about traditions from all over the world, have the children discuss what happens at their houses and how it might be different in another country. If the children have penpals in another country, make that a topic in the next letter and see if more traditions are uncovered.

Activities for the Intermediate and Middle Levels

1. Children can evaluate the informational books they use. Questions such as these will get them started: What are the author's credentials? Are the ideas presented clearly? How is the book organized? Is one book on the subject better than another? Why?

2. History is enlivened by stories of how children worked, played, and made their contributions to family and society (Whitman & Whitman, 2001). Books that offer a child's point of view are *We Were There Too! Young People in U.S. History* (Hoose, 2001) and Russell Freedman's classic *Kids at Work: Lewis Hine and the Crusade Against Child Labor* (1994), as well as recent Orbis Pictus books, *Hurry Freedom: African Americans in Gold Rush California* (Stanley, 2000) and *Osceola: Memories of a Sharecropper's Daughter* (Govenar, 2000).

3. Antarctica is the subject of several recent and notable books, *My Season with Penguins* (Webb, 2000) among them. A unit on Antarctica, or a theme-related reading period in a middle school classroom, could be built on these books: *Shipwreck at the Bottom of the World: The Extraordinary True Story of Shackleton and the Endurance* (Armstrong, 1998), *Antarctic Journal: Four Months at the Bottom of the World* (Dewey, 2001), *Four to the Pole: The American Women's Expedition to Antarctica 1992–1993* (Loewen & Bancroft, 2001) and *Spirit of Endurance* (Armstrong, 2000).

4. While studying pioneers and the westward movement, some children in a fifth-grade classroom made calendars that depicted pioneer and Native American life on the Great Plains. Using information from several sources, 12 realistic scenes were drawn to correspond to the months of a 19th-century year.

A fifth-grader's pioneer calendar using informational material.

REFERENCES

Children's Works

Aliki. (1999). *William Shakespeare and the Globe*. New York: HarperCollins.

Armstrong, J. (1998). *Shipwreck at the bottom of the world: The extraordinary true story of Shackleton and the Endurance*. New York: Crown.

Armstrong, J. (2000). *Spirit of Endurance*. New York: Crown.

Aronson, M. (2000). *Sir Walter Ralegh and the quest for El Dorado*. New York: Clarion.

Beeler, S. (1998). *Throw your tooth on the roof: Tooth traditions from around the world*. Boston: Houghton Mifflin.

Beil, K. M. (1999). *Fire in their eyes: Wildfires and the people who fight them*. New York: Harcourt.

Bishop, N. (2000). *Digging for bird-dinosaurs: An expedition to Madagascar*. Boston: Houghton Mifflin.

Brallier, J. (2001a). *No sweat projects: Hairy science*. New York: Planet Dexter.

Brallier, J. (2001b). *No sweat projects: Thumbs up science*. New York: Planet Dexter.

Branley, F. (2000). *Snow is falling*. New York: HarperCollins.

Casey, P. (2001). *One day at the Wood Green animal shelter*. Cambridge: Candlewick.

Chrisp, P. (2000). *Welcome to the Globe! The story of Shakespeare's Theatre*. New York: DK Ink.

Christelow, E. (1999). *What do illustrators do?* New York: Clarion.

Collard, S. B. III. (2000). *Making animal babies*. Boston: Houghton Mifflin.

Cooper, E. (2001). *Dance!* New York: Greenwillow.

Dash, J. (2000). *The longitude prize*. New York: Foster/Farrar.

Dewey, J. O. (2001). *Antarctic journal: Four months at the bottom of the world*. New York: HarperCollins.

Duffy, T. (2000). *The clock*. New York: Atheneum.

DuPrau, J. (2000). *Cloning*. New York: Raintree.

Floca, B. (2000). *Dinosaurs at the ends of the earth: The story of the central Asiatic expedition*. New York: DK Ink/Jackson.

Fradin, D. B. (2000). *Bound for the north star: True stories of fugitive slaves*. New York: Clarion.

Frazee, M. (Ill.). (1999). *Hush, little baby: A folk song with pictures*. New York: Harcourt Brown Deer.

Freedman, R. (1994). *Kids at work: Lewis Hine and the crusade against child labor*. New York: Clarion.

Freedman, R. (2000). *Give me liberty! The story of the Declaration of Independence*. New York: Holiday.

Gaines, A. G. (1998) *Terrorism*. New York: Chelsea.

Gardner, R. (2000a). *Science projects about the physics of toys and games*. New York: Enslow.

Gardner, R. (2000b). *Science projects about solids, liquids, and gases*. New York: Enslow.

Gardner, R. (2000c). *Science projects about sound*. New York: Enslow.

Govenar, A. (ed.) (2000). *Osceola: Memories of a Sharecropper's daughter*. New York: Hyperion Books for Children.

Harris, R. H. (1994). *It's perfectly normal: Changing bodies, growing up, sex and sexual health*. Cambridge: Candlewick.

Harris, R. H. (1999). *It's so amazing: A book about eggs, sperm, birth, babies, and families*. Cambridge: Candlewick.

Hoose, P. (2001). *We were there too! Young people in U. S. history*. New York: Kroupa/Farrar.

Jackson, D. (2001). *Twin tales: The magic and mystery of multiple birth*. Boston: Tingley/Little.

Koscielniak, B. (2000). *The story of the incredible orchestra*. Boston: Houghton Mifflin.

Leedy, L. (2000). *Subtraction action*. New York: Holiday.

Loewen, N., & Bancroft, A. (2001). *Four to the pole: The American women's expedition to Antarctica 1992–1993*. New York: Linnet.

Macaulay, D. (1973). *Cathedral: The story of its construction*. Boston: Houghton Mifflin.

Macaulay, D. (1977). *Castle*. Boston: Houghton Mifflin.

Macaulay, D. (2000). *Building big*. Boston: Houghton Mifflin.

MacDonald, M. R., & Jaeger, W. (1999). *The round book: Rounds kids love to sing*. New York: Linnet.

Mathews, R. (2000). *The Renaissance*. New York: Bedrick.

Michelson, R. (2000). *Ten times better*. New York: Cavendish.

Murphy, J. (2000). *Blizzard!* New York: Scholastic.

Myers, W. D. (1999). *At her majesty's request: An African princess in Victorian England*. New York: Scholastic.

Nagda, A. W., & Bickel, C. (2000). *Tiger math: Learning to graph from a baby tiger*. New York: Holt.

Older, J. (2000). *Telling time*. New York: Charlesbridge.

Orenstein, R. (2001). *New animal discoveries*. New York: Millbrook.

Patent, D. H. (2000). *Shaping the earth*. New York: Clarion.

Pellant, C. (2000). *The best book of fossils, rocks, and minerals*. New York: Kingfisher.

Ride, S. & O'Shaughnessy, T. (1999). *The mystery of Mars*. New York: Crown.

St. George, J. (2000). *So you want to be president?* New York: Philomel.

Schmandt-Besserat, D. (1999). *The history of counting.* New York: Morrow.

Schwartz, D. (1998). *G is for googol: A math alphabet book.* New York: Tricycle.

Schwartz, D. (1999). *If you hopped like a frog.* New York: Scholastic.

Simon, S. (1987/2000). *Destination: Mars.* New York: HarperCollins.

Skurzynski, G. (2000). *On time: From seasons to split seconds.* New York: National.

Sneve, V. D. H. (1996). *The Cherokees.* New York: Holiday.

Stanley, J. (2000). *Hurry freedom: African Americans in gold rush California.* New York: Crown.

Street, M. (2001). *Lucky 13: Solitaire games for kids.* New York: Sea Star.

Tang, G. (2001). *The grapes of math.* New York: Scholastic.

Van Loon, F. (1922). *The story of mankind.* London: George G. Harrap & Co. Ltd.

Warren, A. (1996). *Orphan train rider: One boy's true story.* Boston: Houghton Mifflin.

Webb, S. (2000). *My season with penguins.* Boston: Houghton Mifflin.

Whitman, S. (2001). *What's cooking: The history of American food.* New York: Lerner.

Winick, J. (2000). *Pedro and me: Friendship, loss, and what I learned.* New York: Holt.

Yount, L. (2000). *Epidemics.* New York: Lucent.

Yue, C., & Yue, D. (2000). *The wigwam and the longhouse.* Boston: Houghton Mifflin.

Professional Works

Allan, K. K., & Miller, M. S. (2000). *Literacy and learning: Strategies for middle and secondary school teachers.* Boston: Houghton Mifflin.

Bamford, R. A., & Kristo, J. V. (2000). *Checking out nonfiction K–8: Good choices for best learning.* Norwood, MA: Christopher Gordon.

Carr, J. (1982). (Ed.). *Beyond fact: Nonfiction for children and young people.* Chicago: American Library Association.

Fisher, M. (1972). *Matters of fact: Aspects of nonfiction for children.* New York: Crowell.

Kerper, R. M. (1998). Choosing quality nonfiction literature: Features for accessing and visualizing information. In R. A. Bamford & J. V. Kristo (Eds.), *Making*

facts come alive: Choosing quality nonfiction literature K–8. Norwood, MA: Christopher Gordon, pp. 55–74.

Leu, D. J., & Kinzer, C. K. (1999). *Effective reading instruction, K–8* (4th ed.). Upper Saddle River, NJ: Merrill/Prentice Hall.

Richardson, J. S., & Morgan, R. F. (1997). *Reading to learn in the content areas* (3rd ed.). Belmont, CA: Wadsworth.

Smith, L. (1953). *The unreluctant years.* New York: Viking.

Tompkins, G. (2001). *Literacy for the 21st century.* Upper Saddle River, NJ: Merrill/Prentice Hall.

Whitman, J., & Whitman, N. (2001). Child's work? In *Book Links,* vol. 10, no. 4, Feb/Mar, pp. 54–59.

Additional Resources

For more pedagogical ideas, see the following two texts:

Donoghue, M. R. (2001). *Using literature activities to teach content areas to emergent readers.* Needham Heights, MA: Allyn & Bacon.

Harvey, S. (1998). *Nonfiction matters: Reading, writing, and research in grades 3–8.* York, ME: Stenhouse.

Magazines for children cover a wide range of nonfiction, and special interests may be encouraged and supported through magazines, online and in print. Following are some popular and well-regarded magazines. Check at your library (public and school) for more.

Calliope world history for kids. Cobblestone Publishing, 7 School Road, Peterborough, NH 03458.

Cobblestone: The history magazine for young people. Cobblestone Publications, 7 School Road, Peterborough, NH 03458.

Cricket. P.O. Box 58342, Boulder, CO 80332.

Dolphin Log. The Cousteau Society, 870 Greenbrier Circle, Chesapeake, VA 23320.

Dramatics. Educational Theater Association, 3368 Central Parkway, Cincinnati, OH 45225.

Faces: People, places and culture. Cobblestone Publishing, 7 School Road, Peterborough, NH 03458.

Kids discover. Kids Discover, 170 Fifth Avenue, New York, NY 10010.

Muse (Smithsonian Museum magazine for children). Box 7468, Red Oak, IA 51591.

National Geographic World. National Geographic Society, 17th and M Streets NW, Washington, DC 20036.

Ranger Rick. National Wildlife Federation, 8925 Leesburg Pike, Vienna, VA 22184.

Sports Illustrated for Kids. Time, Inc. Magazine Co., 1271 Avenue of the Americas, New York, NY 10020.

3–2–1 contact. Children's Television Workshop, P.O. Box 53051, Boulder, CO 80322.

Time for kids. Time, Inc., Time Life Building, Rockefeller Center, New York, NY 10020.

Wildlife conservation. The International Wildlife Park, Bronx, NY 10460.

Zillions: Consumer reports for kids. Consumers Union, 101 Truman Avenue, Yonkers, NY 10703.

Zoobooks San Diego. Wildlife Education Ltd., 9820 Willow Creek Road, San Diego, CA 92131.

Children's Book Awards

Each year the Children's Services Division of the American Library Association selects one children's book to be honored with the **Newbery Medal** and a children's picture book to be honored with the **Caldecott Medal.** These awards are the highest honors in children's book publishing in the United States. They celebrate significant contributions to children's literature by notable people—namely, John Newbery, a noted British bookseller of the 18th century, and Randolph Caldecott, the British artist of the 19th century who raised the picture book to an art form (see Chapter 2 for more information about these two notable figures).

First, the Newbery Medal books and Honor books are listed, followed by the Caldecott Medal winners and Honor books. The Caldecott Medal is earned by the illustrator, not the author (although often the author is also the illustrator). The date on the left indicates the year of the award; all books were published in the preceding year.

The Coretta Scott King award-winning books are then listed. The Social Responsibilities Round Table of the American Library Association designates an outstanding African-American author and illustrator to receive the **Coretta Scott King Award** yearly. Begun in 1970, this award, founded to commemorate Dr. Martin Luther King Jr. and his wife, Coretta Scott King, are given to books published in the preceding year that make inspirational and educational contributions to literature for children and adolescents.

The Association for Library Service to Children, the arm of the American Library Association that deals directly with issues of concern to children and youth, has published a valuable resource entitled *The Newbery and Caldecott Awards: A Guide to the Medal and Honor Books* (2001). Criteria for the awards, a history of the awards, information on John Newbery and Randolph Caldecott, and thoughts from the chair of the 2000 committee make this a desirable reference and reader advisory.

Newbery Medal Winners and Honor Books

1922   *The Story of Mankind,* Hendrik Willem van Loon, Liveright.

HONOR BOOKS: *The Great Quest,* Charles Hawes, Little, Brown; *Cedric the Forester,* Bernard Marshall, Appleton; *The Old Tobacco Shop: A True Account of What Befell a Little Boy in Search of Adventure,* William Bowen, Macmillan; *The Golden Fleece and the Heroes Who Lived Before Achilles,* Padraic Colum, Macmillan; *Windy Hill,* Cornelia Meigs, Macmillan.

1923 *The Voyages of Doctor Dolittle,* Hugh Lofting, Lippincott.

HONOR BOOKS: No record.

1924 *The Dark Frigate,* Charles Hawes, Atlantic/Little, Brown.

HONOR BOOKS: No record.

1925 *Tales from the Silver Lands,* Charles Finger, Doubleday.

HONOR BOOKS: *Nicholas: A Manhattan Christmas Story,* Anne Carroll Moore, Putnam; *Dream Coach,* Anne Parrish, Macmillan.

1926 *Shen of the Sea,* Arthur Bowie Chrisman, Dutton.

HONOR BOOKS: *Voyagers: Being Legends and Romances of Atlantic Discovery,* Padraic Colum, Macmillan.

1927 *Smoky, the Cowhorse,* Will James, Scribner.

HONOR BOOKS: No record.

1928 *Gayneck, the Story of a Pigeon,* Dhan Gopal Mukerji, Dutton.

HONOR BOOKS: *The Wonder Smith and His Son: A Tale from the Golden Childhood of the World,* Ella Young, Longmans; *Downright Dencey,* Caroline Snedeker, Doubleday.

1929 *The Trumpeter of Krakow,* Eric P. Kelly, Macmillan.

HONOR BOOKS: *Pigtail of Ah Lee Ben Loo,* John Bennett, Longmans; *Millions of Cats,* Wanda Gag, Coward-McCann; *The Boy Who Was,* Grace Hallock, Dutton; *Clearing Weather,* Cornelia Meigs, Little, Brown; *Runaway Papoose,* Grace Moon, Doubleday; *Tod of the Fens,* Elinor Whitney, Macmillan.

1930 *Hitty, Her First Hundred Years,* Rachel Field, Macmillan.

HONOR BOOKS: *Daughter of the Seine: The Life of Madame Roland,* Jeanette Eaton, HarperCollins; *Pran of Albania,* Elizabeth Miller, Doubleday; *Jumping-Off Place,* Marian Hurd McNeely, Longmans; *Tangle-Coated Horse and Other Tales,* Ella Young, Longmans; *Vaino: A Boy of New England,* Julia Davis Adams, Dutton; *Little Blacknose,* Hildegarde Swift, Harcourt Brace Jovanovich.

1931 *The Cat Who Went to Heaven,* Elizabeth Coatsworth, Macmillan.

HONOR BOOKS: *Floating Island,* Anne Parrish, HarperCollins; *The Dark Star of Itze: The Story of a Pagan Princess,* Alida Malkus, Harcourt Brace; *Queer Person,* Ralph Hubbard, Doubleday; *Mountains Are Free,* Julia Davis Adams, Dutton; *Spice and the Devil's Cave,* Agnes Hewes, Knopf; *Meggy Macintosh,* Elizabeth Janet Gray, Doubleday; *Garram the Hunter: A Boy of the Hill Tribes,* Herbert Best, Doubleday; *Ood-Le-Uk the Wanderer,* Alice Lide and Margaret Johansen, Little, Brown.

1932 *Waterless Mountain,* Laura Adams Armer, Longmans.

HONOR BOOKS: *The Fairy Circus,* Dorothy P. Lathrop, Macmillan; *Calico Bush,* Rachel Field, Macmillan; *Boy of the South Seas,*

Eunice Tietjens, Coward-McCann; *Out of the Flame,* Eloise Lownsbery, Longmans; *Jane's Island,* Marjorie Allee, Houghton Mifflin; *Truce of the Wolf and Other Tales of Old Italy,* Mary Gould Davis, Harcourt Brace.

1933 *Young Fu of the Upper Yangtze,* Elizabeth Foreman Lewis, Winston.

HONOR BOOKS: *Swift Rivers,* Cornelia Meigs, Little, Brown; *The Railroad to Freedom: A Story of the Civil War,* Hildegarde Swift, Harcourt Brace; *Children of the Soil: A Story of Scandinavia,* Nora Burglon, Doubleday.

1934 *Invincible Louisa: The Story of the Author of 'Little Women,'* Cornelia Meigs, Little, Brown.

HONOR BOOKS: *The Forgotten Daughter,* Caroline Snedeker, Doubleday; *Swords of Steel,* Elsie Singmaster, Houghton Mifflin; *ABC Bunny,* Wanda Gag, Coward-McCann; *Winged Girl of Knossos,* Eric Berry, Appleton; *New Land,* Sarah Schmidt, McBride; *Big Tree of Bunlahy: Stories of My Own Countryside,* Padraic Colum, Macmillan; *Glory of the Seas,* Agnes Hewes, Knopf; *Apprentice of Florence,* Ann Kyle, Houghton Mifflin.

1935 *Dobry,* Monica Shannon, Viking.

HONOR BOOKS: *Pageant of Chinese History,* Elizabeth Seeger, Longmans; *Davy Crockett,* Constance Rourke, Harcourt Brace; *Day on Skates: The Story of a Dutch Picnic,* Hilda Van Stockum, HarperCollins.

1936 *Caddie Woodlawn,* Carol Ryrie Brink, Macmillan.

HONOR BOOKS: *Honk, the Moose,* Phil Stong, Dodd, Mead; *The Good Master,* Kate Seredy, Viking; *Young Walter Scott,* Elizabeth Janet Gray, Viking; *All Sails Set: A Romance of the Flying Cloud,* Armstrong Sperry, Winston.

1937 *Roller Skates,* Ruth Sawyer, Viking.

HONOR BOOKS: *Phoebe Fairchild: Her Book,* Lois Lenski, Stokes; *Whistler's Van,* Idwal Jones, Viking; *Golden Basket,* Ludwig Bemelmans, Viking; *Winterbound,* Margery Bianco, Viking; *Audubon,* Constance Rourke, Harcourt Brace; *The Codfish Musket,* Agnes Hewes, Doubleday.

1938 *The White Stag,* Kate Seredy, Viking.

HONOR BOOKS: *Pecos Bill,* James Cloyd Bowman, Little, Brown; *Bright Island,* Mabel Robinson, Random House; *On the Banks of Plum Creek,* Laura Ingalls Wilder, HarperCollins.

1939 *Thimble Summer,* Elizabeth Enright, Rinehart.

HONOR BOOKS: *Nino,* Valenti Angelo, Viking; *Mr. Popper's Penguins,* Richard and Florence Atwater, Little, Brown; *"Hello the Boat!"* Phyllis Crawford, Holt; *Leader by Destiny: George Washington, Man and Patriot,* Jeanette Eaton, Harcourt Brace; *Penn,* Elizabeth Janet Gray, Viking.

1940 *Daniel Boone,* James Daugherty, Viking.

HONOR BOOKS: *The Singing Tree,* Kate Seredy, Viking; *Runner of the Mountain Tops: The Life of Louis*

Agassiz, Mabel Robinson, Random House; *By the Shores of Silver Lake,* Laura Ingalls Wilder, HarperCollins; *Boy with a Pack,* Stephen W. Meader, Harcourt Brace.

1941   *Call It Courage,* Armstrong Sperry, Macmillan.

HONOR BOOKS: *Blue Willow,* Doris Gates, Viking; *Young Mac of Fort Vancouver,* Mary Jane Carr, Crowell; *The Long Winter,* Laura Ingalls Wilder, HarperCollins; *Nansen,* Anna Gertrude Hall, Viking.

1942   *The Matchlock Gun,* Walter D. Edmonds, Dodd, Mead.

HONOR BOOKS: *Little Town on the Prairie,* Laura Ingalls Wilder, HarperCollins; *George Washington's World,* Genevieve Foster, Scribner; *Indian Captive: The Story of Mary Jemison,* Lois Lenski, Lippincott; *Down Ryton Water,* Eva Roe Gaggin, Viking.

1943   *Adam of the Road,* Elizabeth Janet Gray, Viking.

HONOR BOOKS: *The Middle Moffat,* Eleanor Estes, Harcourt Brace; *Have You Seen Tom Thumb?* Mabel Leigh Hunt, Lippincott.

1944   *Johnny Tremain,* Esther Forbes, Houghton Mifflin.

HONOR BOOKS: *The Happy Golden Years,* Laura Ingalls Wilder, HarperCollins; *Fog Magic,* Julia Sauer, Viking; *Rufus M.,* Eleanor Estes, Harcourt Brace; *Mountain Born,* Elizabeth Yates, Coward-McCann.

1945   *Rabbit Hill,* Robert Lawson, Viking.

HONOR BOOKS: *The Hundred Dresses,* Eleanor Estes, Harcourt Brace; *The Silver Pencil,* Alice Dalgliesh, Scribner; *Abraham Lincoln's World,* Genevieve Foster, Scribner; *Lone Journey: The Life of Roger Williams,* Jeanette Eaton, Harcourt Brace Jovanovich.

1946   *Strawberry Girl,* Lois Lenski, Lippincott.

HONOR BOOKS: *Justin Morgan Had a Horse,* Marguerite Henry, Rand; *The Moved-Outers,* Florence Crannell Means, Houghton Mifflin; *Bhimsa, the Dancing Bear,* Christine Weston, Scribner; *New Found World,* Katherine Shippen, Viking.

1947   *Miss Hickory,* Carolyn Sherwin Bailey, Viking.

HONOR BOOKS: *Wonderful Year,* Nancy Barnes, Messner; *Big Tree,* Mary and Conrad Buff, Viking; *The Heavenly Tenants,* William Maxwell, HarperCollins; *The Avion My Uncle Flew,* Cyrus Fisher, Appleton; *The Hidden Treasure of Glaston,* Eleanor Jewett, Viking.

1948   *The Twenty-One Balloons,* William Pene du Bois, Viking.

HONOR BOOKS: *Pancakes-Paris,* Claire Hutchet Bishop, Viking; *Le Lun: Lad of Courage,* Carolyn Treffinger, Abingdon; *The Quaint and Curious Quest of Johnny Longfoot, the Shoe-King's Son,* Catherine Besterman, Bobbs-Merrill; *The Cow-Tail Switch, and Other West African Stories,* Harold Courlander,

Holt, Rinehart & Winston; *Misty of Chincoteague,* Marguerite Henry, Rand McNally.

1949 *King of the Wind,* Marguerite Henry, Rand McNally.

HONOR BOOKS: *Seabird,* Holling C. Holling, Houghton Mifflin; *Daughter of the Mountains,* Louise Rankin, Viking; *My Father's Dragon,* Ruth S. Gannett, Random House; *Story of the Negro,* Arna Bontemps, Knopf.

1950 *The Door in the Wall,* Marguerite de Angeli, Doubleday.

HONOR BOOKS: *Tree of Freedom,* Rebecca Caudill, Viking; *The Blue Cat of Castle Town,* Catherine Coblentz, Longmans Green; *Kildee House,* Rutherford Montgomery, Doubleday; *George Washington,* Genevieve Foster, Scribner; *Song of the Pines: A Story of Norwegian Lumbering in Wisconsin,* Walter and Marion Havighurst, Winston.

1951 *Amos Fortune, Free Man,* Elizabeth Yates, Aladdin.

HONOR BOOKS: *Better Known as Johnny Appleseed,* Mabel Leigh Hunt, Lippincott; *Gandhi, Fighter Without a Sword,* Jeanette Eaton, Morrow; *Abraham Lincoln, Friend of the People,* Clara Ingram Judson, Follett; *The Story of Appleby Capple,* Anne Parrish, HarperCollins.

1952 *Ginger Pye,* Eleanor Estes, Harcourt Brace Jovanovich.

HONOR BOOKS: *Americans Before Columbus,* Elizabeth Baity, Viking; *Minn of the Mississippi,* Holling C.

Holling, Houghton Mifflin; *The Defender,* Nicholas Kalashnikoff, Scribner; *The Light at Tern Rock,* Julia Sauer, Viking; *The Apple and the Arrow,* Mary and Conrad Buff, Houghton Mifflin.

1953 *Secret of the Andes,* Ann Nolan Clark, Viking.

HONOR BOOKS: *Charlotte's Web,* E. B. White, HarperCollins; *Moccasin Trail,* Eloise McGraw, Coward-McCann; *Red Sails to Capri,* Ann Weil, Viking; *The Bears on Hemlock Mountain,* Alice Dalgliesh, Scribner; *Birthdays of Freedom,* Vol. 1, Genevieve Foster, Scribner.

1954 *. . . and Now Miguel,* Joseph Krumgold, Crowell.

HONOR BOOKS: *All Alone,* Claire Hutchet Bishop, Viking; *Shadrach,* Meindert DeJong, HarperCollins; *Hurry Home, Candy,* Meindert DeJong, HarperCollins; *Theodore Roosevelt, Fighting Patriot,* Clara Ingram Judson, Follett; *Magic Maize,* Mary and Conrad Buff, Houghton Mifflin.

1955 *The Wheel on the School,* Meindert DeJong, HarperCollins.

HONOR BOOKS: *The Courage of Sarah Noble,* Alice Dalgliesh, Scribner; *Banner in the Sky,* James Ullman, Lippincott.

1956 *Carry On, Mr. Bowditch,* Jean Lee Latham, Houghton Mifflin.

HONOR BOOKS: *The Secret River,* Marjorie Kinnan Rawlings, Scribner; *The Golden Name Day,* Jennie

Linquist, HarperCollins; *Men, Microscopes, and Living Things,* Katherine Shippen, Viking.

1957   *Miracles on Maple Hill,* Virginia Sorensen, Harcourt Brace Jovanovich.

HONOR BOOKS: *Old Yeller,* Fred Gipson, HarperCollins; *The House of Sixty Fathers,* Meindert DeJong, HarperCollins; *Mr. Justice Holmes,* Clara Ingram Judson, Follett; *The Corn Grows Ripe,* Dorothy Rhoads, Viking; *Black Fox of Lorne,* Marguerite de Angeli, Doubleday.

1958   *Rifles for Watie,* Harold Keith, Crowell.

HONOR BOOKS: *The Horsecatcher,* Mari Sandoz, Westminster; *Goneaway Lake,* Elizabeth Enright, Harcourt Brace Jovanovich; *The Great Wheel,* Robert Lawson, Viking; *Tom Paine, Freedom's Apostle,* Leo Gurko, Crowell.

1959   *The Witch of Blackbird Pond,* Elizabeth George Speare, Houghton Mifflin.

HONOR BOOKS: *The Family Under the Bridge,* Natalie Savage Carlson, HarperCollins; *Along Came a Dog,* Meindert DeJong, HarperCollins; *Chucaro: Wild Pony of the Pampa,* Francis Kalnay, Harcourt Brace Jovanovich; *The Perilous Road,* William O. Steele, Harcourt Brace Jovanovich.

1960   *Onion John,* Joseph Krumgold, Crowell.

HONOR BOOKS: *My Side of the Mountain,* Jean George, Dutton; *America Is Born,* Gerald W. Johnson,

Morrow; *The Gammage Cup,* Carol Kendall, Harcourt Brace Jovanovich.

1961   *Island of the Blue Dolphins,* Scott O'Dell, Houghton Mifflin.

HONOR BOOKS: *America Moves Forward,* Gerald W. Johnson, Morrow; *Old Ramon,* Jack Schaefer, Houghton Mifflin; *The Cricket in Times Square,* George Selden, Farrar, Straus & Giroux.

1962   *The Bronze Bow,* Elizabeth George Speare, Houghton Mifflin.

HONOR BOOKS: *Frontier Living,* Edwin Tunis, World; *The Golden Goblet,* Eloise McGraw, Coward-McCann; *Belling the Tiger,* Mary Stolz, HarperCollins.

1963   *A Wrinkle in Time,* Madeleine L'Engle, Farrar, Straus & Giroux.

HONOR BOOKS: *Thistle and Thyme: Tales and Legends from Scotland,* Sorche Nic Leodhas, Holt, Rinehart & Winston; *Men of Athens,* Olivia Coolidge, Houghton Mifflin.

1964   *It's Like This, Cat,* Emily Cheney Neville, HarperCollins.

HONOR BOOKS: *Rascal,* Sterling North, Dutton; *The Loner,* Ester Wier, McKay.

1965   *Shadow of a Bull,* Maia Wojciechowska, Atheneum.

HONOR BOOKS: *Across Five Aprils,* Irene Hunt, Follett.

1966   *I, Juan de Pareja,* Elizabeth Borten de Trevino, Farrar, Straus & Giroux.

HONOR BOOKS: *The Black Cauldron,* Lloyd Alexander, Holt, Rinehart &

Winston; *The Animal Family,* Randall Jarrell, Pantheon; *The Noonday Friends,* Mary Stolz, HarperCollins.

1967   *Up a Road Slowly,* Irene Hunt, Follett.

HONOR BOOKS: *The King's Fifth,* Scott O'Dell, Houghton Mifflin; *Zlateh the Goat and Other Stories,* Isaac Bashevis Singer, HarperCollins; *The Jazz Man,* Mary H. Weik, Atheneum.

1968   *From the Mixed-Up Files of Mrs. Basil E. Frankweiler,* E. L. Konigsburg, Atheneum.

HONOR BOOKS: *Jennifer, Hecate, Macbeth, William McKinley, and Me, Elizabeth,* E. L. Konigsburg, Atheneum; *The Black Pearl,* Scott O'Dell, Houghton Mifflin; *The Fearsome Inn,* Isaac Bashevis Singer, Scribner; *The Egypt Game,* Zilpha Keatley Snyder, Atheneum.

1969   *The High King,* Lloyd Alexander, Holt, Rinehart & Winston.

HONOR BOOKS: *To Be a Slave,* Julius Lester, Dial; *When Shlemiel Went to Warsaw and Other Stories,* Isaac Bashevis Singer, Farrar, Straus & Giroux.

1970   *Sounder,* William Armstrong, HarperCollins.

HONOR BOOKS: *Our Eddie,* Sulamith Ish-Kishor, Pantheon; *The Many Ways of Seeing: An Introduction to the Pleasures of Art,* Janet Gaylord Moore, World; *Journey Outside,* Mary O. Steele, Viking.

1971   *Summer of the Swans,* Betsy Byars, Viking.

HONOR BOOKS: *Kneeknock Rise,* Natalie Babbitt, Farrar, Straus & Giroux; *Enchantress from the Stars,* Sylvia Louise Engdahl, Atheneum; *Sing Down the Moon,* Scott O'Dell, Houghton Mifflin.

1972   *Mrs. Frisby and the Rats of NIMH,* Robert C. O'Brien, Atheneum.

HONOR BOOKS: *Incident at Hawk's Hill,* Allan W. Eckert, Little, Brown; *The Planet of Junior Brown,* Virginia Hamilton, Macmillan; *The Tombs of Atuan,* Ursula LeGuin, Atheneum; *Annie and the Old One,* Miska Miles, Atlantic/Little, Brown; *The Headless Cupid,* Zilpha Keatley Snyder, Atheneum.

1973   *Julie of the Wolves,* Jean Craighead George, HarperCollins.

HONOR BOOKS: *Frog and Toad Together,* Arnold Lobel, HarperCollins; *The Upstairs Room,* Johanna Reiss, Crowell; *The Witches of Worm,* Zilpha Keatley Snyder, Atheneum.

1974   *The Slave Dancer,* Paula Fox, Bradbury.

HONOR BOOKS: *The Dark Is Rising,* Susan Cooper, Atheneum.

1975   *M. C. Higgins, the Great,* Virginia Hamilton, Macmillan.

HONOR BOOKS: *Figgs and Phantoms,* Ellen Raskin, Dutton; *My Brother Sam Is Dead,* James Lincoln Collier and Christopher Collier, Four Winds; *The Perilous Gard,* Elizabeth Marie Pope, Houghton Mifflin; *Philip Hall Likes Me, I Reckon Maybe,* Bette Greene, Dial.

1976   *The Grey King,* Susan Cooper, Atheneum.

HONOR BOOKS: *The Hundred Penny Box,* Sharon Bell Mathis, Viking; *Dragonwings,* Laurence Yep, HarperCollins.

1977   *Roll of Thunder, Hear My Cry,* Mildred D. Taylor, Dial.

HONOR BOOKS: *Abel's Island,* William Steig, Farrar, Straus & Giroux; *A String in the Harp,* Nancy Bond, Atheneum.

1978   *Bridge to Terabithia,* Katherine Paterson, Crowell.

HONOR BOOKS: *Ramona and Her Father,* Beverly Cleary, Morrow; *Anpao: An American Indian Odyssey,* Jamake Highwater, Lippincott.

1979   *The Westing Game,* Ellen Raskin, Dutton.

HONOR BOOKS: *The Great Gilly Hopkins,* Katherine Paterson, Crowell.

1980   *A Gathering of Days: A New England Girl's Journal 1830–1832,* Joan Blos, Scribner.

HONOR BOOKS: *The Road from Home: The Story of an Armenian Girl,* David Kherdian, Greenwillow.

1981   *Jacob Have I Loved,* Katherine Paterson, Crowell.

HONOR BOOKS: *The Fledgling,* Jane Langton, HarperCollins; *A Ring of Endless Light,* Madeleine L'Engle, Farrar, Straus & Giroux.

1982   *A Visit to William Blake's Inn: Poems for Innocent and Experienced Travelers,* Nancy Willard, Harcourt Brace Jovanovich.

HONOR BOOKS: *Ramona Quimby, Age 8,* Beverly Cleary, Morrow; *Upon the Head of a Goat: A Childhood in Hungary 1939–1944,* Aranka Siegel, Farrar, Straus & Giroux.

1983   *Dicey's Song,* Cynthia Voigt, Atheneum.

HONOR BOOKS: *Blue Sword,* Robin McKinley, Morrow; *Dr. DeSoto,* William Steig, Farrar, Straus & Giroux; *Graven Images,* Paul Fleischman, HarperCollins; *Homesick: My Own Story,* Jean Fritz, Putnam; *Sweet Whispers, Brother Rush,* Virginia Hamilton, Philomel.

1984   *Dear Mr. Henshaw,* Beverly Cleary, Morrow.

HONOR BOOKS: *The Sign of the Beaver,* Elizabeth George Speare, Houghton Mifflin; *A Solitary Blue,* Cynthia Voigt, Atheneum; *The Wish Giver,* Bill Brittain, HarperCollins.

1985   *The Hero and the Crown,* Robin McKinley, Greenwillow.

HONOR BOOKS: *Like Jake and Me,* Mavis Jukes, Knopf; *Sugaring Time,* Kathryn Lasky, Macmillan; *The Moves Make the Man,* Bruce Brooks, HarperCollins; *One-Eyed Cat,* Paula Fox, Bradbury.

1986   *Sarah, Plain and Tall,* Patricia MacLachlan, HarperCollins.

HONOR BOOKS: *Commodore Perry in the Land of the Shogun,* Rhoda Blumberg, Lothrop, Lee & Shepard; *Dogsong,* Gary Paulsen, Bradbury.

1987 *The Whipping Boy,* Sid Fleischman, Greenwillow.

HONOR BOOKS: *A Fine White Dust,* Cynthia Rylant, Bradbury; *On My Honor,* Marion Dane Bauer, Clarion; *Volcano,* Patricia Lauber, Bradbury.

1988 *Lincoln: A Photobiography,* Russell Freedman, Clarion.

HONOR BOOKS: *After the Rain,* Norma Fox Mazer, Morrow; *Hatchet,* Gary Paulsen, Bradbury.

1989 *Joyful Noise: Poems for Two Voices,* Paul Fleischman, HarperCollins.

HONOR BOOKS: *In the Beginning: Creation Stories from Around the World,* Virginia Hamilton, Harcourt Brace Jovanovich; *Scorpions,* Walter Dean Myers, HarperCollins.

1990 *Number the Stars,* Lois Lowry, Houghton Mifflin.

HONOR BOOKS: *Afternoon of the Elves,* Janet Taylor Lisle, Orchard; *Shabanu, Daughter of the Wind,* Susan Fisher Staples, Knopf; *The Winter Room,* Gary Paulsen, Orchard.

1991 *Maniac Magee,* Jerry Spinelli, Little, Brown.

HONOR BOOKS: *The True Confessions of Charlotte Doyle,* Avi, Orchard.

1992 *Shiloh,* Phyllis Reynolds Naylor, Atheneum.

HONOR BOOKS: *Nothing but the Truth,* Avi, Orchard; *The Wright Brothers,* Russell Freedman, Holiday.

1993 *Missing May,* Cynthia Rylant, Orchard.

HONOR BOOKS: *The Dark Thirty: Southern Tales of the Supernatural,* Patricia McKissack, Knopf; *Somewhere in the Darkness,* Walter Dean Myers, Scholastic; *What Hearts,* Bruce Brooks, HarperCollins.

1994 *The Giver,* Lois Lowry, Houghton Mifflin.

HONOR BOOKS: *Crazy Lady,* Jane Leslie Conly, HarperCollins; *Eleanor Roosevelt,* Russell Freedman, Clarion; *Dragon's Gate,* Laurence Yep, HarperCollins.

1995 *Walk Two Moons,* Sharon Creech, HarperCollins.

HONOR BOOKS: *Catherine, Called Birdy,* Karen Cushman, Clarion; *The Ear, the Eye and the Arm,* Nancy Farmer, Jackson/Orchard.

1996 *The Midwife's Apprentice,* Karen Cushman, Clarion.

HONOR BOOKS: *What Jamie Saw,* Carolyn Coman, Front Street; *The Watsons Go To Birmingham—1963,* Christopher Paul Curtis, Delacorte; *Yolonda's Genius,* Carol Fenner, McElderry; *The Great Fire,* Jim Murphy, Scholastic.

1997 *The View from Saturday,* E. L. Konigsburg.

HONOR BOOKS: *A Girl Named Disaster,* Nancy Farmer, Jackson/Orchard; *The Moorchild,* Eloise McGraw, McElderry; *The Thief,* Megan Whalen Turner, Greenwillow; *Belle Prater's Boy,* Ruth White, Farrar, Straus & Giroux.

1998   *Out of the Dust,* Karen Hesse, Scholastic.

HONOR BOOKS: *Ella Enchanted,* Gail Carson Levine, HarperCollins; *Lily's Crossing,* Patricia Reilly Giff, Delacorte; *Wringer,* Jerry Spinelli, Joanna Cotler/HarperCollins.

1999   *Holes,* Louis Sachar, Foster/Farrar.

HONOR BOOKS: *A Long Way to Chicago,* Richard Peck, Dial.

2000   *Bud, Not Buddy,* Christopher Paul Curtis, Delacorte.

HONOR BOOKS: *Getting Near to Baby,* Audrey Couloumbis, Putnam; *26 Fairmount Avenue,* Tomie de Paola, Putnam; *Our Only May Amelia,* Jennifer L. Holm, HarperCollins.

2001   *A Year Down Yonder,* Richard Peck, Dial.

HONOR BOOKS: *Hope Was Here,* Joan Bauer, Putnam; *The Wanderer,* Sharon Creech, Cotler/HarperCollins; *Because of Winn-Dixie,* Kate DiCamillo, Candlewick; *Joey Pigza Loses Control,* Jack Gantos, Farrar.

2002   *A Single Shard,* Linda Sue Park, Clarion.

HONOR BOOKS: *Everything on a Waffle,* Polly Horvath, Farrar; *Carver: A Life in Poems,* Marilyn Nelson, Front Street.

Caldecott Medal Winners and Honor Books

1938   *Animals of the Bible,* Helen Dean Fish, ill. by Dorothy P. Lathrop, Stokes.

HONOR BOOKS: *Seven Simeon: A Russian Tale,* Boris Artzybasheff,

Viking; *Four and Twenty Blackbirds: Nursery Rhymes of Yesterday Recalled for Children of Today,* Helen Dean Fish, ill. by Robert Lawson, Stokes.

1939   *Mei Li,* Thomas Handforth, Doubleday.

HONOR BOOKS: *The Forest Pool,* Laura Adams Armer, Longmans; *Wee Gillis,* Munro Leaf, ill. by Robert Lawson, Viking; *Snow White and the Seven Dwarfs,* Wanda Gag, Coward-McCann; *Barkis,* Clare Newberry, HarperCollins; *Andy and the Lion: A Tale of Kindness Remembered or the Power of Gratitude,* James Daugherty, Viking.

1940   *Abraham Lincoln,* Ingri and Edgar Parin d'Aulaire, Doubleday.

HONOR BOOKS: *Cock-a-Doodle Doo: The Story of a Little Red Rooster,* Berta and Elmer Hader, Macmillan; *Madeline,* Ludwig Bemelmans, Simon & Schuster; *The Ageless Story,* Lauren Ford, Dodd, Mead.

1941   *They Were Strong and Good,* Robert Lawson, Viking.

HONOR BOOKS: *April's Kittens,* Clare Newberry, HarperCollins.

1942   *Make Way for Ducklings,* Robert McCloskey, Viking.

HONOR BOOKS: *An American ABC,* Maud and Miska Petersham, Macmillan; *In My Mother's House,* Ann Nolan Clark, ill. by Velino Herrera, Viking; *Paddle-to-the-Sea,* Holling C. Holling, Houghton Mifflin; *Nothing at All,* Wanda Gag, Coward-McCann.

1943   *The Little House,* Virginia Lee Burton, Houghton Mifflin.

HONOR BOOKS: *Dash and Dart,* Mary and Conrad Buff, Viking; *Marshmallow,* Clare Newberry, HarperCollins.

1944   *Many Moons,* James Thurber, ill. by Louis Slobodkin, Harcourt Brace.

HONOR BOOKS: *Small Rain: Verses from the Bible,* Jessie Orton Jones, ill. by Elizabeth Orton Jones, Viking; *Pierre Pigeon,* Lee Kingman, ill. by Arnold E. Bare, Houghton Mifflin; *The Mighty Hunter,* Berta and Elmer Hader, Macmillan; *A Child's Good Night Book,* Margaret Wise Brown, ill. by Jean Charlot, Scott, Foresman; *Good Luck Horse,* Chih-Yi Chan, ill. by Plato Chan, Whittlesey.

1945   *Prayer for a Child,* Rachel Field, ill. by Elizabeth Orton Jones, Macmillan.

HONOR BOOKS: *Mother Goose: Seventy-Seven Verses with Pictures,* ill. by Tasha Tudor, Walck; *In the Forest,* Marie Hall Ets, Viking; *Yonie Wondernose,* Marguerite de Angeli, Doubleday; *The Christmas Anna Angel,* Ruth Sawyer, ill. by Kate Seredy, Viking.

1946   *The Rooster Crows . . .,* ill. by Maud and Miska Petersham, Macmillan.

HONOR BOOKS: *Little Lost Lamb,* Golden MacDonald, ill. by Leonard Weisgard, Doubleday; *Sing Mother Goose,* Opal Wheeler, ill. by Marjorie Torrey, Dutton; *My Mother Is the Most Beautiful Woman in the World,* Becky Reyher, ill. by Ruth Gannett, Lothrop, Lee & Shepard; *You Can Write Chinese,* Kurt Wiese, Viking.

1947   *The Little Island,* Golden MacDonald, ill. by Leonard Weisgard, Doubleday.

HONOR BOOKS: *Rain Drop Splash,* Alvin Tresselt, ill. by Leonard Weisgard, Lothrop, Lee & Shepard; *Boats on the River,* Marjorie Flack, ill. by Jay Hyde Barnum, Viking; *Timothy Turtle,* Al Graham, ill. by Tony Palazzo, Viking; *Pedro, the Angel of Olvera Street,* Leo Politi, Scribner; *Sing in Praise: A Collection of the Best Loved Hymns,* Opal Wheeler, ill. by Marjorie Torrey, Dutton.

1948   *White Snow, Bright Snow,* Alvin Tresselt, ill. by Roger Duvoisin, Lothrop, Lee & Shepard.

HONOR BOOKS: *Stone Soup: An Old Tale,* Marcia Brown, Scribner; *McElligot's Pool,* Dr. Seuss, Random House; *Bambino the Clown,* George Schreiber, Viking; *Roger and the Fox,* Lavinia Davis, ill. by Hildegard Woodward, Doubleday; *Song of Robin Hood,* Anne Malcolmson (ed.), ill. by Virginia Lee Burton, Houghton Mifflin.

1949   *The Big Snow,* Berta and Elmer Hader, Macmillan.

HONOR BOOKS: *Blueberries for Sal,* Robert McCloskey, Viking; *All Around the Town,* Phyllis McGinley, ill. by Helen Stone, Lippincott; *Juanita,* Leo Politi, Scribner; *Fish in the Air,* Kurt Weise, Viking.

1950   *Song of the Swallows,* Leo Politi, Scribner.

HONOR BOOKS: *America's Ethan Allen,* Stewart Holbrook, ill. by Lynd Ward, Houghton Mifflin; *The Wild Birthday Cake,* Lavinia Davis, ill. by

Hildegard Woodward, Doubleday; *The Happy Day,* Ruth Krauss, ill. by Marc Simont, HarperCollins; *Bartholomew and the Oobleck,* Dr. Seuss, Random House; *Henry Fisherman,* Marcia Brown, Scribner.

1951   *The Egg Tree,* Katherine Milhous, Scribner.

HONOR BOOKS: *Dick Whittington and His Cat,* Marcia Brown, Scribner; *The Two Reds,* William Lipkind, ill. by Nicholas Mordvinoff, Harcourt Brace; *If I Ran the Zoo,* Dr. Seuss, Random House; *The Most Wonderful Doll in the World,* Phyllis McGinley, ill. by Helen Stone, Lippincott; *T-Bone, the Babysitter,* Clare Newberry, HarperCollins.

1952   *Finders Keepers,* William Lipkind, ill. by Nicholas Mordvinoff, Harcourt Brace.

HONOR BOOKS: *Mr. T. W. Anthony Wood: The Story of a Cat and a Dog and a Mouse,* Marie Hall Ets, Viking; *Skipper John's Cook,* Marcia Brown, Scribner; *All Falling Down,* Gene Zion, ill. by Margaret Bloy Graham, HarperCollins; *Bear Party,* William Pene du Bois, Viking; *Feather Mountain,* Elizabeth Olds, Houghton Mifflin.

1953   *The Biggest Bear,* Lynd Ward, Houghton Mifflin.

HONOR BOOKS: *Puss in Boots,* Charles Perrault, ill. and trans. by Marcia Brown, Scribner; *One Morning in Maine,* Robert McCloskey, Viking; *Ape in a Cape: An Alphabet of Odd Animals,* Fritz Eichenberg, Harcourt Brace; *The Storm Book,* Charlotte Zolotow, ill.

by Margaret Bloy Graham, HarperCollins; *Five Little Monkeys,* Juliet Kepes, Houghton Mifflin.

1954   *Madeline's Rescue,* Ludwig Bemelmans, Viking.

HONOR BOOKS: *Journey Cake, Ho!* Ruth Sawyer, ill. by Robert McCloskey, Viking; *When Will the World Be Mine?* Miriam Schlein, ill. by Jean Charlot, Scott, Foresman; *The Steadfast Tin Soldier,* Hans Christian Andersen, ill. by Marcia Brown, Scribner; *A Very Special House,* Ruth Krauss, ill. by Maurice Sendak, HarperCollins; *Green Eyes,* A. Birnbaum, Capitol.

1955   *Cinderella, or the Little Glass Slipper,* Charles Perrault, ill. and trans. by Marcia Brown, Scribner.

HONOR BOOKS: *Book of Nursery and Mother Goose Rhymes,* ill. by Marguerite deAngeli, Doubleday; *Wheel on the Chimney,* Margaret Wise Brown, ill. by Tibor Gergely, Lippincott; *The Thanksgiving Story,* Alice Dalgliesh, ill. by Helen Sewell, Scribner.

1956   *Frog Went A-Courtin',* ed. by John Langstaff, ill. by Feodor Rojankovsky, Harcourt Brace Jovanovich.

HONOR BOOKS: *Play with Me,* Marie Hall Ets, Viking; *Crow Boy,* Taro Yashima, Viking.

1957   *A Tree Is Nice,* Janice May Udry, ill. by Marc Simont, HarperCollins.

HONOR BOOKS: *Mr. Penny's Race Horse,* Marie Hall Ets, Viking; *1 Is One,* Tasha Tudor, Walck; *Anatole,* Eve Titus, ill. by Paul Galdone, McGraw-Hill; *Gillispie and the*

Guards, Benjamin Elkin, ill. by James Daugherty, Viking; *Lion,* William Pene du Bois, Viking.

1958 *Time of Wonder,* Robert McClosky, Viking.

HONOR BOOKS: *Fly High, Fly Low,* Don Freeman, Viking; *Anatole and the Cat,* Eve Titus, ill. by Paul Galdone, McGraw-Hill.

1959 *Chanticleer and the Fox,* adapted from Chaucer and ill. by Barbara Cooney, Crowell.

HONOR BOOKS: *The House that Jack Built: A Picture Book in Two Languages,* Antonio Frasconi, Harcourt Brace Jovanovich; *What Do You Say, Dear?* Sesyle Joslin, ill. by Maurice Sendak, Scott, Foresman; *Umbrella,* Taro Yashima, Viking.

1960 *Nine Days to Christmas,* Marie Hall Ets and Aurora Labastida, ill. by Marie Hall Ets, Viking.

HONOR BOOKS: *Houses from the Sea,* Alice E. Goudey, ill. by Adrienne Adams, Scribner; *The Moon Jumpers,* Janice May Udry, ill. by Maurice Sendak, HarperCollins.

1961 *Baboushka and the Three Kings,* Ruth Robbins, ill. by Nicolas Sidjakov, Parnassus.

HONOR BOOKS: *Inch by Inch,* Leo Lionni, Obolensky.

1962 *Once a Mouse . . . ,* Marcia Brown, Scribner.

HONOR BOOKS: *The Fox Went Out on a Chilly Night: An Old Song,* Peter Spier, Doubleday; *Little Bear's Visit,* Else Holmelund Minarik, ill. by

Maurice Sendak, HarperCollins; *The Day We Saw the Sun Come Up,* Alice E. Goudey, ill. by Adrienne Adams, Scribner.

1963 *The Snowy Day,* Ezra Jack Keats, Viking.

HONOR BOOKS: *The Sun Is a Golden Earring,* Natalia M. Belting, ill. by Bernarda Bryson, Holt, Rinehart & Winston; *Mr. Rabbit and the Lovely Present,* Charlotte Zolotow, ill. by Maurice Sendak, HarperCollins.

1964 *Where the Wild Things Are,* Maurice Sendak, HarperCollins.

HONOR BOOKS: *Swimmy,* Leo Lionni, Pantheon; *All in the Morning Early,* Sorche Nic Leodhas, ill. by Evaline Ness, Holt, Rinehart & Winston; *Mother Goose and Nursery Rhymes,* ill. and edited by Philip Reed, Atheneum.

1965 *May I Bring a Friend?,* Beatrice Schenk de Regniers, ill. by Beni Montresor, Atheneum.

HONOR BOOKS: *Rain Makes Applesauce,* Julian Scheer, ill. by Marvin Bileck, Holiday; *The Wave,* Margaret Hodges, ill. by Blair Lent, Houghton Mifflin; *A Pocketful of Cricket,* Rebecca Caudill, ill. by Evaline Ness, Holt, Rinehart & Winston.

1966 *Always Room for One More,* Sorche Nic Leodhas, ill. by Nonny Hogrogian, Holt, Rinehart & Winston.

HONOR BOOKS: *Hide and Seek Fog,* Alvin Tresselt, ill. by Roger Duvoisin, Lothrop, Lee & Shepard; *Just Me,* Marie Hall Ets, Viking; *Tom Tit Tot,* Evaline Ness, Scribner.

1967   *Sam, Bangs, and Moonshine,* Evaline Ness, Holt, Rinehart & Winston.

HONOR BOOKS: *One Wide River to Cross,* Barbara Emberley, ill. by Ed Emberley, Prentice Hall.

1968   *Drummer Hoff,* Barbara Emberley, ill. by Ed Emberley, Prentice Hall.

HONOR BOOKS: *Frederick,* Leo Lionni, Pantheon; *Seashore Story,* Taro Yashima, Viking; *The Emperor and the Kite,* Jane Yolen, ill. by Ed Young, World.

1969   *The Fool of the World and the Flying Machine,* Arthur Ransome, ill. by Uri Shulevitz, Farrar, Straus & Giroux.

HONOR BOOKS: *Why the Sun and the Moon Live in the Sky: An African Folktale,* Elphinstone Dayrell, ill. by Blair Lent, Houghton Mifflin.

1970   *Sylvester and the Magic Pebble,* William Steig, Windmill.

HONOR BOOKS: *Goggles!* Ezra Jack Keats, Macmillan; *Alexander and the Wind-Up Mouse,* Leo Lionni, Pantheon; *Pop Corn and Ma Goodness,* Edna Mitchell Preston, ill. by Robert Andrew Parker, Viking; *Thy Friend, Obadiah,* Brinton Turkle, Viking; *The Judge: An Untrue Tale,* Harve Zemach, ill. by Margot Zemach, Farrar, Straus & Giroux.

1971   *A Story—A Story: An African Tale,* Gail Haley, Atheneum.

HONOR BOOKS: *The Angry Moon,* William Sleator, ill. by Blair Lent, Atlantic–Little, Brown; *Frog and Toad Are Friends,* Arnold Lobel, HarperCollins; *In the Night Kitchen,* Maurice Sendak, HarperCollins.

1972   *One Fine Day,* Nonny Hogrogian, Macmillan.

HONOR BOOKS: *If All the Seas Were One Sea,* Janina Domanska, Macmillan; *Moja Means One: Swahili Counting Book,* Muriel Feelings, ill. by Tom Feelings, Dial; *Hildilid's Night,* Cheli Duran Ryan, ill. by Arnold Lobel, Macmillan.

1973   *The Funny Little Woman,* retold by Arlene Mosel, ill. by Blair Lent, Dutton.

HONOR BOOKS: *Anansi the Spider: A Tale for the Ashanti,* adapted by Gerald McDermott, Holt, Rinehart & Winston; *Hosie's Alphabet,* Hosea Tobias and Lisa Baskin, ill. by Leonard Baskin, Viking; *Snow White and the Seven Dwarfs,* trans. by Randall Jarrell, ill. by Nancy Ekholm Burkert, Farrar, Straus & Giroux; *When Clay Sings,* Byrd Baylor, ill. by Tom Bahti, Scribner.

1974   *Duffy and the Devil,* Harve Zemach, ill. by Margot Zemach, Farrar, Straus & Giroux.

HONOR BOOKS: *Three Jovial Huntsmen,* Susan Jeffers, Bradbury; *Cathedral: The Story of Its Construction,* David Macaulay, Houghton Mifflin.

1975   *Arrow to the Sun,* adapt. and ill. by Gerald McDermott, Viking.

HONOR BOOKS: *Jambo Means Hello: A Swahili Alphabet Book,* Muriel Feelings, ill. by Tom Feelings, Dial.

1976   *Why Mosquitoes Buzz in People's Ears,* retold by Verna Aardema, ill. by Leo and Diane Dillon, Dial.

HONOR BOOKS: *The Desert Is Theirs,* Byrd Baylor, ill. by Peter Parnall, Scribner; *Strega Nona,* retold and ill. by Tomie de Paola, Prentice Hall.

1977   *Ashanti to Zulu: African Traditions,* Margaret Musgrove, ill. by Leo and Diane Dillon, Dial.

HONOR BOOKS: *The Amazing Bone,* William Steig, Farrar, Straus & Giroux; *The Contest,* retold and ill. by Nonny Hogrogian, Greenwillow; *Fish for Supper,* M. B. Goffstein, Dial; *The Golem: A Jewish Legend,* Beverly Brodsky McDermott, Lippincott; *Hawk, I'm Your Brother,* Byrd Baylor, ill. by Peter Parnall, Scribner.

1978   *Noah's Ark,* Peter Spier, Doubleday.

HONOR BOOKS: *Castle,* David Macaulay, Houghton Mifflin; *It Could Always Be Worse,* retold and ill. by Margot Zemach, Farrar, Straus & Giroux.

1979   *The Girl Who Loved Wild Horses,* Paul Goble, Bradbury.

HONOR BOOKS: *Freight Train,* Donald Crews, Greenwillow; *The Way to Start a Day,* Byrd Baylor, ill. by Peter Parnall, Scribner.

1980   *Ox-Cart Man,* Donald Hall, ill. by Barbara Cooney, Viking.

HONOR BOOKS: *Ben's Trumpet,* Rachel Isadora, Greenwillow; *The Treasure,* Uri Shulevitz, Farrar, Straus & Giroux; *The Garden of Abdul Gasazi,* Chris Van Allsburg, Houghton Mifflin.

1981   *Fables,* Arnold Lobel, HarperCollins.

HONOR BOOKS: *The Bremen-Town Musicians,* Ilse Plume, Doubleday; *The Grey Lady and the Strawberry Snatcher,* Molly Bang, Four Winds; *Mice Twice,* Joseph Low, Atheneum; *Truck,* Donald Crews, Greenwillow.

1982   *Jumanji,* Chris Van Allsburg, Houghton Mifflin.

HONOR BOOKS: *A Visit to William Blake's Inn: Poems for Innocent and Experienced Travelers,* Nancy Willard, ill. by Alice and Martin Provensen, Harcourt Brace Jovanovich; *Where the Buffaloes Begin,* Olaf Baker, ill. by Stephen Gammell, Warner; *On Market Street,* Arnold Lobel, ill. by Anita Lobel, Greenwillow; *Outside Over There,* Maurice Sendak, HarperCollins.

1983   *Shadow,* Blaise Cendrars, ill. by Marcia Brown, Scribner.

HONOR BOOKS: *When I Was Young in the Mountains,* Cynthia Rylant, ill. by Diane Goode, Dutton; *A Chair for My Mother,* Vera B. Williams, Morrow.

1984   *The Glorious Flight: Across the Channel with Louis Bleriot,* Alice and Martin Provensen, Viking.

HONOR BOOKS: *Ten, Nine, Eight,* Molly Bang, Greenwillow; *Little Red Riding Hood,* retold and ill. by Trina Schart Hyman, Holiday House.

1985   *St. George and the Dragon,* retold by Margaret Hodges, ill. by Trina Schart Hyman, Little, Brown.

HONOR BOOKS: *Hansel and Gretel,* retold by Rika Lesser, ill. by Paul O. Zelinsky, Dodd, Mead; *Have You Seen My Duckling?* Nancy Tafuri,

Greenwillow; *The Story of Jumping Mouse,* John Steptoe, Lothrop, Lee & Shepard.

1986   *The Polar Express,* Chris Van Allsburg, Houghton Mifflin.

HONOR BOOKS: *King Bidgood's in the Bathtub,* Audrey Wood, ill. by Don Wood, Harcourt Brace Jovanovich; *The Relatives Came,* Cynthia Rylant, ill. by Stephen Gammell, Bradbury.

1987   *Hey, Al,* Arthur Yorinks, ill. by Richard Egielski, Farrar, Straus & Giroux.

HONOR BOOKS: *Alphabatics,* Suse MacDonald, Bradbury; *Rumpelstiltskin,* retold and ill. by Paul O. Zelinsky, Dutton; *The Village of Round and Square Houses,* Ann Grifalconi, Little, Brown.

1988   *Owl Moon,* Jane Yolen, ill. by John Schoenherr, Philomel.

HONOR BOOKS: *Mufaro's Beautiful Daughters: An African Tale,* John Steptoe, Lothrop, Lee & Shepard.

1989   *Song and Dance Man,* Karen Ackerman, ill. by Stephen Gammell, Knopf.

HONOR BOOKS: *The Boy of the Three-Year Nap,* Diane Stanley, ill. by Allen Say, Houghton Mifflin; *Free Fall,* David Wiesner, Lothrop, Lee & Shepard; *Goldilocks and the Three Bears,* adapted and ill. by James Marshall, Dial; *Mirandy and Brother Wind,* Patricia McKissack, ill. by Jerry Pinkney, Knopf.

1990   *Lon Po Po: A Red Riding Hood Story from China,* adapted and ill. by Ed Young, Philomel.

HONOR BOOKS: *Bill Peet: An Autobiography,* Bill Peet, Houghton Mifflin; *Color Zoo,* Lois Ehlert, Lippincott; *Herschel and the Hanukkah Goblins,* Eric Kimmel, ill. by Trina Schart Hyman, Holiday; *The Talking Eggs,* Robert D. San Souci, ill. by Jerry Pinkney, Dial.

1991   *Black and White,* David Macaulay, Houghton Mifflin.

HONOR BOOKS: *Puss in Boots,* Charles Perrault, trans. by Malcolm Arthur, ill. by Fred Marcellino, Farrar, Straus & Giroux; *"More More More," Said the Baby,* Vera B. Williams, Greenwillow.

1992   *Tuesday,* David Wiesner, Clarion.

HONOR BOOKS: *Tar Beach,* Faith Ringgold, Crown.

1993   *Mirette on the High Wire,* Emily Arnold McCully, Putnam.

HONOR BOOKS: *Seven Blind Mice,* Ed Young, Philomel; *The Stinky Cheese Man and Other Fairly Stupid Tales,* Jon Scieszka, ill. by Lane Smith, Viking; *Working Cotton,* Sherley Anne Williams, ill. by Carole Byard, Harcourt Brace Jovanovich.

1994   *Grandfather's Journey,* Allen Say, Houghton Mifflin.

HONOR BOOKS: *Peppe the Lamplighter,* Elisa Bartone, ill. by Ted Lewin, Lothrop, Lee & Shepard; *In the Small, Small Pond,* Denise Fleming, Holt, Rinehart & Winston; *Owen,* Kevin Henkes, Greenwillow; *Raven: A Trickster Tale from the Pacific Northwest,* Gerald McDermott, Harcourt Brace

Jovanovich; *Yo! Yes?* Christopher Raschka, Jackson/Orchard.

1995   *Smoky Night,* Eve Bunting, ill. by David Diaz, Harcourt.

HONOR BOOKS: *Swamp Angel,* Anne Isaacs, ill. by Paul O. Zelinsky, Dutton; *John Henry,* Julius Lester, ill. by Jerry Pinkney, Dial; *Time Flies,* Eric Rohmann, Crown.

1996   *Officer Buckle and Gloria,* Peggy Rathmann, Putnam.

HONOR BOOKS: *Alphabet City,* Stephen T. Johnson, Viking; *Zin! Zin! Zin! A Violin,* Lloyd Moss, ill. by Marjorie Priceman, Simon; *The Faithful Friend,* Robert D. San Souci, ill. by Brian Pinkney, Simon & Schuster; *Tops and Bottoms,* Janet Stevens, Harcourt Brace.

1997   *Golem,* David Wisniewski, Clarion.

HONOR BOOKS: *Hush! A Thai Lullaby,* Minfong Ho, ill. by Holly Meade, Kroupa/Orchard; *The Graphic Alphabet,* David Pelletier, Orchard; *The Paperboy,* Dav Pilkey, Orchard; *Starry Messenger,* Peter Sis, Farrar, Straus & Giroux.

1998   *Rapunzel,* Paul O. Zelinsky, Dutton

HONOR BOOKS: *The Gardener,* Sarah Stewart, ill. by David Small, Farrar, Straus, & Giroux; *Harlem,* Walter Dean Myers, ill. by Christopher Myers, Scholastic; *There Was an Old Lady Who Swallowed a Fly,* Simms Taback, Viking.

1999   *Snowflake Bentley,* Jacqueline Briggs Martin, ill. by Mary Azarian, Houghton Mifflin.

HONOR BOOKS: *Duke Ellington,* Andrea Davis Pinkney, ill. by Brian Pinkney, Hyperion; *No, David,* David Shannon, Blue Sky/Scholastic; *Snow,* Uri Shulevitz, Farrar, Straus & Giroux; *Tibet: Through the Red Box,* Peter Sis, Farrar, Straus & Giroux.

2000   *Joseph Had a Little Overcoat,* Simms Taback, Viking.

HONOR BOOKS: *Sector 7,* David Wiesner, Clarion; *The Ugly Duckling,* Jerry Pinkney, Morrow; *When Sophie Gets Angry—Really, Really Angry,* Molly Bang, Scholastic; *A Child's Calendar,* John Updike, ill. by Trina Schart Hyman, Holiday House.

2001   *So You Want to Be President?* Judith St. George, ill. by David Small, Philomel.

HONOR BOOKS: *Casey at the Bat: A Ballad of the Republic Sung in the Year 1888,* Ernest Lawrence Thayer, ill. by Christopher Bing, Handprint; *Click, Clack, Moo: Cows that Type,* Doreen Cronin, ill. by Betsy Lewin, Simon & Schuster; *Olivia,* Ian Falconer, Atheneum.

2002   *The Three Pigs,* David Wiesner, Clarion.

HONOR BOOKS: *The Dinosaurs of Waterhouse Hawkins,* Barbara Kerley, ill. by Brian Selznick, Scholastic; *Martin's Big Words,* Doreen Rappaport, ill. by Bryan Collier, Jump at the Sun/Hyperion; *The Stray Dog,* Marc Simont, HarperCollins.

Coretta Scott King Awards

Note: Awards for illustration began in 1974.

1970   *Martin Luther King, Jr.: Man of Peace,* Lillie Patterson, Garrard.

1971   *Black Troubadour: Langston Hughes,* Charlemae Rollins, Rand.

HONOR BOOKS: *I Know Why the Caged Bird Sings,* Maya Angelou, Random House; *Unbought and Unbossed,* Shirley Chisholm, Houghton Mifflin; *I Am a Black Woman,* Mari Evans, Morrow; *Every Man Heart Lay Down,* Lorenz Graham, Crowell; *The Voice of the Children,* June Jordan and Terri Bush, Holt, Rinehart & Winston; *Black Means,* Gladys Groom and Bonnie Grossman, Hill & Wang; *Ebony Book of Black Achievement,* Margaret W. Peters, Johnson; *Mary Jo's Grandmother,* Janice May Udry, Whitman.

1972   *17 Black Artists,* Elton C. Fax, Dodd.

HONOR BOOKS: None.

1973   *I Never Had It Made: The Autobiography of Jackie Robinson* (as told to) Alfred Duckett, Putnam.

HONOR BOOKS: None.

1974   AUTHOR: *Ray Charles,* Sharon Bell Mathis, Crowell.

HONOR BOOKS (AUTHOR): *A Hero Ain't Nothing but a Sandwich,* Alice Childress, Coward-McCann; *Don't You Remember?* Lucille Clifton, Dutton; *Ms. Africa: Profiles of Modern African Women,* Louise Crain, Lippincott; *Guest in the Promised Land,* Kristin Hunter, Scribner; *Mukasa,* John Nagenda, Macmillan.

ILLUSTRATOR: George Ford, *Ray Charles* by Sharon Bell Mathis, Crowell.

HONOR BOOKS (ILLUSTRATOR): None.

1975   AUTHOR: *The Legend of Africana,* Dorothy Robinson, Johnson.

HONOR BOOKS (AUTHOR): None.

ILLUSTRATOR: Herbert Temple, *The Legend of Africana* by Dorothy Robinson, Johnson.

HONOR BOOKS (ILLUSTRATOR): None.

1976   AUTHOR: *Duey's Tale,* Pearl Bailey, Harcourt.

HONOR BOOKS (AUTHOR): *Julius K. Nyerere: Teacher of Africa,* Shirley Graham, Messner; *Paul Robeson,* Eloise Greenfield, Crowell; *Fast Sam, Cool Clyde and Stuff,* Walter Dean Myers, Viking; *Song of the Trees,* Mildred D. Taylor, Dial.

HONOR BOOKS (ILLUSTRATOR): None.

1977   AUTHOR: *The Story of Stevie Wonder,* James Haskins, Lothrop.

HONOR BOOKS (AUTHOR): *Everett Anderson's Friend,* Lucille Clifton, Holt; *Roll of Thunder, Hear My Cry,* Mildred D. Taylor, Dial; *Quiz Book on Black America,* Clarence N. Blake and Donald F. Martin, Houghton Mifflin.

ILLUSTRATOR: None.

1978   AUTHOR: *Africa Dream,* Eloise Greenfield, Day/Crowell.

HONOR BOOKS (AUTHOR): *The Days when the Animals Talked,* William J. Faulkner, Follett; *Marvin and Tige,* Frankcina Glass, St. Martin's; *Mary McCleod Bethune,* Eloise Greenfield,

Crowell; *Barbara Jordan,* James Haskins, Dial; *Coretta Scott King,* Lillie Patterson, Garrard; *Portia: The Life of Portia Washington Pittman, the Daughter of Booker T. Washington,* Ruth Ann Stewart, Doubleday.

ILLUSTRATOR: Carole Bayard, *Africa Dream,* by Eloise Greenfield, Day/Crowell.

HONOR BOOKS (ILLUSTRATOR): None.

1979   AUTHOR: *Escape to Freedom,* Ossie Davis, Viking.

HONOR BOOKS (AUTHOR): *Skates of Uncle Richard,* Carol Fenner, Random House; *Justice and Her Brothers,* Virginia Hamilton, Greenwillow; *Benjamin Banneker,* Lillie Patterson, Abingdon; *I Have a Sister, My Sister Is Deaf,* Jeanne W. Peterson, Harper.

ILLUSTRATOR: Tom Feelings, *Something on My Mind,* Nikki Grimes, Dial.

HONOR BOOKS (ILLUSTRATOR): None.

1980   AUTHOR: *The Young Landlords,* Walter Dean Myers, Viking.

HONOR BOOKS (AUTHOR): *Movin' Up,* Berry Gordy, Harper; *Childtimes: A Three-Generation Memoir,* Eloise Greenfield and Leslie Jones Little, Harper; *Andrew Young: Young Man with a Mission,* James Haskins, Lothrop; *James Van Der Zee: The Picture Takin' Man,* James Haskins, Dodd; *Let the Lion Eat Straw,* Ellease Southerland, Scribner.

ILLUSTRATOR: Carole Bayard, *Cornrows* by Camille Yarbrough, Coward, McCann, & Geoghegan.

HONOR BOOKS (ILLUSTRATOR): None.

1981   AUTHOR: *This Life,* Sidney Poitier, Knopf.

HONOR BOOKS (AUTHOR): *Don't Explain: A Song of Billie Holiday,* Alexis DeVeaux, Harper.

ILLUSTRATOR: Ashley Bryan, *Beat the Story-Drum, Pum Pum,* Atheneum.

HONOR BOOKS (ILLUSTRATOR): Carole Bayard, *Grandmama's Joy,* by Eloise Greenfield, Philomel; Jerry Pinkney, *Count on Your Fingers African Style* by Claudia Zaslavsky, Crowell.

1982   AUTHOR: *Let the Circle Be Unbroken,* Mildred D. Taylor, Dial.

HONOR BOOKS (AUTHOR): *Rainbow Jordan,* Alice Childress, Coward-McCann; *Lou in the Limelight,* Kristin Hunter, Scibner; *Mary: An Autobiography,* Mary E. Mebane, Viking.

ILLUSTRATOR: John Steptoe, *Mother Crocodile: An Uncle Amadou Tale from Senegal* by Rosa Guy, Delacorte.

HONOR BOOKS (ILLUSTRATOR): Tom Feelings, *Daydreamers* by Eloise Greenfield, Dial.

1983   AUTHOR: *Sweet Whispers, Brother Rush,* Virginia Hamilton, Philomel.

HONOR BOOKS (AUTHOR): *This Strange New Feeling,* Julius Lester, Dial.

ILLUSTRATOR: Peter Mugabane, *Black Child,* Knopf.

HONOR BOOKS (ILLUSTRATOR): John Steptoe, *All the Colors of the Race* by Arnold Adoff, Lothrop; Pat Cummings, *Just Us Women* by Jeannette Caines, Harper.

1984   AUTHOR: *Everett Anderson's Goodbye,* Lucille Clifton, Holt.

SPECIAL CITATION: *The Words of Martin Luther King, Jr.,* compiled by Coretta Scott King, Newmarket.

HONOR BOOKS (AUTHOR): *The Magical Adventures of Pretty Pearl,* Virginia Hamilton, Harper; *Lena Horne,* James Haskins, Coward-McCann; *Bright Shadow,* Joyce Carol Thomas, Avon; *Because We Are,* Mildred Pitts Walter, Lothrop.

ILLUSTRATOR: Pat Cummings, *My Mama Needs Me* by Mildred Pitts Walter, Lothrop.

HONOR BOOKS (ILLUSTRATOR): None.

1985   AUTHOR: *Motown and Didi,* Walter Dean Myers, Viking.

HONOR BOOKS (AUTHOR): *Circle of Gold,* Candy Dawson Boyd, Apple/Scholastic; *A Little Love,* Virginia Hamilton, Philomel.

ILLUSTRATOR: None.

1986   AUTHOR: *The People Could Fly: American Black Folktales,* Virginia Hamilton, Knopf.

HONOR BOOKS (AUTHOR): *Junius Over Far,* Virginia Hamilton, Harper; *Trouble's Child,* Mildred Pitts Walter, Lothrop.

ILLUSTRATOR: Jerry Pinkney, *Patchwork Quilt* by Valerie Flournoy, Macmillan.

HONOR BOOKS (ILLUSTRATOR): Leo and Diane Dillon, *The People Could Fly: American Black Folktales* by Virginia Hamilton, Knopf.

1987   AUTHOR: *Justin and the Best Biscuits in the World,* Mildred Pitts Walter, Lothrop.

HONOR BOOKS (AUTHOR): *Lion and the Ostrich Chicks and Other African Folk Tales,* Ashley Bryan, Atheneum; *Which Way Freedom?* Joyce Hansen, Walker.

ILLUSTRATOR: Jerry Pinkney, *Half Moon and One Whole Star* by Crescent Dragonwagon, Macmillan.

HONOR BOOKS (ILLUSTRATOR): Ashley Bryan, *Lion and the Ostrich Chicks and Other African Folk Tales,* Atheneum; Pat Cummings, *C.L.O.U.D.S.,* Lothrop.

1988   AUTHOR: *The Friendship,* Mildred D. Taylor, Dial.

HONOR BOOKS (AUTHOR): *An Enchanted Hair Tale,* Alexis DeVeaux, Harper; *The Tales of Uncle Remus: The Adventures of Brer Rabbit,* Julius Lester, Dial.

ILLUSTRATOR: John Steptoe, *Mufaro's Beautiful Daughters,* Lothrop.

HONOR BOOKS (ILLUSTRATOR): Ashley Bryan, *What a Morning! The Christmas Story in Black Spirituals,* sel. by John Langstaff, Macmillan; Joe Sam, *The Invisible Hunters: A Legend from the Miskito Indians of Nicaragua,* comp. by Harriet Rohmer, Children's Book Press.

1989   AUTHOR: *Fallen Angels,* Walter Dean Myers, Scholastic.

HONOR BOOKS (AUTHOR): *A Thief in the Village and Other Stories,* James Berry, Orchard; *Anthony Burns: The Defeat and Triumph of a Fugitive Slave,* Virginia Hamilton, Knopf.

ILLUSTRATOR: Jerry Pinkney, *Mirandy and Brother Wind* by Patricia McKissack, Knopf.

HONOR BOOKS (ILLUSTRATOR): Amos Ferguson, *Under the Sunday Tree* by Eloise Greenfield, Harper; Pat Cummings, *Storm in the Night* by Mary Stolz, Harper.

1990 AUTHOR: *A Long Hard Journey,* Patricia C. and Fredrick L. McKissack, Walker.

HONOR BOOKS (AUTHOR): *Nathaniel Talking,* Eloise Greenfield, Black Butterfly; *The Bells of Christmas,* Virginia Hamilton, Harcourt; *Martin Luther King, Jr., & the Freedom Movement,* Lillie Patterson, Facts on File.

ILLUSTRATOR: Jan Spivey Gilchrist, *Nathaniel Talking* by Eloise Greenfield, Black Butterfly.

HONOR BOOKS (ILLUSTRATOR): Jerry Pinkney, *The Talking Eggs* by Robert D. San Souci, Dial.

1991 AUTHOR: *Road to Memphis,* Mildred D. Taylor, Dial.

HONOR BOOKS (AUTHOR): *Black Dance in America,* James Haskins, Crowell; *When I Am Old with You,* Angela Johnson, Orchard.

ILLUSTRATOR: Leo and Diane Dillon, *Aida,* retold by Leontyne Price, Harcourt.

HONOR BOOKS (ILLUSTRATOR): None.

1992 AUTHOR: *Now Is Your Time! The African-American Struggle for Freedom,* Walter Dean Myers, HarperCollins.

HONOR BOOKS (AUTHOR): *Night on Neighborhood Street,* Eloise Greenfield, Dial.

ILLUSTRATOR: Faith Ringgold, *Tar Beach,* Crown.

HONOR BOOKS (ILLUSTRATOR): Ashley Bryan, *All Night, All Day! A Child's First Book of African American Spirituals,* Atheneum; Jan Spivey Gilchrist, *Night on Neighborhood Street* by Eloise Greenfield, Dial.

1993 AUTHOR: *The Dark-Thirty: Southern Tales of the Supernatural,* Patricia McKissack, Knopf.

HONOR BOOKS (AUTHOR): *Mississippi Challenge,* Mildred Pitts Walter, Bradbury; *Sojourner Truth: Ain't I a Woman?* Patricia C. McKissack and Fredrick McKissack, Scholastic; *Somewhere in the Darkness,* Walter Dean Myers, Scholastic.

ILLUSTRATOR: Kathleen Atkins Smith, *Origins of Life on Earth: An African Creation Myth* by David A. Anderson, Sight Productions.

HONOR BOOKS (ILLUSTRATOR): Wil Clay, *Little Eight John* by Jan Wahl, Lodestar; Brian Pinkney, *Sukey and the Mermaid* by Robert D. San Souci, Four Winds; Carole Byard, *Working Cotton* by Sherley Anne Williams, Harcourt.

1994 AUTHOR: *Toning the Sweep,* Angela Johnson, Orchard.

HONOR BOOKS (AUTHOR): *Brown Honey in Broomwheat Tea,* Joyce Carol Thomas, HarperCollins; *Malcolm X: By Any Means Necessary,* Walter Dean Myers, Scholastic.

ILLUSTRATOR: Tom Feelings, *Soul Looks Back in Wonder* by Phyllis Fogelman, Dial.

HONOR BOOKS (ILLUSTRATOR): Floyd Cooper, *Brown Honey in Broomwheat Tea* by Joyce Carol Thomas, HarperCollins; James Ransome, *Uncle Jed's Barbershop* by Margaret King Mitchell, Simon & Schuster.

1995   AUTHOR: *Christmas in the Big House, Christmas in the Quarters,* Patricia C. McKissack and Fredrick L. McKissack, Scholastic.

HONOR BOOKS (AUTHOR): *Black Diamond: The Story of the Negro Baseball Leagues,* Patricia C. McKissack and Fredrick L. McKissack, Scholastic; *I Hadn't Meant to Tell You This,* Jacqueline Woodson, Delacorte; *The Captive,* Joyce Hansen, Scholastic.

ILLUSTRATOR: James E. Ransome, *The Creation* by James Weldon Johnson, Holiday.

HONOR BOOKS (ILLUSTRATOR): Floyd Cooper, *Meet Danitra Brown* by Nikki Grimes, Lothrop; Terea Shaffer, *The Singing Man* by Angela Shelf, Holiday House.

1996   AUTHOR: *Her Stories,* Virginia Hamilton, Scholastic.

HONOR BOOKS (AUTHOR): *The Watsons Go to Birmingham—1963,* Christopher Paul Curtis, Delacorte; *Like Sisters on the Homefront,* Rita Williams-Garcia, Lodestar; *From the Notebooks of Melanin Sun,* Jacqueline Woodson, Blue Sky.

ILLUSTRATOR: Tom Feelings, *The Middle Passage: White Ships, Black Cargo,* Dial.

HONOR BOOKS (ILLUSTRATOR): Leo and Diane Dillon, *Her Stories* by Virginia Hamilton, Blue Sky; Brian Pinkney, *The Faithful Friend* by Robert D. San Souci, Simon & Schuster.

1997   AUTHOR: *Slam!* Walter Dean Myers, Scholastic.

HONOR BOOKS (AUTHOR): *Rebels Against Slavery: American Slave Revolts,* Patricia C. McKissack and Fredrick L. McKissack, Scholastic.

ILLUSTRATOR: Jerry Pinkney, *Minty: A Story of Young Harriet Tubman* by Alan Schroeder, Dial.

HONOR BOOKS (ILLUSTRATOR): Gregory Christie, *The Palm of My Heart: Poetry by African American Children* by Davida Adedjouma, Lee & Low; Reynold Ruffins, *Running the Road to A B C* by Denize Lauture, Simon & Schuster; Synthia Saint James, *Neeny Coming, Neeny Going* by Karen English, Bridgewater.

1998   AUTHOR: *Forged by Fire,* Sharon M. Draper, Atheneum/Simon & Schuster.

HONOR BOOKS (AUTHOR): *I Thought My Soul Would Rise and Fly: The Diary of Patsy, a Freed Girl,* Joyce Hansen, Scholastic; *Bayard Rustin: Behind the Scenes of the Civil Rights Movement,* James Haskins, Hyperion.

ILLUSTRATOR: Javaka Steptoe, *In Daddy's Arms I Am Tall: African Americans Celebrating Fathers,* Lee & Low.

HONOR BOOKS (ILLUSTRATOR): Ashley Bryan, *Ashley Bryan's A B C of African American Poetry,* Atheneum/Simon & Schuster; Baba Wague Diakite, *The Hunterman and the Crocodile: A West African Folktale,* Scholastic; Christopher Myers, *Harlem* by Walter Dean Myers, Scholastic.

1999 AUTHOR: *Heaven,* Angela Johnson, Simon & Schuster.

HONOR BOOKS (AUTHOR): *Jazmin's Notebook,* Nikki Grimes, Dial; *Breaking Ground, Breaking Silence,* Joyce Hansen, Holt; *The Other Side: Shorter Poems,* Angela Johnson, Orchard.

ILLUSTRATOR: Michelle Wood, *I See the Rhythm* by Toyomi Igus, Children's Book Press.

HONOR BOOKS (ILLUSTRATOR): Floyd Cooper, *I Have Heard of a Land* by Joyce Carol Thomas, HarperCollins; E. B. Lewis, *The Batboy and His Violin* by Gavin Curtis, Simon & Schuster; Brian Pinkney, *Duke Ellington* by Andrea Davis Pinkney, Hyperion.

2000 AUTHOR: *Bud, Not Buddy,* Christopher Paul Curtis, Delacorte.

HONOR BOOKS (AUTHOR): *Francie,* Karen English, Farrar, Straus & Giroux; *Black Hands, White Sails,* Patricia C. McKissack and Fredrick L. McKissack, Scholastic; *Monster,* Walter Dean Myers, HarperCollins.

ILLUSTRATOR: Brian Pinkney, *In the Time of the Drums* by Kim Siegelson, Jump at the Sun/Hyperion.

HONOR BOOKS (ILLUSTRATOR): E. B. Lewis, *My Rows and Piles of Coins* by Tololwa M. Mollel, Clarion; Christopher Myers, *Black Cat,* Scholastic.

2001 AUTHOR: *Miracle's Boys,* Jacqueline Woodson, Putnam.

HONOR BOOK (AUTHOR): *Let It Shine! Stories of Black Women Freedom Fighters,* Andrea Davis Pinkney, Gulliver/Harcourt.

ILLUSTRATOR: Bryan Collier, *Uptown,* Holt.

HONOR BOOKS (ILLUSTRATOR): Bryan Collier, *Freedom River* by Doreen Rappaport, Jump at the Sun/Hyperion; E. B. Lewis, *Virgie Goes to School with Us Boys* by Elizabeth Fitzgerald Howard, Simon & Schuster; R. Gregory Christie, *Only Passing Through: The Story of Sojourner Truth,* by Anne Rockwell, Knopf.

2002 AUTHOR: *The Land,* Mildred D. Taylor, Fogelman.

HONOR BOOKS (AUTHOR): *Money Hungry,* Sharon G. Flake, Jump at the Sun/Hyperion; *Carver: A Life in Poems,* Marilyn Nelson, Front Street.

ILLUSTRATOR: Pinkney, *Go in Someplace Special,* by Patricia C. McKissack, Schwartz/Atheneum.

HONOR BOOK (ILLUSTRATOR): Bryan Collier, *Martin's Big Words,* by Doreen Rappaport, Jump at the Sun/Hyperion.

Internet Addresses and Additional Resources

Internet Addresses

Each chapter includes specific website addresses. Following are some general addresses covering a wide range of children's book information. Many link to others, as well. Every effort has been made to keep these up to date, but addresses may change over time. Resources for author and illustrator websites are listed in the Additional Resources section at the end of Chapter 11.

Children's Literature Web Guide—
www.ucalgary.ca/~dkbrown/index.html
Literally hundreds of Internet resources related to children's literature are here.

Children's Book Council—www.CBCBooks.org
Information about children's books, authors, publishers, and events are given.

Bookwire Navigator—www.bookwire.com
Children's best-seller lists from Publisher's Weekly, information about conferences and book fairs, and children's authors on tour make up the information on this website. Adult as well as children's books are touted through this navigator.

The Bulletin of the Center for Children's Books—
www.lis.uiuc.edu/~ccb
The home page of the bulletin includes monthly online features such as starred reviews of the month, quote of the month, the Bulletin Dozen (a theme-based list of titles), a rising star (author to watch), archive reviews and features, and information about the center.

Internet Public Library—www.ipl/org
Maintained by the University of Michigan's School of Information, this site has a youth division that includes information about children's literature.

DCF Children's Book Award—
www.mps.k12.vt.us/msms/dcf/2002/DCF02.html
The home page for the Dorothy Canfield Fisher Children's Book Award includes the yearly lists (30 recommended books each) from the last three years, a DCF Discussion, and a DCF Quiz. Winners from previous years are listed.

Carol Hurst's Children's Literature Site—
www.carolhurst.com
Oriented toward using books in classrooms, Carol Hurst's website includes articles, suggestions, and a variety of thematic lists of books and activities.

American Library Association—www.ala.org and
www.ala.org/alsc
*The ALA has much information available about
its range of services; the ALSC (second address,
above) is the ALA's Library Service to Children
branch that contains children's literature
notable books and awards, cool sites for kids,*
*resources for librarians and teachers, and
much more.*
Red Clover award—www.vermontbook.org
*This is a children's choice award for children
in grades K–4. Top picture books are selected,
then children vote.*

Additional Resources

While each chapter closed with some ideas and
directions for further study, there remain some
fairly new resources of a general nature. The
first is a new *International Companion Encyclopedia of Children's Literature,* edited by Peter Hunt, a well-known voice in children's literature publications. This is a reference tool of
over 900 pages devoted to theory and critical
approaches, types and genres, the international
scene, children's book design and publishing,
and teaching applications. It is available
through Routledge Publishers, whose U.S. office is at 7625 Empire Drive, P.O. Box 6904, Florence, KY 41022.

Another encyclopedia, *The Continuum Encyclopedia of Children's Literature* (2001), edited by Bernice E. Cullinan and Diane G. Person, is available through the International
Reading Association, www.reading.org. IRA
also publishes reprints of *Choices* (children's,
teachers', and young adults') in brochures.

Storytelling Resources

Czarnota, L. M. (Ad.) (2000). *Medieval tales that kids
can read and tell.* Little Rock, AR: August
House Publishers.
*A professional storyteller presents stories about
Robin Hood, Boudicca, King Arthur, and many
more heroes and heroines of the distant past.
Each story includes Tips for Telling and a Story
History. Glossary and source notes are given.*
Holt, D., & Mooney, B. (Comp.) (2000). *More
ready-to-tell tales from around the world.* Little
Rock, AR: August House Publishers.
*This eclectic mix includes folktales, fables,
urban legends, and original stories.*

Livo, N. J. (Ad.) (2000). *Moon cakes to maize: Delicious world folktales.* Golden, CO: Fulcrum.
*45 stories about food (there are four variants of
"The Gingerbread Boy") and each has
suggested activities that include cooking and
tasting.*
Rooney, R. C. (2001). *The story performance handbook.* Mahwah, NJ: Lawrence Erlbaum.
*This handbook has practical storytelling
methods for the novice or the experienced
storyteller, with an emphasis on evaluating the
performance and selecting the tale.*

Spanish-Speaking Resources

Schon, I. (2000). *Recommended books in Spanish
for children and young adults: 1996 through
1999.* Lanham, MD: Scarecrow.
*Nearly 1,000 books in Spanish are presented
with annotated bibliographies. Reference,
fiction, and nonfiction are included.*

Vigil, A. (Ad.) (2000). *The eagle on the cactus: traditional stories from Mexico/El aguila encima del
nopal: cuentos tradicionales de Mexico.* Englewood, CO: Libraries Unlimited.
*This is a bilingual resource of traditional
stories.*

Glossary

allegory a prose or poetry narrative in which people or objects represent general concepts or abstractions.

alliteration repetition of initial consonant sounds in consecutive words.

allusion an indirect reference to a well-known person or event.

antagonist character or force that opposes the main character (the protagonist) in a literary work.

archetype universal images, situations, plots, characters, and themes found in traditional literature and repeated in modern literature, either consciously or unconsciously.

assonance a repetition of vowel sounds in a line of prose or poetry.

authentic biography a biography in which almost every fact is documented. The work has no invented characters, scenes, or events.

autobiography a factual account of someone's life written by that person.

ballad a narrative poem in short stanzas with or without music.

battledore a large piece of paper folded in thirds, printed with the alphabet, numerals, and ditties, or phonograms. This cheaply produced paper, popular in the 1700s, contained early reading lessons for children.

bibliotherapy the use of books to promote emotional healing in an individual.

biographical fiction a realistic or fanciful story that includes some biographical (factual) material.

biography a written factual account of someone's life.

blank verse unrhymed iambic pentameter, such as that used by William Shakespeare in his dramas.

booktalks brief oral presentations (not reports, analyses, or critiques) about books; teachers and librarians use them to stimulate and motivate children to read and to generate interest in the book and the topic.

canon a list of especially meritorious literary works.

cartoon a style of artwork that is reminiscent of cartoons in newspapers.

chapbook cheaply made story booklets crudely illustrated with woodcuts; they were popular from the 15th through the 17th centuries.

character a person, or a personified animal or object, who creates a role in literature.

cinquain a five-line poem that does not rhyme, but follows a pattern that defines each line.

cliffhanger unresolved suspense that concludes a chapter.

climax the emotional high point of a story when tension breaks and conflict is at its height.

collage a design made by pasting nonpainterly materials on a surface.

comedy   when used in literary analysis, the central idea of comedy is rebirth or renewal after obstacles are overcome. *Cinderella* is a perfect example of the comic structure.

concrete poetry   a poem written to represent visually the shape or the meaning of the poem.

conflict   tension between two opposing forces.

consonance   a kind of slant rhyme that occurs when consonant sounds are alike but vowels differ, as in "chitter" and "chatter."

contemporary realism   realistic stories set in contemporary times.

couplet   two lines that end in rhyming words.

cross-hatching   a technique in which artists cover a drawing with fine black lines. Cross-hatching can be light or heavy; it adds depth and texture to a picture.

cubism   a style of art in which paintings of the human figure and landscape are represented by geometrical shapes, often cubes.

cumulative plot   a plot structure in which something is added to the basic pattern in successive events.

diamante   a seven-line poem, shaped like a diamond, that follows a pattern for each line.

didactic   primarily intended to teach a moral lesson, with any entertainment or amusement value being secondary.

didacticism   the heavy-handed message in a literary work.

double-page spread   the design or drawing spreads over both pages when a book is opened. Also called double-spread.

dynamic   a character who changes as a result of the story. Also, changes that occur when forces in the story collide.

endpapers   the paper sheets immediately inside the front and back covers of a book.

engraved plate   (see *intaglio*) a sheet of copper, usually, upon which a design is engraved.

episodic plot   a plot structure that is somewhat disconnected. Each part may be independent.

explicit theme   a stated, obviously articulated, unifying idea (see also *implicit theme*).

expository prose   written material of a factual, informative nature, such as that found in encyclopedias or textbooks.

expressionistic art   art that leans toward abstraction, expressing the emotional subjectivity of objects.

fable   a brief narrative with a pointed moral that takes abstract ideas of behavior and makes them concrete through the actions of animal characters.

fantasy   a genre of modern literature; it includes an impossible element.

fictionalized biography   a biography based on fact that includes a significant amount of fiction.

figurative language   the use of words outside of their literal meaning to add beauty or force.

first person   the point of view of a character using "I" to tell a story.

flashback   looking back at a previous event, out of chronological order.

flat character   a character who has very few traits.

foil   character who has traits contrasting those of the main character.

folklore   the traditional beliefs, legends, customs, and so on, of a community or society.

folktale   a story passed down the generations through the oral tradition.

foreshadowing   a hint of an upcoming event.

free verse   poetry free of traditional or "formal" metrical and stanzaic patterns.

genre   a large category of literary works that has a set of similar characteristics.

haiku   Japanese lyric verse form with counted syllables of five, seven, and five in three unrhymed lines.

high fantasy   a subgenre of fantasy that has the characteristics of medieval metrical romance.

historical realism   literary stories that are realistic and set in a past time.

hornbook   a wooden paddle about 2¾ by 5 inches, on which was pasted a lesson sheet of vellum and parchment. The sheet began with a cross, followed by the alphabet, syllables, and prayers. This was covered with a thin layer of transparent horn and bound along the edges with strips of brass. It was sometimes worn around the neck, suspended by a leather thong strung through a hole in the handle.

humor   a play on words, ambiguity, or slapstick; something funny that occurs.

implicit theme   a unifying idea that is not directly stated (see also *explicit theme*).

impressionism   relying on the play of light on an object or scene, impressionism hints at and suggests reality. A dreamlike quality is often achieved.

information   a genre of children's literature that refers to factual writing about school subjects.

intaglio a process of engraving used in the production of early picture books.

internal rhyme words that rhyme inside a line of verse.

irony deliberately saying the opposite of what one means; insinuating the opposite theme throughout a literary work.

irony–satire as a form of literary analysis, irony–satire reflects the discrepancy between what is and what ought to be. It parodies the romance. Sometimes revealing a bitter picture of human or humanlike existence, "The Gingerbread Boy" is an example of irony–satire.

limerick a humorous poem of five lines that follows the rhyme scheme a, a, b, b, a.

linear plot narration that advances the action.

lithography a printing method in which pictures are drawn with oil-based chalk or paint on a limestone plate. After the plate is submerged in water, ink adheres to the chalk or paint; when heavy pressure joins the design to paper, the design prints.

lyrical poetry poetry that is descriptive and personal and follows no prescribed form or pattern. It can be set to music.

media paper, paint, ink, cardboard, or other items that are used to create art.

metaphor an implied comparison.

montage the combination of several pictures to make a composite picture.

mood a subjective emotional state created by setting and other elements.

motif a recurring pattern of imagery or action.

multicultural literature literature coming from a cultural group that is usually seen as out of the mainstream of political or economic power.

myth a story originating in folk belief; myths often show supernatural forces operating.

narrative poetry a poem that tells a story; narrative poems typically have no refrain and are quite long.

omniscient an all-knowing point of view using a third person; an author tells the story in third person.

onomatopoeia the use of words that sound like their meanings, such as "buzz" or "hiss."

parable a brief narrative that takes abstract ideas and makes a point through the actions of one-dimensional characters.

personification giving human traits to animals or objects.

picture book a book in which artwork and text are equally important; in some cases, the artwork is more important. Also, a genre of children's literature.

picture storybook a picture book that tells a story. *Picture storybook* is sometimes used synonymously with *picture book;* it sometimes just refers to fictional picture books, such as contemporary and historical realistic fiction, traditional literature, and fantasy picture books.

plot the order of events in a story.

poetry a genre of literature with well-defined forms that include, but are not restricted to, rhythm and rhyme.

point of view the narrative direction from which a story is written.

primary world the realistic world as a setting for fiction (realism and fantasy).

problem an event or task that begins the action, conflict, or tension in a story.

protagonist the principal character in a literary work.

realism a genre of literature in which stories mirror reality. Realism can be contemporary or historical. There may be improbable characters and happenings, but not impossible ones.

representational, or realistic, art art that imitates reality in shape, color, proportion, and so on.

response journal a journal in which the reader writes his or her reactions to ideas in books. Usually personal (but sometimes directed by the teacher), these responses encourage critical thinking about a story, plot, or character or an identification with some element in literature.

rhyme scheme a pattern created by the rhyming words of a stanza or poem.

romance a particular kind of literature based on medieval imagery and codes of behavior. When used in literary analysis, the romance involves a quest in three parts: a dangerous journey; a struggle, test, or ordeal; and a successful return to the beginning point. *Shrek* is an example of a romance.

round character a well-developed character, one with many traits.

science-fiction fantasy a subgenre of fantasy; stories are set in a future time and rely on imaginary technological inventions or extensions of today's technology.

setting   the time and place in which the story occurs.

simile   an explicit comparison using "like" or "as."

sonnet   a poem of 14 lines, usually in iambic pentameter; typically has the rhyme scheme abab cdcd efef gg.

static character   a character who does not change over time.

stereotype   a person who possesses only the expected traits of a group.

stock character   flat character with little or no development.

story   a work of fiction.

story grammar   the linear pattern of the events in a story.

story structure   the linear, circular, or episodic pattern of events in a story, from introduction to resolution.

style   aspects of language that create a total effect.

stylistic language   words used in patterns that become familiar over time, such as "Once upon a time."

subgenre   a part of a larger genre, or category, of literature. For example, alphabet books constitute a subgenre of picture books.

surrealistic art   artwork that distorts and plays with images, juxtaposing reality with absurdity.

symbol   someone or something that stands for something else.

tanka   a poetic form of five lines with five syllables in the first line, seven in the second line, five in the third line, and seven syllables in each of the fourth and fifth lines.

text set   a number (usually five or six) of trade books in a classroom that focuses on a single theme or topic.

theme   unifying idea that permeates a literary work.

third person   a point of view from "above" the action, sometimes called "omniscient." The author can project a story from any person's thoughts or by description.

tone   the attitude that permeates a written piece.

touchstone   a book that represents the "best" or highest quality; a book used to evaluate other books by comparison.

trade book   a book such as that sold in bookstores or found in libraries—not a textbook.

traditional literature   stories, proverbs, rhymes, and other linguistic expressions coming from the oral tradition. The names of the authors or originators have been lost in time.

tragedy   a literary form that explores the limits of humankind's power to derive success. Realistic, lifelike stories of catastrophe, death, and loss of innocence are tragedies. *Bridge to Terabithia* (Paterson, 1978) could be considered to be written in the tragic form.

verse   (1) one line of poetry; (2) a stanza, particularly with refrain (as the *verse* of a song); (3) poetry in general; (4) light poetry as opposed to serious.

visual literacy   the reading process as it relates to signs and symbols.

wordless picture book or **wordless book**   a subgenre of picture books in which no text (or minimal text) is used and the story is told through the artwork.

Author and Title Index

Aardema,V., 76, 278
ABC Bunny (Gag), 267
ABC For You and Me (Girnis), 100, 109, 258
ABC Kids (Williams), 100, 109
ABC T-Rex (Most), 100, 109
Abel's Island (Steig), 272
Abigail Adams (Wallner), 232, 241
Abraham Lincoln (d' Aulaire), 274
Abraham Lincoln, Friend of the People (Judson), 269
Abraham Lincoln's World (Foster), 268
Absolutely Lucy (Cooper), 194, 204
Ackamarackus: Julius Lester's Sumptuously Silly Fantastically Funny Fables (Lester), 62
Ackerman, K., 280
Across Five Aprils (Hunt), 210, 224, 223, 270
Adaline Falling Star (Osborne), 218
Adam of the Road (Gray), 268
Adams, H. S., 197
Adams, J. D., 266
Adedjouma, D., 286
Adler, D., 14, 202, 235, 237, 256
Administrative Support for Literature-Based Reading Programs (De Lapp), 18
Adoff, A., 148, 150, 152, 157
Adventures of Marco and Polo, The (Wiesmuller), 130

Adventures of Tom Sawyer, The (Twain), 34, 187, 205
Aesop & Company (Bader), 39
Aesop's Fables (Caxton), 24, 39
Aesop's Fables (Pinkney), 72, 88
Africa Dream (Greenfield), 282, 283
Afternoon of the Elves (Lisle), 273
After the Rain (Mazer), 273
Ageless Story, The (Ford), 274
Agony and the Eggplant, The: Daniel Pinkwater's Heroic Struggle in the Name of Young Adult Literature (Hogan), 205
Aida (Price), 122, 285
Aiken, J., 207
Airfield (Ingold), 61
Alcott, L. M., 33, 186, 187
Alderson, B. 33
Alexander and the Windup Mouse (Lionni), 278
Alexander, L., 159, 164, 270, 271
Alexander, S. H., 258
Alger, H., Jr., 33
Alice's Adventures in Wonderland (Carroll), 33, 35, 39, 162, 163, 179
Alien Brain Fryout: A Wild Willie Mystery (Joose), 14
All Alone (Bishop), 269
Allan, K. K., 249

All Around the Town (McGinley), 275
All by Herself: 14 Girls who Made a Difference (Paul), 144, 158
Allee, M., 267
Allen, D., 56
All Falling Down (Zion), 276
All in the Morning Early (Leodhas), 277
All Night All Day! A Child's First Book of African American Spirituals, 285
All-of-a-Kind Family (Taylor), 210, 225
All Sails Set: A Romance of the Flying Cloud (Sperry), 267
All the Colors of the Race (Adoff), 283
Along Came a Dog (DeJong), 270
Alphabet City (Johnson), 281
Alphabatics (MacDonald), 280
Alphin, E., 196
Alvarez, J., 84
Always Room for One More (Leodhas), 277
Amazing Bone, The (Steig), 279
Amazing Life of Benjamin Franklin, The (Giblin), 239–240, 257
Amber Brown (Danziger), 202
Amber Spyglass, The (Pullman), 168, 181
Amelia Bedelia (Parrish), 202
America Is Born (Johnson), 270
America Moves Forward (Johnson), 270
American Girl, 197

American Picture Books from Noah's Ark to the Beast Within (Bader), 110, 113, 132

American Poetry for Children: The 20th Century (Hopkins), 158

Americans Before Columbus (Baity), 269

America's Champion Swimmer: Gertrude Ederle (Adler), 235, 240, 257

America's Ethan Allen (Holbrook), 275

Amistad: A Long Road to Freedom (Myers), 14

Amos Fortune, Free Man (Yates), 269

Alphabet of Old Friends and the Absurd ABC, An (Crane), 109

American ABC, An (Petersham), 274

Anansi the Spider: A Tale for the Ashanti (McDermott), 278

Anatole (Titus), 276–277

Anatomy Of Criticism (Frye), 64

Andersen, H. C., 33, 35, 40, 68, 161, 162, 276

Andersen's Fairy Tales, 161, 179

Anderson, D. A., 285

Anderson, L. H., 216

Andrew Young: Young Man with a Mission (Haskins), 283

. . . and Now Miguel (Krumgold), 269

Andy and the Lion: A Tale of Kindness Remembered or the Power of Gratitude (Daugherty), 274

An Enchanted Hair Tale (De Veaux), 284

Angelo, V., 267

Angelou, M., 198, 282

Angry Moon, The (Sleator), 278

Angus and the Ducks (Flack), 95

Angus, Thongs, and Full Frontal Snogging: Confessions of Georgia Nicolson (Rennison), 196, 205

Animal Family, The (Jarrell), 271

Animal Fun (Newcome), 108

Animals of the Bible (Fish), 274

Animorphs, 197

Annie and the Old One (Miles), 271

Annotated Jules Verne: From the Earth to the Moon, The (Verne), 180

Anonymous (Lear), 147

Anpao: An American Indian Odyssey (Highwater), 272

Antarctica (Cowcher), 129, 130

Antarctic Antics: A Book of Penguin Poems (Sierra), 130

Antarctic Journal: Four Months at the Bottom of the World (Dewey), 261–262

Anthony Burns: The Defeat and Triumph of a Fugitive Slave (Hamilton), 284

Ape in a Cape: An Alphabet of Odd Animals (Eichenberg), 276

Appelt, K., 107, 108

Apple and the Arrow, The (Buff), 269

Apprentice of Florence (Kyle), 267

April's Kittens (Newberry), 274

Arabian Nights, The, 69

Archambault, J., 99, 101

Are You There, God? It's Me, Margaret (Blume), 188, 204

Arf! Beg! Catch!: Dogs from A to Z (Horenstein), 100, 109

Aries, P., 24

Amer, L. A., 266, 274

Armstrong, J., 261

Armstrong W., 271

Arnold, M., 4

Arnosky, J., 256

Aronson, M., 227–228, 258

Around My Room (Smith), 147, 158

Arrhenius, P., 130

Arrington, F., 216

Arrow to the Sun (McDermott), 278

Arthur Makes the Team, 120, 132

Art of Biography in Eighteenth Century England, The (Stauffer), 241

Art of Keeping Cool, The (Lisle), 220

Art of Realism, The (Walsh), 205

Artzybasheff, B., 274

Asbjornsen, P., 69, 88

Ashanti to Zulu: African Traditions (Musgrove), 279

Ashley Bryan's ABC of African American Poetry (Bryan), 287

At the Back of the North Wind (MacDonald), 158, 179

At Her Majesty's Request: An African Princess in Victorian England (Myers), 14, 257, 262

At the Sign of the Star (Sturtevant), 212, 225

Atwater, F., 130, 267

Atwater, R., 130, 267

Au, K.H., 10

Auch, M. J., 166

Audubon (Rourke), 267

Avi, 167, 216, 226, 273

Avion My Uncle Blew, The (Fisher), 268

Awful Ogre's Awful Day (Prelutsky), 152

Aylesworth, J., 84

Babbit, N., 171,271

Babe (King-Smith), 166, 179

Babe and Me: A Baseball Card Adventure (Gutman), 171

Babe Didrikson Maharius: The Making of a Champion (Freedman), 235, 240

Baboushka and the Three Kings (Robbins), 277

Bad Boy: A Memoir (Myers), 14, 239, 240

Bader, B., 23, 95, 113, 119

Bagdasarian, A., 211

Bailey, C. S., 268

Bailey, P., 282

Baity, E., 269

Baker, O., 279

Baker, S., 137

Balanced Literacy Instruction: A Teacher's Resource Book (Au), 18

Ballerina! (Sis), 100, 109

Balouch, K., 82

Bambino the Clown (Schreiber), 275

Bamford, R.A., 246

Bancroft, A., 261

Bang, M., 279, 281

Banks, L., 174

Banned Books Week Invites Readers to Celebrate the Freedom to Read (Micklos), 205

Banner in the Sky (Ullman), 269

Bannerman, H., 119

Barbara Jordan (Haskins), 283

Bard of Avon The: The Story of William Shakespeare, (Stanley & Vennema), 121, 132

Barkis (Newberry), 274

Barnes, N., 268

Barrie, J., 162, 164

Bartoletti, S. C., 256

Bartholomew and the Oobleck (Dr. Seuss), 276

Bartone, E., 280

Baseball Card Adventure (Gutman), 179

Baseball in April and Other Stories (Soto), 200

Basket Counts, The (Adoff), 152

Baskin, L., 278

Batboy and His Violin, The (Curtis), 287

Bathtub Reading (Jordan), 205

Battle-Lavert, G., 84

Bauer, J., 192, 274

Bauer, M. D., 273

Baum, L. F., 162, 164

Bayard, C., 283

Bayard Rustin: Behind the Scenes of the Civil Rights Movement (Haskins), 286

Baylor, B., 278, 279

Bearing Witness to the Holocaust, Book Links (Rothman), 14

Bear Party (duBois), 276

Bears on Hemlock Mountain, The (Dalgliesh), 269

Beast (Napoli), 179–180

Beat the Story Drum, Pum-Pum (Bryan), 283

Beatrix Potter (Malam), 238–239, 240

Beautiful Butterfly, The (Sierra), 85

Beauty (McKinley), 179, 180

Beauty and the Beast (Hearns), 69, 80, 88

Beauty, Brains & Brawn: The Construction of Gender in Children's Literature (Lehr), 205

Beaverson, A., 171

Because of Winn-Dixie (DiCamillo), 194, 201, 204, 274

Because We Are (Walter), 284

Becoming Felix (Wilson), 203, 205

Beeler, S., 255, 260

Be First in the Universe (Spinner), 172, 180

Beggar's Magic, The: A Chinese Tale (Chang & Chang), 88

Behind the Wheel: Poems About Driving (Wong), 153

Beil, K. M., 256

Bell, A., 85

Belle Prater's Boy (White), 273

Belling the Tiger (Stolz), 270

Bells of Christmas, The (Hamilton), 285

Belting, N. M., 277

Bemelmans, L., 95, 267, 274, 276

Benjamin Banneker (Patterson), 283

Benjamin Bunny, 95

Benson, K., 236

Ben's Trumpet (Isadora), 279

Berger, G., 130

Berger, M., 130

Berry, E., 267

Berry, J., 153, 274

Best Book of Fossils, Rocks, and Minerals, The (Pellant), 254, 262

Best, H., 266

Besterman, C., 268

Bettelheim, B., 23, 69, 75

Better Known as Johnny Appleseed (Hunt), 269

Beyond Fact: Nonfiction for Children and Young People, 263

Beyond Paradise (Hertenstein), 220

Beyond the Western Sea Books (Avi), 216

Beyond the Western Sea-Book One: The Escape from Home (Avi), 224

Beyond the Western Sea-Book Two: Lord Kirkle's Money (Avi), 224

Beyond Words: Picture Books for Older Readers and Writers (Benedict & Carlisle), 132

Beyond Words: Picture Books for Older Readers and Writers (Bishop & Hickman), 132

Bhimsa, the Dancing Bear (Weston), 268

Bianco, M., 267

Bickle, C., 253

Bierhorst, J., 82

Big Box, The (Morrison), 122

Biggest Bear, The (Ward), 276

Big Jabe (Nolen), 78, 88

Big Snow, The (Hader), 275

Big, Spooky House, The (Washington), 84

Big Talk: Poems for Four Voices (Fleischman), 157

Big Tree (Buff), 268

Big Tree Of Buneaby: Stories of My Own Countryside (Colum), 267

Billington, E., 94

Bill Peet: An Autobiography (Peet), 280

Bingham, J., 24

Biography. In *Children's Books and Their Creators* (Burns), 241

Biography Today, 241

Biography Today: Profiles of People of Interest to Young Readers, 241

Birnbaum, A., 276

Birthdays of Freedom, Vol. I (Foster), 269

Bishop, C. H., 268, 269

Bishop, N., 254

Bishop, R.S., 122

Bisson, T., 62

Bjork, C., 200

Black and White (Macaulay), 122, 280

Black Beauty (Sewell), 34

Black Bull of Norroway, The (Huck), 85

Black Cat, The (Myers), 287

Black Cauldron, The (Alexander), 270–271

Black Dance in America (Haskins), 285

Black Diamond: The Story of the Negro Baseball Leagues (McKissack & McKissack), 286

Black Fox of Lorne (de Angeli), 270

Black Hands, White Sails (McKissack & McKissack), 287

Black Means (Groom & Grossman), 282

Black Pearl, The (O'Dell), 271

Black Potatoes: The Story of the Great Irish Famine, 1845–1850 (Bartoletti), 257

Black Stallion, The (Farley), 187, 204

Black Troubador: Langston Hughes (Rollins), 282

Blackwood, G., 215

Blake, C. N., 282

Blake, R. J., 56

Blake, W., 32, 138, 139

Blizzard! (Murphy), 248–249, 258, 262

Block, F. L., 85, 179

Blos, J., 210, 272

Blowin' in the Wind (Kennedy), 142

Blueberries for Sal (McCloskey), 275

Blue Cat of Castle Town, The (Coblentz), 269

Blue Fairy Book, The (Lang), 69, 88

Blue Lawn, The (Taylor), 200
*Blues Singers: Ten Who Rocked the
        World, The* (Lester), 234,
        240
Bluestem (Arrington), 216, 224
Blue Sword (McKinley), 272
Blue Willow (Gates), 268
Blumberg, R., 235, 272
Blume, J., 17, 188, 198
Boats on the River (Flack), 275
Bobbsey Twins, The, 197
Body of Christopher Creed
        (Plum-Ucci), 195, 205
Bond, N., 272
Bone from a Dry Sea, A (Dickinson),
        224
Bontemps, A., 269
Book of Coupons, A (Morgenstern),
        196, 204
Book of Greek Myths (D'Aulaire), 84,
        88
*Book of Nursery and Mother Goose
        Rhymes,* 276
Book of The Lion, The (Cadnum), 215,
        224
Book of Martyrs (Foxe), 25
Book of Monsters (Rowling), 163
Book of Nonsense (Lear), 138
*Book of Nursery Rhymes and Mother
        Goose* (de Angeli), 109
Books, Children and Men (Hazard), 40
*Books Without Bias: Through Indian
        Eyes* (Slapin & Seale), 181
Boorstin, D., 231
Borden, L., 61, 126, 216
Borrowers, The (Norton), 164, 174, 180
*Bound for the North Star: True Stories
        of Fugitive Slaves* (Fradin),
        256, 262
Bowdish, L., 217
Bowen, W., 265
Bowman, J. C., 267
Boyd, C. D., 284
Boy in the Burning House, The
        (Wynne-Jones), 193
Boy of the South Seas, (Tietjens), 267
Boy of the Three-Year Nap, The
        (Stanley), 280
Boy Who Was, The (Hallock), 266
*Boy Who Couldn't Obey, The: A
        Mayan Legend* (Rockwell),
        84
Boy with a Pack (Meader), 268
Bradley, K. B., 258

Brallier, J., 254
Branford, H., 215
Branley, F., 254
Breadwinner, The (Ellis), 200
Breaking Ground, Breaking Silence
        (Hansen), 287
Breman-Town Musicians, The
        (Plume), 279
Brennan, J. H., 214
Brer Rabbit (Harris), 81
Brian's Winter (Paulsen), 192, 205
Bridges, R., 229, 256
Bridge to Terabithia (Paterson), 188,
        205, 272
Bright Island (Robinson), 267
Bright Shadow (Thomas), 284
Brimstone Journals (Koertge), 143,
        157
Brink, C., 210, 267
Brittain, B., 272
Bronze Bow, The (Speare), 210, 225,
        270
Brooke, P., 217
Brooklyn, Bugsy, and Me (Bowdish),
        217, 227
Brooks, B., 272
Brooks, W., 14
Brothers Grimm, 28, 68, 73, 85
Brown, D., 235
Brown Honey in Broomwheat Tea
        (Thomas), 285
Brown, M., 116, 120, 275, 276, 277
Brown, M. W., 1, 276
Browning, R., 138. 139, 144
Bruchac, J., 76, 153, 200
Bryan, A., 284, 285, 287
Bubblegum Delicious (Lee), 145, 157
Buddha Stories (Demi), 72, 88
Bud, Not Buddy (Curtis), 207–208,
        222, 224, 274, 287
Buff, C., 268, 269, 275
Buff, M., 268, 269, 275
Buffy, the Vampire Slayer, 197
*Bug in Teacher's Coffee: And Other
        School Poems* (Dakos), 152
Building Big (Macaulay), 253, 262
*Bulletin of the Center for Children's
        Books,* The, 55, 151, 222
*Bulletin of the Center for Children's
        Books* (Stevenson), 65, 225
Bunting, E., 281
Bunyan, J., 27, 28
Burglon, N., 267
Burkert, N. E., 24

Burleigh, R., 122
Burnett, F. H., 187
Burns, M. M., 229
Burton, J., 56
Burton, V. E., 275
Bush, T., 152, 282
Buttons (Cole), 132
Byard, C., 285
Byars, B., 202, 271
By the Shores of Silver Lake (Wilder),
        268

Caddie Woodlawn (Brink), 210, 224,
        267
Cadnum, M., 211, 215
Caged Eagles (Walters), 220
Cairney, T., 13
*Caldecott on the Net: Reading and
        Internet Activities* (Story-
        Huffman), 132
Caldecott, R., 34, 35, 93, 95, 123
Calico Bush (Field), 266
Calliope World History for Kids, 263
Call It Courage (Sperry), 268
Cameron, A., 202
Cameron, E., 159
Cam Jensen (Adler), 202
Campbell, J., 69
*Canadian Children's Books: A
        Critical Guide to Authors
        and Illustrators* (Jones &
        Stott), 241
Candy Corn (Stevenson), 152
Can Story Grammar Speak Japanese
        (Matsuyama), 89
Canterbury Tales (Chaucer/
        McCaughrean), 23
*Captain Underpants and the Perilous
        Plot of Professor
        Poopypants* (Pilkey), 174,
        180
Capturing Objects in Words (Worth),
        158
Carbone, E., 211
Carle, E., 103, 104
Carlson, J., 188
Carlson, N. S., 270
Carmi, D., 200
*Carmine's Story: A Book about a Boy
        Living with AIDS*
        (Shulman), 120, 132
Carpenter, H. 138
Carr, J., 244, 268
Carroll, J.H., 10

Carroll, L., 33, 138, 162

Carry on, Mr. Bowditch (Latham), 269

Carter G. Woodson: The Man Who put "Black" in American History (Haskins & Benson), 236, 240

Carver: A Life in Poems (Nelson), 145, 158, 274

Casanova, M., 82

Casey at the Bat: A Ballad of the Republic Sung in the Year 1888 (Thayer), 281

Casey, P., 255

Castillo, A., 153

Castle (Macaulay), 244, 262, 279

Catcher in the Rye (Salinger), 187, 205

Cathedral: The Story of Its Construction (Macaulay), 244, 262, 278

Catherine, Called Birdy (Cushman), 210, 224, 273

Cat Who Went to Heaven, The (Coatsworth), 266

Caudill, R., 269, 277

Caxton, W., 24

Cedric the Forester (Marshall), 265

Celebration of Bees, A (Esbensen), 158

Cello of Mr. O, The (Cutler), 219

Cendrars, B., 279

Censorship of Children's Books in Battling Dragons (McClure), 205

Centuries of Childhood (Aries), 39

Chair for my Mother, A (Williams), 279

Chambers, A., 3

Chameleon Wore Chartreuse, The (Hall), 14

Chan, C-Y., 275

Chandler, E., 196

Chang, M., 69

Chang, R., 69

Chanticleer and the Fox (Chaucer) 277

Charlotte's Web (White), 1–5, 15, 18, 41–43, 48, 50, 64, 164, 166 180, 269

Checking Out Nonfiction K–8: Good Choices for Best Learning (Bamford & Kristo), 263

Cherokees, The (Sneve), 263

Cherokee Sister (Dadey), 218

Chicaro: Wild Pony of the Pampa (Kalnay), 270

Chicka Chicka Boom Boom (Martin & Archambault), 99, 101–103, 109

Child As Critic, The (Sloan), 65

Childhood and Society (Erikson), 18

Childhood's Future (Louv), 18

Children and Books (Sutherland), 40, 89

Children and Literature: Views and Reviews (Haviland), 241

Children of the Soil: A Story of Scandinavia (Burglon), 267

Children Remember the Holocaust, 224

Children's Book Authors and Illustrators on the Web. In Book Links (Feldman), 241

Children's Books and Their Creators (Silvey), 19

Children's Books from Other Countries (Tomlinson), 89

Children's Books in Print, 132

Children's Books: Interacting with the Curriculum (Johnson & Giorgis), 14

Children's Literature: An Anthology 1802–1902 (Hunt), 40, 65

Children's Literature and Critical Theory (May), 64

Children's Literature Association Quarterly (Children's Literature Association), 40

Children's Literature in the Classroom: Weaving Charlotte's Web (Hickman & Cullinan), 18

Children's Literature in Education (Human Sciences Press), 40

Children's Literature in the Elementary School (Huck et al.), 18, 241

Children's Literature: Its Discipline and Content (Cullinan), 64

Children's Poetry Preferences (Terry), 158

Childress, A., 282, 283

Childress, G., 9

Child's Calendar, A (Updike), 281

Child's Garden of Verses (Stevenson), 139, 158

Child's Good Night Book, A (Brown), 275

Child's Work? (Whitman & Whitman), 263

Childtimes: A Three-Generation Memoir (Greenfield & Little), 283

Chisholm, S., 282

Choices, 290

Choldenko, G., 194

Choosing Quality Nonfiction Literature: Features for Accessing and Visualizing Information (Kerper), 263

Chorao, K., 107, 108

Chrisman, A. B., 266

Chrisp, P., 253, 260

Christelow, E., 253

Christie, G., 286, 287

Christmas Anna Angel, The (Sawyer), 275

Christmas Carol, A (Dickens), 33, 35, 39

Christmas in the Big House, Christmas in the Quarters (McKissack & McKissack), 286

Christopher, M., 195

Chukovsky, K., 75

Ciardi, J., 138, 147, 150

Cinderella, 23, 28, 68, 69, 80, 86

Cinderella: A Casebook (Dundes), 88

Cinderella, or the Little Glass Slipper (Perrault), 276

Cinderella Skeleton (San Souci), 86, 88

Circle of Gold (Boyd), 284

Civil War on Sunday (Osborne), 172, 180

Clancy, T., 195

Clara Schumann: Piano Virtuso (Reich), 257

Clark, A. N., 269, 274

Clark, L., 137

Clarke, J., 200

Classic Fairy Tales, The (Opie & Opie), 181

Classics of Children's Literature (Griffith & Frey), 40

Clay (Rodowsky), 258

Clay, W., 285

Clearing Weather (Meigs), 266

Cleary, B., 135, 188, 196, 202, 272

Cleopatra VII: Daughter of the Nile (Gregory), 232, 240

Clement-Davies, D., 160

Click, Clack, Moo: Cows that Type (Cronin), 281

Clifton, L., 282, 284

Climo, S., 84

Clock, The (Duffy), 253, 262

Cloning (DuPrau), 255, 262

C.L.O.U.D.S., 284

Coatsworth, E., 266

Coblentz, C., 269

Coburn, B., 236

Cock-A-Doodle Doo: The Story of a Little Red Rooster (Hader), 274

Cobblestone: The History Magazine for Young People, 263

Cobwebs to Catch Flies: Illustrated Books for the Nursery and Schoolroom (Whalley), 110

Codfish Musket, The (Hewes), 267

Cod's Tale, The (Kurlansky), 257

Cognitive Development (Flavell), 18

Cohn, A., 72

Cold Feet (De Felice), 85

Cole, B., 192

Cole, J., 120

Collard, S. B., III., 254

Collier, B., 287

Collier, J., 223, 271

Collected Poems Langston Hughes (Hughes), 157

Collodi, C., 69, 162

Colonial Williamsburg Foundation adaptation, 31

Color Me Dark: The Diary of Nellie Lee Love-The Great Migration North (McKissack), 218

Color of My Words, The (Joseph), 200

Colors (Diggory), 104

Colors (Nordine), 152

Colors (Shields), 109

Color Zoo (Ehlert), 280

Colum, P., 266, 267

Coman, C., 273

Combs, M., 130

Comenius, J., 26, 32

Come with Me: Poems for a Journey (Nye), 152

Commodore Perry in the Land of the Shogun (Blumberg), 272

Comparison of the Treatment of the Negro in Children's Literature in the Periods 1929–1938 and 1959–1968 (Carlson), 205

Complete Works of Lewis Carroll, The (Carroll), 39

Composition, The (Skarmeta), 199

Conly, J., 217, 273

Conover, C., 56

Conrad, P., 223

Contest, The (Hogrogian), 279

Continuum Encyclopedia of Children's Literature, The, 290

Coolidge, O., 270

Cooper, E., 253

Cooper, F., 286, 287

Cooper, I., 142, 194

Cooper, J. F., 187

Cooper, S., 164, 271, 272

Coretta Scott King (Patterson), 283

Corey, D., 100

Cormier, R., 198

Corn Grows Ripe, The (Rhoads), 270

Cornrows (Yarbrough), 283

Cosmo and the Robot (Pinkney), 132

Cotton, J., 27, 28

Couloumbis, A., 193, 274

Counterfeit Son (Alphin), 196, 204

Counting Kisses (Katz), 104, 109

Count on Your Fingers African Style (Zaslovsky), 283

Courage of Sarah Noble, The (Dalgliesh), 269

Courlander, H., 268

Cowcher, H., 130

Cowell, C., 107

Cowley, J., 173

Cow-Tail Switch, and Other West African Stories (Courlander), 268

Cox, C., 12

Crago, H., 6

Crago, M., 6

Crain, L., 282

Crane, W., 35, 93, 94

Crawford, P., 267

Crazy Lady (Conly), 273

Crazy Loco (Rice), 199

Creation, The (Johnson), 286

Creech, S., 46, 50, 183–184, 201, 273, 274

Cremation of Sam McGee, The (Service), 158

Crews, D., 279

Cricket, 263

Cricket in Times Square (Selden), 270

Crist-Evans, C., 150

Critical Handbook of Children's Literature, A (Lukens), 18 64, 158

Critical History of Children's Literature, A (Meigs et al.), 40

Criticism, Theory, and Children's Literature (Hunt), 18, 64

Cronin, D., 281

Crossley-Holland, K., 69

Crow Bay (Yashima), 156, 158, 276

Crows (McCord), 156

Crutcher, C., 195

Cubes, Cones, Cylinders, and Spheres (Hoban), 99, 103, 109

Cuckoo: A Mexican Folktale (Ehlert), 84

Cullinan, B., 50, 209

Cummings, P., 192, 236, 284

Cummins, J., 61

Cunningham, P., 56, 57

Curtis, C. P., 207–208, 209, 222, 273, 274, 286, 287

Curtis, J., 287

Cushman, D., 14

Cushman, K., 210, 215, 273

Cutler, J., 219

Daddy's Roommate (Wilhoite), 120, 132

Dadey, D., 218

Dahl, R., 17

Dakos, K., 152

Dalgliesh, A., 268, 269, 276

Daly, J., 87

Dance! (Cooper), 253, 262

Dancing in the Wings (Allen), 56

Dancing Rig, The (Sierra), 82

Daniel Boone (Daugherty), 229, 240, 267

Daniels, H., 221

Danziger, P., 202

Dark Angel, 197

Dark Frigate, The (Hawes), 266

Dark is Rising, The (Cooper), 271

Darkness Be My Friend (Marsden), 173, 180

Dark Portal, The (Jarvis), 167, 179

Dark Secrets (Chandler), 196, 204

Dark Star of Itze, The: The Story of a Pagan Princess (Malkus), 266

Dark Thirty, The: Southern Tales of the Supernatural (McKissack), 273, 285

D' Armancourt, P., 28

Dash and Dart (Buff), 275

Dash, J., 236, 258

Dateline: Troy (Fleischman), 224

Daugherty, J., 229, 267, 274

Daughter of the Mountains (Rankin), 269

Daughter of the Seine: The Life of Madame Roland (Eaton), 266

D'Aulaire, E., 84, 95, 274

D'Aulaire, I., 84, 95, 274

Davis, L., 275

Davis, M. G., 267

Davis, O., 283

Davy Crockett (Rourke), 267

Day, A Dog, A (Vincent), 132

Daydreamers (Greenfield), 283

Day on Skates: The Story of a Dutch Picnic (Stockum), 267

Dayrell, E., 278

Days When the Animals Talked, The (Faulkner), 282

Day We Saw the Sun Come Up, The (Goudey), 277

de Angeli, M., G., 210, 269, 270, 275

Dear Genius: The Letters of Ursula Nordstrom (Marcus), 18

Dear Ellen Bee: A Civil War Scrapbook of Two Union Spies (Lyons & Branch), 218

Dear Mr. Henshaw (Cleary), 188, 204, 272

DeFelice, C., 85

Defence of Fantasy, The (Swinfen), 181

Defender, The (Kalashnikoff), 269

Defoe, D., 30, 32, 186

DeJong, M., 269, 270

de la Mare, W., 138, 139

De Lapp, S., 12

Delta Education Media Treasures, 226

De Luca, G., 230

Demarest, C., L., 100

Demi, 72, 236

de Paola, T., 236, 238, 239, 274, 279

Desert is Theirs, The (Baylor), 279

Destination: Mars (Simon), 254, 260, 263

Deuker, C., 195

DeVeaux, A., 283, 284

Developmental Psychology Today (Hoffman et al.), 7, 18

Devil and His Boy, The (Horowitz), 215, 224

Dewey, J., 261

De Worde, W., 24, 25

Diakite, B. W., 287

Diary of a Young Girl (Frank), 229, 231, 240

DiCamillo, K., 194, 201, 274

Dicey's Song (Voigt), 272

Dickens, C., 33, 35, 187

Dickinson, E., 137

Dickinson, P., 164, 223

Dick Whittington and His Cat (Brown), 276

Digging for Bird-Dinosaurs: An Expedition to Madagascar (Bishop), 254, 262

Dillon, D., 284, 285, 286

Dillon, L., 284, 285, 286

Dinosaurs at the Ends of the Earth: The Story of the Central Asiatic Expedition (Floca), 254, 262

Dinosaurs Before Dark (Osborne), 177, 180

Dinosaurs: Magic Tree House Research Guide #1 (Osborne & Osborne), 238

Dinosaurs of Waterhouse Hawkins: An Illuminating History of Mr. Waterhouse Hawkins, Artist and Lecturer, The (Kerley), 257, 281

D is for Duck, 92

Dobry (Shannon), 267

Dodge, M. M., 34, 187

Dog, A Day, A (Vincent), 121

Dogsong (Paulsen), 272

Dolphin Log, 263

Domanska, J., 278

Do Monkeys Tweet? (Walsh), 107, 109

Donelson, K., 10

Donoghue, M. R., 56

Don Quixote and Sancho Panza (Hodges), 122

Don't Expect to Depend on Anybody Else. . .: The Frontier as Portrayed in the Little House Books (Fellman), 225

Don't Explain: A Song of Billie Holiday (DeVeaux), 283

Don't You Remember? (Dutton), 282

Door in the Wall, The (de Angeli), 210224, 269

Do Penguins Get Frostbite? Questions and Answers About Polar Animals (Berger & Berger), 128, 130

Dotkich, R, K., 100

Doucet, S. A., 218, 223

Downright Dencey (Snedeker), 266

Down Ryton Water (Gaggin), 268

Doyle, A. C., Sir, 187

Do You Remember the Color Blue? And Other Questions Kids Ask About Blindness (Alexander), 258

Dr. De Soto (Steig), 272

Dragon's Gate (Yep), 273

Dragon Wings (Yep), 272

Draper, S. M., 286

Dream Coach (Parrish), 266

Dream Keeper and Other Poems, The (Hughes), 139, 157

Dream Soul (Yep), 211, 218, 225

Dresang, E. T., 198

Drill, Ye Tarriers, Drill (Cooper), 142–143, 150

Drummer Hoff (Emberley), 115, 132, 278

du Bois, W. P., 268, 276, 277

Duckett, A., 282

Duey's Tale (Bailey), 282

Duffy and the Devil (Zemach), 278

Duffy, T., 253

Duke Ellington (Pinkney), 281, 287

Dunbar, P. L., 153

Dundes, A., 69

Dunn, O., 108

Dunning, S. 156

DuPrau, J., 255

Eagle Boy: A Pacific Northwest Native Tale (Vaughn), 82

Eagle on the Cactus, The: Traditional Stories from Mexico (Vigil), 290

Eagleton, T., 44

Eaton, J., 266, 267, 269

Ear, the Eye and the Arm, The (Farmer), 164, 179, 273

Early American Children's Books (Rosenbach), 40

East O' the Sun and West O' the Moon (Asbjornsen), 88

Ebony Book of Black Achievement (Johnson), 282

Eckert, A. W., 271

Edmonds, W. D., 268

Effective Literacy Instruction (Leu & Kinzer), 221, 225

Effective Reading Instruction K–8 (Leu & Kinzer), 18, 263

Egg Tree, The (Milhous), 276

Egoff, S., 35, 37, 188

Egypt Game, The (Snyder), 271

Ehlert, L., 84, 99, 101, 103, 280

Ehrlich, A., 28

Eichenberg, F., 276

Eight Seconds (Ferris), 200

Eleanor Roosevelt (Freedman), 273

Elffers, J., 258

Elisabeth (Nivola), 120, 132

Elkin, B., 277

Ella Enchanted (Levine), 274

Ellis, D., 200

Elsie Dinsmore (Finley), 33, 39

Elympics (Kennedy), 152

Emberley, B., 278

Emberley, R., 99, 104, 115

Emilie (Rousseau), 32

Emperor and the Kite, The (Yolen), 278

Emperor's Egg, The (Jenkins), 130

Emperor's New Clothes, The, 33, 161

Empress of the World (Ryan), 200

Enchanted Castle, The (Nesbitt), 162, 180

Enchanted Runner, The (Little), 200

Enchantress from the Stars, The (Engdahl), 173, 179, 271

Encyclopedia Brown and the Case of the Slippery Salamander (Sobol), 196, 205

Endter, M., 27

Engdahl, S., 173, 271

English, K., 286, 287

Enright, E., 267, 270

Epidemics (Yount), 255, 263

Erasmus, 24, 25

Ereth's Birthday (Avi), 167, 179

Erikson, E., 6

Esbensen, B., 145, 148, 150

Escape from Home, The (Avi), 216

Escape South (Sigelson), 218

Escape to Freedom (Davis), 283

Escape to the Forest: Based on a True Story of the Holocaust (Radin), 14

Esperanza Rising (Ryan), 217, 225

Estes, D., 268, 269

Ets, M. H., 275, 276, 277

Eva (Dickinson), 164, 179

Evans, E., 34, 35, 94, 123

Evans, M., 282

Everett Anderson's Friend (Clifton), 282, 284

Every Man Heart Lay Down (Graham), 282

Everyone's Guide to Children's Literature (West), 65

Everything Book, The (Fleming), 100, 109

Everything on a Waffle (Horvath), 196, 204, 274

Every Time a Rainbow Dies (Williams-Garcia), 199

Everywhere Babies (Meyers), 100, 109

Ewing, J. H., 187

Executioner's Daughter (Williams), 211, 225

Expiration Date: Never (Spinner & Bisson), 62

Extraordinary Friends (Rogers), 258

Fables (Label), 279

Face First, A (Cummings), 204

Faces: People, Places and Culture, 263

Facts and Fictions of Minna Pratt, The (MacLachlan), 203–204

Fair, Brown and Trembling: An Irish Cinderella Story (Daly), 87–88

Fairmont Avenue (de Paola), 274

Fairy Circus, The (Lathrop), 266

Faithful Elephants (Touchiya), 121, 132

Faithful Friend, The (San Souci), 281, 286

Falconer, I., 116, 281

Fallen Angels (Myers), 284

Falling Star (Alyssa), 83

Falling Up (Silverstein), 158

Faltis, C., 80, 83

Family of Stories, The (Moss & Stott), 181

Family Under the Bridge, The (Carlson), 270

Fannie in the Kitchen (Hopkinson), 239–240

Farley, W., 187

Farmer, N., 164, 273

Fast Sam, Cool Clyde and Stuff (Myers), 282

Fat Camp Commandos (Pinkwater), 196, 205

Fated Sky, The (Branford), 215, 224

Faulkner, W. J., 282

Favorite Nursery Rhymes (Caldecott), 34, 94

Fax, E. C., 282

Fearless Jack (Johnson), 84

Fearnley, J. T., 10, 11

Fearsome Inn, The (Singer), 271

Feather Mountain (Olds), 276

Feathers, Flaps & Flops: Fabulous Early Fliers (Zaunders), 62–63

Feelings, M., 278

Feelings, T., 286

Feely, J. T., 10, 11

Fellman, A.C., 210

Fenner, C., 273, 283

Ferguson, A., 285

Ferocious Girls, Steamroller Boys, and Other Poems in Between (Bush), 152

Ferris, J., 200

Fever 1793 (Anderson), 216, 224

Fiddle Back (Honey), 200

Fiddle Fever (Doucet), 218, 223–224

Field, R., 266, 275

Fifteen Centuries of Children's Literature (Bingham & Scholdt), 39

Fifty Years of Children's Books (Smith), 205

Figgs and Phantoms (Raskins), 271

Fighting Ruben Wolfe (Zusak), 195, 205

Final Journey, The (Pausewang), 224–225

Finders Keepers (Lipkind), 276

Finding Hattie (Warner), 218

Fine White Dust, A. (Rylant), 273

Finger, C., 266

Finley, M. F., 33

Fire Bringer (Clement-Davies), 159–160, 166, 179

Firefighters A to Z (Demarest), 100, 109

Fire in Their Eyes: Wildfires and the People Who Fight Them (Beil), 256, 262

First Air Voyage in the United States: The Story of Jean-Pierre Blanchard, The (Wallner), 57, 60

First Day On A Strange New Planet (Yaccarino), 173, 180

F is for Fabuloso (Lee), 199

Fish, H. D., 274

Fisher, A., 150

Fisher, C., 139, 268

Fisher, M., 246

Fisherman and His Wife, The, (Brothers Grimm/Manheim), 73, 74, 75

Fisherman and His Wife, The: A Brand New Version (Wells), 88

Fish for Supper (Gaffstein), 279

Fishing for a Dream: Ocean Lullabies and Night Verses (Keisler), 107

Fish in the Air (Weise), 275

Fitzhugh, L., 187

Five Chinese Brothers (Bishop), 120, 132

Five Little Monkeys (Kepes), 276

Five Little Piggies (Martin), 108–109

Five Owls, The (Jara Society), 40

Flack, M., 95, 275

Flake, S. G., 287

Flavell, J., 8

Fledgling, The (Blake), 56

Fledgling, The (Langton), 272

Fleet, T., 29

Fleischman, P., 139, 157, 192, 224, 272, 273

Fleischman, S., 273

Fleming, D., 100, 280

Flicker Flash (Graham), 147, 157

Floating Island (Parrish), 266

Floca, B., 254

Floodland (Sedgewick), 173, 180

Florian, D., 151, 152, 155

Flowers, A., 230, 244

Fly High, Fly Low (Freeman), 277

Fly High: The Story of Bessie Coleman (Border & Kroeger), 61

Fogelman, P., 286

Fog Magic (Sauer), 268

Fool of the World and the Flying Machine (Ransome), 278

Forbes, E., 210, 215, 268

Ford, L., 274

Foresman, S., 276

Forest Pool, The (Armer), 274

Forged By Fire (Draper), 286

Forging Freedom: A True Story of Heroism (Talbot), 14

Forgotten Daughter, The (Snedeker), 267

Forgotten Fire (Bagdasarian), 211, 224

Foster, G., 268, 269

Four and Twenty Blackbirds: Nursery Rhymes of Yesterday Recalled for Children of Today (Fish), 274

Four Corners of the Sky, The: Creation Stories and Cosmologies from Around the World (Zeitlin), 76, 88

Four or Fourteen or Forty: Picture Books Are for Everyone (Bishop & Hickman), 132

Four Perfect Pebbles: A Holocaust Story (Perl & Lazen), 223, 225

Four to the Pole: The American Women's Expedition to Antarctica 1992–1993 (Loewen & Bancroft), 261–262

Fox, P., 271, 272

Foxe, J., 25

Fox Went Out on a Chilly Night, The: An Old Song (Spier), 277

Fradin, D. B., 256

Frames of Mind (Gardner), 18

Francie (English), 287

Franco, B., 151

Frank, A. 229, 230

Frankenstein (Shelley/Carpenter & Pritchard), 172, 180

Frank O. Gehry: Outside In (Greenberg & Jordan), 235, 240

Frasconi, A. 277

Frazee, M., 252

Freddy and the Dragon (Brooks), 14

Frederick (Lionni), 116, 132, 278

Freeburg, R. E., 142

Freedman, R., 61, 230, 231, 235, 237, 256, 261, 272, 273

Freedom Like Sunlight: Praisesongs for Black Americans (Lewis), 153

Freedom River (Rappaport), 287

Freeman, D., 277

Freewill (Lynch), 193

Freight Train (Crews), 279

French, F., 122

Frey, C., 33

Freymann, S., 258

Friedman, C., 223

Friedman, I., 14

Friends and Enemies (Gaeddert), 220

Friendship; The (Taylor), 284

Fritz, J., 232, 235, 237, 272

Frog and Toad Are Friends (Lobel), 271, 278

Frog Went-A-Courtin', 276

From Cover to Cover: Evaluating and Reviewing Children's Books (Horning), 158

From Mythic to Linear: Time in Children's Literature (Nikolajeva), 181

From the Notebooks of Melanin Sun (Woodson), 286

From Sea to Shining Sea: A Treasury of American Folklore and Folk Songs (Cohn), 72, 88

From the Mixed-Up Files of Mrs. Basil E. Frankweiler (Konigsburg), 271

From Two to Five (Chukovsky), 88

Frontier Living (Tunis), 270

Frost, Robert, 137

Frye, N., 44, 50, 137

Funny Little Woman, The (Mosel), 278

Gaeddert, L., 200

Gag, W., 266, 267, 274

Gaggin, E. R., 268

Gaines. A. G., 256

Galda, L., 209

Gallaz, C., 122

Gammage Cup, The (Kendall), 270

Gandhi (Demi), 236

Gandhi, Fighter without a Sword (Eaton), 269

Gannett, R. S., 269

Gantos, J., 192, 258, 274

Gardener, The (Stewart), 281

Garden of Abdul Gasazi, The (Allsburg), 279

Gardiner, J., 222

Gardner, H., 12

Gardner, R., 255

Garram the Hunter: A Boy of the Hill Tribes (Best), 266

Gates, D., 268

Gathering Blue (Lowry), 172, 179

Gathering of Days, A: A New England Girl's Journal 1830–1832 (Blos), 272

Gauthier, G., 217

Gayneck, The Story of a Pigeon (Mukerji), 266

Gender Gap in the Library: Different Choices for Boys and Girls (Childress), 18

George, J. C., 192, 270, 271

George, K. O. 152

George Washington (Foster), 269

George Washington & The Founding of a Nation (Marrin), 235, 239, 240

George Washington's World (Foster), 268

Geras, A., 214

Gershator, P., 81

Getting Near to Baby (Couloumbis), 193, 274

Ghost Wings (Joose), 61, 63

Gib and the Grey Ghost (Snyder), 223, 225

Gibbons, G., 114, 126, 130

Giblin, J., 91, 239, 256

Giff, P. R., 211, 216, 220, 274

Gift from Zeus, A (Steig), 76, 88

Gift of the Crocodile, The: A Cinderella Story (Sierra), 86, 88

Gilchrist, J. S., 285

Giles, H., 69

Gillespie and the Guards (Elkin), 276–277

Gillespie, M., 29, 32, 34

Gilmore, R., 218

Giorgis, C. 14

Ginger Pye (Estes), 269

Gipson, F., 270

Girl Named Disaster, A, (Farmer), 273

Girl Got Game: Sports Stories and Poems (Macy), 195, 204

Girl Who Loved Wild Horses, The (Gable), 279

Girl Who Spun Gold, The (Hamilton), 84

Girnis, M., 100, 258

G is for Googol: A Math Alphabet Book (Schwartz), 253, 263

Give Me Liberty! The Story of the Declaration of Independence (Freedman) 256, 262

Giver, The (Lowry), 172, 179

Glass, F., 282

Glorius Flight: Across the Channel with Louis Bleriot (Provensen), 279

Glory of the Seas (Hewes), 267

Giver, The (Lowry), 273

Go Ask Alice (Anonymous), 188, 204

Goats, The (Cole), 192, 204, 206

Goble, P., 82, 83, 121, 279

Goffstein, M. B., 279

Goggles! (Keats), 278

Go In Someplace Special (McKissack), 287

Gold, A. L., 236

Gold Dust (Lynch), 195, 204

Golden Basket (Bemelmans), 267

Golden Compass, The, (Pullman), 168, 169, 180

Golden Fleece and the Heroes Who Lived Before Achilles (Colum), 265

Golden Goblet (McGraws), 270

Golden Name Day (Linquist), 269–270

Goldilocks (Opie & Opie), 161

Goldilocks and the Three Bears (Marshall), 280

Goldsmith, O., 31

Golem: A Jewish Legend (McDermott), 279

Golem (Wisniewski), 281

Goneaway Lake (Enright), 270

Good Luck Horse (Chan), 275

Good Master, The (Seredy), 267

Goodnight Moon (Brown), 1

Goodrich, S., 33

Goody Two Shoes, 31

Goosebumps (Stine), 197–198

Goose Chase (Kindl), 85

Gordy, B., 283

Gorrell, G. K., 236

Goudy, A. E., 277

Govenar, A., 256, 261

Grace, The (Heneghan), 179

Graham, A., 275

Graham, B., 59

Graham, J. B., 147

Graham, L., 282

Graham, S., 282

Grahame, K., 162, 164

Grandfather's Journey (Say), 280

Grandmama's Joy (Greenfield), 283

Grapes of Math, The (Tang), 253, 263

Graphic Alphabet, The (Pelletier), 281

Grave, The (Heneghan), 171

Graven Images (Fleischman), 272

Gray, E. J., 266, 267, 268

Greatest, The: Muhammed Ali (Myers) 236, 240

Great Fairy Tale Tradition, The: From Straparola and Basile to the Brothers Grimm (Zipes), 89

Great Fire, The (Murphy), 273

Great Gilly Hopkins, The (Paterson), 272

Great Little Madison, The (Fritz), 235, 240

Great Quest, The (Hawes), 265

Great Wheel, The (Lawson), 270

Green and Burning Tree, The (Cameron), 181

Greenaway, K., 35, 93–94, 110

Greenberg, J., 235

Greene, B., 281

Greene, E., 85

Green Eyes (Birnbaum), 276

Greenfield, E., 150, 282, 283, 285

Gregory, K., 232

Grey King, The (Cooper), 164, 179, 272

Grey Lady and the Strawberry Snatcher, The (Bang), 279

Grifalconi, A., 280

Griffith, J., 33

Grimes, N., 135, 287

Grimm, J., 33, 35, 40, 85

Grimm's Fairy Tales, 33

Grimms' Tales for Young and Old (Manheim), 89

Grimm Tales in English (Alderson), 39

Grimm, W., 33, 35, 40,

Groom, G., 282

Grossman, B., 147, 282

Group of One, A (Gilmore), 218

Grutman, J., 211, 218

Guest in the Promised Land (Hunter), 282

Guinness Book of World Records, The, 247

Gulliver in Lilliput (Hodges), 30

Gulliver's Travels (Swift), 30, 32, 174, 180

Guns: What You Should Know (Shulson), 120, 132

Gurko, L., 270

Gus and Gertie and the Missing Pearl (Nixon), 130

Gutman, D., 171

Guts: The True Stories Behind Hatchet and the Brian Books (Paulsen), 238, 240

Guy, R., 283

Haas, J., 194

Hader, B., 274, 275

Hader, E., 274, 275

Haldane, S., 237

Hale, B., 14

Haley, G., 278

Half Moon and One Whole Star
(Crescent Dragonwagon),
284

Hall, A. G., 268

Hall, D., 279

Hall, E., 7, 8, 9

Hallock, G., 266

Hamilton, V., 22, 23, 84, 188, 271,
273, 283, 284, 285, 286

Handford, T., 274

*Hannah's Journal: The Story of an
Immigrant Girl* (Moss),
216, 225

Hannah's Winter of Hope (Leeuwen),
216, 225

*Hans Brinker, or the Silver Skates: A
Story of Life in Holland*
(Dodge), 187, 204

*Hans Christian Andersen: The
Complete Fairy Tales and
Stories* (Haugaard), 88

Hansel and Gretel (Lesser), 279

Hansen, J., 284, 286, 287

Hansi (Bemelmans), 95, 132

Happy Day (Krauss), 276

Happy Golden Years (Wilder), 268

Hardy Boys, The, 197

Harlem (Myers), 281, 287

Harlow, J. H., 223

Harper Handbook to Literature, The
(Frye et al.), 158

Harriet the Spy (Fitzhugh), 187, 204

*Harriet the Spy: Milestone,
Masterpiece?* (Wolf), 205

Harris, R. H., 254, 255

Harrison, B., 220

Harry Potter (Rowling), 37, 160, 162,
164, 168, 170

*Harry Potter and the Chamber of
Secrets* (Rowling), 163, 164,
180

Harry Potter and the Goblet of Fire
(Rowling), 164, 180

Harry Potter and the Phoenix
(Rowling), 164, 180

*Harry Potter and the Prisoner of
Azkaban* (Rowling), 164,
180

Harry Potter and the Sorcerer's Stone
(Rowling), 164, 178, 180

Haskins, J., 236, 282, 283, 284, 285,
286

Hatchet (Paulsen), 205, 226, 273

Haugaard, E., 68

Hautman, P., 173

Have You Seen My Duckling? (Tafuri),
279–280

Have You Seen Tom Thumb? (Hunt),
268

Havighurst, M., 269

Havighurst, W., 269

Haviland, V., 233

Hawes, C., 265, 266

Hawk, I'm Your Brother (Baylor), 279

Hayward, C., 138

Hazard, P., 33

Headless Cupid, The (Snyder), 271

Hear My Cry (Scales), 206

Hearn, M. P., 31

Hearne, B., 31, 69, 80, 196

*Heart and Soul: The Story of Florence
Nightingale* (Gorrell), 236

Heaven (Johnson), 287

Heavenly Tenants, The (Maxwell), 268

Heidi (Spyri), 187, 205, 222, 225

"Hello the Boat!" (Crawford), 267

Helper, S., 1, 231

Henny Penny (Wattenberg), 85

Henry and Mudge (Rylant), 202

Henry Fisherman (Brown), 275

Henry, M., 187, 268, 269

Henry, O., 187

Herculeah Jones (Byars), 202

Here Comes Mother Goose (Opie), 72,
88

Here We All Are (de Paola), 236, 238,
240

Hero ain't Nothing but a Sandwich, A
(Childress), 282

Hero and the Crown, The (McKinley),
272

Heroes (Mochizuki), 122

*Heroine of the Titanic: The Real
Unsinkable Molly Brown*
(Landau), 232, 240

Hero of Ticonderoga, The (Gauthier),
217, 224

Hero with a Thousand Faces
(Campbell), 88

Herrerra, J. F., 236

Herron, C., 120

Herschel and the Hanukkah Goblins
(Kimmel), 280

Her Stories (Hamilton), 286

Hertenstein, J., 220

Hesse, K., 145, 210, 274

Hewes, A., 266, 267

Hey, Al (Yorinks), 280

Hiawatha (Longfellow), 157

Hickman, J., 1, 121, 122, 223, 231,

Hicyilmaz, G., 200

Hidden Arrow of Maether, The
(Beaverson), 171, 179

Hidden Treasure of Glaston, The
(Jewett), 268

Hide and Seek Fog (Tresselt), 277

Higgensen, V., 72

High King, The (Alexander), 164, 179,
271

High, L., 111, 112

High Rise Private Eyes, The (Rylant),
14, 167, 178, 180

Highwater, J., 272

Highwayman, The (Noyes), 144, 157,
158

Hildilid's Night (Ryan), 278

Hillerman, T., 195

Hillman, C., 121, 139, 140

Hindenburg, The (O'Brien), 56

Hines, A. G., 152

Hinton, S.E., 188

*Hippety Hop Hippety Hay: Growing
with Rhymes from Birth to
Age Three* (Dunn), 108, 109

Hiroshima No Pika (Maruki), 122

His Dark Materials (Pullman), 37, 169

*His Dark Materials: Book One:
Northern Lights* (Pullman),
180

*His Dark Materials: Book Three: The
Amber Spyglass* (Pullman),
180

*His Dark Materials: Book Two: The
Subtle Knife* (Pullman), 180

History and Friends (Gillespie), 39

History of Counting, The (Schmidt-
Besserat), 253, 263

History of Reading, A (Manguel), 40

History of Reynard The Fox (Caxton),
24

Hite, S., 211

Hitty, Her First Hundred Years (Field),
266

Ho, M. O., 153, 281

Hoban, R., 167

Hoban, T., 99, 103, 104

Hobbie, H., 104

*Hobbit, The: Or, There and Back
Again* (Tolkien), 164, 180

Hodges, M., 30, 122, 227, 279

Hoffman, L., 7, 8–9

Hofmeyr, D., 81

Hogrogian, N., 278, 279

Holbrook, S., 275

Hole in the Sky (Hautman), 173, 179

Holes (Sachar), 180, 274

Holling, H. C., 269, 274

Holm, J. L., 274

Holocaust, Materials and Resources, 14

Holocaust Survivors, Rescuers and Bystanders, Book Links (Rochman), 14

Holt, K. W., 193

Holy Twins: Benedict and Scholastica (Norris), 235, 240

Holzworth, W., 200

Homeless Bird (Whelan), 200

Honey, E., 200

Honk, the Moose (Stong), 2, 67

Hoose, P., 261

Hope Was Here (Bauer), 192, 274

Hopkins, L. B., 138, 151, 152

Hopkinson, D., 239

Horenstein, H., 100

Horn Book Guide, 86, 230, 244

Horn Book Magazine, The, (Sutton), 55, 65, 151

Horn Book: Sambo, Babaji, and Sam (Bader), 132

Horning, K. T., 139, 140

Horowitz, A., 215

Horrible Harry (Kline), 202

Horsecatcher, The (Sandoz), 270

Hort, L., 107, 152

Horvath, P., 196, 274

Hosie's Alphabet (Tobias & Baskin), 278

House of Dies Drear, The, 226

House of Sixty Fathers, The (De Jong), 270

Houses from the Sea (Goudey), 277

House that Jack Built, The, (Winter), 74, 88

House that Jack Built, The: A Picture Book in Two Languages (Frasconi), 277

Howard, E. F., 287

How Are You Peeling? Foods with Moods (Freymann & Elffers), 258

How Chipmunk Got His Stripes (Bruchac & Bruchac), 76, 88

Hubbard, R., 266

Huck, C., 1, 85, 230, 231

Hughes, L., 138–139, 145

Hughes, M., 173

Hughes, T., 152

Hugo, V., 21

Humpty Dumpty, 29

Hundred Dresses, The (Estes), 268

Hundred Penny Box, The (Mathis), 272

Hunt, I., 210, 223, 270, 271

Hunt, M. L., 268, 269

Hunt, P., 5, 43

Hunter, K., 282, 283

Hunter, R. A., 56

Hunter, The: A Chinese Folktale (Casanova), 82

Hunterman and the Crocodile: A West African Folktale (Diakite), 287

Hurry Freedom: African Americans in Gold Rush California (Stanley), 230–231, 241, 257, 261, 263

Hurry Home, Candy (De Jong), 269

Hush! A Thai Lullaby (Ho), 281

Hush, Little Baby: A Folk Song with Pictures (Frazee), 252, 262

Hutchins, P., 99

Hyman, T. S., 279

I Am a Black Woman (Evans), 282

I Am Morgan le Fay: A Tale from Camelot (Springer), 171, 180

I Am the Cat (Schertle), 152

Ibbotson, E., 171

If All the Seas were One Sea (Domanska), 278

If I Ran the Zoo (Dr. Seuss), 276

If You Hopped Like a Frog (Schwartz), 263

Igus, T., 287

I Hadn't Meant to Tell You This (Woodson), 286

I Have a Sister, My Sister Is Deaf (Peterson), 283

I Have Heard of a Land (Thomas), 287

I, Juan de Pareja (de Trevino), 270

I Know Why the Caged Bird Sings (Angelou), 282

Iktomi and the Coyote: A Plains Indian Story (Goble), 82

Imig, W., 142

I'm Jose and I'm Okay: Three Stories from Bolivia (Holzworth), 200

I'm Now the Girlfriend of a Sex God: Further Confessions of Georgia Nicholson (Rennisson), 196

I'm Small, and Other Verses (Moore), 108, 109

Inch by Inch (Lionni), 277

Incident at Hawk's Hill (Eckert), 271

Incredible Journey, The (Bumford), 204

In Daddy's Arms I am Tall: African Americans Celebrating Fathers (Steptoe), 153

Indian Captive: The Story of Mary Jemison (Lenski), 268

Indian in the Cupboard, The (Banks), 174, 179

I Never Had It Made: The Autobiography of Jackie Robinson (Duckett), 282

In Every Tiny Grain of Sand: A Child's Book of Prayers (Lindbergh), 151

Ingold, J., 61

In My Mother's House (Clark), 274

Innocenti, R., 122

In Real Life: Six Women Photographers (Sills), 236, 241

Inspector Hopper (Cushman), 14

Intellectual Freedom Manual (American Library Association), 205

International Companion Encyclopedia Of Children's Literature, 290

Interpreting the Past: Reflections of An Historical Novelist (Aiken), 225

In the Beginning: Creation Stories from Around the World (Hamilton), 22, 273

In the Forest (Ets), 275

In the Moonlight Mist: A Korean Tale (San Souci), 82

In the Night Kitchen (Sendak), 95, 109, 278

In the Rainfield: Who Is the Greatest? (Olaleye), 81

In the Small, Small Pond (Fleming), 280

In the Time of the Drums (Siegelson), 287

In the Time of the Knights (Tanaka), 235, 241

Introducing Books to Children (Chambers), 18

Introduction to Fantasy: The Perilous Realms in Innocence and Experience (Levin), 181

Introduction to Poetry (Kennedy), 149, 158

Invincible Louisa: The Story of the Author of 'Little Women' (Meigs), 240, 269

Invisible Hunters: A Legend from the Miskito Indians of Nicaragua (Rohmer), 284

I See the Rhythm (Igus), 287

Isaacs, A., 220, 281

Isadora, R., 100, 279

Ish-Kishor, S., 271

Island of the Blue Dolphins (O'Dell), 5, 15, 18, 41–43, 270, 48–49, 55, 64, 210, 225–226

Isn't My Name Jorge: On Both Sides of the River (Medina), 153

Isn't My Name Magical: Sister and Brother Poems (Berry), 153

Island of the Aunts (Ibbotson), 171

It Could Always Be Worse (Zemach), 279

I Thought My Soul Would Rise and Fly: The Diary of Patsy, A Freed Girl (Hansen), 286

It's Like This, Cat (Neville), 270

It's Perfectly Normal: Changing Bodies, Growing Up, Sex and Sexual Health (Harris), 255, 262

It's Raining Pigs and Noodles (Prelutsky), 152

It's So Amazing! A Book about Eggs, Sperm, Birth, Babies, and Families (Harris), 254, 262

Ivanhoe (Scott), 210, 225

I Was a Rat (Pullman), 174, 180

I Was a Third Grade Spy (Auch), 166, 179

Jabberwocky (Carroll), 149

Jack and Jill, 29

Jack and The Beanstalk: An English Fairy Tale (Bell), 85–87

Jackaroe (Siegmeister), 144

Jackson, D., 255

Jacob Have I Loved (Paterson), 188, 205, 272

Jacobs, P. S., 218, 232

Jacques, B., 166

Jaeger, W., 253, 260

Jakarta Missing (Kurtz), 200

Jake and Honeybunch Go to Heaven (Zemach), 120, 132

Jake's Orphan (Brooke), 217, 224

Jambo Means Hello: A Swahili Alphabet Book (Feelings), 278

James, P. D., 195

James, W., 266

James Printer: A Novel of Rebellion (Jacobs), 218, 232, 240

James Van Der Zee: The Picture Takin' Man (Haskins), 283

Janeczko, P. B., 146, 147

Jane's Island (Allie), 267

Jane Yolen's Mother Goose Songbook (Yolen), 109

Jarrell, R., 271, 278

Jarvis, R., 167

Jazmin's Notebook (Grimes), 287

Jazz Kid, The (Collier), 223–224, 271

Jeffers, S., 278

Jenkins, M., 130

Jenkins, S., 256

Jennifer, Hecate, Macbeth, William McKinley, and Me, Elizabeth (Konigsburg), 271

Jericho (Hickman), 223–224

Jessie De La Cruz: A Profile of a United Farm Worker (Soto), 237

Jewett, E., 268

Jip His Story (Paterson), 216, 225

Joan Baez Songbook, The (Siegmeister), 158

Joey Pigza Loses Control (Gantos), 193, 258, 274

Johansen, M., 266

John Gilpin's Ride and Other Stories (Caldecott), 93, 109

John Henry (Lester), 281

John Newbery and His Books: Trade and Plumb-Cake Forever, Huzza (Townsend), 38, 40

John Newbery, "Friend of All Mankind" (Hearn), 40

Johnny Tremain (Forbes), 210, 215, 224, 268

Johnson, A., 285, 287

Johnson, D., 151

Johnson, G.W., 270

Johnson, J. W., 286

Johnson, N. J., 14

Johnson, P. B., 84

Johnson, S. A., 256

Johnson, S. T., 281

Join Fostering (Faltis), 88

Jones, I., 267

Jones, J. O., 275

Joose, B. M., 14, 61, 63

Jordan, A.D., 197

Jordan, J., 282

Jordan, S., 235

Joseph Had a Little Overcoat (Taback), 281

Joseph, L., 200

Joslin, S., 277

Journal of Biddy Owens, The: The Negro Leagues (Myers), 14, 218

Journal of Scott Pendleton Collins, The (Myers), 220

Journal of Wong Ming Chung, The: A Chinese Miner (Yep), 218

Journey Cake, Ho! (Sawyer), 276

Journey Outside (Steele), 271

Jovanovich, B, 273

Joyful Noise: Poems for Two Voices, (Fleischman), 139, 157, 273

Juan Bobo Goes to Work: A Puerto Rican Folktale (Montes), 84

Juanita (Politi), 275

Judge, The: An Untrue Tale (Zemach), 278

Judson, C. I., 269, 270

Juice (Watson), 200

Jukes, M., 272

Julian, Huey and Glorida (Cameron), 202

Julie of the Wolves (George), 271

Julius K. Nyerere: Teacher of Africa (Messner), 282

Jumanji (Van Allsburg), 132, 279

Jumping-off Place (McNeely), 266

Jumping Tree, The: A Novel (Saedana), 199

Jung, C., 69

Junius Over Far (Hamilton), 284

Justice and Her Brothers (Hamilton), 283

Justin and the Best Biscuits in the World (Walter), 284

Justin Morgan Had a Horse (Rand), 268
Just Me (Ets), 277
Just Us Women (Caines), 283

Kalashnikoff, N., 269
Kalnay, F., 270
Kaminsky, M., 236
Kaplan, H., 120, 258
Karr, K., 216
Kate and the Beanstalk (Osborne), 85
Katz, K., 104
Keats, E. J., 100, 277, 278
Keeper of the Isis Light (Hughes), 173
Keillor, G., 203
Keith, H., 270
Kelly, E. P., 210, 266
Kendall, C., 270
Kennedy, D., 142, 143, 146
Kennedy, X. J., 142, 143, 146, 149, 152
Kepes, J., 276
Kerley, B., 256, 281
Kerper, R. M., 246
Kerr, M.E., 188
Kessler, C., 200
Ketteman, H., 202
Key Is Lost, The (Vos), 14
Kherdian, D., 272
Kids at Work: Lewis Hine and the Crusade Against Child Labor (Freedman), 261–262
Kids Discover, 263
Kiefer, B., 1, 18, 98, 113, 116, 121, 231
Kiesler, K., 107
Kildee House (Montgomery), 269
Kimmel, E., A., 82, 84, 280
Kindl, P., 85
Kinderlager: An Oral History of Young Holocaust Survivors (Nieusma), 14
King And Three Thieves, The: A Persian Tale (Balouch), 82
King Bidgood's in the Bathtub (Wood), 280
King, C. S., 284
King Henry's Primers, 25
Kingman, L., 275
King of the Wind (Henry), 187, 204, 269
King's Fifth, The (O'Dell), 271
Kingsley, C., 162
Kinzer, C. K., 13, 221, 247
Kipling, R., 162

Kit's Wilderness (Almond), 200
Klein, N., 188
Kline, S., 202
Klise, K., 196
Kneeknock Rise (Babbitt), 271
Knock at a Star (Kennedy), 142–143, 147, 157
Knock at the Door: And Other Baby Action Rhymes (Chorao), 107–108
Koertge, R., 145
Konigsburg, E. L., 195, 209, 271, 273
Koscielniak, B., 252
Koss, A., 192
Kozar, R., 237
Krauss, R., 276
Krensky, S., 56, 60, 61
Kristo, J.V., 246
Kroeger, M. K., 61
Krull, K., 237
Krumgold, J., 269, 270
Kurlansky, M., 256
Kurtz, J., 200
Kuskin, K., 150
Kutiper, K. S., 139
Kyle, A., 267

Lakota Hoop Dancer (Left Hand Bull & Haldane), 237
Land, The (Taylor), 211, 225, 287
Landau, E., 232
Lang, A., 69
Langstaff, J., 276, 284
Langton, J., 17, 272
Larson, R., 218
Lasky, K., 223, 272
Last Book in the Universe, The (Philbrick), 173, 180
Last of the Mohicans, The (Cooper), 187
Latham, J. L., 269
Lathrop, D. P., 266
Lauber, P., 273
Laugh-Eteria (Florian), 152
Lauture, D., 286
Lawson, R., 268, 270, 274
Lazen, M. B., 223
Leader by Destiny: George Washington, Man and Patriot (Eaton), 267
Leaf by Leaf: Autumn Poems (Rogasky), 152
Leaf, M., 274
Lear, E., 138, 146
Lear's Nonsense (Hayward), 158

Lee, D., 145
Lee, M., 199
Leedy, L., 253
Left Hand Bull, J., 237
Legend of Africana, The (Robinson), 282
Le Guin, U., 164, 271
Lehn, B., 122
Le Lun: Lad of Courage (Treffinger), 268
Lena Horne (Haskins), 284
L'Engle, M., 17, 164, 270, 272
Lenski, L., 267–268
Leodhas, S. N., 270, 277
Leonardo da Vinci (Stanley), 230–231, 235, 241
Leprechaun Who Wished He Wasn't, The (Parkinson), 175, 180
Lerner, C., 61
Les Misérables (Hugo), 21
Lesser, R., 279
Lester, H., 130, 234,
Lester, J., 62, 119, 193, 214, 271, 281, 283, 284
Let It Shine! Stories of Black Women Freedom Fighters (Pinkney), 287
Let the Circle Be Unbroken (Taylor), 283
Let the Lion Eat Straw (Southerland), 283
Leu, D. J., 13, 221, 247
Levin, B., 162
Levine, G. C., 274
Lewis, C.S., 162, 164, 168, 170
Lewis, E. B., 287
Lewis, E. F., 266
Lewis, J. P., 153
Lide, A., 266
Life and Adventures of Robinson Crusoe, The (Defoe), 30, 39, 204
Life and Art of Madeline's Creator, The (Marciano), 110
Life and Death of Crazy Horse, The (Freedman), 230, 240
Life in Poems, A (Nelson), 287
Life of Samuel Johnson (Boswell), 229
Light at Tern Rock, The (Sauer), 269
Like Jake And Me (Jukes), 272
Like Sisters on the Homefront (Williams-Garcia), 286
Lily's Crossing (Giff), 220, 274

Lincoln: A Photobiography (Freedman), 230–231, 240, 273
Ling, P. S., 69
Lion (duBois), 277
Lion and the Mouse, and Other Aesop's Fables, The (Orgel), 72, 88, 284
Lion and the Unicorn, The (Johns Hopkins University Press), 40
Lionni, L., 116, 277, 278
Lion's Share, The (Conover), 56
Lion, The Witch and the Wardrobe, The (Lewis), 164, 169, 179
Lindbergh, R., 151
Lindgren, A., 164
Lindquist, J., 270
Lipkind, W., 276
Lirael: Daughter of the Clayr (Nix), 180
Lisle, J. T., 220, 273
Listen and Read: Songs of Innocence and Experience (Blake), 157
Literacy and Learning: Strategies for Middle and Secondary School Teachers (Allan & Miller), 263
Literacy Development in the Early Years: Helping Children Read and Write (Morrow), 64
Literacy for the 21st Century: A Balanced Approach (Tompkins), 18, 65, 221, 225, 263
Literacy Heritage of Childhood, The (Frey & Griffith), 39
Literary Theory: An Introduction (Eagleton), 64
Literature and the Child (Galda & Cullinan), 225
Literature Circles Resource Guide: Teaching Suggestions, Forms, Sample Book Lists and Databases (Hill, Noe, & Johnson), 65
Literature Circles: Voice and Choice in the Student-Centered Classroom (Daniels), 221, 225
Literature for Today's Young Adults (Nilsen), 18
Little Bear's Visit (Minarik), 277
Little Blackhorse (Swift), 266

Little Eight John (Wahl), 285
Little Golden Lamb, The (Greene), 85
Little Gold Star: A Spanish American Cinderella Tale (San Souci), 87–88
Little House, The (Burton), 275
Little House in the Big Woods (Wilder), 205, 210, 216, 225
Little House on the Prairie (Wilder), 36, 187
Little House series (Wilder), 210, 216
Little Island, The (MacDonald), 275
Little, K. G., 200
Little, L. J., 283
Little Lost Lamb (MacDonald), 275
Little Love, A (Hamilton), 284
Little Mermaid, The (Andersen), 161
Little Miss Muffet, 29
Little Miss Spider (Kirk), 132
Little Pretty Pocket-Book, A (Newbery), 31–32, 186
Little Pretty Pocket-Book: Milestones in Children's Literature (Newbery), 204
Little Red Hen, The (Makes a Pizza), (Sturges), 74, 88
Little Red Riding Hood (Ehrlich), 28
Little Red Riding Hood (Hyman), 279
Little Tales for Children and for the Family Collected by the Brothers Grimm, 33, 35
Little Town on the Prairie (Wilder), 268
Little Women (Alcott), 33, 39, 187, 204
Lives of Extraordinary Women: Rulers, Rebels (and What the Neighbors Thought) (Krull), 237
Livingston, M. C., 135, 136, 150
Lizzie at Last (Mills), 196, 204
Lobel, A., 271, 278, 279
Locke, J., 27, 28, 32
Locust Pocus! A Book to Bug You (McKelvey), 151
Loewen, N., 261
Lofting, H., 164, 266
London, J., 100
Lone Journey: The Life of Roger Williams (Eaton), 268
Loner, The (Wier), 270
Longfellow, H. W., 144
Long Hard Journey, A (McKissack), 285
Longitude Prize, The (Dash), 258, 262
Longmans, J. B., 265

Long Way to Chicago, A (Peck), 274
Long Winter, The (Wilder), 268
Lon Po Po: A Red Riding Hood Story from China (Young), 280
Lookin' for Bird in the Big City (Burleigh), 122
Look Whooo's Counting (MacDonald), 100, 109
Lord Brocktree (Jacques), 166, 179
Lord Kirkle's Money (Avi), 216
Lord of the Deep (Salisbury), 200
Love, D. A., 211
Love Flute (Goble), 83, 88, 121, 132
Love to Mama: A Tribute to Mothers (Mora), 153
Lou in the Limelight (Hunter), 283
Louv, R., 9
Low, J., 279
Lownsbery, E., 266
Lowry, L., 172, 196, 220, 226, 273
Lucky Thing, A (Schertle), 145, 158
Lucky 13: Solitaire Games for Kids (Street), 253, 263
Lueders, E., 156
Lukens, R., 3, 5, 46, 140
Lyddie (Paterson), 216, 225
Lynch, C., 193, 195
Lyons, M. E., 218
Lytle Book of Good Manners for Children, A (Erasmus/Whittington), 24–25

Mabela, The Clever (MacDonald), 81
Mabingion, The, 69
Macaulay, D., 122, 244, 253, 278, 279, 280
MacDonald, G.,162, 168, 275
MacDonald, M. R., 81, 87, 108, 253, 260
MacDonald S., 100, 280
Machinery for the Muse: Computers and Poetry (Marcus), 158
MacLachlan, P., 203, 272
Macy, S., 195
Madeline (Bemelmans), 95, 132, 274, 276
Magical Adventures of Pretty Pearl, The (Hamilton), 284
Magic and Mischief: Tales from Cornwall (Climo), 84
Magic Can Be Murder (Vande Velde), 175, 180
Magic Maize (Buff), 269

Magic Paintbrush, The (Yep), 175, 180

Magic Tree House (Osborne & Osborne), 178

Maguire, G., 170

Mahy, M., 200

Make Way for Ducklings (McCloskey), 95, 274

Making Animal Babies (Collard), 254, 262

Malam, J., 238, 239

Malcolmson, A., 275

Malcolm X: By Any Means Necessary (Myers), 285

Malkus, A., 266

Man and His Symbols (Jung), 88

Manguel, A., 21

Manheim, R., 73

Maniac Magee: Homer on George Street (Spinelli), 174, 180, 181, 273

Many Moons (Thurber), 275

Many Stories (Coman), 192

Many Ways of Seeing, The: An Introduction to the Pleasures of Art (Moore), 271

Maples in the Mist: Children's Poems from the Tang Dynasty (Ho), 153

Mapping the World (Johnson), 257

Marc Brown Arthur Chapter Book Series, 120

Marcellino, F., 119

Marco's Millions (Sleator), 173, 180

Marcus, S., 94 140

Marguerite Makes a Book (Robertson), 215, 225

Marianna and the Merchild: A Folktale from Chile (Pitcher), 84

Marrin, A., 235, 237, 239

Marsden, J., 173

Marshall, B., 265

Marshall, J., 280

Marshmallow (Newberry), 275

Martian Rock (Shields), 130

Martin, B., Jr., 99, 101

Martin, D., 108, 282

Martin, J. B., 281

Martin Luther King Jr.: Man of Peace (Patterson), 282

Martin Luther King, Jr. & the Freedom Movement (Patterson), 285

Martin's Big Words: The Life of Dr. Martin Luther King, Jr. (Rappaport), 257, 281, 287

Maruki, T., 122

Marvin and Tige (Glass), 282

Marvin Redpost (Sachar), 202

Mary: An Autobiography (Mebane), 283

Mary Jo's Grandmother (Uldry), 282

Mary Poppins (Travers), 164, 180

Master Man: A Tale of Nigeria (Shepard), 81, 88

Matchlock Gun, The (Edmonds), 268

Mathis, S. B., 272, 282

Matilda Bone (Cushman), 215, 224

Matsuyama, U., 81

Matters of Fact: Aspects of Nonfiction for Children (Fisher), 263

Matthaei, G., 211, 218

Matthews, R., 253

Max (Graham), 56, 59

Maxwell, W., 268

May I Bring a Friend? (de Regniers), 277

Maynard, B., 192

Mazer, N. F., 273

McCaughrean, G., 23, 175

McCleod Bethune (Greenfield), 282–283

McCloskey, R., 95, 274

McClure, A., 198

McCord, D., 138, 150, 156

McCully, A., 280

McDermott, B. B., 279

McDermott, G., 278, 280

McElligot's Pool (Dr. Seuss), 275

McGinley, P., 275, 276

McGraw, E., 174, 215, 269, 270, 273

M.C. Higgins, the Great (Hamilton), 271

McKelvey, D. K., 151

McKinley, R., 85, 179, 272

McKissack, F., 285, 286, 287

McKissack, P., 215, 218, 273, 280, 285, 286, 287

McNaughton, C., 152

McNeely, M. H., 266

Meader, S. W., 268

Means, F. C., 268

Mebane, M. E., 283

Medal Man: Randolph Caldecott and the Art of the Picture Book (Marcus), 110

Medieval Knight-Read Me A Book (Anderson), 226

Medieval Tales that Kids Can Read and Tell (Czarnota), 290

Medina, J., 153

Meet Danitra Brown (Grimes), 286

Meggy Macintosh (Gray), 266

Meigs, S., 229, 230, 265, 266, 267

Mei Li (Handforth), 274

Meltzer, M., 230, 237

Memorabia (Florian), 151, 155, 157

Men, Microscopes, and Living Things (Shippen), 270

Men of Athens (Coolidge), 270

Mermaid's Purse, The (Hughes), 152

Merriam, E., 150

Meyer, S. E., 92, 95

Meyers, S., 100

Mice Twice (Low), 279

Michael J. Fox (Kozar), 237

Michelangelo (Stanley), 235, 241, 257

Michelson, R., 253

Micklos, J., 198

Middle Moffat, The (Estes), 268

Middle Passage: White Ships, Black Cargo, The, 286

Midnight Ride of Paul Revere, The (Longfellow), 144, 157

Midnight Train Home, The (Tamar), 217, 223, 225

Midwife's Apprentice, The (Cushman), 273

Mighty Hunter, The (Hader), 275

Mikkelsen, N., 43, 72

Mildred Taylor's Story of Cassie Logan: A Search for Law and Justice in a Rascist Society (Bosmajian), 226

Miles, M., 271

Milhous, K., 276

Milk for Babes Drawn Out of Breasts of Both Testaments, Chiefly for the Spiritual Nourishment of Boston Babes in Either England, But May Be of Like Use to Any Children (Cotton), 27–28

Miller, E., 266

Miller, M.S., 249

Millions of Cats (Gag), 266

Millman, I., 114, 258

Mills, C., 196

Milne, A.A., 138, 139, 164, 174

Minarik, E., 277

Minn of the Mississippi (Holling), 269

Minty: A Story of Young Harriet Tubman (Shroeder), 232, 240, 286

Miracle's Boys (Woodson), 199, 287

Miracles on Maple Hill (Sorensen), 270

Mirandy and Brother Wind (McKissack), 280, 285

Mirette on the High Wire (McCully), 280

Miss Hickory (Bailey), 268

Missing May (Rylant), 273

Mississipi Challenge (Walter), 285

Miss Mouse Takes Off (Ormerod), 56

Miss Rumphius (Cooney), 132

Misty of Chincoteague (Henry), 269

Moccasin Trail (McGraw), 269

Mochizuki, K., 122

Moe, J., 69, 88

Moja Means One: Swahili Counting Book (Feelings), 278

Mollel, T. M., 81, 287

Money Hungry (Flake), 287

Monkey King (Young), 81, 88

Monster (Myers), 10, 14, 18, 287

Montes, M., 84

Montgomery, L. M., 226

Montgomery, R., 269

Montgomery, S., 256

Moon, G., 266

Moon and Riddles Diner and the Sunnyside Café, The (Willard), 152

Moon Cakes to Maize: Delicious Worlds Folktales (Livo), 290

Moorchild, The (McGraw), 180, 273

Moon Jumpers, The (Udry), 277

Moon Over Tennessee: A Civil War Journal (Crist-Evans), 150, 157

Moore, A. C., 266

Moore, C., 139

Moore J.G., 271

Moore, L., 108, 144, 150

Mora, P., 153

Mordvinoff, N., 276

"More More More," Said the Baby (Williams), 280

More Ready-to-Tell Tales from Around the World (Holt & Mooney), 290

Morgan, R. F., 247

Morganstern, S., 196

Morning Girl (Dorris), 224

Morphology of the Folktale (Propp), 64, 69, 89

Morris, G., 171

Morrison, T., 122

Morrow, L. M., 56, 57, 59

Morte D'Arthur (Caxton), 24

Mosel, A., 278

Moser, B., 85

Moses Goes to a Concert (Millman), 114, 132, 258

Moss, A., 162, 180

Moss, M., 216

Most, B., 100

Most Wonderful Doll in the World, The (McGinley), 276

Mother Crocodile: An Uncle Amadou Tale from Senegal (Guy), 283

Mother Goose, 29, 38, 71, 99

Mother Goose and Nursery Rhymes, 277

Mother Goose: Seventy-Seven Verses with Pictures, 275

Mother Goose's Melodies (Gillespie), 29, 32

Mother Goose Tales, 28

Motown and Didi (Myers), 284

Mountain Born (Yates), 268

Mountains are Free (Adams), 266

Mouse and His Child, The (Hoban), 167, 179

Moved-Outers, The (Means), 268

Moves Make the Man, The (Brooks), 272

Moving Forward with Literature: Basals, Books, and Beyond (Wepner & Feeley), 18

Movin': Teen Poets Take Voice (Johnson), 151

Movin' Up (Harper), 283

Mozart Season, The (Wolff), 203–204

Mr. Justice Holmes (Judson), 270

Mr. L.W. Anthony Wood: The Story of a Cat and a Dog and a Mouse (Ets) 276

Mr. Penny's Race Horse (Ets), 276

Mr. Popper's Penguins (Atwater & Atwater), 125, 130, 267

Mr. Rabbit and the Lovely Present (Zolotow), 277

Mrs. Frisby and the Rats of NIMH (O'Brien), 166, 180, 271

Mr. Wolf's Pancakes (Fearnley), 85

Ms. Africa: Profiles of Modern African Women (Crain), 282

Mufaro's Beautiful Daughters (Steptoe), 114, 132, 280, 284

Mukerji, D. G., 266

Multicultural Folktales: Readers' Theatre for Elementary Students (Barchers), 84

Murphy, J., 237, 248, 258, 273

Murphy, M., 130

Murphy, R., 62, 174

Muse: Smithsonian Museum Magazine for Children, 263

Musgrove, M., 279

Music in Our Life (Cooper et al.), 157

My America: A Poetry Atlas of the United States (Hopkins), 151

My Brother Sam is Dead (Collier & Collier), 271

My Colors/Mis Colores (Emberley), 99, 104, 109

My Daniel (Conrad), 223–224

My Daughter, My Son, the Eagle, the Dove: An Aztec Chant (Castillo), 153

My Dog (Jessica), 148

Myers, A., 222

Myers, C., 56, 58, 287

Myers, W. D., 10, 13, 14, 218, 220, 236, 239, 256, 273, 281, 282, 283, 284, 285, 286, 287

My Father's Dragon (Gannett), 269

My First Nursery Rhymes (Whatley), 100, 109

My Mama Needs Me (Walter), 284

My Mother is the Most Beautiful Woman in the World (Reyher), 275

My Numbers/Mis Numeros, 104

My Opposites/Mis Opuestos, 104

My Own Story (Fritz), 272

My Parents' Divorce (Cole), 120, 132

My Rows and Piles of Coins (Mollel), 287

My Season with Penguins: An Arctic Journal (Webb) 127, 129 130, 245, 248–249, 258, 261, 263

My Shapes/Mis Formas, 104

My Side of the Mountain Trilogy (George), 192, 204, 270

Mystery of Mars, The (Ride & O'Shaughnessy), 254, 260, 262

My Very First Mother Goose (Opie), 99, 109

Na, A., 199, 218
Nagda, A. W., 253
Nagenda, J., 282
Naidoo, B., 200
Nancy Drew, 197, 201
Nansen (Hall), 268
Napoli, D., 85, 179
Nappy Hair (Herron), 120, 132
Narnian Chronicles (Lewis), 169
Natarella, M. A., 139
Nate the Great (Sharmat), 202
Nathaniel Talking (Greenfield), 285
National Geographic World, 264
Natov, R., 230
Nature and Science of Wings, The
    (Burton and Taylor), 56, 60
Naylor, P. R., 194, 273
Neeny Coming, Neeny Going
    (English), 286
Neilson, K., 95
Nelson, M. 145, 274, 287
Nesbit, E., 162
Ness, E., 277, 278
Neville, C., 270
New Animal Discoveries (Orenstein),
    254, 262
Newbery, J., 31–32, 38, 186
Newberry, C., 274, 275, 276
Newcome, Z., 108
New England Primer, 27–28, 39
New Found World (Shippen), 268
New Kid on the Block, The (Prelutsky),
    62–63, 138, 158
New Land (Schmidt), 267
Newman, L., 120
New Tales for Old: Folktales As
    Literary Fiction for Young
    Adults (DeVos), 89
New Zealand Penguins, 130
Nichelason, M. G., 202
Nicholas: A Manhattan Christmas
    Story (Moore), 266
Nieuwsma, M. J., 14
Night Before Christmas, The (Moore),
    158
Nightfather (Friedman), 223–224
Night Flying (Murphy), 62, 174, 180
Night Garden: Poems from the World
    of Adams (Wong), 153
Night Hoops (Deuker), 195, 204
Night Journey, The (Lasky), 223, 225
Night on Neighborhood Street
    (Greenfield), 285
Night Train (Clarke), 200

Nilsen, A., 10
Nilsson, J. L., 203
Nine Days to Christmas (Ets), 277
Nine Spoons: A Chanukah Story
    (Stillerman), 120, 132
Nino (Angelo), 267
Nivola, C. A., 120
Nix, G., 171
Nixon, J. L., 130
Noah's Ark (Speir), 279
No Condition is Permanent (Kessler),
    200
No, David (Shannon), 281
Nodelman, P., 3, 97, 185
No Dinner! The Story of the Old
    Woman and the Pumpkin
    (Souhami), 82
Nolen, J., 78
Nonfiction Matters: Reading, Writing,
    and Research in Grades
    3–8 (Harvey), 263
Nonsense Poems of Edward Lear
    (Lear), 157
Noonday Friends, The (Stolz), 271
Nordholm, H., 142
Nordstrom, U., 18
Norman, H., 83
Norris, K., 235
North, S., 270
Norton, D., 116
Norton, M., 164, 174
Nory Ryan's Song (Giff), 211, 216, 224
No Sweat Projects: Hairy Science and
    No Sweat Projects: Thumbs
    Up Science (Brallier), 254,
    262
Notes from a Liar and Her Dog
    (Choldenko), 194, 204
Nothing at All (Gag), 274
Nothing But the Truth (Avi), 273
Not One Damsel in Distress: World
    Folktales for Strong Girls
    (Yolen), 86, 88
Now Is Your Time! The African-
    American Struggle for
    Freedom (Myers), 285
Noyes, A., 144, 157
Number the Stars (Lowry), 220, 273
Nye, N. S., 151, 152
Nzingha: Warrior Queen of Matamba
    (McKissack), 215, 225

O'Brien, P., 56, 61
O'Brien, R., 166, 271

O'Dell, S., 5, 15, 41, 42, 49, 210, 270,
    271
Odin's Family: Myths of the Vikings
    (Philip), 84, 88
Officer Buckle and Gloria (Rathman),
    281
Off to the Sweet Shores of Africa: And
    Other Talking Drum Rhymes
    (Unobagha), 100, 109, 153
Ola, 95
Olaleye, I. O., 81
Old, W. C., 62
Older, J., 254
Old Ramon (Schaefer), 270
Old Tobacco Shop: A True Account of
    What Befell a Little Boy in
    Search of Adventure, The
    (Bowen), 265
Old Yeller (Gipson), 270
Olivia (Falconer), 116, 132, 281
Once a Mouse (Brown), 277
Once Upon a Time: The Story of
    Benny Goodman (Winter),
    237
One Day at the Wood Green Animal
    Shelter (Casey), 255, 262
One-Eyed Cat (Fox), 272
One Fine Day (Hogrogian), 278
145ᵗʰ Street: Short Stories (Myers), 14
100 Most Popular Picture Book
    Authors and Illustrators:
    Biographical Sketches and
    Bibliographies (McElmeel),
    110, 241
1 Is One (Walck), 276
One Morning in Maine (McCloskey),
    276
One More Bunny: Adding from One
    to Ten (Walton), 100, 109
One Red Sun (Keats), 100, 109
123 Pop! (Isadora), 100, 109
One Wide River to Cross (Emberley),
    278
Onion John (Krumgold), 270
Only Connect (Egoff & Sutton), 39,
    158
Only One Cowry: A Dahomean Tale
    (Gershator), 81
Only Passing Through: The Story of
    Sojourner Truth
    (Rockwell), 237, 287
On Market Street (Label), 279
On My Honor (Bauer), 273
On My Way (De Paola), 236, 239, 240

On the Banks of Plum Creek (Wilder), 267

On the Bright Side, I'm Now the Girlfriend of a Sex God: Further Confessions of Georgia Nicholson (Rennison), 196, 205

On the Same Day in March: A Tour of the World's Weather (Singer), 132

On the Trail of Elder Brother: Glous'gap Stories of the Micmac Indians (Running Wolf), 82

On the Wing: American Birds in Migration (Lerner), 61

On Time: From Seasons to Split Seconds (Shurzynski), 254, 263

On Top of Old Smoky (Kennedy), 142

Oort-Le-Uk the Wanderer (Lide & Johansen), 266

Opening Statement to "The Perilous Realms: A Colloquy" (Alexander), 181

Opie, I., 29, 71, 72, 99, 161

Opie P., 29, 71, 161

Oranges on Golden Mountain (Partridge), 211, 225

Orbis Pictus (Comenius), 26–28

Oppel, K., 167

Orbis Sensualism Pictus (Comenius), 26, 92, 244

Orenstein, R., 254

Orgel, D., 72

Orgill, R., 234

Origins of Intelligence in Children, The (Piaget), 18

Origins of Life on Earth: An African Creation Myth (Anderson), 285

Ormerod, J., 56

Orphan Train Rider: One Boy's True Story (Warren), 246, 263

Osborne, D., 178

Osborne, M. P., 85, 172, 177, 178, 218

Osceola: Memories of a Sharecropper's Daughter (Govenar), 261–262

O'Shaughnessy, T., 254, 260

Other Side, The (Woodson), 114, 132

Other Side of Truth, The (Naidoo), 200

Other Side: Shorter Poems, The (Johnson), 287

Other Victims, The: First Person Stories of Non-Jews Persecuted by the Nazis (Friedman), 14

Other Worlds: The Endless Possibilities of Literature (Cairney), 18

Otto of the Silver Hand (Pyle), 209–210, 225

Our Eddie (Ish-O Kishor), 271

Our Neighbor is a Strange, Strange Man (Seymour), 57, 239–240

Our Only May Amelia (Holm), 274

Out of the Dust (Hesse), 145, 157, 274

Out of the Flame (Townsbery), 267

Outside Over There (Sendak) 95, 109, 122, 132, 279

Outsiders, The (Hinton), 188, 204

Owl and the Pussycat, The (Lear), 138, 157

Owl Moon (Yolen), 280

Ox-Cart Man (Hale), 279

Oxford Companion to Children's Literature (Carpenter & Pritchard), 158, 181

Oxford Dictionary of Nursery Rhymes (Opie & Opie), 40, 89

Paddle-to-the-Sea (Halling), 274

Pageant of Chinese History (Seeger), 267

Palm of My Heart: Poetry by African American Children (Adedjourma), 286

Pancakes-Paris (Bishop), 268

Paperboy, The (Pilkey), 281

Parcel of Patterns, A (Walsh), 211, 225

Paris, S., 7, 8, 9

Park, L. S., 274

Park Beat: Rhymin' Through the Seasons (London), 100, 109

Parkinson, S., 175

Parrish, A., 266, 269

Parrish, P., 202

Parsifal's Page (Morris), 171, 180

Partridge, E., 211

Patchwork Quilt (Flournoy), 284

Patent, D. H., 254

Paterson, K., 135, 188, 198, 216, 272

Patterson, L., 282, 283, 285

Paul, A. W., 144

Paul Robeson (Greenfield), 282

Paulsen, G., 192, 238, 272

Pausewang, G., 224

Peacock Pie (de la Mare), 139, 157

Pearce, P., 171,

Peck, R., 210, 274

Pecos Bill (Bowman), 267

Pedro, The Angel of Olivera Street (Politi), 275

Pedro and Me: Friendship, Loss, and What I Learned (Winick), 258, 263

Peet, B., 280

Pellant, C., 254

Pelletier, D., 281

Penguin Power!, 12–13, 123–124

Penguin Quartet, The (Arrhenius), 130

Penguins! (Gibbons), 114, 126, 128–130, 132

Penguins (Easy Make-and-Learn Projects Series) (Silver), 130

Penguins (Eyes on Nature Series) (Resnick), 130

Penguins (Peterson), 126, 130

Penguins (Silver and Wynne), 129

Penn (Gray), 267

People Could Fly, The: American Black Folktales (Hamilton), 284

People with 5 Fingers, The: A Native California Creation Tale (Bierhorst), 82

Peppe the Lamplighter (Bartone), 280

Perilous Gard, The (Pope), 271

Perilous Road, The (Steele), 270

Perkins, G., 137

Perl, L., 223

Perrault, C., 28, 40, 276, 280

Peter and the Blue Witch Baby (San Souci), 85

Peter Pan (Barrie), 162, 164, 179

Peters, M. W., 282

Petersham, M., 274, 275

Peterson, G. W., 283

Peterson, R. T., 126, 130

Pharaoh's Daughter: A Novel of Ancient Egypt (Lester), 214, 225

Philbrick, R., 173

Philip Hall Likes Me, I Reckon Maybe (Greene), 271

Philip Pullman's Quest (Zipes), 181

Phillip, N., 84, 152

Phoebe Fairchild: Her Book (Lenski), 267

Phonics They Use: Words for Reading and Writing (Cunningham), 64

Piaget, J., 6, 8, 9

Pick and Shovel Poet: The Journeys of Pascal D'Angelo (Murphy), 237

Picture Books for Children (Cianciolo), 133

Pieces: A Year in Poems and Quilts (Hines), 152

Pied Piper of Hamelin, The (Browning), 138, 144, 157

Pierre Pigeon (Kingman), 275

Pigtail of Ah Lee Ben Loo (Bennett), 266

Pilgrim's Progress (Bunyan), 27–28, 39

Pilkey, D., 174, 281

Pinkney, A.D., 281, 287

Pinkney, B., 285, 286, 287

Pinkney, J., 72, 119, 283, 284, 285

Pinkwater, D., 196

Pinocchio, (Collodi), 40, 88, 162, 179

Pippi Long Stocking (Lindgren), 164, 179

Pitcher, C., 84

Planet of Junior Brown (Hamilton), 271

Play with Me (Ets), 276

Please Be Quiet! (Murphy), 109, 130

Pleasures of Children's Literature (Nodelman), 18, 110, 205

Plume, I., 279

Plum-Uchi, C., 195

Pocahontas (Film), 80

Pocketfull of Cricket, A (Caudill), 277

Poem (Hughes), 145

Poetry Instruction and Assessment in the Middle Grades (Hillman), 158

Poetry Splash, 156

Poetry Unfettered (in) Children and Their Literature: A Readings Book (Clark), 158

Pogany, W., 100

Poitier, S., 283

Poke in the I, A: A Collection of Concrete Poems (Janeczko), 157

Polar Express, The (Allsburg), 280

Politi, L., 275

Pondfire (Maynard), 204

Pop Corn and Ma Goodness (Preston), 278

Pope, E. M., 271

Portia: The Life of Portia Washington Pittman, The Daughter of Booker T. Washington (Stewart), 283

Potential of Picture Books: From Visual Literacy to Aesthetic Understanding (Kiefer), 110, 133

Potter, B., 95

Power of Poetry, The (Grimms), 158

Powling, C., 238, 239

Pran of Albania (Miller), 266

Prayer for a Child (Field), 275

Precepts, Pleasures and Portents: Changing Emphases in Children's Literature (Egoff et al.), 39

Prelude to Literacy: A Preschool Child's Encounter with Picture and Story (Crago & Crago), 18

Prelutsky, J., 135, 138, 151, 152

Preston, E. M., 278

Price, L., 122, 285

Princess and the Goblin, The (MacDonald), 162, 179

Problem Novel, The (Egoff), 205

Profiles in Children's Literature: Discussions with Authors, Illustrators, and Editors (Weiss), 241

Propp, V., 41, 69

Proud Taste for Scarlet and Miniver, A (Konigsburg), 209, 225

Provensen, A., 279

Provensen, M., 279

Pullman, P., 37, 169–170, 175

Puss in Boots, (Perrault), 28, 276, 280

Pyle, H., 209

Quaint and Curious Quest of Johnny Longfoot, the Shoe-King's Son, The (Besterman), 268

Queen of Atolia (Turner), 175, 180

Queer Person (Hubbard), 266

Quiz Book on Black America (Blake & Martin), 282

Rabbit Hill (Lawson), 268

Rabbit's Bride, The (Grimm), 85

Rackham, Arthur, 95

Radin, R. Y., 14

Ragged Dick (Alger), 33, 39

Railroad to Freedom: A Story of the Civil War (Swift), 267

Rainbow Boys (Sanchez), 200

Rainbow Jordan (Childress), 283

Rainbow Wings (Ryder), 57

Rain Drop Splash (Tresselt), 275

Rain Makes Applesauce (Scheer), 277

Ramona and Her Father (Cleary), 272

Ramona Quimby, Age 8 (Cleary), 272

Ramona's World (Cleary), 202, 204

Randolph Caldecott Treasury (Billington), 110

Random House Book of Fairy Tales (Ehrlich), 39

Ranger Rick, 264

Rankin, L., 269

Ransome, A., 278

Ransome, J. E., 286

Rappaport, D., 256, 281, 287

Rapunzel (Zelinsky), 68, 281

Rascal (North), 270

Raschka, C., 281

Raskin, E., 271, 272

Rathmann, P., 100, 281

Raven: A Trickster Tale from the Pacific Northwest (McDermott), 280

Raven of the Waves (Cadnum), 211, 224

Rawlings, M. K., 187, 269

Rawls, W., 187

Ray Charles (Mathis), 282

Readers and Writers in Primary Grades (Combs), 130

Reader, the Text, The Poem. The Transactional Theory of the Literary Work (Rosenblatt), 18, 64

Reading and Writing Literary Genres (Buss & Karnowski), 65

Reading Magic: Why Reading Aloud to Our Children Will Change Their Lives Forever (Fox), 18

Reading Today (Micklos), 198

Reading to Learn in the Content Areas (Richardson & Morgan), 263

Read to Me: Raising Kids Who Love to Read (Cullinan), 110

Rebels Against Slavery: American Slave Revolts (McKissack & McKissack), 286

Recommended Books in Spanish for Children and Young Adults: 1996 Through 1999 (Schon), 290
Red-Dirt Jessie (Myers), 222, 225
Red Fairy Book (Lang), 69
Red Sails to Capri (Weil), 269
Red Swan: Myths and Tales of the American Indians (Bierhorst), 88
Redwall (Jacques), 166
Reed, P., 277
Reef, C., 237
Reflections On a Gift of Watermelon Pickle (Dunning et al.), 157
Reich, S., 256
Reiss, J., 271
Relatives Came, The (Rylant), 280
Renaissance, The (Mathews), 253, 262
Rennison, G., 196
Resnik, J. P., 129, 130
Retellings Too Good to Miss, 87
Rey, M., 130
Reyher, B., 275
Rhea, R., 142
Rhoads, D., 270
Rice, D., 199
Richardson, J. S., 247
Ride, S., 254, 260
Rifles for Watie (Keith), 270
Rimshots: Basketball Pix, Rolls, and Rhythm (Smith), 152
Ringgold, F., 280, 285
Ring of Endless Light, A (L' Engle), 272
Road from Home: The Story of an Armenian Girl (Kherdian), 272
Road to Home, The (Auch), 215, 224
Road to Memphis (Taylor), 285
Roald Dahl (Powling), 238, 240
Robbins, R., 277
Robertson, B., 215
Robinson, D., 282
Robinson, L., 115
Robinson, M., 267, 268
Robinson Crusoe, (Defoe), 32, 186
Rochelle, B., 153
Rochman, H., 14
Rockwell, A., 84, 237, 287
Rodda, E., 171
Rodwosky, C., 258
Rogasky, B., 152
Roger and the Fox (Davis), 275
Rogers, F., 258

Rohmann, E., 281
Rohmer, H., 284
Roller Skates (Sawyer), 267
Rollins, C., 282
Roll of Thunder (Scales), 206
Roll of Thunder, Hear My Cry (Taylor), 217
Rookery, The: A Penguin Place, 130
Rooster (Weaver), 225, 258, 272, 282
Rooster Crows, The, 275
Rose and the Beast, The: Fairy Tales Retold (Block), 85, 179
Rose Blanche (Gallaz & Innocenti), 122
Rosenbach, A. S. W., 27
Rosenblatt, L., 11, 12
Rossetti, C., 138, 139, 145
Roughing It On the Oregon Trail (Stanley), 172, 180, 209, 222, 225
Round Book: Rounds Kids Love to Sing, The (MacDonald & Jaeger), 253, 260, 262
Rourke, C., 267
Rousseau, J. J., 32
Rover Boys, The 197
Rowan of Rin (Rodda), 171, 180
Rowling, J. K., 37, 159, 162–164
Royal Diaries series, 232
Rubalcaba, J., 214
Ruby, L., 216
Rufus M. (Estes), 268
Rumpelstiltskin (Zelinsky), 280
Rumpelstiltskin Problem, The (Vande), 85
Runaway Bunny, The (Brown), 116, 132
Runaway Papoose, The (Moon), 266
Runaway Radish, The (Haas), 194, 204
Runaway Tortilla (Kimmel), 84
Runner of the Mountain Tops: The Life of Louis Agassiz (Robinson), 268
Running the Road to A B C (Lauture), 286
Running Wolf, M. B., 82
Ryan, C. D., 278
Ryan, P. M., 217
Ryan, S., 200
Ryder, J., 57
Rylant, C., 14, 167, 178, 202, 273, 279, 280

St. George and the Dragon (Hodges), 279

St. George, J., 255, 281
St. Nicholas (M. M. Dodge), 34–35
Sachar, L., 274
Saldana, R., Jr., 199
Salinger, J. D., 187, 198
Salisbury, G., 200
Salting the Ocean: 100 Poems By Young Poets (Nye), 151
Sam and the Tigers (Lester), 119, 132
Sam, Bangs, and Moonshine (Ness), 278
Samir and Yonatan (Carmi), 200
Sam, J., 284,
Sammy Keyes and the Curse of Moustache Mary (Van Draanen), 14
Sammy Keyes and the Hollywood Mummy (Van Draanen), 196, 205
Sammy Sosa: Heroe do los Jonromes (Savage), 236, 240
Sanchez, A., 200
Sandoz, M., 270
Sandy Bottom Orchestra, The (Keillor & Nilsson), 203–204
San Souci, D., 82
San Souci, R. D., 85, 86, 87, 280, 281, 285, 286
Sarah, Plain and Tall (Maclachlan), 222, 225, 272
Sathre, V., 84
Sauer, J., 268, 269
Savage, J., 236
Sawyer, R., 267, 276
Sawyer, S., 275
Say, A., 280
Schaefer, J., 270
Scheer, J., 277
Schell, R., 7, 8, 9
Schenk de Regniers, B., 277
Schertle, A., 145, 152
Scheu, J. A., 10
Schickedanz, J. A., 97
Schlein, M., 276
Schmandt-Besserat, D., 253
Schmidt, S., 267
Schneider, D., 140
Scholt, G., 24
School Censorship in the 21st Century: A Guide for Teachers and School Library Media Specialists (Simmons & Dresant), 205

Schreiber, G., 275

Schroeder, A., 232, 286

Schulman, A., 120

Schulson, R. E., 120

Schwarcz, C., 111

Schwarcz, J., 111

Schwartz, A., 104

Schwartz, D., 253

Schwartz, V. F., 218

Science Projects About Solids, Liquids, and Gases, and *Science Projects About Sound,* and *Science Projects About the Physics of Toys and Games* (Gardner), 255, 262

Scieszka, J., 51, 87, 171, 280

Scorpions (Myers), 273

Scott, W., 210

Seabird (Holling), 269

Seale, D., 120, 174

Seals on the Bus, The (Hort), 107

Seashore Story (Yashima), 278

Secret Footprints, The (Alvarez), 84

Secret Garden, The (Burnett), 187, 204

Secret of the Andes (Clark), 269

Secret River (Rawlings), 269

Sector 7 (Weisner), 122, 281

Sedgwick, M., 173

Seeger, E., 267

Seek (Fleischman), 204

See You Later, Gladiator (Scieszka), 5, 64, 171, 180

Selden, G., 270

Selecting Books for the Elementary School Library Media Center: A Complete Guide (Van Orden), 19

Sendak, M., 8, 49, 95, 114, 116, 122, 135, 277, 278, 279

Send One Angel Down (Schwartz), 218

Seredy, K., 267

Serposs, E. H., 142

Service, R. W., 144

Seuss, Dr., 141, 275, 276

Seven Blind Mice (Young), 280

Seven Simeon: A Russian Tale (Artzybasheff), 274

17 Black Artists (Fax), 282

Sewell A., 34

Seymour, T., 57, 239

Shabanu, Daughter of the Wind (Staples), 273

Shadow (Cendrars), 279

Shadow and Substance (Sims), 64

Shadow of a Bull (Wojciechowska), 270

Shadrack (De Jong), 269

Shaffer, T., 286

Shake It Up Tales: Stories to Sing, Dance, Drum and Act Out (McDonald), 87–88, 108, 110

Shakespeare's Scribe (Blackwood), 215, 224

Shaking Bag, The (Battle-Lavert), 84

Shannon, D., 281

Shannon, M., 267

Shaping the Earth (Patent), 254, 262

Sharmat, M. W., 202

Shelf, A., 286

Shelley, M., 172

Shen of the Sea (Chrisman), 266

Shepard, A., 81

Sherwood: Original Stories from the World of Robin Hood (Yolen), 85

Shields, C. D., 130

Shiloh Season (Naylor), 194, 204, 273

Shingebiss: An Ojibwe Legend (Van Laan), 83

Shining Company, The (Sutcliff), 225

Ship Ahoy! (Sis), 100, 109

Shippen, K., 268, 270

Shipwreck at the Bottom of the World: The Extraordinary True Story of Shackleton and the Endurance (Armstrong), 261–262

Shipwrecked! The True Adventures of a Japanese Boy (Blumberg), 235, 240

Shiva: An Adventure of the Ice Age (Brennan), 214, 224

Shiva's Fire (Staples), 200

Shoes (Nichelson), 202, 205

Shoeshine Whittaker (Ketteman), 202, 204

Shout, Sister, Shout! Ten Girl Singers Who Shaped a Century (Orgill), 234, 240

Shrek (Steig), 72, 88

Shulevitz, U., 98, 279, 281

Siegel, A., 272

Siegelson, K., 218, 287

Sierra, J., 82, 85, 86, 130, 131

Sigmund Freud: Pioneer of the Mind (Reef), 237

Sign of the Beaver, The (Speare), 215, 223, 225, 272

Silent to the Bone (Konigsburg), 195, 204

Sills, L., 236

Silver, D. M., 130

Silver Pencil, The (Dalgliesh), 268

Silverstein, S., 135, 138

Simmons, J. S., 198

Simon, S., 254, 260

Simont, M., 281

Sims, R., 44

Sing a Song of Sixpence, 29

Sing Down the Moon (O'Dell), 271

Singer, I. B., 271

Singer, M., 152

Singing Man, The (Shelf), 286

Singing Tree, The (Seredy), 264

Sing In Praise: A Collection of the Best Loved Hymns (Wheeler), 275

Single Shard, A (Park), 274

Singmaster, E., 267

Sing Mother Goose (Wheeler), 275

Sing-Song (Rossetti), 139, 158

Sir Walter Ralegh and the Quest for El Dorado (Aronson), 227–228, 240, 258, 262

Sis, P., 100, 281

Sitting Bull and His World (Marrin), 237

Skarmeta, A., 199

Skates of Uncle Richard (Fenner), 283

Skeleton Man (Bruchac), 200

Sketchbook of Thomas Blue Eagle, The (Matthaei & Grutman), 211, 218, 225

Skipper John's Cook (Brown), 276

Skullduggery (Karr), 216, 224

Skurzynski, G., 254

Slam! (Myers), 286

Slapin B., 120, 174

Slave Dancer, The (Fox), 271

Sleator, W., 173, 278

Sleds on Boston Common: A Story from the American Revolution (Borden), 216

Sleds on Boston Common (Borden), 224

Sleeping Beauty, 23, 28, 80, 87

Slender Ella and Her Fairy Hog Father (Sathre), 84

Sloan, G., 44, 50

Small Rains: Verses from the Bible (Jones), 275

Smiling for Strangers (Hicyilmaz), 200

Smith, C. R., 152, 195
Smith, D., 187
Smith, H., 156
Smith, K. A., 285
Smith, L., 244
Smith, W. J., 147
Smoky Night (Bunting), 132, 281
Smoky, the Cowhorse (Scibner), 266
Snake Scientist, The (Montgomery), 257
Snedeker, C., 266, 267
Snell, G., 199
Snow (Shulevitz), 98, 109, 281
Snowflake Bentley (Briggs), 132
Snowflake Bentley (Martin), 281
Snow Is Falling (Branley), 262
Snow White, 23, 68
Snow White (Film), 80
Snow White and the Seven Dwarfs (Gag), 274
Snow White and the Seven Dwarfs (Jarrell), 278
Snow White in New York (French), 122
Snowy Day (Keats), 277
Snyder, Z. K., 223, 271
Sobol, D., 196
Soccer Duel (Christopher), 195, 204
Soderburgh, P., 197
Sojourner Truth: Ain't I a Woman? (McKissack & McKissack), 285
Soldier (Wulffson), 220
Solitary Blue, A (Voigt), 272
Some Babies (Schwartz), 104, 109
Something Beautiful: Reading Picture Books, Writing Poetry (Schneider), 158
Something Big Has Been Here (Prelutsky), 138, 158
Something On My Mind (Grimes), 283
Some Thoughts Concerning Education (Locke), 27–28
Somewhere in the Darkness (Myers), 273, 285
Song and Dance Man (Ackerman), 280
Song for a Dark Queen (Sutcliff), 214, 225
Song of Hiawatha (Longfellow), 144
Song of Robin Hood, 275
Song of the Pines: A Story of Norwegian Lumbering in Wisconsin (Havighurst), 269
Song of the Swallows (Politi), 275

Song of the Trees (Taylor), 282
Songs of Innocence (Blake), 32, 39, 138–139
Soon Be Free (Ruby), 217, 225
Sorenson, V., 270
Soto, G., 135, 200, 237
Souhami, J., 82
Soul Looks Back in Wonder (Fogelman), 286
Sounder (Armstrong), 271
Southerland, E., 283
Southey, R., 161
So You Want to Be President? (St. George), 255, 263, 281
Speare, E. G., 210, 215, 223, 270, 272
Special Fate, A: Chiune Sugihara, Hero of the Holocaust (Gold), 236
Sperry, A., 267, 268
Spice and the Devil's Cave (Hewes), 266
Spier, P., 277, 279
Spindle's End (McKinley), 85
Spinelli, J., 174, 193, 273, 274
Spinner, S., 62, 172
Spinners (Napoli), 85
Spirit of Endurance (Armstrong), 261–262
Sports Illustrated for Kids, 264
Sports! Sports! Sports! A Poetry Collection (Hopkins), 152
Spotting the Leopard (Myers), 222, 225
Springer, N., 171
Sproule, A., 62
Spy Masters: Unmask the Prankster Website, 15
Spyri, J., 187
Squire: Protector of the Small (Pierce), 171, 180
Squirrel Nutkin, 95
Stanley, D., 121, 172, 209, 222, 230, 231, 235, 256, 280
Stanley, J., 231, 256, 261
Staples, S. F., 200, 273
Star-Bearer, The: A Creation Myth from Ancient Egypt (Hofmeyr), 81
Starbright and Dream Eater (Cowley), 173, 179
Star girl (Spinelli), 193
Star in the Storm (Harlow), 223–224
Starry Messenger (Sis), 281
Stars, E., 145–146
Stauffer, D., 229

Steadfast Tin Soldier, The, 33, 276
Steele, M., 271
Steele, W. O., 270
Steig, J., 76, 277
Steig, W., 72, 272, 279
Steinbeck, J., 17
Step From Heaven, A (Na), 199, 218
Steptoe, J., 114, 152, 280, 283, 284, 286
Stevens, J., 281
Stevenson, J., 152
Stevenson, R. L., 138, 139, 209
Stewart, R. A., 283
Stewart, S., 281
Stewig, J. W., 115
Stick and Whittle (Hite), 211, 224
Sticks and Stones: The Trouble Some Success of Children's Literature from Slovenly Peter to Harry Potter (Zipes), 89
Stillerman, M., 120
Stine, R. L., 197
Stinky Cheese Man and Other Fairly Stupid Tales (Scieszka), 87–88, 280
Stoltz, M., 270, 285
Stone Bench in an Empty Park (Janeczko), 146, 157
Stone Fox (Gardiner), 222, 224
Stonehouse, B., 130
Stones Are Hatching, The (McCaughrean), 175, 179
Stone Soup: An Old Tale (Brown), 275
Stong, P., 267
Storm Book, The (Zolotow), 276
Storm in the Night (Stolz), 285
Storm Warriors (Carbone), 211, 224
Story About Ping, The (Flack), 95
Story-A Story, A: An African Tale (Haley), 278
Story of Appleby Capple, The (Parrish), 269
Story of Jumping Mouse (Steptoe), 280
Story of Little Babaji, The (Bannerman), 119, 132
Story of Little Black Sambo, The (Bannerman), 119, 132
Story of Mankind, The (Van Loon), 244, 263, 265
Story of the Incredible Orchestra, The (Koscielniak), 252, 262
Story of the Negro (Bontemps), 269
Story of Stevie Wonder, The (Haskins), 282

Story Performance Handbook, The (Rooney), 290
Stranger in Dadland (Koss), 204
Stratemeyer, E., 197
Stratemeyer Strain: Educators and the Juvenille Series Book (Soderburgh), 205
Strawberry Girl (Lenski), 268
Stray Dog, The (Simont), 281
Street, M., 253
Strega Nona (dePaola), 279
String in the Harp, A (Bond), 272
Striped Ships, The (McGraw), 215, 225
Struggling Middle School Readers and Multicultural Picture Books (Hillman), 133
Stuart Little (White), 166, 180
Stuck in Neutral (Trueman), 193
Sturges, P., 74
Sturtevant, K., 212
Subira Subira (Mollell), 81
Subtle Knife, The (Pullman), 169, 170
Subtraction Action (Leedy), 253, 262
Sugaring Time (Lasky), 272
Suitcase of Seaweed and Other Poems (Wong), 153
Sukey and the Mermaid (San Souci), 285
Summer of the Swans (Byars), 271
Sundiata Lion King of Mali (Wisniewski), 78, 88
Sun Is a Golden Earring (Belting), 277
Sunwing (Oppel), 167, 180
Survey of the Adolescent Poetry Preferences of Seventh, Eighth, and Ninth Graders (Kutiper), 158
Surviving Hitler: A Boy in the Nazi Death Camps (Warren), 14
Sutcliff, R., 77, 214
Sutherland, Z., 25, 27, 68
Sutton, W., 37
Swamp Angel (Isaacs), 281
Sweet Valley High, 197
Sweet Valley Twins, 197
Sweet Valley University, 197
Sweet Whispers, Brother Rush (Hamilton), 272, 283
Swift, H., 266, 267
Swift, J., 30, 32
Swift Rivers (Meigs), 267
Swimmy (Lionni), 277

Swinfen, A., 164
Sword of the Samurai: Adventure Stories from Japan (Kimmel), 82
Swords of Steel (Singmaster), 267
Sylvester and the Magic Pebble (Steig), 278
Sylvia Long's Mother Goose (Long), 109

Taback, S., 281
Tacky and the Emperor (Lester), 130
Tafuri, N., 279
Take Off! (Hunter), 56
Taking Flight: The Story of the Wright Brothers (Krensky), 56, 60
Talbott, H., 14
Tale of Tricky Fox, The: A New England Trickster Tale (Aylesworth), 84
Tale of Peter Parley (Goodrich), 33
Tales from the Abington (Thomas), 88
Tales from the Silver Lands (Finger), 266
Tales of Uncle Remus: The Adventures of Brer Rabbit (Lester), 284
Talking Eggs, The (San Souci), 280, 285
Talking with Artists (Cummings), 236
Tall Tales: Six Amazing Basketball Dreams (Smith), 195, 205
Tamar, E., 216, 223
Tanaka, S., 235
Tang, G., 253
Tangle-Coated Horse and Other Tales (Young), 266
Tar Beach (Ringgold), 280, 285
Taylor, K., 56
Taylor, M., 211, 217, 218, 272, 282, 284, 285, 287
Taylor, S. 210
Taylor, W., 200
T-Bone, the Babysitter (Newberry), 276
Teacher Resources for the Holocaust, 14
Teaching Banned Books: Twelve Guides for Young Readers (Scales), 206
Teaching Reading with Children's Literature (Cox & Zarillo), 18
Teaching with Picture Books in the Middle School (Tiedt), 133

Teens Movin' with Poetry (Taachi), 158
Telling Time (Older), 254, 262
Tell Me About series, 239
10 Minutes Till Bedtime (Rathmann), 100, 109
Tenniel, John, 95
Ten, Nine, Eight (Bang), 279
Tennis Ace (Christopher), 195, 204
Ten Red Apples (Hutchins), 99, 109
Ten Times Better (Michelson), 253, 262
Terrific Connections with Authors, Illustrators, and Storytellers: Real Space and Virtual Links (Buzzeo & Kurtz), 241
Terrorism (Gaines), 256, 262
Terry, A., 139
Thanksgiving Story, The (Dalgliesh), 276
Thayer, E. L., 281
Theo (Harrison), 220
Theodore Roosevelt, Fighting Patriot (Judson), 269
There Is No Rhyme for Silver (Merriam), 157
There Was an Old Lady Who Swallowed a Fly (Taback), 281
There Was a Young Lady Whose Nose (Lear), 146
These Happy Golden Years (Wilder), 216, 225
They Were Strong and Good (Lawson), 274
Thicker Than Water: Coming of Age Stories by Irish and American Writers (Snell), 199
Thief, The (Turner), 273
Thief in the Village and Other Stories, A (Berry), 284
Thimble Summer (Enright), 267
Things I Have to Tell You: Poems and Writings by Teenage Girls (Franco), 151
Think, Pair and Tomorrow/Today Share (Cunningham et al.), 56, 58
This Is My Song: A Collection of Gospel Music for the Family (Higginsen), 72, 88

This Life (Poitier), 283

This Strange New Feeling (Lester), 283

Thistle and Thyme: Tales and Legends from Scotland (Leodhas), 270

Thomas, G., 69

Thomas, J. C., 284, 285, 286, 287

Thoroughbreds, 197

Thought and Language (Vygotsky), 110, 118

Three Bears, The (Southey), 161, 180

Three Billy Goats Gruff, The, 87

Three Jovial Huntsmen (Jeffers), 278

Three Little Pigs, The (Moser), 85, 87

Three Little Pigs, The (Weisner), 85, 87, 281

3-2-1 Contact, 264

Three Voices: An Invitation to Poetry Across the Curriculum (Cullinan), 158

Through My Eyes (Bridges), 229, 240, 257

Through the Eyes of a Child (Norton), 133

Through the Looking Glass (Carroll), 33, 157, 162

Throw Your Tooth on the Roof: Tooth Traditions from Around the World (Beeler), 255, 260, 262

Thumbelina, 33

Thurber, J., 275

Thy Friend, Obadiah (Turkle), 278

Tibet: Through the Red Box (Sis), 281

Tietjens, E., 267

Tie Your Socks and Clap Your Feet: Mixed-Up Poems (Hort), 152

Tiger Math: Learning to Graph from a Baby Tiger (Nagda & Bickel), 253, 262

Time Flies (Rohrmann), 281

Time for Kids, 264

Time of Wonder (McClosky), 277

Time Warp Trio Series (Scieszka), 51, 171

Timothy Tunny Swallowed a Bunny (Grossman), 147, 157

Timothy Turtle (Graham), 275

Titus, E., 276, 277

Toasting Marshmallows: Camping Poems (George), 152

To Be a Slave (Lester), 271

Tobias, H., 278

Toddlerobics (Newcome), 108, 109

Toddler Two-Step (Appelt), 107–108

Tod of the Fens (Whitney), 266

Tolkien, J.R.R., 162, 164, 168

Tomboy of the Air: Daredevil Pilot Blanche Stuart Scott (Cummins), 61

Tombs of Atuan, The (Le Guin), 271

Tom Paine Freedom's Apostle (Gurko), 270

Tompkins, G.E., 1, 62, 221, 247

Tom's Midnight Garden (Pearce), 171, 180

Tom Swift, 197

Tom Swift, Nancy Drew and Pals All Had the Same Dad (Watson), 205

Tom Thumb: His Life and Death (Sutherland), 25

Tom Tit Tot (Ness), 277

Toni Morrison: The Magic of Words (Haskins), 236, 240

Toning the Sweep (Johnson), 285

Too Far Away to Touch (Newman), 120, 132

Toot and Puddle: Puddle's ABC (Hobbie), 104, 109

Top of the World: Climbing Mount Everest, The (Jenkins), 257

Tops and Bottoms (Stevens), 281

Torn Thread (Isaacs), 220

To the Young Scientist: Reflections on Doing and Living Science (Bortz), 240

Touch Magic: Fantasy, Faerie & Folklore in the Literature of Childhood (Yolen), 181

Touch the Poem (Adoff), 148, 157

Townsend, J. R., 32, 38, 95

Travers, P. L., 164

Treasure, The (Shulevitz), 279

Treasure Island (Stevenson), 40, 209, 222, 225

Treasury of the Great Children's Book Illustrators, A (Meyer), 110

Tree Fall (Wiesner), 280

Tree Is Nice, A (Uldry), 276

Tree of Freedom (Caudill), 269

Treffinger, C., 268

Trends in Children's Books Today (Giblin), 110

Tresselt, A., 275, 277

Trial By Jury/Journal (Klise), 196, 204

Trickster and the Fainting Birds (Norman), 83

Triumph of Everest: A Photobiography of Sir Edmund Hillary (Cobum), 236

Trouble's Child (Walter), 284

Troy (Geras), 214, 224

Truce of the Wolf and Other Tales of Old Italy (Davis), 267

Truck (Crews), 279

True Believer (Wolff), 145, 158, 193

True Confessions of Charlotte Doyle, The (Avi), 273

Trueman, T., 193

Trumpeter of Krakow, The (Kelly), 210, 224, 266

Tsuchiya, Y., 121

Tuck Everlasting (Babbitt), 161, 171, 179

Tuesday (Wiesner), 280

Tunis, E., 270

Turkle, B., 278

Turner, M. W., 175, 273

Twain, M., 34, 187

Twas the Night Before Christmas (Moore), 144

20th Century Children's Poetry Treasury, The (Prelutsky), 151

24 Hours (Mahy), 200

Twenty-One Balloons, The (du Bois), 268

Twin Tales: The Magic and Mystery of Multiple Birth (Jackson), 255, 262

Two Mountains: An Aztec Legend, The (Kimmel), 84

Two Reds, The (Lipkind), 276

Udry, J. M., 276, 277, 282

Ugly Duckling, The, 33, 161, 281

Ullman, J., 269

Umbrella (Yashima), 277

Unobagha, U., 100, 153

Unbought and Unboxed (Chisholm), 282

Uncle Jed's Barbershop (Mitchell), 286

Uncommon Champions: Fifteen Athletes who Battled Back (Kaminsky), 236, 240

Uncommon Traveler: Mary Kingsley in Africa (Brown), 235, 240
Under New York (High), 111–112, 132
Understanding Children and Adolescents (Schickedanz), 110
Under the Sunday Tree (Greenfield), 285
Unreluctant Years (Smith), 263
Up a Road Slowly (Hunt), 271
Updike, J., 152, 281
Upon the Head of a Goat: A Childhood in Hungary 1939–1944 (Siegal), 272
Upside Down Boy, The/El Nino de Cabeza (Herrera), 236
Upstairs Room, The (Reiss), 271
Uptown (Collier), 287
Urban, B., 216
Uses Of Enchantment, The (Bettelheim), 39, 69, 88
Using Literature Activities to Teach Content Areas to Emergent Readers (Donoghue), 64, 263

Vaino: A Boy of New England (Adams), 266
Valentine and Orson (Burkert), 24–25, 39
Van Allsburg, C., 279, 280
Vande Velde, V., 85, 175
Van Draanen, W., 14, 196
Van Laan, N., 83
Van Leeuwen, J., 216
Van Loon, F., 244, 265
Van Stockum, H., 267
Vaugelade, A., 220
Vaughan R. L., 82
Velveteen Rabbit, The (Williams), 174, 180
Vendella in Venice (Bjork), 200
Vennema, P., 121
Verne, J., 172
Very Lonely Firefly, The (Carle), 103, 109
Very Special House, A (Krauss), 276
Very Truth, The. In Celebrating Children's Books (Fritz), 241
Victorian Horizens: The Reception of the Picture Books of Crane, Caldecott and Greenaway (Lundin), 110

View from Saturday, The (Konigsburg), 273
Village of Round and Square Houses, The (Grifalconi), 280
Vincent, G., 121
Virgie Goes to School with Us Boys (Howard), 287
Visit to William Blake's Inn, A (Willard), 139, 144, 158, 279
Visual Introduction to Penguins, A (Stonehouse), 130
Voice of the Children, The (Jordan & Bush), 282
Voice of the Heart (Young), 122
Voigt, C., 272
Volcano (Lauber), 273
Vos, I., 14
Voyagers: Being Legends and Romances of Atlantic Discovery (Colum), 266
Voyages of Dr. Dolittle (Lofting), 164, 179, 266
Voyage to the Center of the Earth (Verne), 172
Vygotsky, L. S., 6, 97

Wadjet Eye, The (Rubalcaba), 214, 225
Wahl, J., 285
Waiting for Deliverance (Urban), 216, 225
Waiting to Sing (Kaplan), 120, 132, 258
Walk Two Moons (Creech), 50, 64, 204, 273
Wallner, A., 57, 60, 61, 232
Walsh, J. P., 5, 185, 211
Walsh, M., 107
Walter, M. P., 284, 285
Walters, E., 220
Walton, R., 100
Wanderer, The (Creech), 64, 183–184, 201, 204, 274
Wanderings of Odysseus, The: The Story of the Odyssey (Sutcliff), 77, 88
War, The: A Fable (Vaugelade), 220
Ward, L., 276
War and the Pity of War (Philip), 152
Warner, S., 218
Warren, A., 14, 246
Washington, D., 84
Water Babies (Kingsley/Townsend), 162, 179

Waterless Mountain (Armer), 266
Watson, B., 197
Watson, K., 200
Watsons Go to Birmingham—1963 (Curtis), 209, 224, 273, 286
Wattenburg, J., 85
Wave, The (Hodges), 277
Wayfinder, The (Pattison), 180
Way to Start a Day, The (Baylor), 279
Weaver, B. N., 258
Weaver's Daughter, The (Bradley), 216, 224, 258
Webb, S., 127, 130, 245, 248, 258, 261
Wee Gillis (Leaf), 274
Weik, M., 271
Weil, A., 269
Weismuller, D., 130
Welcome to the Globe: The Story of Shakespeare's Theatre (Chrisp), 253, 260, 262
Well, The (Taylor), 218
Wells, R., 73, 99
Welsh History Makers (Wrenn), 89
Wepner, S. B., 10, 11
Westing Game (Raskin), 272
Weston, C., 268
We Were There Too! Young People in U.S. History (Hoose), 261–262
Whale Talk (Crutcher), 195, 204
Whalley, J. I., 92
What a Morning! The Christmas Story in Black Spirituals (Langstaff), 284
What Do Illustrators Do? (Christelow), 253, 262
What Do You Say, Dear? (Joselin), 277
Whately, B., 100
What Happened on Planet Kid (Conly), 217, 224
What Hearts (Brooks), 273
What I Know Now (Larson), 218
What In the World? (Merriam), 149–150
What Is a Picture Book? (Shulevitz), 110
What Is a Teacher? (Lehn), 122
What Is a Triangle? (Dotkich), 100, 109
What Jamie Saw (Coman), 273
What's Cooking: The History of American Food (Whitman), 256, 263

What Shall We Do with the Boo-Hoo Baby? (Cowell), 107

What's Inside (Ashbe), 109

Wheeler, O., 275

Wheel on the Chimney (Brown), 276

Wheel on the School, The (De Jong), 269

Whelan, G., 200

When Children Went to War, 13, 219

When Clay Sings (Baylor), 278

When Dad Killed Mom (Lester), 193

When I Am Old with You (Johnson), 285

When I Was Young in the Mountains (Rylant), 279

When Kambia Elaine Flew in from Neptune (Williams), 199

When Shlemiel Went to Warsaw and Other Stories (Singer), 271

When Sophie Gets Angry—Really, Really Angry (Bang), 281

When the Rain Sings: Poems by Young Native American (National Museum Of The American Indian), 153

When We Were Very Young (Milne), 139, 157

When Will the World Be Mine? (Schlein), 276

When Zachery Beaver Came to Town (Holt), 193

Where the Buffaloes Begin (Baker), 279

Where the Red Fern Grows (Rawls), 187, 205

Where the Sidewalk Ends, (Silverstein), 138, 158

Where the Wild Things Are (Sendak), 8, 18, 49, 64, 95, 109, 114, 116, 132 277

Which Way Freedom? (Hansen), 284

Whipping Boy, The (Fleischman), 273

Whistler's Van (Jones), 267

White, E. B., 1, 15, 41, 50, 164–166, 269

White, R., 273

Whiteback the Penguin Sees the World (Rey), 130

White Snow, Bright Snow (Tresselt), 275

White Stage, The (Seredy), 267

Whitman, J., 260

Whitman, N., 260

Whitman, S., 256

Whitney, E., 266

Whittington, R., 24

Who Has Seen the Wind? (Rossetti), 144–145, 157

Who's in the Hall? A Mystery in Four Chapters (Hearne), 196, 204

Why I Value Literature (Hoggart), 3

Why Mosquitoes Buzz in People's Ears (Aardema), 76, 88, 278

Why Not, Lafayette? (Fritz), 235, 240

Why the Sun and the Moon Live in the Sky: An African Folktale (Dayrell), 278

Wiese, K., 275

Wiesner, D., 85, 122, 280

Wiggin, K. D., 187

Wigwam and the Longhouse, The (Yue & Yue), 256, 263

Wild and Swampy: Exploring with Jim Arnosky (Arnosky), 257

Wild Birthday Cake, The (Davis), 275–276

Wilder, L. I., 36, 210, 216, 226, 267, 268

Wilhoite, M., 120

Willard, N., 139, 152, 272, 279

William Shakespeare and the Globe (Aliki), 260, 262

Williams, L., 100

Williams, L A., 199

Williams, L E., 211

Williams, M., 174

Williams, S. A., 280, 285

Williams, V., 279, 280

Williams-Garcia, R., 199, 286

Willy Pogany's Mother Goose, 100, 109

Wilson, N. H., 203

Wind in the Willows, The (Grahame), 162, 164, 179

Windy Hill (Meigs), 265

Winged Girl of Knossos (Berry), 267

Wings (Myers), 55, 56, 57, 58

Winick, J., 258

Winnie-the-Pooh (Milne), 164, 174, 180

Winter, J., 74, 237

Winterbound (Bianco), 267

Winter Eyes (Florian), 152

Winter Room, The (Paulsen), 273

Wishes, Lies and Dreams (Koch), 158

Wish Giver (Brittain), 272

Wisniewski, D., 78, 81, 281

Witches of Worm, The (Snyder), 271

Witch of Blackbird Pond, The (Speare), 210, 215, 225, 270

Witness (Hesse), 211, 224

Wizard of Earthsea, A (Le Guin), 164, 179

Wojciechowska, M., 270

Wolf, V., 187

Wonderful Stories for Children (Andersen), 161

Wonderful Year (Barnes), 268

Wonderful Wizard of Oz (Baum), 162, 164, 179

Wonder Smith and His Son, The: A Tale from the Golden Childhood of the World (Young), 26

Wong, J., 153

Wood, A., 280

Woodson, J., 114, 199, 286, 287

Woodward, H., 276

Wolff, V. E., 145, 193, 203

Word Dance, 156

Words and Pictures: Lessons in Children's Literature and Literacies (Mikkelsen), 64, 89

Words of Martin Luther King, Jr., The (King), 284

Words with Wings: A Treasury of African American Poetry and Art (Rochelle), 153

Working Cotton (Williams), 280, 285

World at Her Fingertips, The: The Story of Helen Keller (Dash), 236

World Illustrated, The (Comenius), 26, 244

Worth, V., 137, 150

Wrenn, D., 69

Wright Brothers, The (Freedman), 273

Wright Brothers, The: The Birth of Modern Aviation (Sproule), 62

Wright Brothers, The: How They Invented the Airplane (Freedman), 61

Wright Brothers, The: Inventors of the Airplane (Old), 62

Wringer (Spinelli), 274

Wrinkle in Time, A (L'Engle), 164, 179, 270

Written for Children (Townsend), 40, 110, 181

Wulffson, D., 220

Wyeth, N.C., 95

Wynne, P. J., 129, 130
Wynne-Jones, T., 193

Yaccarino, D., 173
Yashima, T., 156, 277
Yates, E., 268, 269
Year Down Yonder, A (Peck), 210, 225, 274
Yearling, The (Rawlings), 187, 205
Year without Rain, A (Love), 211, 225
Yep, L., 175, 211, 218, 272, 273
Yolonda's Genius (Fenner), 273
Yolen, J., 85, 86, 108, 278, 280
Yonge, C., 187
Yonie Wonder Nose (de Angeli), 275
Yorinks, A., 280
You Can Write Chinese (Wiese), 275
You Go Away (Corey), 100, 109
Young, E., 81, 122, 266, 280

Young Cam Jansen and the Pizza Shop (Adler), 14
Young Children's Preferences in Poetry: A National Survey of First, Second, and Third Graders (Fisher), 158
Young Fu of the Upper Yangtze (Lewis), 267
Young Landlords, The (Myers), 283
Young Mac of Fort Vancouver (Carr), 268
Young Walter Scott (Gray), 267
Yo! Yes? (Raschka), 280
Yount, L., 255
Yue, C., 256
Yue, D., 256

Zarillo, J., 12
Zaslavsky, C., 283

Zaunders, B., 62, 63
Zeely (Hamilton), 188, 204
Zeitlin, S., 76
Zelinsky, P. O., 280, 281
Zemach, H., 278
Zemach, M., 120, 279
Zillions: Consumer Reports for Kids, 264
Zindel, P., 188
Zion, G., 276
Zin! Zin! Zin! A Violin (Moss), 281
Zipes, J., 170
Zlateh the Goat and Other Stories (Singer), 271
Zolotow, C., 276, 277
Zoobooks San Diego, 264
Zooman Sam (Lowry), 196, 204
Zusack, M., 195

Subject Index

action books, for infants and toddlers, 107
activities,
    about fantasy, 177–179
    about realism, 202–204
    and picture books, 17–18
    for folktales, 87
    for infants and toddlers, 108
    for middle levels, 131–132, 156–157, 178–179
    for primary levels, 155–156, 177–178
    for preschoolers, 108
ADHD (Attention Deficit Hyperactivity Disorder), a book on, 258
adolescence, 9–10
adventure stories, 30, 187, 190, *See Also* Mysteries and adventures
Aesop's Fables, 23, 39
African-American books, 199, 218
African,
    folklore, 80–81
    literature, 80–81
    poetry, 153
alliteration, 50
allusions, 50
alphabet books, 99–100
alphabet/dictionary sheet, 62–63
American Library Association, website, 290, *See Also* Newberry Medal
American publishing, 95

ancient world, the, books of, 214
Andersen, Hans Christian, 38, 68
animal fantasy, 35, 159–160, 165–167, a175–176
animal realism, 193–194
antagonists, 48
Antarctica, books on, 261
anthropomorphizing, *See* personification
archetype, 50
archetypes (psychological), 53
art, in picture books, 105
artistic elements, of picture books, 101–104, 112–113, 115–116
Asian-American, books, 199, 218
Asian,
    literature, 81–82
    poetry, 153
Association For Library Service To Children, 265
asthma, book on, 258
authors,
    list of, 17
    on tour, 289
autism, book on, 258
autobiography, 44, 228–229, 237, *See also* biography

baby books, 91, *See Also* infants and toddlers

balance,
    as a literary element, 51–52
    and point-of-view, 53
ballads, 142–144
battledores, 31
bedtime books, 107
behavioral markers, 95–96
Bemelmans, Ludwig, 110
best-seller lists, 289
bibliotheraphy, 188
biographical writing,
    definition of, 227–228, 231–232
    evaluating, 233–234
    history of, 229–231
    subgenres of, 234–237
    value of, for children, 232–233
biographies,
    activities for, 239–240
    and autobiography, 44–45
    as a genre, 44
    for children, 240–241
    of contemporary figures, 236
    of historical figures, 235, 236–237
    professional works on, 241
    projects in, 238
blindness, book on, 258
board books, 107
book buddies, *See* buddy reading
books, for professionals,
    about censorship, 205
    about children's literature, 18, 39, 64–65

about myths and tales, 87–88
about picture books, 132–133, 110
and fantasy, 181
and poetry, 158
books, in classrooms, website for, 289–290
books, of information,
    for children, 262–263
    for professionals, 263–264
books, on fantasy, 179–181
Bookwire Navigator, 289
brainstorming activity, 57
brevity, of poetry, 142
Brothers Grimm, 28, 33, 35
buddy reading, 57, 62, 132
Bulletin Of The Center For Children's
        Books, The,
    website, 289

Caldecott Medal, 35, 93, 265, 274–281
Caldecott, Randolph, 93–94, 110, 265
canon, 3
Carol Hurst's Children's Literature
        Site, 289
cause/effect, in expository writing, 249
Caxton, William, 24
censorship, 184–185, 190
    and ALA, 198
    book challenges, 198
    children's awareness of, 203
    and reality, 201
cerebral palsy, book on, 258
chapbooks, 25, 28
characters, 46, 173–175
    activities about, 202
    child/adolescent, 192
    definition of, 48
    development of 52, 189–190
    focus on, 190–191, 194
    one-dimensional, 54
    as role models, 186
    well-known, 183
characterization,
    and point-of-view, 53
    and realism/fantasy, 54
child development, 23
    and behavioral markers, 95–96
    and children's literature, 6–10
    in infancy and toddlerhood, 91–94
    in medieval times, 24
    theorists, 32
childhood,
    concepts of, 27

contemporary views of, 36–38
    historical views, 24
children, as poets, 135–136
children's books,
    about fantasy, 179–180
    about penguins, 130
    about poetry, 154–157
    a few classics, 64
    folktales, 88
    for the very young, 109–110
    historical books, 39
    on Flight, 61–62
    on realism, 204–205
    picture books, 17–18
Children's Book Council website, 289
children's literature, See Also
        evaluation; History of
        Children's Literature; Literature
        units and
    specific genres,
    audience of, 41
    characters of, 4–5
    classics of, 35
    and classrooms, 11
    critical theory of, 65
    defining, 2–3
    genres of, 15, 210
    history of, 21–23
    interdisciplinary, 1
    webguide, 289
Children's Services Division of the
        American
        Library Association Awards,
        265–290
Chinese folklore translated, 69
Cinderella,
    and archetypes, 53
    first published, 28
    variations on, 86–87
cinquain, 148–149
classification of literature, 43–44, See
        Also genre; evaluation
classification schemes, 42–44, 55
classroom activities,
    for biographies, 239–240
    for middle levels, 223–224
    for primary level, 222–223
    on books of information, 260–261
classroom projects, 38, 177
    about poetry, 154
    book club, 17
    for classrooms, 89
    for primary grades, 55–57,
        124–131

of historical fiction, 222
    on books of information,
        259–260
    reading list, 16
    to create a text set, 17
    with picture books, 123
cliffhangers, 47
color, as an artistic element, 102
comedy, 44
Comenius, John, 26
coming-of-age novels, 52, 187, 191
compare/Contrast, in expository
        writing, 248
concept books, 96, 99–100, 247
concept web, 62
concrete poetry, 147–148
conferences, and book fairs, 289
confessional stories, 196
conflict, 47, 54
contemporary realism, 35, 45
    as a genre, 44–45
contemporary realistic fiction,
        183–185, 201
    controversies in, 184
    definition of, 185–186
    evaluation of, 189, 190–198
    examples of subgenres, 184–185,
        190
    more realism in, 188–189
Coretta Scott King Award, 265,
        282–290
Cotton, John, 28
counting books, 99–100
couplet, 150
courtesy books, 23–24
Crane, Walter, 93–94
creation myths, 76–77
creation stories, 22–23
cumulative plots, 47
cumulative tales, 74

Dame Goose, 29
DEAR (Drop Everything and Read), 59
death, book on, 258
description, in expository writing, 248
descriptors of plots, 46–47
development of literacy, 21–23, 91
development, of literature, 21–22, 25
developmental theories, 6–7
diamante, 148–149
didactic, 3
    books, 27
    poetry, 140
    stories, 188

didacticism, 25, 33, *See Also* scientific didacticism; religious didacticism
dieties, in literature, 22
Disney's versions, of folklores, 80
ditties, 28–29
diversity, 188, 199–201
Dorothy Canfield Fisher Children's Book Award, website, 289
double-entry journal technique, 255
Down syndrome, book on, 258
DRTA (A Directed Reading Thinking Activity), 221
dynamic characters, 48

easy readers, 185
Edgar Award From The Mystery Writers Of America, website, 195–196
educational theorists, 32
Elizabeth Nesbitt Room, and website, 39
emotions and poetry, 142
encyclopedias, on children's literature, 290
episodic plots, 47
engraved plates, 92
enumeration, in expository writing, 248
essays, 62
European - American diversity, 199
European,
    fairy tales, 89
    folklore, 84–85
    folktales, 89
exploration and colonization, books on, 215–216
expository writing,
    definitions and patterns, 248
    graphic overviews of, 250
    patterns of, 248–250
    structures of, 247
extraordinary characters, 173–175
evaluation, *See Also* literary elements; specific elements,
    of children's books, 5–6
    issues and trends in, 119–121
    of literary elements, 51
    of picture books, 104–105, 117–121
    two types of, 52–53
expository text profile, 62

fables, 70, 72, 79
fact books, 247

facts, help with, 249
fairy tales, 28–29, 35, 72, 79
    definition of, 70
    first, 68
family dramas, 82
family and school stories, 192
family stories, 187–190, 193
fantasy, 35, 43, 53–54, 176–177, *See Also* individual types
    bibliography of, 164
    in books, 114
    definition of, 44–45, 159–160
    evaluation of, 175–176
    examples of, 159
    as a genre, 44–45
    history of, 162
    and literary elements, 54
    sacred or ethical, 162
    subgenres, 165–172, 190
fiction, 37, *See Also* evaluation
    defined, 185
    examples, 187
    forms of, 44
    genre of, 15
    point-of-view, 52
    series books, 196–197
    versus nonfiction, 60
figurative language, 49
first books, 24
first person narration, 51
first printed Bible, 24
flashbacks, 47, 54, 190
flat character, 48, 53, 191
Flight unit, 61–64
foil, 48
folk literature, 24
folklore, 68–69, 72, 79 *See Also* traditional literature
folk rhymes, 71–72, 79
folk songs, 71–72, 79
folktales, 33, 72–76
    European, 162
    and fairy tales, 70, 79
    and fantasy, 161
    of the world, 290
    scripts from, 89
foreshadowing, 47
format, as an artistic element, 2
free verse poetry, 145
freshness, as a literary element, 51–53

gay and lesbian books, 200, 218
gender differences and roles, 188–189
genesis myths, 23

genres, *See Also* specific genres and subgenres, 44–45
    classified, 15, 41, 43–45
    evaluations of, 6
    focus on character, 184, 190–194
    focus on plot, 184, 194–195
    most popular, 183
    of the 1800s, 35
    similiar characteristics of, 45
    theory of, 65
girls and women, 21, 86
golden age, 33–34, 40, 187
good versus evil
    in Harry Potter, 162–163
    in Lord Brocktree, 166
Goosefooted Bertha, 29
grand conversation, 221
Greenaway Medal, 93–94

haiku, 145–146
hard-to-find books, 140
Harry Potter activities, 178, *See Also* high fantasy
hearing-impaired, book on, 258
hero myths, 77–78
high fantasy,
    and good versus evil, 54
    and Harry Potter, 164, 167–171, 175
    characters of, 53
    definition and examples of, 167–171
    evaluation of, 175
Hispanic literature,
    folklore, 83–84
    poetry, 153
Hispanic poetry, 153
Hispanics, and diversity, 199
historical,
    fantasy, 209
    fiction, 35, 42, 186–187, 208–218
    realism, 37, 43–45, 207–213, 218–219
history, of children's literature, 27–29, 36–37, 187–188, *See Also* Traditional literature,
    Golden Age of, 33–34, 40
    themes of, 37–38
history, of literacy, 21–23
Hogwarts, 159
Holocaust, the, 13–14
Holocaust Teacher Resource Center, 14
hornbooks, 25–26, 28

humanities (the arts), books, 252–253
humor, 50–51, 196
Humpty Dumpty, 29

illuminated manuscripts, 23
illustrated information books, 247
illustrations, 92–95, *See Also* picture
    books
industrial revolution, 34
infancy, 6–7
infants and toddlers, 91–110
information books, 44–45, 259, *See
    Also* books of information
intaglio process, 92
interactive books, 96
intergenerational stories, 188
intermediate and middle levels, *See*
    middle levels
internal rhyming, 150
International Reading Association, 198
Internet addresses, 289–290, *See Also*
    individual topics for
    addresses
inventions, 173–175
Internet Public Library, website, 289
irony, 50
irony-satire, 44
Island Of The Blue Dolphins versus
    Charlotte's Web, 41–42
Italian folklore, 69

Jack and Jill, 29
journaling, 220
juvenile literature, 196

King Henry's Primers, 25
K-W-L chart, 253–254

language,
    and patterns, 73–74
    markers of development, 7
    of poetry, 142
Latin American literature, See
    Hispanic literature
learning, through literature, 186
learning, to play a musical
    instrument, 203
legends, 77–79
limericks, 146–147, 150
limited omniscient, 51
line, as an artistic element, 102
linear plots, 46–47, 54
linguistics, 33
literacy, 10–11, 110

literacy elements, *See Also* characters;
        setting; style; theme,
    and classifying, 54
    and theme, 52
    in picture books, 114–116, 122
    projects on, 55
literary forms, 44
literary maps, 55, 81
literary milestones, 25, 28, 32, 35
literature,
    based classroom, 12–13
    based programs, 10, 13–15
    circles, 221
    definition of, 44
    Flight unit, 61–63
    Penguins unit, 124–131
    units, 12–13
    Wings unit, 56–61
lithography, 92
Little Miss Muffet, 29
Little Red Riding Hood, 28
Locke, John, 28
lyrical poetry, 144–145

magazine, for children, 35
magic numbers, 76
manipulative books, 96
manuscripts, 23
mathematics and technology, books
        in, 253–254
media, 101–102
medieval and renaissance worlds,
        books about, 215
medieval,
    tales for children, 290
    times, 24
mentally disabled neighbor, book
        about, 258
metaphors/similies, 49–50
middle childhood,
    markers of, 7
mixed media, 115
modern fantasy, 162–165
monogenesis, 68
mood, 49
Mother Goose, 28–30
    Melodies, 32
    nursery rhymes, 71–72, 99–100
    Tales, 28
multicultural,
    books, 43
    folktales, 89
    literature, 80–85
    stories, 67

multiculturalism, *See Also* Diversity
multimedia, 37
mysteries, 14, *See* mystery and
        adventure
mystery and adventure, 195–196
mythical beasts, 76
mythology, 76–77
myths,
    and dreams, 69
    and legends, 70, 79
    definition of, 70
    evaluation of, 79

narrative poetry, 144
Native American,
    activity, on life of, 261
    and creole books, 218
    bibliography on diversity, 200
    folklore, 82–83
    poetry, 153
nature versus nurture, 28
Newbery, John, 31–32, 38, 265
Newbery Medal, 31, 265–274
New England Primer, 27–28, 39
nonfiction, 37, 114
    books of information, 243–246,
        249–255, 256–258
    chapter books, 246
    genre of, 15
    point-of-view, 52
    series books, 197
nonsense poetry, 138
nursery rhymes, 28, 34, 71, 99–100

Office For Intellectual Freedom Of
    The American Library
    Association, and censorship, 198
older readers, 85, 195, *See* intermediate
        and middle level
omniscient, 51
Orbis Pictus Awards, for non-fiction,
        257
onomatopoeia, 149
oral tradition, 22–24, 28, *See Also*
        traditional literature

panchatantra fables, 23
parables, 70, 72, 79
parents, and censorship, 201
partner Reading, 57
peekaboo books, 96
penguins, unit for, 123–131
Perrault, Charles, 28, 40
personification, 50, 165

photo essays, 247
picture books, 24–28, 34–37
    artistic elements in, 101
    as a genre, 44–45
    bibliography of, 100, 110, 122
    definition of, 98
    early development of, 110
    evaluating, 104–105, 52
    forms of, 15
    for older children, 111, 113–114,
        121–122, 133
    history of, 92–95
    subgenres, 99
    style and media, 112, 115–116
    styles of, 115–116
pioneers,
    books on, 216
    calendar, 261
plot, 46–47
    and genres, 53
    and realism/fantasy, 54
    as literary element, 51
    in fantasy, 54
    in realistic fiction, 189, 191, 194
    profile of, 62
poetry, 137–150, 151–153, 157–158
    as a genre, 44–45
    elements of, 149
    forms of, 15, 142
    preferences, 139–140
    standard for, 32
    subgenres, 190
    versus verse, 140
    writing of, 62
poets, 150–151
plot, structures and patterns, 47
point-of-view, 46, 51–55
polygenesis, 68
pourquoi stories, 76–77
pretend and parallel play, 96
primary childhood, 7–9
primary level, 55–60, 87
primary and secondary worlds,
        159, 165
printing press, invention of, 24
printing process, 93
problems, 73, 190
professional resources, 290
prose, 15
protagonist, 48, 190
proverbs, 67,
    definition of, 70–71
    evaluation of, 79
psychosocial development, 95–96

psychosocial markers, of language
        development, 6–7
publishing industry, See American
        publishing

rascism, 119–121, 188
reader-response theory, 11
reading, 10, 91, 109
reading programs, See literature-based
        programs
realism, 36–37, 53–54, 114
realistic,
    animal stories, 187, 189, 190,
        193–194
    fiction, 187
    plots, 54
    prose fiction, 53
Red Clover Award website, 290
religious didacticism, 24–25, 27–28,
        31–32
retelling Center, 59
retellings, 85–86, 179
rhymes, 28–29
rhymes,
    about politics, 38
    evaluation of, 79
    scheme, of limericks, 146
rites of passage themes, 191
Robert F. Sibert Award, 258
romance, 44
round characters, 48, 191
Rousseau, Jean-Jacques, 32
royalty and nobility, 29
rural American folktales, 84
Russian folktales, 69

satires, 30
school stories, 190
science, books in, 254–255
science fiction, and good over evil, 54
science-fiction/fantasy, 37, 165,
        172–173, 175
scientific didacticism, 31
Scott O'Dell Awards website, 210
second golden age, 95
sensitive issues books, 258
sequence of events, 202–203
series books, 189
setting, 46, 49
    and realism/fantasy, 54
    as a literary element, 51
sexuality, 188–189
shape, as an artistic element, 102
similes, 49

singing books, and toy books, 107
social issues, 118–122, 187–189,
        192–1193
Social Studies, books in, 255–256
Spanish books, for children and
        young adults, 290
special needs books, 258
spells of enchantment, 76
sports stories, 195
SSR (Sustained Silent Reading), 59
static character, 48
stereotypes, 33, 48
stock characters, 75
story,
    grammar, 68
    line, 172
story retelling, 57, 60, See Also
        retelling
story structure, 74, See linear plot
storytellers, 23, 67, See Also
        Goosefooted Bertha
storytelling, 23, 290
Stratemeyer Syndicate, 197–198
style, 46, 49, 101–102
    as a literary element, 51
    in picture books, 115–116
stylistic devices, 190
subgenres, 45, See Also Specific genres
survival stories, 189, 192
symbol, 49–50

tabula rasa, 27
tall tales, 77–78
teaching, with books, 99
technology, uses of, 165
television game shows, 204
texture, of books, 102
themes, 46, 189, 191
    and genres, 53
    and realism/fantasy, 54
    as a literary element, 52
    explicit versus implicit, 46
    in fantasy, 53
    in historical fiction, 211
think, Pair, and Tomorrow/Today
        Share, 57–58
time fantasy, 165, 171–172, 175, 177
time sequence, in expository writing,
        248
Time Warp Trio series, 51
tone, 50
trade books, 2
traditional literature, 53, 71–74, 114
    and fantasy, 161

and point-of-view, 54
and printing press, 24
as a genre, 44–45
definition of, 22
evaluation of, 78–80
influenced modern, 69
subgenres of, 70–78
tragedy, 44
transitional books, 185, 202
twentieth century, 36–37, 217

United States Holocaust Memorial
    Museum, 14

urban survival stories, 192

verses, 29
Victorian era, 34–35
violence, 189
visual elements, of picture books, *See*
    artistic elements
visual literacy, 97
vitality, as a literary element, 51–52
websites, *See Also* individual topics
    for websites
    for the Holocaust, 14
    for picture books, 110

Western expansion and
    industrialization, books of,
    216–217
whole class meeting, 62
Wings unit, 55–60
woodcuts, 27
Word Dance magazine, 156
wordless picture books, 99–100
word Wall, 57, 60
word Web, 57–58

young adult literature, 10, 54
younger readers, mysteries for, 196

About the Author

Dr. Judith Hillman, professor of Education at Saint Michael's College, Colchester, Vermont, teaches graduate and undergraduate children's literature courses, reading and language arts methodology, and reading assessment. She also supervises student teachers and graduate reading teacher interns. Children's literature has always been at the center of her professional interests, and working with teachers, librarians, parents, and children in schools allows her to explore this interest wholeheartedly. Teachers know her as a tireless advocate of literacy through the enjoyment of literature.

Complementing the school and college-based aspects of her professional life are professional organizations to which she belongs and contributes: The New England Reading Association (past president and board member), The International Reading Association (former state counselor), National Council of Teachers of English, Children's Literature New England, and the Children's Literature Association. She has served on the Dorothy Canfield Fisher Book Award Committee, a children's preference award in Vermont upon which other state programs are based. She frequently speaks to parents and teachers about children's literature and the importance of reading to children; publishes articles in periodicals devoted to children, reading, and literature; reviews children's fantasy for the Vermont Department of Libraries; and reviews professional literature for the New England Reading Association's Journal.